DUNKIRK

JULIAN THOMPSON

DUNKIRK

Retreat to Victory

SIDGWICK & JACKSON

First published 2008 by Sidgwick & Jackson
an imprint of Pan Macmillan Ltd
Pan Macmillan, 20 New Wharf Road, London N1 9RR
Basingstoke and Oxford
Associated companies throughout the world
www.panmacmillan.com

ISBN 978-0-283-07021-1

PICTURE ACKNOWLEDGEMENTS
Bettmann / Corbis: 28, 21
Corbis: 34
Getty Images: 1, 2, 3, 5, 7, 14, 16, 17, 19, 20, 29, 31, 35, 39, 40, 41, 42
Hulton-Deutsch Collection / Corbis: 32, 26
Imperial War Museum: 6, 8, 9, 10, 11, 12, 13, 18, 24, 27, 38, 43, 44, 45, 47, 48
PA Photos: 15, 23, 25, 37
popperfoto.com: 22, 33, 36
Time & Life Pictures / Getty Images: 4, 30, 31, 39, 46

1 3 5 7 9 8 6 4 2

A CIP catalogue record for this book is available from
the British Library.

Typeset by SetSystems Ltd, Saffron Walden, Essex
Printed and bound in the UK by
CPI Mackays, Chatham ME5 8TD

Contents

List of Maps

NORTH-WEST EUROPE AND SOUTHERN UK

Birmingham

UNITED KINGDOM

Norwich

Gloucester

Harwich

Swansea

Newport

London

Barry   Avonmouth

Camberley

Dover

Southampton

Calais

Weymouth

Portsmouth

Boulogne

Plymouth

Falmouth

English Channel

Abbevill

Somme

Dieppe

Fécamp   St Valery-en-Caux

Cherbourg

Havre

Rouen

Channel Islands

Caen

Dives

Seine

Conches

St Malo

Argentan

Verneuil

Dinard

Brest

Mortagne

Rennes

Le Mans

Lorient

Quiberon Bay

Angers

Loire

St Nazaire

Nantes

Saumur

16 kilometres

10 miles

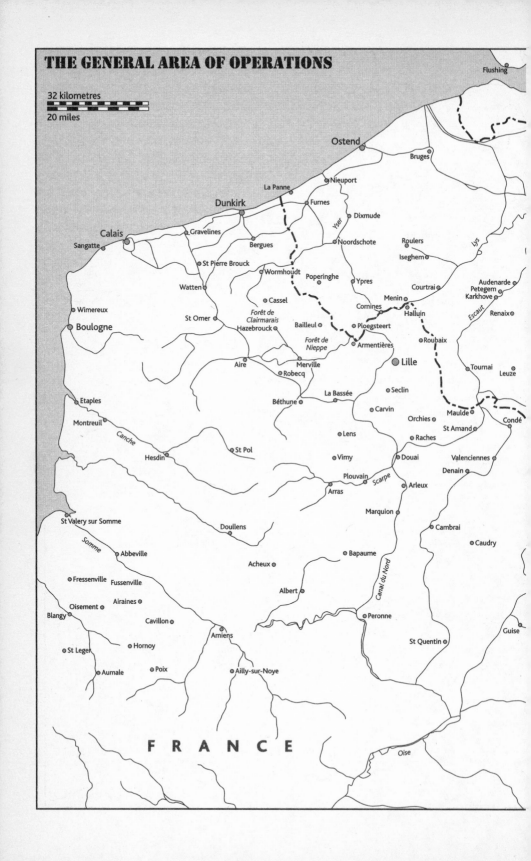

THE GENERAL AREA OF OPERATIONS

32 kilometres

20 miles

Flushing

Ostend

Bruges

Nieuport

La Panne

Furnes

Dunkirk

Dixmude

Yser

Gravelines

Calais

Bergues

Noordschote

Roulers

Sangatte

St Pierre Brouck

Iseghem

Lys

Wormhoudt

Watten

Poperinghe

Ypres

Courtrai

Audenarde
Petegem
Karkhove

Wimereux

Cassel

Menin

Forêt de
Clairmarais

St Omer

Cornines

Halluin

Renaix

Escaut

Boulogne

Hazebrouck

Bailleul

Ploegsteert

Roubaix

Forêt de
Nieppe

Armentières

Aire

Merville

Lille

Tournai

Leuze

Robecq

La Bassée

Seclin

Etaples

Béthune

Carvin

Maulde

Montreuil

Orchies

Condé

Canche

Lens

St Amand

St Pol

Vimy

Douai

Valenciennes

Hesdin

Raches

Plouvain

Scarpe

Denain

Arras

Arleux

St Valery sur Somme

Marquion

Cambrai

Somme

Doullens

Caudry

Abbeville

Bapaume

Canal du Nord

Acheux

Fressenville   Fussenville

Airaines

Albert

Peronne

Oisement

Blangy

Cavillon

Guise

Amiens

St Leger

Hornoy

Poix

St Quentin

Aumale

Ailly-sur-Noye

F R A N C E

Oise

Preface

This book tells the story, from the point of view of the British Expeditionary Force (BEF), of the campaign in France and Flanders in 1940 that led to the evacuation from Dunkirk. It does not quite end there, for the British Army also participated in the fighting south of the Somme, a campaign almost unknown to most British readers. This was followed by yet another evacuation of nearly 150,000 British soldiers of what was sometimes called the 'Second BEF'.

The story of the saving of the BEF at Dunkirk has been told often, perhaps too often in the context of 'the dithering of Hitler and the immortal exploits of the "little ships" – to quote Brian Bond, a distinguished historian of the period. Less well known is the narrative of continuous hard fighting experienced by the main body of the BEF in the three weeks between the German invasion of France on 10 May 1940 and the end of the evacuation from Dunkirk on 4 June. When I mentioned that I was writing a book about the campaign to a field marshal, a distinguished veteran of the Second World War (but not of Dunkirk), his reaction was that there was plenty to say about the actual evacuation. He added, 'But the trouble is that the BEF did so little fighting before the evacuation.' The implication was that there was little to say on the subject. It has been my purpose to show that not only did the BEF have to fight hard, it had to do so while carrying out that most difficult phase of war, a withdrawal while in contact with a ruthless enemy. Many armies in history have found retreat more than they can handle and have disintegrated before surrendering, or have been cut to pieces with huge loss. The former was the fate of both of Britain's allies in this campaign.

The BEF of 1940 was not the best-trained or best-equipped army that has left our shores to fight overseas. Years of political dithering had seen to that. It was certainly nothing like as well trained as the superb German Army, throughout the Second World War perhaps one of the finest fighting organizations the world has ever seen. Viewed overall the BEF in 1940 lacked that difficult-to-define flair that marks out brilliant soldiers from plain practitioners of the art. Or put another way they were not 'quick enough on the draw' tactically speaking. Of course there were exceptions – some individuals and units showed this flair – but it did not run through the whole force like a common thread. This comes only with training and good leadership. The BEF did not have enough time to train. It was not the fault of the soldiers, and the reasons for it are made plain in this book.

But, despite that, the BEF gave the Germans a testing run for their money, and this is made clear in the German assessment of the British soldier as a 'fighter of high value', in the report quoted in my final chapter. How much more challenging it would have been for the Germans had the BEF been better equipped and trained. It is hard to fault much of the leadership of the BEF – some of it was outstanding, as the reader will discover. From the ashes of the 1940 campaign in France and Flanders emerged many of the successful senior commanders in the British Army in the Second World War, starting with the man who would be the Chief of the Imperial General Staff from 1941 to the end of the war, Field Marshal Sir Alan Brooke (later Viscount Alanbrooke). The others include, and the list is not exhaustive, future army commanders Montgomery, Alexander, McCreery and Dempsey; corps commanders Lumsden, Horrocks, Ritchie (who briefly commanded Eighth Army) and Crocker; and divisional commanders Adair, Rennie and Whistler. These officers proved themselves in moments of the utmost danger in 1940, which would have broken lesser men, and sometimes did.

The soldiers they led were indomitable and were no different from their predecessors, in the words of Field Marshal Wavell writing of an earlier war, 'whose humorous endurance of time and chance lasts always to the end'. Of course there were instances where discipline broke down, of cowardice and of failure, but in the main these were a tiny minority. The manner in which they fought earned the respect of their opponents, which could not be said of their French and Belgian allies. It cannot be said too often that the retreat was not caused by failure on the part of the BEF; it was the consequence of their allies on either flank losing the battle. But in the end for the BEF it was a retreat to victory like that at Corunna in Spain in 1809 or Burma in 1942. Throughout, the soldiers of the BEF thought of themselves as better than their opponents, and this bloody-minded conceit sustained them in the darkest moments.

This is their story.

1

TWENTY WASTED YEARS

History provides many examples of a British Army being asked to operate under appalling handicaps by the politicians responsible for British policy, but I doubted that the British Army had ever found itself in a graver position than that in which the governments of the last twenty years had placed it.

Major General Noel Mason-MacFarlane briefing the press, 15 May 1940[1]

At 1334 hours on 3 June 1940, Admiral Jean Abrial, the French commander of the Dunkirk area, was ordered by the French high command to leave and embark for England. The British evacuation, less some of the more seriously wounded in hospitals and dressing stations, was complete. In peacetime Dunkirk was a busy commercial port; now chaos reigned in the town. The beaches were under German artillery fire, while French soldiers, sailors and civilians looted the burning buildings. British destroyers waited until darkness before heading for the moles to take off the French rearguard. Vice Admiral Bertram Ramsay, the Flag Officer Dover, asked that 'in return for the British effort on behalf of the French Army' the maximum number of British wounded should be included in the evacuation.

At about 2200 hours, Abrial burned his codes and embarked but, reluctant to leave his command, remained off the port and beaches until 0200 hours the next morning, before his ship steamed for Dover. Meanwhile all night crowds of weary men boarded a miscellany of craft including tugs, pleasure craft, cross-Channel ferries, launches, motorboats and destroyers that came alongside the moles at Dunkirk. At first light, on the orders of General Barthélemy, commanding the Flanders fortified sector, the French 68th Infantry Division that had been holding ground to the south-west of Dunkirk disengaged and withdrew to the port. Few of the division got away: a flood of deserters from the First, Seventh and Ninth French Armies, who had hidden in the town, emerged and blocked the route of Barthélemy's rearguard to the last ships. In desperation, some officers sent their men to the dunes in the hope of eventually finding ships off the beaches.

That morning the Germans entered Dunkirk to find the moles and approaches packed with enemy soldiers. For miles along the beaches lay a trail of military impedimenta: steel helmets, guns, trucks, small arms of all descriptions, boots and clothing, gas masks, wireless sets – and the bodies of men caught in the open on the beaches, killed in the fighting to hold the perimeter, or washed in by the tide from ships and vessels bombed and machine-gunned by the Luftwaffe. Off the beaches the wreckage of all manner of vessels protruded above the surface of the sea, or lay like stranded whales at low tide, their hulls and decks littered with dead French and British soldiers.

Before the French commanders surrendered to the Germans at the Hôtel de Ville, they signalled General Weygand, the French Supreme Commander, that nothing more could be done, adding that 'Admiral Abrial considers the operation of the English [sic] this night magnificent'. Admiral Darlan, the French Chief of the Naval Staff, signalled his thanks to the British Admiralty and to Admiral Ramsay. Nearly half as many French troops as British had been evacuated, but thousands more were marched off to Germany as prisoners. Perhaps some of them overheard the remark made by an unknown German officer: 'Where are the Tommies? Tommies gone and you here. You crazy?' The recriminations that ensued among the Allies were bitter, stoked among others by the Anglophobes Darlan and Marshal Philippe Pétain, the latter soon to be the head of the French government.

The arguments last to this day, and can be traced back to a misalignment of French and British perceptions about the situation as the Battle of France unfolded in May 1940. The French government, believing that the war was lost, with their army totally defeated and heading for destruction, a successful military outcome was unimaginable. They wanted the British to fight long enough in northern France, and eventually at Dunkirk, to buy time for both France and Britain to obtain an acceptable peace for both nations. The French did not articulate this desire, they merely hinted at it, hoping that this was what the British would do. The British had no intention of falling in with this vague and probably fruitless concept; they had an escape route and would take it, to live to fight another day. Brigadier Swayne, head of the British Military Mission to General Georges, commander of the French North-East Front, remarked: 'We who live in a small island regard the sea as a high road. For the French it is the limit of their country. To take to the sea would be to abandon their country and would be disgraceful.' To the British the evacuation at Dunkirk was a 'miracle'; to the French it was desertion. How did it come about?

*

The words of General Mason-MacFarlane quoted at the head of this chapter provide part of the clue to the situation in which the British found themselves in May and June 1940. Although often forgotten now, it was not until February 1939, only seven months before the outbreak of the Second World War, that the British government decided to commit a small part of the army to the continent in the event of German aggression in the west. This field force was to consist of four regular infantry divisions, the first two to arrive in their assembly area in France thirty days after mobilization. It was smaller than the British Expeditionary Force (BEF) of 1914, less well trained and lacking much essential equipment.

Britain had ended the First World War twenty years earlier with the best-trained, best-equipped and best-commanded army in her history. In the space of three months in the autumn of 1918, this army had fought and won a series of battles, each bigger than any in which it was to engage in the Second World War. By November 1918, the British Army had soundly defeated the German Army, taking more prisoners and guns than the French and American armies put together. No other army was in the same league. This was to change as the years passed. With the 'war to end all wars' won, Britain rapidly disarmed, while others talked about it and did nothing, or – like Germany – having disarmed, secretly rearmed. Starting in 1918, successive British governments assumed that there would be no major war for ten years, and from 1928, as each year passed, the assumed decade of peace was moved forward with it. The armed services were reduced, and for thirteen years these small forces were kept starved of equipment. In March 1932, seeing that others had not followed this example, leaving Britain dangerously weak, the government abandoned the ten-year policy and a policy of rearmament was discussed, though little was actually done.

> One would have lingering wars with little cost;
> Another would fly swift, but wanteth wings;
> A third thinks, without expense at all,
> By guileful fair words peace may be obtain'd.[2]

In January 1933 Hitler became German chancellor. The following year the British finally decided on a measure of rearmament, but by 1936, when Hitler's troops reoccupied the Rhineland in breach of the 1925 Locarno Treaty, there was little to show for it. By then Italy and Germany had formed the Axis alliance and were beginning to build large armies, while Japan – which joined the Axis a year later – was spending 46 per cent of her national income on armaments. In April 1938 London concluded that in the event of war with Germany the British contribution to the Allied response should be provided mainly by naval and air forces. A large army would not be sent to the continent of Europe; instead its role would be confined to defending the United Kingdom and her overseas territories. So priority in the way of equipment for the army was given to anti-aircraft guns and coastal batteries. The five divisions of the field force trained and were fitted out for imperial defence, not for continental warfare against a first-class enemy. The Territorial Army (TA) was to be supplied only with training equipment. This was the state to which successive governments had reduced the British Army.

This army had been the first to use the tank in battle, in September 1916. After the First World War two men, Captain Basil Liddell Hart and Major General J. F. C. Fuller, preached that the future lay in massed formations of fast tanks, supported by mobile self-propelled artillery and infantry carried in tracked armoured vehicles. Instead of hammering away at a wide sector of front, as in 1914–18, the armoured formations would exploit a weak spot in the enemy defences and pour through in what Liddell Hart and Fuller called an 'expanding torrent', to attack vital points in the enemy's rear and paralyse him. In 1926, the British Army set up an experimental mechanized force to practise and develop these theories of armoured warfare. But two years later the conservative element within the army disbanded the force. Mechanization was eventually carried out but far too late for the whole army to assimilate the changed tactics that might have brought success in the ensuing campaign in France and Flanders in 1940.

Once the British government woke up to the dangerous situation that faced the country thanks to the failure to rearm, the Royal Navy and the Royal Air Force were rapidly, if belatedly, re-equipped (not always with the happiest results, but that is outside the scope of this book). The tasks envisaged for the Royal Navy did not impinge on operations ashore in France and Flanders in 1940. The role assigned to the RAF most certainly did. The 1938 re-armament programme called for a greatly expanded RAF capable of defending Britain and mounting bombing offensives against Germany. There was no provision for support of land operations that would have meant sending a large, mobile air force overseas. Although a proportion of the RAF's bombers might be stationed forward in France to decrease the range to German targets, these were expressly not in support of ground operations. The RAF had stoutly defended its independent existence since its creation in April 1918, and preached a doctrine called the indivisibility of air power. In essence, the RAF would decide where and how air power would be exerted. Simply expressed, the RAF's thinking was 'We will win the war on our own, and certainly will not waste our time supporting you brown jobs' – or, if addressing the Royal Navy, 'you blue jobs'.[3]

Rearmament in Britain was boosted by the aftermath of the Munich meeting in the autumn of 1938, when it became apparent that despite the appeasement of Hitler by the British Prime Minister, Neville Chamberlain, peace was not at hand. The snag with rapid rearmament is that putting it into effect is considerably more difficult and time-consuming than deciding to go ahead with it. This is especially true if, as was the case with Britain, the armaments industry had been allowed to run down. Factories have to be geared up for a hugely increased rate of production, while new workshops may have to be built to augment existing ones that could not cope with the expanded output required. Weapons and equipment that are still in the trial stage of development, or even just a gleam in the eye of the inventor, may need further trials before production in quantity can begin. Finally soldiers have to be trained to use and maintain the new equipment. But it does not end there. Introducing a new gun into service usually involves designing and manufacturing a new type of ammunition. So yet more plant is required, and a workforce trained to operate it. Equipment needs spares to ensure that it is kept serviceable. These have to be manufactured too, sometimes in vast quantities. Rearming on a large scale involved placing orders abroad to supplement British production, or even to manufacture every piece, from complete equipments to spares. As in 1914–18, the bulk of these orders went to the United States. The British government should have been well aware of all the hurdles that had to be overcome in the great rearmament catch-up effort. Britain had undergone exactly the same experience in the First World War only twenty years earlier. There were plenty of people around in senior government posts who could remember this, and there was no excuse for being caught out a second time.

In February 1939, in addition to committing the army to deploying in France, and therefore to a war for which it was not equipped or trained, the British government doubled the size of the TA to 340,000, creating twelve new infantry divisions with supporting arms – thus compounding the problem the country already faced in the race to rearm. If that was not enough, a limited form of conscription was introduced. The conscripts needed equipment on which to train too.

Events now speeded up. On 14 March 1939, German troops invaded what had been left of Czechoslovakia after the dismemberment of the country at Munich the previous year. On 29 March, six months before the outbreak of war, Anglo-French staff talks began. The French made clear that the defence of their own territory was their first priority in the event of invasion by Germany. When this had been secured, they intended remaining on the defensive until they had built up sufficient resources for a counter-offensive, while at the same time maintaining an economic blockade of Germany. The British had no difficulty in agreeing this strategy; indeed, since their contribution was so small, they could hardly do otherwise. At this stage in the talks the British revealed that there would be a gap of eleven months between the arrival in France of the first two divisions and the advent of the second two. The build-up for the counter-offensive would, the Allies agreed, be a matter of years not months, given that there was so much ground to make up in terms of equipment and manpower. They had to assume that they could force a stalemate on the Germans and ensure a repetition of the static warfare on the Western Front of most of the years 1914–18. This assumption was made despite the advances in warfare and equipment since 1918, especially in tanks and aircraft. It was a strategy based on the hope that the enemy would do what suited the Allies.

As the weeks went by, the British were able to tell the French that their proposed contribution was a general headquarters and two corps, each of two regular divisions, and an air component of the RAF. When the French Commander-in-Chief, General Gamelin, visited London in June 1939, he was told that the first two divisions of the British field force would now be able to arrive nineteen days after mobilization, and the whole of the rest of the regular contingent of the BEF in thirty-four days. British follow-up forces would consist of one armoured division, which would be available in early 1940, followed by another much later. As the TA divisions became ready for overseas service between four and six months hence, they too would be made available.

The French would have eighty-four to eighty-six divisions, of which twelve would be needed to guard the Italian frontier. So seventy-two to seventy-four would be available to garrison the Maginot Line, and to stem the German offensive wherever this took place. Along with the four British divisions the Allies could muster at minimum seventy-six divisions. Germany would be able to field 116 divisions. It was assumed that the Germans would attack Poland first, and that it was unlikely that France would be attacked until Poland was defeated. The Germans, having the initiative, would be able to deploy their greater strength at their main point of effort, whereas the Allies would be forced to cover the whole 500 miles of front from Switzerland to the North Sea until the Germans showed their hand.

The Germans also outnumbered the Allies in the air. At this stage, with four months to go before war broke out, the Germans could muster a total of 3,700 aircraft of all types against the Allied total of 2,634. If

Italy came into the war she would bring another 1,400 aircraft into the battle.

Staff talks were not held with Belgium or Holland. Both countries hoped that their neutrality would protect them from invasion. The Belgians believed that any staff talks with France and Britain would give the Germans the excuse to attack them when the time came to invade France. The Belgians had failed to learn the lessons of history: neutrality in 1914 had not deterred the Germans from attacking them when it suited them to do so as part of their attempt to outflank the French Army. Holland, having managed to retain its neutrality in the First World War, imagined that it could do likewise in any subsequent conflict.

In the months before war broke out, in an atmosphere of growing menace, Britain introduced full conscription, and partially mobilized the Fleet and the Royal Air Force.

*

On 1 September 1939 Germany invaded Poland after bombing her airfields without warning. Britain ordered full mobilization and, honouring her undertaking to come to Poland's assistance if she were attacked, sent an ultimatum to Germany timed to expire on 3 September. The Germans did not respond and, at 11.00 that morning, the Second World War began.

The British government made two other important decisions that day. The first was to appoint General the Viscount Lord Gort as Commander-in-Chief of the BEF. Gort, who was then fifty-three years old, was a highly decorated Grenadier Guardsman who had served with distinction in the First World War, eventually commanding in turn the 4th and 1st Battalions of his regiment and briefly 3rd Guards Brigade. He had been wounded four times, mentioned in despatches on nine occasions and awarded the Military Cross, the Distinguished Service Order with two bars and the Victoria Cross. A man of great personal and moral courage, he was not suited to high command and had been promoted well above his ceiling. It would be hard to better the description of his character by that very great soldier, then Lieutenant General Alan Brooke, commanding II Corps in the BEF, whose diary entry for 21 November 1939 reads: 'Gort's brain has lately been compared to that of a glorified boy scout! Perhaps unkind but there is a great deal of truth in it.'[4] On 22 November 1939 his criticism is more measured:

Gort is queer mixture [sic], perfectly charming, very definite personality, full of vitality, energy and joie de vivre, and gifted with great powers of leadership. But he just fails to see the big picture and is continually returning to those trivial details that counted a lot when commanding a battalion, but which should not be the concern of a Commander-in-Chief.[5]

The second decision was to determine how Gort should conduct British operations in France. The British government placed him under the orders of General Georges, commanding the French North-East Theatre of Operations. Gort was told, 'You will carry out loyally any instructions issued by him.' He had the right of appeal to his own government if at any time an order given by Georges appeared to imperil the BEF. Gort was also told that, if General Georges wished to detach part of the BEF for operations elsewhere, such an arrangement should only be temporary.

As the Second World War began less than twenty-one years after the end of the First, there were plenty of officers in the British Army with a wealth of fighting experience. Thanks to the slow pace of promotion in peacetime, men who had fought the Germans in the previous contest could be found down to the rank of major. The commanders of I and II Corps were both older than Gort, and had been senior to him before his sudden and unexpected elevation to C-in-C of the BEF. Lieutenant General Sir John Dill of I Corps, who was five years older, had risen in the First World War to be a Brigadier General Staff (BGS) under Haig, and had been a key planner of Haig's final and highly successful offensives in the autumn of 1918. Lieutenant General Alan Brooke of II Corps was three years older than Gort, had a keen brain and was to prove the star corps commander in the BEF.

One of the youngest divisional commanders, at forty-seven, was Major General the Hon. Harold Alexander, commanding the 1st Division in I Corps, lately of the Irish Guards, having commanded a battalion of that regiment at the age of twenty-five in France in the First World War. Always immaculately turned out, nothing ever seemed to worry him. Major General Bernard Montgomery, commanding the 3rd Division in II Corps, was nearly fifty-two years old, and had already crossed swords with Gort when chief instructor at the Staff College at Quetta in what was then India. Gort, director of training on the staff of C-in-C India, had taken exception to Montgomery's self-assertive instructional style. Montgomery never left anyone, however senior, in any doubt about what he thought of them. Brooke was one of the few people he was in awe, and if anything his admiration for him increased as the war progressed. Brigadiers, colonels and lieutenant colonels with fine fighting records in the First World War were plentiful in the 1939–40 BEF. Some would go on to high command later in the war. Others would fade out of the picture.

The transportation of the BEF to France by the Merchant Navy, escorted by the Royal Navy, took place without the loss of a single life. The main ports through which the BEF landed were Cherbourg, Nantes and Saint-Nazaire in western France, the Channel ports through which the 1914–18 BEF had disembarked being deemed too vulnerable to air attack. The two corps of the BEF were deployed hundreds of miles to the east near the Belgian border and took over French positions between Maulde and Armentières, with French First Army on the right and French Seventh Army on the left. This was only the start. As the months passed, the build-up of the BEF continued, until a third corps was operational. By early May 1940, the BEF had grown from four divisions in two corps to ten divisions in three corps. The corps commanders were: I Corps, Lieutenant General M. G. H. Barker, who had taken over from Lieutenant General Sir John Dill on his appointment as Vice Chief of the Imperial General Staff (VCIGS); II Corps, Lieutenant General A. F. Brooke; and III Corps, Lieutenant General Sir Ronald Adam Bt. Meanwhile everybody waited for Hitler to begin his assault in the west, having carved up Poland in less than a month with his new ally the Soviet Union.

The German Army had used the opportunity of sending 'volunteers' to fight on Franco's side in the Spanish Civil War of 1936–9 to practise some of its techniques and theories. But, much more important, the war in Poland provided an excellent live-firing rehearsal for what was to follow in France six months later. The Germans learned a number of useful lessons, and were able to hone their procedures for employing battle groups, infantry–tank co-operation tactics, and the use of aircraft to provide intimate support for ground formations, as well as the necessary liaison and communications to orchestrate the modern all-arms battle.

The British were more up to date than the Germans in just one aspect, that of mechanization or motorization. The BEF that went to France in 1939 was a totally mechanized army. Like the German and French armies it had tanks, but in addition every infantry battalion had ten small open-topped tracked vehicles called Bren-gun carriers designed to provide some mobile protected firepower for the troops. Specially designed motorized vehicles towed all the BEF's guns, and all its supplies were carried in trucks, as were some of the troops. Cars, small vans and motorcycles were provided for commanders, for liaison and for carrying messages. On the outbreak of war, many of these vehicles were requisitioned from civilian firms. Like most other British formations, Major General Montgomery's 3rd Division went to war with laundry and bakers' vans. None of these commandeered vehicles were really suitable for military use – they were often underpowered and because they did not have four-wheel drive were almost useless across country – but they were better than nothing.

The German Army on the other hand had many horsed formations and units, and persevered with them until the end of the war in 1945. Indeed, the vast majority of formations were not mechanized. Infantry divisions marched on foot, and although each had some 942 motor vehicles, the bulk of their supplies was carried in horse-drawn wagons, 1,200 per division. In addition horse-drawn artillery hugely outnumbered motor-towed pieces. Slow-moving horse-drawn transport should be allo-cated dedicated roads to avoid blocking the route for its motorized counterpart, but this was not always possible, and the resulting traffic jams sometimes impeded the progress of the army as a whole. Horses consume bulky fodder – yet another unwelcome problem for the logisti-cians. This horse–motor mix created a quartermaster's nightmare and was to contribute to the failure of the German campaign in Russia that was launched in 1941. Tactically there were two German armies: one fast and mobile, the other slow and plodding. This Achilles heel in the mighty German war machine was to be amply demonstrated in 1940. Only operational and tactical ineptness, principally on the part of the French, prevented the Allies from exploiting this fundamental weakness in the German way of making war.

The French pinned their defence hopes on the Maginot Line, named after the War Minister from 1929 to 1932 who as Sergeant Maginot had been wounded at Verdun early in the First World War. A great deal of the fighting at Verdun in the eleven-month battle of 1916, in which Maginot did not participate, had taken place in and around forts and concrete strongpoints on vital ground defending the city. Paradoxically, before the First World War, the French had scorned the concept of fighting from fortresses, opting instead for aggressive tactics out in the open, attacking the enemy with infantry and light guns regardless of casualties. During the Verdun fighting of 1916, the nature of the terrain and the determination of the French not to cede an inch of ground brought home to them just how important the fortress system was. Loss of some of the key forts nearly cost them the battle. That experience and the terrible losses the French had incurred in the First World War, not only at Verdun but also in numerous engagements both before and after that bloodletting, persuaded them that fortresses and artillery were the answer in any future war. In effect they fell into the age-old trap of planning to fight the next war on the basis of the last one. In 1921, Marshal Pétain, then Supreme Commander, set the scene for the French Army's doctrine on the use of armour, saying, 'Tanks assist the advance of the infantry, by breaking static obstacles and active resistance put up by the enemy.'[6] This was not the last time that Pétain, the saviour of Verdun, was to have a baleful influence on his country.

Constructed between 1930 and 1935, and extending from Luxembourg in the north to the Swiss border in the south, the Maginot Line was not really a line, but a string of concrete forts built about three miles apart, interspersed by smaller casemates. Both types were well buried, with only observation cupolas and gun turrets visible, and even these in many cases could be lowered flush with the roof. Advanced warning posts, anti-tank obstacles, wire and mines screened the forts. The garrisons varied from twelve to thirty men in the casemates, and from 200 to 1,200 in the forts. The latter were like underground villages, with barracks, kitchens, generators, magazines and even electric railways to transport men and ammunition from barrack and magazine to the gun positions. Casemates contained machine guns and one 47mm anti-tank gun, with heavy artillery in the forts.

Belgium was still an ally of France while the Maginot Line was under construction and so extending the line to cover the 250 miles of the Franco-Belgian border was considered tactless, as it would send a signal of no confidence in Belgium's capability to resist invasion, and would isolate her on the 'wrong' side of the wall. An added disincentive to extending the line was the expense. The eighty-seven miles completed by 1935 had cost 4,000 million francs in excess of the 3,000 million allocated in the budget. Finally, an extension of the line would run through the heavily industrialized region of Lille–Valenciennes on the Belgian border, causing major disruption to French industry. Experience in the First World War had persuaded the French that, if they were to avoid losing this northern industrial region, they would have to stop the invader before he crossed the French frontier. So when Belgium elected for a policy of strict neutrality, the French realized that they would have to enter Belgian territory from the west the moment the Germans invaded it from the east. In this event, instead of fighting from behind the concrete and steel of the Maginot Line on which so much treasure had been spent, the French would be forced to engage in a mobile battle of encounter in open country, a contest for which they were neither mentally prepared nor organized.

The French aimed to fight a methodical battle under a system of rigid centralization and adherence to orders from the top. Unit and formation commanders were supposed to remain at their command posts – the theory being that here, at the centre of communications, they were best placed to receive information and orchestrate the battle. This of course begged the question what one should do if the communications did not work. It was a question that demanded an answer, but the French failed to provide one, and it was a key ingredient in their defeat. For there were few radios in French units and formations, and communication was mainly by messengers or by telephone, using either the civilian system or lines laid by the military. Initiative in subordinate commanders at whatever level was frowned upon. No one was trained to react to the unexpected, and therefore how to work through the chaos. The French doctrine ignored the German commander Helmuth von Moltke's dictum that 'no plan of operations will ever extend, with any sort of certainty, beyond the first encounter with the hostile main force', and that success in battle was, and still is, gained by the commander's ability 'to recognize the changed situation, to order its foreseeable course and to execute this energetically'.

French planning envisaged that as soon as the enemy attacked he was to be stopped by concentrated artillery fire and static defence, rather than by counter-attack. Local reserves would be placed in front of enemy penetrations to slow him down and eventually stop him. Meanwhile local superiority of men and equipment would be assembled, and then, and only then, would counter-attacks be mounted. The armour would not be employed in mass, but in penny packets accompanying the infantry as mobile pillboxes. Even had the communications worked, this rigid, pedestrian operational concept was hardly the best way to fight a mobile enemy. Once the two-way flow of communications was slowed by enemy interdiction, or even brought to a complete standstill, commanders sitting in their command posts would be completely out of touch and unable to influence events.

The German system was totally the opposite, and stressed personal initiative and what modern soldiers call mission command. Subordinates were told what their superior's mission was, and were expected to adapt their plans and the execution of them to achieve it, and to exploit a changing situation to their advantage, while their superiors supported them with all the means at their disposal. Everybody was trained to command at least one if not two levels above their own, and therefore able to take over when superiors became casualties. The leaders of Nazi Germany knew that their country was not well placed economically to fight a long war, but instead had to win swiftly. Thus was born the principle of lightning war, *Blitzkrieg*, which, following Moltke's teachings, demanded flexibility and the will to win. The German Army was adept at combining mass and aggressive tactics, and in achieving this the commander's mental alertness and drive were essential factors, for the force of his personality affected the whole of his command.

The Germans often used a tactic that today we would call recce pull. Armoured battle groups preceded by reconnaissance would find, or lever open, the weak spots in the enemy defence and, using radio communications, 'pull' the main force through behind them; if necessary the main force would switch its axis on to the new line. This is the opposite of everybody bashing forward in a setpiece attack supported by a mass of artillery, only to come up against a rock-like defence. The success of mission command and recce pull depended not only on commanders being well forward where they could 'read' the battle, but also on their being in a position to communicate the necessary orders to take account of the changing situation, either face to face with subordinates or by radio. The German system demanded good secure radio communications, and they had them. In addition, German commanders were able to call upon support from their air force, not least dive-bombers that they used in lieu of artillery, particularly if they had advanced beyond the range of their guns. In this way the Germans fought a true all-arms battle, with infantry, armour, artillery and air. Their armour and mechanized infantry were concentrated in elite armoured (panzer) formations, with tanks used in mass.

For the Germans had taken note of British writings and experimentation on armour. Above all, Captain Heinz Guderian, who in the First World War had been on the staff of the German Crown Prince at Verdun, had become convinced that any future war should be fought very differently. He studied the works of Liddell Hart and Fuller and saw the importance of armoured formations, with tanks taking the leading role, not just as adjuncts to infantry. By 1931 he was commanding a motorized battalion equipped with dummy tanks – all that Germany was allowed under the terms of the 1919 Treaty of Versailles. He kept abreast of experiments by Brigadier Hobart's British 1st Tank Brigade on Salisbury Plain in 1934 by employing a local tutor to translate the articles Liddell Hart wrote reporting these exercises. The following year Guderian published a book *Achtung – Panzer!*, which analysed the successes and failures of the Allied use of tanks during the First World War – the Germans having used tanks only fitfully during that war, and those mainly captured Allied ones. He concluded that what was needed was a fast-moving, medium 'breakthrough' tank, not a heavy infantry-support tank of the kind fielded by the French Army. Hitler's accession to power saw Guderian's theories turned into reality, and by 1935 he was commanding the 2nd Panzer Division. The first pamphlets issued to the new panzer divisions were based on British Army manuals on the use of armour, not on the French equivalent, because of the rigidity of the latter's doctrine on the relationship between armour and infantry. *Achtung – Panzer!* was never translated into French or English, nor was it studied at staff colleges or by the general staffs of either country, although it foretold precisely how Guderian would carry out the breakthrough at Sedan in 1940.

At this point it might be helpful to lay to rest some of the myths about the relative strengths and types of armour on both sides. The ultimate German success has been ascribed to superiority in the numbers and types of equipment, especially tanks. The French possessed some 4,000 armoured fighting vehicles of all types. Of these around 2,000 were fit for modern warfare. A good proportion of these modern tanks were the S-35s (known as Somuas from the initials of the maker). This was one of the best tanks in service in the world, with a 47mm turret-mounted gun. The French also had some slower but more heavily armoured Char B1s, with a hull-mounted short-barrelled 75mm gun, and a 47mm in the turret. The Somuas were grouped in three light mechanized divisions (*divisions légères méchaniques* – DLMs), very like the German light divisions in that they comprised motorized infantry with a powerful tank element. The excellent Somua medium tank was more heavily armoured, as fast as any contemporary German tank and, except for the *Panzer Kampfwagon* Mk IV, had a heavier gun. The Char B1s were grouped in three armoured divisions (*divisions cuirassées*). These had only recently formed and had undergone little or no collective training. A DLM had 220 tanks compared with only 150 in a *division cuirassée*. The DLMs were allocated to separate armies, and the *divisions cuirassées* to the reserve: one to the general reserve and two to the reserves of the French First Army Group in the centre, and deployed piecemeal.

The Germans had 2,539 tanks at their disposal when they started their offensive in the west, but of these 1,478 were obsolete Mk Is and Mk IIs, whose main armament consisted only of machine guns or 20mm cannon. The only battleworthy tanks were 349 Mk IIIs with a 37mm gun main armament, 334 Czech tanks also with 37mm guns, and 278 Mk IVs, which in 1940 had a short-barrelled 75mm and were intended as a close-support tank for the Mk IIIs. The Mk IVs were not upgunned until later in the war. So the French outnumbered the Germans in battleworthy tanks.

The British fielded three types of tank: the light Mk VI with one .303in and one .55in machine gun; three Marks of cruiser tank each with a 2-pounder main armaments; and two Marks of infantry tank. The Mk I infantry tank had a .303in machine gun, and the far heavier Mk II or Matilda had a 2-pounder and a .303 machine gun. One of the legacies of the preaching by Liddell Hart and Fuller on the subject of armoured warfare was that the British went to war with these three types of tanks: light tanks for reconnaissance; with cruiser tanks grouped in armoured divisions, highly mobile but weak in firepower; and infantry tanks suitable only for infantry support. The correct answer, which took the British most of the war to arrive at, was a medium or main battle tank, combining firepower, protection and mobility in one type of tank. For technical reasons this was a difficult balancing act, but it was one which the Germans achieved long before the British. The tanks produced by the British were undergunned and, except for the Matildas, lacked armoured protection. Wedded to the 2-pounder gun, the British built tanks with turret rings far too small to accept any bigger-calibre guns. The 2-pounder was too small calibre to produce an effective high-explosive (HE) round, and fired only solid shot, which was useless against infantry and bunkers. Dual-capability and larger-calibre tank guns did not feature in the British inventory until the American tanks arrived (Lee-Grants and Shermans).

One of Liddell Hart's notions of future warfare, propounded in the inter-war period, was of 'fleets' of fast tanks, like ships at sea, roaming the area behind the enemy lines causing so much mayhem, especially by destroying his communications and headquarters, that the enemy was unable to continue the contest. Hence the British term 'cruiser' tank, following Liddell Hart's nautical analogy. This happy state of affairs could, so Liddell Hart predicted, be achieved at a low cost in casualties, provided the correct tactical formulae were applied. Unfortunately, Liddell Hart's theories of the 'indirect approach' (not attacking the enemy at his strongest point but finding a way round, or attacking a vital point in the rear), and the vision he dreamed up of 'fleets' of tanks swanning about, begged a number of questions: how did one break through the enemy in order to burst out into the open country beyond without a tough fight, especially if there were no open flanks; and what if the enemy was equally agile and mobile but reacted correctly, that is with a force of all arms, artillery, anti-tank guns, infantry and air? The British were to learn that armour must be accompanied by infantry (to deal with the enemy infantry, especially if equipped with anti-tank weapons) and by artillery (to destroy anti-tank guns, or at least neutralize them by killing and wounding their crews or by forcing them to keep their heads down in the interests of survival).

The French Army either had not read Liddell Hart or, in typically Gallic fashion, deemed any idea, military or otherwise, that had not originated in France as unworthy of a second thought. Whatever the reason, as mentioned earlier, the French also arrived at a flawed concept for the use of armour.

Almost all tanks, British, French and German, were vulnerable to all the types of artillery employed by either side. The exceptions were the British infantry tanks and the Char B1, which were so heavily armoured they were proof against the German 37mm gun, although not against heavier guns. As the Battle of France was to show, as were later encounters in North Africa, tanks could be destroyed by 2-pounders, 75mm and 18-pounder field artillery, 105mm howitzers, 3.7in mountain guns, 25-pounder guns, and of course the 88mm anti-aircraft guns, provided that all these guns were firing using direct laying (pointing directly at the tank, not being fired from a position out of sight, directed by a spotter).

No Second World War tank could withstand a direct hit by a medium artillery shell, a 155mm or 5.5in gun. Tanks caught in artillery concentrations that included medium shells, even if not hit directly, could be set on fire, have tracks blown off and turrets jammed by shell splinters. Artillery fire could severely punish infantry and towed artillery accompanying armoured attacks, blow off radio aerials from tanks, and force commanders to shut down inside their turrets, which restricted their vision. Most commanders liked to move and fight with their heads out of the top of the turret, and the more thrusting ones would sit on the rim of the hatch to get the best view possible. Well-sited and resolutely handled field artillery batteries could repel a tank attack – a technique that the British practised before the war. The British 25-pounder was provided with an anti-tank sight, and when in action with its wheels on the round metal platform with which it was eventually fitted could be trained round quickly to a flank. The French 75mm field gun had been specifically designed to fire direct, which reduced its capability as a field gun, but made it a first-class anti-tank gun. In short, tanks often achieved their effect by appearing to be all-powerful, but they could be stopped.

It is sometimes forgotten that Hitler was not averse to building fixed defences, but for a rather different reason from that favoured by France. In the Rhineland, he constructed a line of concrete forts opposite the Maginot Line, known as the West Wall or Siegfried Line. In 1936, Churchill predicted how the Germans would use this line, which because of its intrinsic strength could be held by fewer troops than defences consisting of trenches, to release sufficient troops to 'swing round through Belgium and Holland'. The Siegfried Line would deter France and Britain from rendering aid to their eastern allies, first Czechoslovakia and subsequently Poland. Hitler could dispose of his enemies in the east at his leisure, before turning on the French with his rear secure.

In November 1939 Allied planners, expecting the Germans to outflank the Maginot Line and attack through Belgium, came up with what was known as Plan D. This called for the French 1st Army Group under General Billotte and the BEF to rush into Belgium and create stop lines to slow down and eventually halt the Germans in accordance with current French tactical principles. This would, it was hoped, buy time to build up reserves for a counter-attack. The stop lines were based on river courses, particularly the Escaut (Scheldt to the Belgians) and the Dyle. The Dyle, further east than the Escaut, was where the initial stop line would be established – hence Plan D for Dyle being preferred to Plan E for Escaut. The Belgians were fully aware of the plan but, clinging to their neutrality, would allow only a few British officers in plain clothes to carry out reconnaissance.

The command arrangements were entirely of French design, the French being senior partner in the forthcoming campaign in France and Flanders by virtue of their overwhelming superiority in numbers over their British allies. The Supreme Commander, the sixty-eight-year-old General Maurice Gamelin, had no radio contact with the commanders in the field. He gave orders by messenger from his headquarters in the Château de Vincennes outside Paris. It would be misleading to imagine Gamelin as an earlier version of Eisenhower, the Supreme Commander of the Allied Expeditionary Force that fought in north-west Europe in 1944–5. Unlike Eisenhower, Gamelin did not have a staff of Allied officers working together to produce a common and agreed strategy. Instead a military mission under Major General Sir Richard Howard-Vyse was appointed to Gamelin's headquarters to represent the British Chief of the Imperial General Staff (CIGS); this was known as the Howard-Vyse Mission. Furthermore there was no Anglo-French equivalent to the Anglo-American Combined Chiefs of Staff, introduced after America came into the war at the end of 1941, to which Eisenhower as Supreme Allied Commander reported. Gamelin reported to the French government, and the British Chiefs of Staff effectively had no influence whatever over his decisions, other than representations by the Howard-Vyse Mission or personal visits by CIGS.

The outline command structure is shown in Appendix A. In addition to his responsibilities for the defence of France against German attack, Gamelin also commanded French troops in the Alps (facing Italy), Syria and North Africa. His deputy General Georges commanded the North-East Front, stretching from Switzerland to the Channel. Georges had three army groups under him, of which Billotte's French 1st Army Group was earmarked for operations in Belgium. This army group consisted of three French armies and with it, but directly under command of Georges, would go the BEF. Also directly under Georges was the French Seventh Army, which had an independent role operating behind and to the left of the Belgians at Antwerp to cover their left flank and also, if possible, to link them to the Dutch. It was a complicated and muddled set-up, with the BEF and French Seventh Army out on Billotte's flank, and having to co-ordinate their activities with his, which given the French paucity of communications was not going to be easy. A mission under Brigadier J. G. de R. Swayne (known as the Swayne Mission) was sent to Georges' headquarters to represent Gort.

At the outbreak of war, the German offensive was under way in the east, carving up Poland. Poland's allies France and Britain did almost nothing, despite Gamelin having assured the Poles in May 1939 that immediately war broke out the French Army would take the offensive against Germany, and that by the fifteenth day after mobilization it would throw in the majority of its forces. The so-called Saar Offensive that Gamelin authorized in September was a pathetic affair. The trumpeting in the British press of a major attack on the Siegfried Line, and stories of secret 70-ton French tanks crashing through German lines, turned out to be eyewash. No more than nine divisions took part in the Saar operation. They were ordered not to advance beyond the outposts of the Siegfried Line, and to avoid casualties at all costs. Apart from taking some abandoned villages, the French gains were negligible. Not one German formation was diverted from Poland. When Poland capitulated, Gamelin ordered a withdrawal to the Maginot Line. When the Germans obligingly allowed the French to retreat unscathed, Gamelin sighed with relief.

The Germans were amazed and relieved. They had expected a full-blooded assault. The Siegfried Line was nothing like as strong as the Maginot Line, and was anyway not complete. As the frontier from Aachen to Switzerland was held by only twenty-five reserve divisions, with not one tank, and with sufficient ammunition for only three days' fighting, many German generals assessed that the French would be on the Rhine within fourteen days, and might even have won the war by then. Neutral observers noted how low morale was in Berlin, 'facing war with something approaching abject terror', in the words of Joseph Hersch, Berlin editor of the *Christian Science Monitor*. They were convinced that Hitler's bluff was about to be called at last; but they were wrong again. So began a period known as the Phoney War. During the Saar Offensive the morale of French soldiers had been high, but it sagged when this was called off. Arthur Koestler was an intellectual who fled Germany and was temporarily interned by the French as a suspicious alien in October 1939. He witnessed the French attitude first-hand:

> We talked to many of the soldiers. They were sick of the war before it started ... they wanted to go home and did not care a bean for Dantzig and the Corridor ... They rather liked La France, but they did not actually love her; they rather disliked Hitler for all the unrest he created, but they did not actually hate him. The only thing they really hated was the idea of war.[7]

Danzig was created a free city on the Baltic by the Treaty of Versailles in 1919, the aim being to give the Poles access to the sea through the territory called the Polish corridor. The city's population was overwhelmingly German and this played an important part in Hitler's case for going to war with Poland.

As the months of the Phoney War passed with no German attack, some British formations were sent to help man the French sector in the area of the Maginot Line. When it came to the 4th Division's turn, Lieutenant James Hill, a platoon commander in the 2nd Battalion Royal Fusiliers, spent Christmas 1939 in the *ligne de contact* (contact line) forward of the Maginot Line. It was bitterly cold that winter, and the forward companies lived in trenches dug by the French. The ground was covered by snow and one could see almost as well by night as by day. The nearest Germans were about four miles away. In the event of a heavy attack, the troops in the contact line would withdraw to the Maginot Line. Hill remembers that British troops manning the contact line were taken round the Maginot Line and were very impressed by what they saw.

The Germans patrolled, as did the British, in section strength (eight soldiers led by a non-commissioned officer), in the hope of capturing a prisoner. Hill did not seize any prisoners, but another company in the 2nd Royal Fusiliers managed to bag a couple. The French were not as aggressive as their opponents or their allies – in Hill's opinion, they did not want to stir things up. Winston Churchill, then First Lord of the Admiralty, commented:

> The prevailing atmosphere of calm aloofness often struck visitors to the French front, by the seemingly poor quality of the work in hand, by the lack of visible activity of any kind. The emptiness of the roads behind the line was in great contrast to the continual coming and going which extended for miles behind the British sector.[8]

Frenchmen also noted that their troops were occupied growing roses to pretty up the Maginot Line and painting the steps white, and that they seemed to have plenty of time for football instead of training.

Second Lieutenant Peter Martin, serving in the 2nd Battalion the Cheshire Regiment, a machine-gun battalion in Barker's I Corps, also had a low opinion of the French soldiers he came across. Martin had joined his battalion just before war broke out, but to his chagrin was not allowed to accompany them to France. He was deemed too young, the lower age limit for deployment on war service being nineteen and a half in those days. Having completed a machine-gun course, and still desperate to get to France, he was ordered to the Regimental Depot. There he learned from the adjutant that anyone who made advances to the niece of the depot commanding officer got sent out straight away. So he made advances, which was not a chore as she was pretty and charming. Within three weeks he was on his way, joining his battalion in the Lille area. A machine-gun battalion had forty-eight Vickers medium machine guns. Martin took over number 7 platoon, consisting of two sections, each of two guns. In his own words he 'was raw and useless. I had some wonderful sergeants who "carried" me. The Platoon Sergeant really took charge. The soldiers were wonderful – if they liked you they "carried" you, if they didn't, they ditched you.'

More senior British officers were also less than satisfied with what they saw of the French during the long months of the Phoney War. The commander of II Corps, Lieutenant General Alan Brooke, who had a fine First World War record, recorded in his diary a visit to the Maginot Line on 20 December 1939. It is important to remember that these were his opinions at the time and were not written with the wisdom of hindsight: 'It gave me but little feeling of security, and I consider that the French would have done better to invest the money in the shape of mobile defences such as more and better aircraft and more heavy armoured divisions than to sink all this money into the ground.'9

Subsequent trips to the line did nothing to alter Brooke's view that the money could have been better spent. After inspecting the forts in the line, he went to visit 12th Infantry Brigade, which included Hill's battalion:

> We first went to the Black Watch [6th Battalion] in the 'Ligne de Recueil' [literally Line of Collection, a French expression referring to the line to which the outposts retire when pushed back by an attack], some 3,000 yards in front of the Maginot Line. This line has no defence and a rotten anti-tank ditch. From there we went up to the PWV [Prince of Wales's Volunteers – 1st Battalion the South Lancashire Regiment] holding the outpost line some 6,000 yards further forward. A line with no power of resistance, a few isolated posts far apart and only lightly wired in. German patrols penetrate right in behind our posts at dusk and at night. A no-man's land of some 1,500 to 2,000 yards exists between ill-defined fronts. But practically no activity on either side, a certain amount of shelling was going on either side and an air battle in the afternoon, otherwise absolute peace. The defence does not inspire me with confidence.10

Nor did the French soldiers he saw impress Brooke: 'French slovenliness, dirtyness [sic] and inefficiency are I think worse than ever.'11 After attending a service to commemorate the Armistice that ended the First World War, he stood alongside General Corap, commanding French Ninth Army, to take the salute:

I can still see those troops now. Seldom have I seen anything more slovenly and badly turned out. Men unshaven, horses ungroomed, clothes and saddlery that did not fit, vehicles dirty, and complete lack of pride in themselves or their units. What shook me most was the look on the men's faces, disgruntled and insubordinate looks, and although ordered to give 'eyes left', hardly a man bothered to do so.[12]

Brooke was no Francophobe. He had been born in France and had spent his early years there, loved the country, and spoke French before he learned to speak English. He had visited Verdun in 1916, during the time of France's greatest trial, and had come away deeply imbued with the lionhearted spirit of the French soldier and the people. What he saw now devastated him.

He was just as critical of the state of training of the BEF, although not of its spirit, writing in his diary on 1 November that his corps still needed months of training before it could be considered fit for war.[13] After visiting the 4th Battalion The Gordon Highlanders on 26 November, he observed, 'It is totally unfit for war in every respect and it will take at least 2 months to render it fit. It would be sheer massacre to commit it to action in its present state in addition to endangering the lives of others.'[14]

The lamentable state of training of the BEF was of course a direct result of the way the British Army had been starved of funds by successive governments for twenty years. For example it was commonplace on pre-war field exercises to find flags representing anti-tank guns and football rattles taking the place of machine guns. Restrictions on the use of land resulted in exercises that lacked realism. Therefore when Brooke's II Corps arrived in France, having been promised a much needed period of intensive training, only to be told by Gort to take over part of the French defensive positions south of Lille, he was extremely put out. In this as in other matters Gort was deficient as a commander. During the whole eight months of the Phoney War, he did nothing to prepare the BEF headquarters for war, not once conducting a signals, command-post or movement exercise. An army, like any other military unit or formation, is the creation of and reflects its commander. Gort failed to give the lead required to ensure that his army used the precious time available to put right all the many deficiencies in training that had piled up in the locust years of the 1920s and 1930s. Brooke was the only senior commander who did prepare for the time ahead; taking his cue from him, Major General Bernard Montgomery, commanding the 3rd Division, did so too. Montgomery wrote later that 'in September 1939, the British Army was totally unfit to fight a first class war on the Continent of

Europe'. The other division in II Corps, the 4th, was not so well trained, and curiously Brooke did not sack the divisional commander. Montgomery trained his division rigorously, practising it in moving by day and night over similar distances that it would encounter during the advance into Belgium when the balloon went up. His exercises were designed to shake down his division into a fighting team so that it would hold together under the shock of battle and the chaos it brings in its train. For a collection of soldiers, however well trained in individual skills, does not make a unit or formation – it is the articulation of the whole that counts.

Training was not helped by the French insistence on radio silence, which severely limited the scope of command-post exercises that are so important in achieving the cohesion without which an army cannot exert its full fighting power. This ridiculous ruling by the French was not such a hindrance to training at battalion level as it would be today; in the British Army at that stage in the war there were no radios from battalion headquarters to companies, and on down to platoons and sections. Communication forward of battalion was by telephone, motor-cycle despatch rider or runner. Lack of radios was to prove a considerable disadvantage in the war of movement that would actually take place, as opposed to the slow pace of most operations in the previous war.

The British regular divisions had a foundation of discipline, skill at arms and tactical proficiency that could serve as a basis for improving standards of training, and they used the long months of the Phoney War to do just that. The territorial divisions, lacking this grounding, and having been sent to France much later than the regular formations, found it more difficult to improve and become battleworthy. The general level of toughness and training was patchy throughout the BEF. To remedy this would have taken a far higher standard of strong leadership from the very top, based on an up-to-date doctrine of tactics and oper-ational-level skills promulgated BEF-wide, than Gort and some of his formation commanders provided.

One of the problems encountered by the BEF during this period was the rising incidence of VD. This is hardly surprising. Brothels flour-ished in all the major towns and larger villages. Most of these were an eye-opener to young British soldiers brought up in what by today's standards were somewhat straitlaced circumstances. Girls and pin-ups in the modest bathing costumes of the time were commonplace, but going topless in public wearing just a thong as today's girls often do was unknown. So the reactions of young men like Bombardier Harding on going into a brothel for the first time are not surprising. 'We'd never seen anything like it. Girls with long black hair down their backs, wearing just G-strings and high-heeled shoes. The G-strings disappeared leaving just their bottoms showing. You couldn't help yourself really. You couldn't get up the stairs fast enough.'

Montgomery's solution was to demand that the troops be educated and to insist that the subject of sex and disease was not buried under a blanket of sanctimoniousness. He issued an order on the subject, requiring that condoms be on sale in the NAAFI canteen and that the men be taught the French for 'French letter', in case they wanted to buy one in a shop. Outraged, the senior chaplain at General Headquarters demanded that Gort take action. Gort was minded to sack Montgomery, but Brooke persuaded him against the idea.

Captain White, the adjutant of the 1st/6th East Surreys, a TA battalion in the 4th Division, also under Brooke, recorded that their newly arrived commanding officer got into trouble when he bought up all the condoms in town and distributed them to the battalion free of charge. The padres were incensed, believing that he was encouraging the men to sin. They seemed oblivious to the outcome of the CO's initiative: the 1st/6th East Surreys had virtually no cases of VD, in contrast to most other units in the 4th Division.

Although morale in the BEF never approached the depths reached by the French, many units and formations succumbed to the boredom of the Phoney War, with the result that their preparations were lackadaisical. This air of unreality also affected some of the top civilians too. The British Prime Minister, Neville Chamberlain, visited the 3rd Division just before Christmas 1939 and whispered to Montgomery, 'I don't think the Germans have any intention of attacking us do you?'[15] Montgomery replied that the Germans would attack when it suited them, probably when the weather improved.

On 10 January 1940 Major Helmuth Reinberger, serving on a German airborne planning staff, flew in a light aircraft to Cologne, carrying with him a briefcase containing top-secret documents. The pilot got disorientated in bad visibility, and then his engine cut out, obliging him to perform a forced landing. To his horror he found himself just inside Belgian territory. Reinberger tried to burn his maps and papers, but only partially succeeded before they were taken from him by a Belgian captain who, accompanied by troops, arrived hotfoot at the crash scene.

The papers were soon at Belgian GHQ and, although badly scorched, were sufficiently legible to reveal that the Germans intended to invade France via Belgium and Holland. The Dutch and French were duly informed. The French Army, in a state of high alert, closed up to the Belgian frontier in appalling weather. The Belgian frontier barriers were raised, and for a moment it looked as if the Belgians were going to invite the Allies in. But King Leopold, whose naivety had led to Belgian neutrality in the first place, rescinded the order, dismissing his chief of staff. By 15 January the flap died down. Spurred on by sight of the German plans, Gamelin strengthened the force that would go into Belgium in the event of a German invasion. Now instead of ten French divisions and the BEF, thirty would go in, among them the best the French Army could offer: two out of France's three new armoured divisions, five out of seven motorized divisions, and all three DLMs.

On the extreme left flank was to be deployed General Giraud's Seventh Army of seven first-class divisions, including one DLM. Until Gamelin made these changes, the Seventh Army was to have constituted the major part of General Georges' operational reserve. Gamelin's decision to commit it in Belgium from the outset was to have dire consequences. On Giraud's right would be Gort's BEF, positioned on the Dyle from four miles north of Louvain to Wavre. South of the BEF would come Blanchard's First Army, tasked with holding the Gembloux Gap down to Namur on the Meuse. Corap's Ninth Army was to occupy the line of the Meuse in the Belgian Ardennes south of Namur. General Huntziger's Second Army would deploy from Sedan to Longwy and the start of the Maginot Line.

Thus the main striking power of the French Army was to be committed to operations in Belgium north of Namur. This, as we shall see, was exactly what Hitler wanted. For years after the Second World War the French believed that the forced landing by Reinberger had been a 'cunning German plan'. It was nothing of the kind.

2

INTO BELGIUM: FIRST SHOCKS

'Hitler has missed the bus,' claimed Chamberlain in a speech on 4 April 1940, at the Central Hall in Westminster. Five days later the Germans occupied Denmark and began the invasion of Norway. The story of the ill-starred Allied campaign in Norway in response to the German invasion has no place in this book, but its last act was still being played out, during and after the evacuation of Dunkirk, and so provided an unwelcome distraction for the British government at that time.

At first light on 10 May, the Luftwaffe attacked Allied airfields, rail centres and other key points in France in an attempt to disrupt communications while the German Army had already started moving west. The British Official History dismisses the attacks, and it certainly did nothing to affect the British plans or moves. The main weight of the Luftwaffe fell on Holland that day, and much of their fighter force was flying top cover over the long columns of tanks, guns and infantry as they streamed forward to the attack, crossing the frontiers of Belgium, Holland and Luxembourg. The BEF's move to its positions on the Dyle went without a hitch. There was a moment of farce, however, when a frontier guard demanded that the leading unit of Montgomery's 3rd Division show him a permit to enter Belgium. The British charged the barrier with a 15-hundredweight truck, and the advance of the division proceeded. The leading mechanized cavalry reached the Dyle that night. The movements that day and the next, although carried out in daylight, were not interrupted by the Luftwaffe, which was busy destroying the Belgian Air Force, most of which was caught on the ground, and supporting the airborne invasion of Holland. Even so, the Germans managed to destroy six of the Blenheim light bombers of the RAF's 114 Squadron at Condé Vraux and render unserviceable the remaining twelve, as well as setting fire to the fuel dump. There was another reason why the German air force did not want to hinder the move of the Allies into Belgium unduly: it suited their plan. Not even the wily Brooke seems to have suspected that the BEF and French Seventh Army were being led into a trap.

As the BEF motored through Belgium, the civilians turned out to cheer. Lieutenant Dunn led his troop of guns of the 7th Field Regiment, part of Montgomery's 3rd Division, through Brussels at about 0800 hours. As the guns bumped and rattled over the cobbled streets, crowds threw flowers, fruit and sweets to the soldiers riding on the gun quads (motor towers). The soldiers waved and grinned. Dunn thought of Wellington's army moving out of the same city on the way to Waterloo.

Eventually Dunn's troop arrived at their designated harbour area in a small village in a valley. A harbour area for any kind of military unit, be it a battery of guns, squadron of tanks or battalion of infantry, is a place where sub-units or units gather while waiting to move forward or back. Replenishment, especially of armoured units, may take place in the harbour area. Sentries will be posted and other defensive measures taken, such as digging slit trenches and siting anti-aircraft guns. But a harbour area is not a position from which one aims to fight – so field artillery, for example, will not be sited for firing. The countryside was green, rolling and wooded, a pleasant change from the industrial region of France where the regiment had spent the winter. As they were camouflaging their guns and vehicles, a German reconnaissance aircraft flew low over the village. The Bren gunners and riflemen blazed away, their shining faces turned to the skies. A quarter of an hour later two aircraft appeared and each dropped a bomb on the village. As far as Dunn was concerned it was the best lesson they could have had. From that moment on, he never saw any of his men fire at an aircraft with a rifle or Bren gun, as both were ineffective except at low level. Thereafter they lay low and kept still, or took cover. Looking up at aircraft is a sure way to be spotted, something that not everybody in the BEF learned.

The BEF deployed with two corps up along seventeen miles of the Dyle. On the right Lieutenant General Barker's I Corps had 1st and 2nd Divisions in the front line, and 48th Division held back; and on the left Brooke's II Corps had the 3rd Division up, and the 4th Division in reserve. Two other divisions, 5th and 50th, were in general reserve (elements of these two had been sent to Norway before the German attack in the west). Two more divisions, 42nd and 44th, were deployed in depth some fifty miles back on the River Escaut under Adam's III Corps. It was a good defensive layout with plenty of depth. Four more divisions of the BEF would be involved in the battles ahead: 12th, 23rd and 46th, which had been sent out for pioneering work (unskilled labour on the lines of communication) and to complete their training. They had no artillery and lacked much other vital equipment. Lastly, the 51st (Highland) Division had been detached in April to the Saar front to gain experience in the Maginot Line under French command, and never rejoined the BEF.

By 11 May, the only confrontation in the BEF's sector involved the

3rd Division which, by agreement of the Allied command, had been ordered to defend Louvain. As the division approached the town at dawn on 11 May, Belgian infantry fired on its machine-gun battalion, 2nd Battalion the Middlesex Regiment. When Montgomery informed the commander of the 10th Belgian Division that Louvain was to be defended by the BEF, the Belgian general said that King Leopold had entrusted the defence of Louvain to him, and that he would never leave his post without orders from his King, despite the agreed deployment that allocated a sector *north* of Louvain to the Belgians. Gort's reaction to this nonsense, instead of immediately taking the matter to Leopold, was to back down and tell Brooke to 'double-bank' the Belgian division. 'Not a satisfactory solution,' Brooke wrote in his diary.[1] Brooke went to see Leopold the next day, addressing him in fluent French, but found him totally under the influence of his malignant ADC, Major General van Overstraeten, and was not able to persuade him to change the order. Overstraeten interposed himself twice between Brooke and Leopold, rudely interrupting him, so that eventually the King stepped to one side and looked out of the window.

> I could not very well force my presence a third time on the King, and I therefore discussed the matter with this individual who I assumed must be the Chief of Staff. I found that arguing with him was a sheer waste of time, he was not familiar with the dispositions of the BEF and seemed to care little about them. Most of his suggestions were fantastic. I finally withdrew.[2]

Brooke found that Montgomery had solved the problem by putting himself unreservedly under the Belgian divisional commander's orders, which thrilled that officer. When asked what he proposed to do when the Germans attacked, Montgomery replied that he would place the Belgian under arrest and take command. In the event Montgomery did not have to carry out his stated intention. As German pressure on Louvain built up, the commander of the Belgian 10th Division decided not to fight but to move out so that he could, in his own words, 'rest his tired troops'. Montgomery was delighted to be shot of them.

That same day, Gort's Chief of the General Staff, Lieutenant General Henry Pownall, also had an audience with King Leopold, who seemed dazed. Pownall found Overstraeten suave, glib and specious. There he also found Generals Georges and Billotte, whose main aim appeared to be to persuade the Belgians that Billotte should co-ordinate the operations of the BEF and the Belgian Army, as a representative of General Georges. Gort should have been told about this change of command relationship long before battle was joined. However, Pownall, speaking

for Gort agreed, as did King Leopold. Gamelin, having been unaware of
what Georges had cooked up, told him that it was 'an abdication', but
did nothing to correct his subordinate's decision.

Gort loyally supported the new command arrangement, and the next
day sent his vice chief of the general staff, Major General Eastwood, to
Billotte to tell him that he was not only willing to accept him as co-
ordinator, but would be glad to receive orders from him. Yet no radio link
was established with Billotte, although the BEF had one with the French
First and Seventh Armies, with Georges' headquarters and with the
British mission at Belgian GHQ near Antwerp. Comparing Appendix B
with Appendix A may give the reader a clearer idea of the alteration in
the chain of command. From now on Gort understood that he had to look
to Billotte for orders, and could no longer expect to receive orders from
Georges. In such a situation, the co-ordinator (in this case Billotte) must
be able to translate the directives from above (Georges) into practical
orders which those he is supposed to be co-ordinating (Gort) can carry out.
Equally important, the commander whose actions are being co-ordinated
(Gort) must have confidence in the co-ordinator's judgement and be willing to act on his orders. The British Official History's understated comment
is: 'In this instance the arrangements worked but haltingly, for neither of
these conditions was ever wholly fulfilled.'[3]

It was a muddled command arrangement and also one that was not in
accordance with the British government's directive to Gort when he was
appointed to command the BEF in September 1939. The change was the
outcome of a unilateral decision made by General Georges without any
discussion with the British government, and Gamelin's reaction is evidence that it was sprung on him unexpectedly. The Allies had had eight
months in which to sort out the command set-up before 11 May, and the
situation they found themselves in after moving into Belgium was no
different from that envisaged by the plan. That Gort's status was now
effectively lower down the chain of command could be lived with in the
interests of Allied solidarity, but much more serious was the confusion
and lack of co-ordination that ensued.

The French high command had assumed that the Belgians' defence of
their frontier and the delaying action of the British and French mechanized cavalry screen would suffice to prevent the Germans reaching the
main defence line, the Dyle, before the Allies' move forward was complete. As far as the French Ninth Army was concerned this assumption
was at fault, because some units of this army were engaged before they
were established on the Dyle Line.

General Blanchard's French First Army, heading for the Gembloux Gap
to the right of the BEF, was in an even unhappier position than the Ninth

Army. As it advanced it met a flood of Belgian refugees heading for France from the Liège area, and the air was thick with rumours of treachery and of a fifth column.[4] General Prioux's Cavalry Corps (2nd and 3rd DLMs, each with 174 tanks), the first to arrive at Gembloux, was disconcerted to find how thinly the Belgians had fortified this area, an open plain and excellent tank country. Worse, news came in that Eben-Emael had fallen. This supposedly impregnable fortress, sited behind the twin obstacles of the River Meuse and the Albert Canal, south of Maastricht, was designed to cover by fire the Albert Canal bridges at Briedgen, Veldwezelt and Vroenhaven west of Maastricht. It was garrisoned by 700 men and was the lynchpin of the Belgian defences on the Dutch border east of Brussels and Antwerp. On 10 May, seventy-eight airborne engineers of the Luftwaffe Koch Assault Detachment landed on top of the fortifications in gliders and, using hollow charges, kept the garrison cowed, while German parachute and glider troops captured the bridges. The following day the German 223rd Infantry Division arrived and captured the remaining fortifications. The Koch Detachment lost six dead and twenty wounded. Not since the German capture of Douaumont at Verdun in February 1916 had a fort been taken with so little loss on the part of the attackers and such pathetically weak resistance by the defenders.

Prioux, in view of the feeble Belgian resistance, and assessing that his corps would not have time to establish good defensive positions before the Germans arrived in strength, suggested to his army commander, Blanchard, that they should now switch the defence to the Escaut, some forty-five miles further back. Blanchard agreed, and told Billotte, who was shocked and told him that revising the plan at this stage was out of the question. Prioux would have to hold on until 14 May, while First Army speeded up its move to support him.

Meanwhile in Holland the situation unravelled with lightning speed. A combination of airborne troops and the 9th Panzer Division prised open the Germans' route to Rotterdam. On 11 May, Giraud's French Seventh Army, heading, as planned by Gamelin, for a link-up with the Dutch at Breda, ran into 9th Panzer at Tilburg. Unnerved by this unexpected turn of events, Giraud fell back towards Antwerp, now being flayed from the air by the Luftwaffe. The link-up with the Dutch, upon which Gamelin had gambled his mobile reserve of seven divisions, including 1st DLM, had now evaporated.

At this stage the BEF did not suffer directly in the way that the French First, Seventh and Ninth Armies did. The main German effort was not directed at the BEF's front, even though the Belgian Army was forced back more quickly than expected. Moreover in the British sector the Dyle position was fairly strong, although three divisions covering some 30,000 yards meant that the defences on the actual river line were quite thin, and in any case the so-called river is only a stream. Furthermore, the banks were wooded in places, which made infantry infiltration by the enemy easier. But the river and the railway, which for most of the sector followed the eastern bank, were together quite effective in slowing down armour, and some stretches of the Dyle valley were flooded, which offered more of an obstacle. A system of dykes in Belgium's low-lying country held water drained from the land. Sluices, or gates, in the dykes could be opened to allow water into the rivers or, as a defensive measure, to flood the terrain. Near Louvain the Belgians had built some pillboxes. All things considered, attacking the BEF between Louvain and Wavre would be no walkover, especially against the well-sited British artillery.

The BEF had three days to prepare their positions on the Dyle, instead of six as planned. The few scattered pillboxes and wire entanglements left by the Belgians were a poor exchange for the numerous concrete defences, well protected by belts of wire and mines, that the British had prepared on the Franco–Belgian border during the winter. But at least there was something of an obstacle in front, which to an army trained to fight a static defensive battle, preferably behind an obstacle, rather than relying on manoeuvre and speed, was some comfort. The BEF also had plenty of support in the form of one heavy and eight medium regiments of artillery and eight machine-gun battalions shared between the three front divisions. In addition each division had its own three field regiments (each of two twelve-gun batteries of 4.5-inch howitzers, or 18-or 25-pounders) and an anti-tank regiment in direct support. The two battalions of the 1st Army Tank Brigade arrived by train and, after unloading off the flat cars on 14 May, rumbled into the Forest of Soignes, between Brussels and the field of the 1815 Battle of Waterloo. Both its battalions, the 4th and the 7th Royal Tank Regiment (RTR), were allocated to I Corps. Each was equipped with the heavy infantry tank. The 4th RTR had fifty of the old Mk I, weighing eleven tons but armed only with one machine gun. The 7th RTR had twenty-seven Mk Is, and twenty-three Mk IIs, the Matilda, weighing twenty-six and a half tons, and armed with a 2-pounder as well as a machine gun. Although slow, with a maximum road speed of 8mph for the Mk I, and 15mph for the Mk II, the British infantry tank was more heavily armoured than every other German or French tank of the period, except the French Char B1.

The air was thick with rumours and uncertainty as the BEF dug in and reconnoitred gun positions. Lieutenant Dunn's harbour area was bombed, but there were no casualties. Several men were shaken, but morale remained high, as it does when one has escaped bombing or shelling without a scratch. Shortly afterwards, a despatch rider appeared with an alarmist message saying that the Germans were seven miles from Louvain, and the battery was to be prepared to pull back to another harbour some five miles away. Dunn listened to the German news in English on his wireless as the battery waited to move; it sounded so sinister that his morale was lower than at any time during the ensuing campaign. It was not the news that the Germans had crossed the Albert Canal, it was not the demoralized Belgians, some of whom were beginning to trickle back through the BEF, that dismayed him so much as the feeling that those who controlled the battery's movements had lost their grip. The battery area had after all been changed at least twice in eight hours. Dunn had heard the expression order-counter-order-disorder, but had never encountered the reality of it before. He was to discover that, throughout the campaign, men would carry out orders provided they were clear. The orders might be unreasonable, they might even be suicidal, but men would simply assume that they were the best possible in the circumstances. However, if they were constantly changing, doubt, fear of the unknown and loss of confidence set in. Dunn went to bed that night exhausted and unhappy. It was his first experience of war and its effects. He was to see plenty more in France in the course of this campaign, and would encounter it subsequently in the desert and again in north-west Europe in 1944–5.

Good leadership was, and is, the key to success in situations such as faced the BEF in May 1940. No less important, it has to be said, is the hardening of the heart and inner toughness that experienced troops acquire so that they expect chaos and learn to work through it. These were early days, and too many of the BEF lacked the demanding, realistic and exhaustive training that is one of the ingredients in inuring soldiers to the unpleasant surprises and shocks of war.

Bringing the guns forward from the harbour into a position in the forward edge of some woods proved a difficult task for Dunn the next day. The roads were completely blocked with Belgian troops and civilians. Eventually, having brought the guns into action, he went to choose an observation post (OP) from which he could spot for the guns, communicating with them by radio. He eventually found it on a hill to the west of Louvain, in such a position that he could see the forward side of the town, the direction from which the enemy would come. Having satisfied himself that his OP was well concealed, he crossed the Dyle and drove through Louvain, to fix targets in what would shortly be German-occupied Belgium. Arriving back at his OP, he found that the hill was now occupied by the King's Company, 1st Grenadier Guards. They were full of rumours: the Americans had given Hitler forty-eight hours to get out of Belgium; Mussolini had shot himself; the King of Italy had abdicated.

One of the rumours that was to plague the BEF throughout this campaign concerned the sudden arrival of enemy parachutists. The use of parachute troops was a new form of warfare, which the Germans had not been slow to exploit, and had done so successfully. Because it was so novel, and neither the British nor French had paratroops in their army, and knew very little about their strengths and limitations, this form of warfare was invested with a mystique far beyond what was feasible. In the event the Germans never used parachute troops against the BEF or the French. But this did not prevent numerous false alarms, such as experienced by Lieutenant Dunn, who had a disturbed night on 12/13 May when some of his young soldiers saw a parachutist behind every tree in the gun position, and fired at them. In the end he had to beat the wood with a lighted torch before they were convinced that no such enemy had descended out of the skies.

The next day refugees were still pouring by, and the scenes of desperation were enough to cause even the most hard-boiled of Dunn's soldiers to remark, 'It makes you want to fucking weep, sir.' That morning reports came in that the British armoured cavalry were in contact with the Germans about ten miles beyond Louvain. Belgian units were withdrawing in a steady stream, some batteries moving at a brisk trot. Presently, a message was passed to the British artillery batteries that the armoured cavalry were clear, and registration of targets could begin.

Soon after the British blew the bridges over the Dyle in the afternoon of 14 May, German motorcyclists from the divisional reconnaissance battalions of three German divisions (19th, 14th and 31st) appeared out in the open beyond the river. Careless about taking cover, having had an easy advance so far, they were assailed by numerous Brens, and 'malleted' soon after by British artillery. German horse-drawn artillery came into action, and shelled some British forward positions, giving the soldiers their first experience of the 'whoeeer' noise of incoming artillery fire, followed by the ringing crump of a shell exploding. The British artillery rapidly replied, which was good for their own side's morale. Lieutenant Dunn felt supremely confident, and enjoyed directing his battery's first shoot in anger. The guns were in a good position, which was being made stronger every hour. He slept dreamlessly and well.

The German infantry first came into action at Louvain, in the form of the 19th Infantry Division, precipitating the Belgian withdrawal that so pleased Montgomery. But the delays caused by the misunderstanding over who was responsible for the defence of Louvain had the effect of impeding the British preparation of defensive positions. However, the

Germans hard on the heels of the fleeing Belgians were given a warm reception by the 3rd Division's Vickers medium machine guns, Brens and rifles, an onslaught soon joined by the division's field artillery. The 2nd Royal Ulster Rifles of the 9th Infantry Brigade, Montgomery's right-hand forward brigade, saw off the German attack with ease. But the 1st Grenadiers of 7th Guards Brigade, the left forward brigade, had been drawn further forward than they wished by the need to conform to the Belgian defensive layout. During the night they withdrew from the railway line to the Dyle Canal, suffering a number of casualties. The Dyle Canal ran north from Louvain a few hundred yards west of the River Dyle and the railway. The enemy managed to infiltrate some warehouses by the canal in 1st Coldstream's sector (7th Guards Brigade), but when they attempted to launch a pontoon bridge it was reduced to matchwood by British 25-pounder high explosive, a cheering sight for the guardsmen.

Soon after dawn the next day, the Germans – having reconnoitred the 1st Royal Ulster's positions by the railway station, goods yards and signal boxes – brought down two hours of artillery fire on them. Then German infantry came skirmishing in supported by their MG 34 machine guns. At the station the fighting swayed back and forth from platform to platform, as shellfire brought the glass roof smashing down on the defenders. Second Lieutenant Garstin, one of the Ulster platoon commanders, used the subway system to bring a Bren into action on the flanks and behind the attackers, forcing the Germans back to their side of the line. One of the signal boxes became the scene of a hectic grenade battle, which held the Germans at bay. At one point the attackers managed to cross the railway line and holed up in a tangle of wrecked and undamaged railway trucks in a goods siding. A brisk counter-attack by the Ulsters and the 1st King's Own Scottish Borderers, supported by the guns of 7th Field Regiment, turfed out the intruders.

The 1st Coldstream also had to mount a counter-attack. Having withdrawn from the riverbank to maintain contact with the Grenadiers when they pulled back, the position had to be retaken. The reserve company was brought up, and following a fifteen-minute 'stonk' by field and medium guns, and supported by two troops of the 5th Royal Inniskilling Dragoon Guards in Mk VI light tanks, the Coldstreamers retook the position with no losses to themselves.

The southern end of the British line also came under attack on the morning of 15 May. The German 31st Infantry Division, having reached the river before dawn on the 14th, had twenty-four hours for reconnaissance, and time to select a good spot for the attack. It chose a bend in the river, just north of Wavre, in the sector held by the 6th Brigade of 2nd Division. As an assembly area the Germans used the cover afforded by the village of Gastuche near the river. Following a brief firestorm bombardment, the enemy infantry charged in soon after dawn on to positions held by the 2nd Durham Light Infantry (DLI), 6th Brigade's right-hand battalion. Before anyone could spot the attack, the Germans overwhelmed a platoon of the centre company holding a château. The Durhams' left-hand company also lost some ground and men. But the left-hand platoon, commanded by Second Lieutenant Annand, held fast at a demolished bridge and frustrated all the German attempts to scramble across on girders and planks. Apparently unconcerned by the mortar bombs and bullets raining down on the position, he repulsed the Germans twice, the second time by himself, rushing forward hurling grenades.

As the DLI were on a forward slope, they found it difficult to move about during daylight without drawing fire. Although a counter-attack by the reserve company managed to seal up the breach in their positions, they were unable to drive all the German infantry back across the river. But the field artillery and the Vickers medium machine guns of the 2nd Manchesters kept the Germans at bay and subdued as the day advanced. A company of the 1st Royal Welch Fusiliers was frustrated in its attempt to eject the enemy by counter-attack on the forward slope, but blocked any further incursion. Meanwhile, as evening approached, Annand was fighting off fresh attempts by the Germans to cross the bridge, dashing in and hurling grenades, although himself wounded. His platoon sergeant remembered that he came to platoon headquarters and asked for another box of grenades, as he could hear the Germans trying to repair the bridge. 'Off he went and must have been having a lovely time, because he was soon back for more. Just like giving an elephant strawberries.' Eventually Annand was ordered to withdraw, and on bringing his men back to the rendezvous he discovered that his batman Private Joseph Hunter was missing. Back he went and, having found Hunter wounded, carried him off in a wheelbarrow. He was making good progress when his path was blocked by a fallen tree. Now weak from loss of blood, he was unable to lift Hunter over. Reluctantly, he left his batman in an empty trench and set off for help. Eventually he collapsed but was later taken to safety and evacuated. For his rescue attempt and his courageous actions, Annand was awarded the VC, the first won for the army in the Second World War. Hunter was captured by the Germans, but died in hospital a month later.

So far the Germans had not succeeded in penetrating the Dyle positions held by the British at any point. However, on the right in the French First Army sector a 5,000-yard breach had been made where there was no river protection. Gort offered the 48th Division from British I

Corps reserve to plug the gap, but Blanchard, the French First Army Commander, preferred to pull back to the line between Châtelet and Ottignies. This meant that the British I Corps had to conform, and swing back from Rhode-Sainte-Agathe along the line of the River Lasne, a tributary of the Dyle about four miles to the west, to link up with the French. Accordingly orders were given to the 2nd Division and right-hand brigade of the 1st to withdraw that night. Unfortunately the notice was short and the enemy were active, especially on the front of the 6th Brigade, all of whose battalions were fully engaged. A withdrawal in war is difficult enough, but hugely more so if one is in contact with the enemy. First-class discipline and control are needed if the operation is not to end up with the enemy following up like wolves tearing down a stricken prey and turning withdrawal into a headlong rout. A clean break covered by heavy fire is the recipe for success. In this case a bombardment by British artillery covered the noise of transport and troops moving to the rear, and kept the enemy distracted and their heads down.

The 1st Royal Berkshires had the most difficult time. Their CO, Lieutenant Colonel Furlong, arrived back from receiving orders at brigade headquarters at 2300 hours, and, finding that his telephone lines to his companies had been cut by shellfire, sent a subaltern on a motorcycle to pass on the orders for the withdrawal. About an hour later, he discovered that the young officer was in the regimental aid post (RAP) dying of wounds. So he himself set off, riding pillion behind a despatch rider. On the way a shell-burst knocked some of the spokes off the back wheel, but they carried on, and Furlong managed to communicate the orders. The Berkshires successfully broke contact, the noise of their transport and that of the other battalions covered by the guns in support. The guns' muzzle flashes lit up the dark night as they fired off stocks of ammunition so carefully built up over the preceding days, and which they would have neither the time nor the trucks to take away.

Although the Lasne was a poor substitute for the Dyle and did not offer any prospect of being held for long, the general situation on the BEF's front was encouraging. At Louvain, where the heaviest attacks had been made, the position was still being held, and everywhere the BEF gained immensely in confidence from these first encounters with the enemy. By now, the morning of 16 May, the Dutch had been out of the fight for two days.

Up until 12 May, Gamelin, along with most other senior commanders, British as well as French, had had their attention firmly fixed on the developments in Belgium and Holland. Gamelin's HQ, Grand Quartier Général (GQG), was convinced that the German main point of effort was between Maastricht and Liège. The London *Times* military correspondent

declared, 'This time there has been no strategic surprise,' an allusion to
the Schlieffen Plan of 1914 which had hoodwinked the British and
French. General Ironside, who was one of Britain's most experienced
battlefield soldiers but was probably past his best when appointed CIGS,
a job for which he was unsuited by temperament, wrote in his diary, 'We
shall have saved the Belgian Army. On the whole the advantage is with
us. A really hard fight this summer . . .' By the time these words were
written, strategic surprise was about to be unleashed upon the Allies. It
was called *Sichelschnitt* by the Germans, in English 'sickle-cut'. It was to
hack through the French, and almost took the British in its deadly swing.

Plan Yellow

The first version of the German plan to attack in the west, Plan Yellow,
was prepared by the Army General Staff and issued on 19 October 1939.
This version stated that the attack would be made on the western front
through Holland, Belgium and Luxembourg, with the aim of defeating as
much as possible of the Allied armies, to win as much as possible of
Holland, Belgium and northern France as a base for air and sea warfare
against 'England' and also to provide a wide protective area in front of
the Ruhr.[5] Having stated the general purpose of the plan, the order dealt
only with operations against Holland, Belgium and Luxembourg, taking
the invading forces up to the northern frontier of France; the scheme for
subsequent operations was not covered. Army Group B, consisting of
three armies, was to attack north and south of Brussels, before heading
for the coast between Ostend and Boulogne.

The plan was changed at the end of October 1939, and in this second
version the aim was changed to defeating as substantial a portion of the
Allied Armies in northern France and Belgium as possible in order to
create favourable conditions for the continuation of the war on land and
in the air.[6] The main emphasis was no longer on the axes north and
south of Brussels; the attack on Holland was omitted (although the
Maastricht appendix would be crossed in the advance on Belgium to the
north of Liège); and the axes of the attacking formations would fan out
from north of Brussels to Sedan. This was the plan the Allies believed
they would face when Hitler attacked, and on which all their plans were
based, including rushing into Belgium.

Colonel General von Rundstedt, on being appointed to command Army
Group A, concluded that Yellow version two was a bad plan. He had not
seen version one because he had only just returned from Poland. His
objection was that it did not cut off the Allies from the Somme but

merely pushed them back, which risked a replay of the stalemate of the First World War. Colonel General von Brauchitsch, the C-in-C of the German Army, did not agree. The argument continued until the end of December, whereupon there was some tinkering with the plan, and it was reissued as version three, but without changing its overall concept. Rundstedt and his brilliant chief of staff, Lieutenant General von Manstein, continually pestered Brauchitsch to strengthen the southern wing with more armour, and to concentrate the main point of effort here, but to no avail. All along, the driving force behind this concept was Manstein. The offensive was ordered for 17 January 1940. The forced landing of Major Reinberger's aircraft, described in Chapter 1, occurred on 10 January, and gave the Allies valuable information on Plan Yellow. But, although this caused much pother in the German camp, the plan was not changed. The offensive was cancelled because of the weather, *not* because the plan had been compromised. Indeed a fourth version of Plan Yellow was issued. Rundstedt, with Manstein supplying the vision, continued to badger Brauchitsch.

Two Army Group A war games were held in early February, a normal part of the German operational planning process.[7] In the course of the one carried out on 7 February, attended by Brauchitsch's chief of staff, General Halder, it seems that the latter began to warm to what Rundstedt wanted. On 17 February, Manstein was dining with Hitler on his way to take up a new job commanding XXXVIII Infantry Corps. After dinner, he took the opportunity to expound his and Rundstedt's views that the whole plan of campaign should be changed by placing the main striking power on the left wing. It is possible that this was the first time that Hitler had heard of this concept, because Brauchitsch had refused to report Rundstedt's views to him. The Führer was immediately taken by the idea. Whether Brauchitsch learned of what had transpired at the dinner is not clear, but the next day he and Halder briefed Hitler that they intended to strengthen the left wing, that is fall in with Rundstedt's wishes. Hitler approved, and in the end Rundstedt got far more armour than he had asked for. The whole weight of the attack was transferred to the left wing. Colonel General von Bock's Army Group B, consisting of twenty-six infantry and three panzer divisions, would still attack into Belgium, distracting the Allies' attention. But Rundstedt's Army Group A, of forty-four divisions, would attack through the thinly defended Ardennes, then turn north and cut off the French and British forces. The armoured sickle of Army Group A consisted of three panzer corps: Hoth's XV (5th and 7th Panzer Divisions); Reinhardt's XLI (6th and 8th Panzer Divisions); and Guderian's XIX Panzer Corps (1st, 2nd and 10th Panzer Divisions). Guderian had the largest corps with over 800 tanks, and was supported by the crack GrossDeutschland Infantry Regiment. Guderian's and Reinhardt's corps were formed into a panzer group under General von Kleist, giving a total of 1,222 tanks, 41,140 vehicles and 134,370 men. Colonel General von Leeb's Army Group C remained behind the Siegfried Line, a threat to the Maginot Line.

Commanding the 7th Panzer Division in Hoth's XV Panzer Corps was the newly promoted Major General Rommel. After commanding Hitler's personal guard battalion, Rommel had been appointed to a panzer formation although he lacked previous experience of armour. He was to give a breathtaking performance in the campaign.

In both November and January, when the Germans had intended to mount Plan Yellow but had subsequently called it off, the Allies had received six days' notice that an attack was impending, mainly from intelligence about troop movement forward to the start positions. This gave rise to the assumption that when the attack finally came the Allies would have six days to prepare positions from the moment movement forward was detected. However, when the final version of Plan Yellow was approved, the Germans did not have to allow time for preliminary moves, because on the previous two occasions when formations had begun advancing, only to have the offensive cancelled, the troops had remained where they were. So, of the six days allowed for movement, three had already taken place. The Germans had also tightened up their security, which allowed them to close up to the frontier in great secrecy. When the order was given to start Yellow at midday on 9 May, the Germans were able to attack at daybreak on 10 May. The Allies reacted only *after* the attack had actually begun.

Guderian crossed into Luxembourg at 0435 hours on 10 May. The French had estimated that it would take an enemy force ten days to reach the Meuse through the Ardennes from the Luxembourg border. In the event 1st Panzer Division arrived at the river at 1400 hours on 12 May. The French detected armour in the Ardennes, but had their eye taken off the ball by Army Group B to the north. The Allies agreed that the Ardennes would not be the main effort. The French in the Ardennes were in such disarray that Sedan was occupied by the Germans along with the north bank of the Meuse by last light on 12 May. The French now expected a pause, as laid down in their manuals, to allow the enemy to concentrate before tackling such a major obstacle. But on 13 May Guderian, in modern soldiers' language, conducted a bounce crossing of the river with all three panzer divisions using massive air support. The Luftwaffe backed the crossing with 310 bombers, 200 Stuka dive-bombers and 200 fighters. A mere seven French aircraft appeared over Sedan, and were seen off. The German commanders were close up behind their leading troops, while the French as required by their doctrine sat in their command posts; while Guderian was overlooking Sedan or on the banks of the river, the commander of French X Corps, General Grandsard, was more than twelve miles away.

It was the German infantry and assault engineers, with Luftwaffe support, who made the crossing and subsequent breakout possible – not the armour. None of Guderian's tanks went over on 13 May. The first to do so, from 1st Panzer Division, crossed the bridge constructed by the assault engineers at 0200 hours on 14 May. Reinhardt at Monthermé, in the centre between Hoth and Guderian, was having a harder time crossing in the face of regulars of the French 102nd Fortress Division, a tougher proposition than the B reservists positioned elsewhere on the Meuse. It was to take Reinhardt another two days to get his armour across. Further north, Hoth at Dinant also started pushing his armour over the Meuse during the night of 13/14 May, a crossing made possible by the drive and bravery of the infantry and assault engineers, and the support of the ubiquitous Luftwaffe. It was here and thereafter in the breakout that the Stuka (Ju 87) was used in lieu of artillery which, being mainly horse-drawn in the German Army, could not keep up with the armoured advance. This development shattered the confidence of the French; they simply could not believe the speed at which the enemy armour moved. Thinking in terms of the First World War, and in particular of the way both sides had used artillery in that war, they believed that the armour would have to wait for the guns to catch up at each phase of the battle.

Early on 14 May, General Georges flung himself into a chair and burst into tears. 'Our front has been broken at Sedan,' he announced. On 15 May, the German armour began its breakout from the Meuse bridgeheads. That day at nightfall Georges heard that Corap's Ninth Army had been routed along a fifty-mile front, and likewise Huntzinger's Second Army. Georges replaced Corap by Giraud; in addition, the remnants of Giraud's own Seventh Army were to come south, passing behind the BEF, in an attempt to plug the hole torn in the French defences. Huntzinger, whose army's defence had been no less ineffective than Corap's and his command style no less unsure, was left in charge.

Holland surrendered on 15 May, adding to the gloom. Her tiny army had been swept away, but it was the bombing of Rotterdam that had shattered Dutch spirit. The Dutch claimed that 30,000 people had perished in Rotterdam in seven and a half minutes. Post-war investigation revealed the true figure to have been 980. But the damage was substantial: a square mile of the centre of the city set alight, 20,000 buildings destroyed and 78,000 people made homeless. Rotterdam was the first city in history whose bombing was the cause of national surrender; the next two were Hiroshima and Nagasaki in 1945.

Also on 15 May, the French Premier, Paul Reynaud, telephoned Winston Churchill, the new British Prime Minister, and told him, 'We are defeated – we have lost the battle.' Churchill decided to fly to Paris the next day. Gort knew very little more about the disaster to his south other than what he could glean from broadcasts over the radio. The supposed co-ordinator on this front, General Billotte, whose duty it was to keep Gort in the picture, was in the same state of despair as Georges. Major Archdale, a liaison officer at Billotte's HQ, was horrified by the lack of order and decision, and by the spectacle of weeping staff officers. Gort knew that the Belgians on his left were on their last legs, and was aware of the serious breach in the French Ninth and Second Armies. His most immediate concern was the withdrawal of the French First Army on his right, and its supine attitude towards mounting a counter-attack. By nightfall he assessed that Louvain might be enveloped, so he sent off Major General Eastwood early on 16 May to ascertain what Billotte intended doing about the situation on the Allied front in Belgium.

Billotte had already moved his HQ once, to Caudry, about eighty miles from Gort's forward command post. Caudry was uncomfortably close to the battle, and actually lay in the direct path of the German armoured thrust, so a further move, to Douai, was ordered. Eastwood arrived at around 0600 hours and found Billotte amid the scurry of preparations to relocate the HQ. He had nevertheless made a plan: his armies were to fall back on the Escaut starting that night, 16/17 May. The withdrawal was to be carried out in two stages, so that over three successive nights the positions would be established as follows:

Night 16/17 May	Charleroi–Brussels–Willebroeck Canal (known to the BEF as the Line of the Senne)
Night 17/18 May	Maubeuge–Mons–Ath–River Dendre to Termonde, thence line of River Escaut to Antwerp and the sea (known to the BEF as the Dendre Line)
Night 18/19 May	The frontier defences to Maulde – the line of the River Escaut to Ghent and thence the canal to Terneuzen (known to the BEF as the Escaut Line)[8]

Gort issued a warning order to the BEF to pull back to the Senne Line that night, 16 May, beginning at 2200 hours. He held a conference at I Corps HQ to give orders for the plan of retirement. Major General Needham, head of the British Military Mission at Belgian Army HQ, attended, and on his way back to report to the Belgians was seriously hurt in a car crash. Several hours elapsed before the Belgians knew of the British withdrawal to comply with Billotte's orders.

When the order to retreat percolated down to the soldiers in the BEF, they were astonished and aggrieved. Only six days before they had advanced sixty miles to meet the enemy. They had encountered them on the Dyle and had so far frustrated all their attempts to break their line. Now they were to fall back. They were in tremendous spirit and the fighting had increased rather than sapped their confidence. Second Lieutenant Martin's men of 7 Platoon, the 2nd Cheshires were typical in being 'staggered' to be told to withdraw. They had experienced some good machine-gun practice shooting German snipers who had tied themselves to trees about 1,000 yards to their front, followed by shooting the men who had been sent to cut them down – 'good fun without much danger'.

In the early evening of 16 May, Lieutenant Dunn's battery was ordered to continue firing until all the dumped ammunition, some 600 rounds per gun, was expended. It appeared that the enemy had broken through on the right of the 1st Division, and the battery was to withdraw to the River Dendre. The regiment was moving at once, but Dunn's troop was to remain in action until 2000 hours under command of the 8th Brigade, the rearguard for the 3rd Division. Dunn was to report to the brigade commander in the scout car at once. The guns were red hot by this time and the gunners stripped to the waist. They could not understand why they were being told to retreat: 'Why, sir? Why? Why don't we advance? If they leave us here, nothing will ever get through this.' Dunn explained that nothing would, but that it was elsewhere that things had gone wrong, and that unless they moved they would be cut off.

Telling them that the French front miles away to the south had been shattered did not seem to the soldiers sufficient reason to pull out. But the pattern was set: now and for the next ten days the position on the flanks of the BEF, rather than the actions of the enemy directly to their front, would chiefly determine events. Gamelin's master plan lay in ruins. On 16 May, Churchill learned just how much of a ruin when he arrived at the Quai d'Orsay in Paris for a meeting with Reynaud and Daladier, Minister of National Defence and War. Churchill had taken over from Chamberlain as Prime Minister only five days before. Gamelin told him that north and south of Sedan German armour had broken through on a fifty- to sixty-mile front. The French Army in front of them was scattered and destroyed and the Germans were advancing at speed either towards the coast via Amiens and Arras or straight for Paris. Behind the armour, eight or ten German divisions, all motorized, were driving onwards, making flanks for themselves against the two separated

French armies on either side. Churchill asked, 'Où est la masse de manoeuvre?' (Where is your strategic reserve?). Gamelin shrugged and replied, 'Aucune' (There isn't one).[9] Churchill, looking out of the window of the Quai d'Orsay, saw clouds of smoke rising from huge bonfires where 'venerable officials' were burning large wheelbarrow-loads of archives. By his own admission, he had experienced one of the greatest surprises of his life: that any commander having to defend 500 miles of front would not have a strategic reserve had never occurred to him. That the British government or War Office had not known about it was inexcusable. Gamelin and the two ministers were convinced that all was lost. The general made some remarks about bringing in divisions from Africa and withdrawing some from the Maginot Line to mount a counter-attack on the flanks of the German penetration, or 'bulge' as he called it, during the next two or three weeks. His remarks carried no conviction. That was the last Churchill saw of Gamelin.

Meanwhile, unaware of events in Paris or of the true magnitude of the French disaster, the BEF withdrew from its positions on the Dyle and Lasne. The general plan for the withdrawal of the BEF was for the two front-line brigades of each division to thin out and finally retire through the reserve line held by the third brigade. This well-practised method of withdrawal by night would be replicated down the chain of command. So brigades would thin out their front-line battalions, which would finally retire through a line held by the rear battalion, and so on through companies and down to platoons and sections. Thinning out usually meant that about half a battalion, company, platoon and section would quietly move back to a rendezvous in rear, perhaps behind the rear reserve line. When joined by the balance of the battalion or company that had held the position until the time for the final withdrawal, everyone would set off for a pre-designated rendezvous at which the whole battalion or formation would assemble before moving off to the new defensive position either on foot, in transport or both.

All formations and units usually send back reconnaissance parties to lay out the new position in rear, and receive their units and sub-units and allocate them to the new locations immediately on arrival, thus saving time. These reconnaissance parties usually consist of the seconds-in-command at all levels from lance-corporals in rifle sections up to majors in battalions and senior staff officers in brigades and divisions, and hence sometimes known colloquially as 'the second eleven'. Reconnaissance parties move back in a body under control, and at a predetermined time probably laid down by divisional HQ. As discussed earlier, conducting a successful withdrawal when in contact with the enemy demands well-trained and disciplined troops, and tight control.

It is usually easier at night. In daytime, if the enemy is alert, well trained and in contact, the forward units and formations may not be able to thin out but may instead have to conduct a fighting withdrawal, with sub-units covering each other by fire as they withdraw in stages covered by fire from artillery and the reserve unit or sub-unit. A daytime withdrawal in contact is one of the most difficult phases of war to conduct successfully, and the ability to do so without losing cohesion in spite of casualties is the mark of a first-class outfit.

Lieutenant Dunn, having been told to support the 8th Brigade, drove up to find Brigadier Woolner and his staff having dinner, and they sent him to Lieutenant Colonel Bull, the CO of the 4th Royal Berkshires, whose battalion was covering the withdrawal of the brigade. Dunn arrived in the middle of the CO's conference, and he got the impression that the CO was a bit 'rattled'. He told Dunn to stay as long as possible, to fire an SOS defensive task at high rate at midnight, and then be in a position to cover the battalion on the eastern outskirts of Brussels at 0300 hours.

At last light units began thinning out, and two hours later forward units and sub-units pulled back through rearguards. Once all forward troops were through, these too pulled out, and except in one or two cases a clean break was achieved. This was a manoeuvre that most had practised, none more assiduously than Montgomery's 3rd Division. The 2nd Royal Ulster Rifles of Montgomery's 9th Brigade, after two days of fighting in Louvain, had no difficulty breaking contact; likewise the 1st Grenadiers of Montgomery's 7th Guards Brigade on their left. The 1st Coldstream, also of 7th Guards Brigade, on the extreme left of the BEF, had it less easy. The Belgians on their left started withdrawing prematurely, in the early afternoon, and the Germans following them up started to work round the Coldstream and engage their left flank and even their centre companies from the rear. Supporting fire from the divisional artillery and the machine-gunners of the 2nd Middlesex took their toll of the Germans, and held them. But any move out in the open by the Coldstream rifle companies drew fire. Here the carriers came into their own, bringing ammunition forward and taking wounded to the rear. At 2100 hours, as planned, the withdrawal began, timed to be complete by 2300 hours. As the first troops came back under cover from their own artillery, the Germans crossed the Dyle canal and entered the town of Herent, through which the withdrawal route lay. The rearguard of reserve and headquarters companies fought desperately to hold the road open, as the forward companies came back with bayonets fixed to turf out the enemy. Streams of tracer arced across the withdrawal route and mortar bombs crumped around the guardsmen. The Coldstream casualties mounted to 120, mostly in the left and centre companies. But the rearguard held Herent, and checked that all the survivors of the forward companies were through, before pulling out itself. The 5th Inniskilling Dragoon Guards now assumed the rearguard, carrying some of the lightly wounded on their tanks.

Dunn's troop in support of the 4th Royal Berkshires, having fired ten rounds per gun at intense rate on each SOS target, limbered up and got away. As they passed the long columns of infantry on the road, the gunners were loudly cheered. At 0240 hours, Dunn's troop came into action in a suburb of Brussels, and he reported to Lieutenant Colonel Bull that he was ready to support him.

The 1st/6th East Surreys, from the 44th Division, were among those units covering the 3rd Division's withdrawal over the River Dendre. Captain White, the adjutant, watched some units of the 3rd Division withdrawing in good order. It was a great fillip to morale to see the soldiers with all their equipment and their immaculate discipline. It provided a strong contrast to the Belgians he had seen earlier retreating through the battalion's position, 'a rabble without rifles or tin hats'.

Some of the closest scrapes were experienced by the divisional cavalry regiments covering their divisions while they fell back. Often covering long sections of front, and spread thinly, they needed initiative and skill at all levels, and sometimes a degree of cunning, not to get cut off. The 4th/7th Royal Dragoon Guards covered the 2nd Division withdrawal from the Dyle in the sector north of Wavre. Just as A Squadron was about to move, having received orders from regimental headquarters to withdraw, it came under fire from about six anti-tank guns at 400 yards' range. As the squadron pulled out of position, they engaged the anti-tank guns, with uncertain results, except that by the end of the scrap only two enemy guns were still firing. 'Bad shooting by the Bosch,' recorded the squadron diary, 'only one carrier hit and overturned.' The crew, although badly shaken, got out and mounted other vehicles. A Squadron rallied at Wavre, and the bridge was 'kept open' and not demolished for an hour in the hope of getting Troop Sergeant Major Emmerton back, one of the troop leaders missing from earlier that day. Although Emmerton did not turn up, Lieutenant Owen did, having also been missing for a while. He had had to take avoiding action and work his way round the enemy by taking a cross-country route. Eventually the bridge had to be blown, as the Germans were getting too close. It was later learned that Emmerton and his crew, as well as a despatch rider, had been taken prisoner. Despatch riders were especially vulnerable in a withdrawal, because as they took messages from one part of the battlefield to another they sometimes found that the sub-unit they were looking for had gone, and been replaced by the enemy, or that the route they were using was suddenly thick with enemy vehicles. That night, 14/15 May, was the first night since crossing into Belgium on 10 May that most of the 4th/7th managed to get some sleep.

Everywhere else in the BEF sector, the withdrawal proceeded without serious loss, although not without some hard marching in cases where the transport arrangements failed. The 6th Brigade of 2nd Division, which had been holding the Lasne position, marched forty miles in twenty-seven hours after being in close contact with the enemy for thirty-six hours. The attack on Herent by the Germans' 19th Infantry Division was the only attempt at frustrating the British withdrawal. All their other formations, as was their custom, closed down operations during the night for rest and reorganization. With a few exceptions, the Germans were to exhibit this reluctance to fight at night throughout the Second World War, in all theatres. As the war progressed, Allied troops who were aggressive and led by bold commanders would take advantage of this habit. On this occasion the Germans must have known something was up, because the British artillery kept up an almost continuous barrage until the withdrawal was complete. The medium guns of I Corps alone fired 12,150 rounds that night, around 150 per gun. The gunners had a demanding time moving their guns to cover one line after another, siting new positions, coming into action and getting out again, handicapped for much of the time by refugees fleeing west.

All through the morning of 17 May, British troops marched through the streets of Brussels on their way to the canalized line of the River Senne, part of which runs through the western half of the city. They were watched by a sullen population, which only six days before had welcomed them as heroes coming to their aid. British remorse was tinged with resentment of the Belgians for their foolishness in maintaining their neutral stance right up to the moment of invasion, and for the poor performance of their troops.

The airmen had also been busy in these first few days of fighting. Although the Luftwaffe was busier over other Allied formations than over the BEF, that is not to say it was not a threat, and the activities of the RAF were crucial to the successful daylight movement and fighting by the BEF. In defending the sky over the BEF, the RAF lost sixty-seven aircraft in the first six days. RAF bombers attacking German columns found them well protected by light anti-aircraft (AA) (20mm and 37mm) guns at low level and by fighters and heavy 88mm guns at high level. The RAF did not have enough fighters deployed in France to cover strikes by their own bombers, so sorties were flown at low level, and the bombers were vulnerable to ground defence as they attacked the long columns of German armour and transport.

The British bombers interdicting German ground forces were the Fairey Battle and the Blenheim. The Fairey Battle, or Battle for short, was a disaster. A single-engine light bomber with a crew of three, it was underpowered and lacked both speed and defensive firepower. It was suspect even before it reached squadron service. The Blenheim was better; it too was a light bomber with a crew of three and was under-gunned, but it was twin-engine, and faster than the Battle. Within hours of the outbreak of war, the inadequacy of the British light bomber force was exposed. On 10 May, beginning at about midday, successive waves of Battles took off to attack German columns advancing through Luxembourg. These waves of four formations of eight bombers each were a puny force compared with the waves of hundreds of aircraft being sent over by the Luftwaffe. Out of thirty-two Battles, thirteen were shot down, and every one of the survivors was damaged. The Battles went in at 250 feet, and most of the losses were due to ground fire. The Battle pilots were greeted with intense fire from German vehicles on the roads, and static targets and key points such as bridges were ringed with AA guns. These missions were suicidal, yet the dedicated aircrews went on flying until the squadrons of Battles were wiped out. The Blenheims did no better. When six Blenheims of No. 600 Squadron attacked the captured Dutch airfield at Waalhaven, five were shot down by Me 110s, a loss rate of 83 per cent. Day after day brought bad news of the fate of Battles and Blenheims thrown in against staggering odds. For example, on 11 May, of eight Battles sent to attack enemy columns near Luxembourg, only one returned and it was badly damaged and beyond repair – a 100 per cent loss rate of airframes. The following day was a bad one for Blenheims: seven out of nine aircraft of No. 139 Squadron were brought down in an attack on German columns near Maastricht, followed directly by ten out of twenty-four Blenheims lost attacking Maastricht itself. But worst of all was No. 12 Squadron's attack on the bridges over the Albert Canal west of Maastricht. Attacks on these had already cost ten out of fifteen Battles of the Belgian Air Force; now volunteers were called for from No. 12 Battle Squadron RAF. The entire squadron stepped forward, and the first six on the duty roster were chosen. Only five aircraft took off, because one proved unserviceable, as was its replacement. One Battle returned to base, crash-landing on arrival. All other aircrew were killed or captured. Flying Officer Garland and his observer Sergeant Gray were both posthumously awarded the VC, the first for the RAF of the war. For some reason, the air gunner, Leading Aircraftman Reynolds, received no award.

These losses are made the more poignant by the fact that the effort that led to them was misdirected. General d'Astier de la Vigerie, commanding the French Air Force, had already reported the mass of armour and other vehicles approaching the Meuse crossings, and said, 'One can assume a very serious enemy effort in the direction of the Meuse.' This was of course the 'sickle', the main body of the German Army. To Vigerie's disgust, the French high command refused to believe him. Billotte continued to allocate air priorities to the Maastricht sector, completely ignoring the threat on the Meuse.

When the penny dropped on 14 May, and the French high command realized the seriousness of the situation on the Meuse, they asked the RAF to provide a maximum effort against the German pontoon bridges and the German armour crossing them at Sedan. Between 1500 and 1600 hours on 14 May, seventy-one light bombers took off protected by around 250 Allied fighters. The Germans had three times that number of fighters protecting that sector, and the bridgeheads were ringed with flak. The result is shown below:

RAF bomber losses on the Meuse, 14 May 1940			
Wing No.	Squadron No.	Aircraft despatched	Losses
71	105	11 Battles	6
	150	4 Battles	4
	114	2 Blenheims	1
	139	6 Blenheims	4
15	88	10 Battles	1
	103	8 Battles	3 (possibly 7)
	218	11 Battles	10
76	12	5 Battles	4
	142	8 Battles	4
	226	6 Battles	3

Out of seventy-one sorties, forty (or forty-four) aircraft were lost, some 56 (or 62) per cent. In addition sixteen Hurricanes were lost that day. For the RAF the Meuse was a valley of death.[10]

The only encouraging news, for the British at least, during these days of air combat and bombing sorties was the overall success of the Hurricanes. At least the Hurricane was a modern fighter, the only one the Allies possessed in France (the Spitfires were not involved over France and Flanders at this stage). The performance of the Hurricane was a marvellous boost to morale of its pilots and ground crew. It was a success that was, as so often, not so evident to the British soldiers on the ground. Because they could not see the Hurricanes above them, they imagined that the RAF was not playing its part; nothing could have been further from the truth.

On 17 May, as the BEF was trudging and motoring back to the Senne, Gort was aware that although Barker's British I Corps was in touch with the French First Army's III Corps on his right, and knew their position, further south the situation was far from clear. Gort knew that the French First Army was engaged in serious fighting with the northern prong of the German armoured advance, and as the Germans proceeded west they threatened the British right flank. To protect this flank, Gort ordered his director of military intelligence, Major General Mason-MacFarlane, to form a scratch force under his command. Macforce, as it was dubbed, consisted of: the 127th Infantry Brigade from the 42nd Division; two regiments of field artillery and an anti-tank battery; the Hopkinson Mission; engineers, signals and elements of the Royal Army Medical Corps (RAMC) and Royal Army Service Corps (RASC). The 1st Army Tank Brigade was to join later. The Hopkinson Mission, under Lieutenant Colonel Hopkinson, was a ground reconnaissance force mounted on armoured cars, trucks and motorcycles whose task was to gather information from corps, division and brigade headquarters and pass this to the RAF headquarters and to Gort's HQ. The mission was fully mobile and equipped with high-powered radios. It was the precursor of what became known later as the highly successful GHQ 'Phantom' Regiment. Macforce's task was to protect the right rear of the BEF. In particular it was to deny the crossings of the River Scarpe from Raches to Saint-Amand, some fifteen miles. Macforce was the first of a rash of ad-hoc forces that Gort formed as the campaign progressed – a habit that was to persist in the British Army after the 1940 campaign in France and Flanders, and right up to August 1942 in the Western Desert in Egypt. Montgomery stamped firmly on the practice when he arrived in the desert.

In retrospect, the formation of Macforce was unnecessary, and the French First Army never gave way. But Gort was not to know that. However, it would have been better to have used a complete division in this role, rather than weakening the 42nd Division. Far more serious, and ultimately detrimental to the command of the BEF, was sending to the force his head of intelligence as well as Lieutenant Colonel Templer, the GSO 1 intelligence. The lack of intelligence at Gort's command post was to be a grave handicap. It was exacerbated by the faulty organization of Gort's HQ staff, which affected other staff branches as well as intelligence. When Gort formed his command post and moved into Belgium, he took with him Mason-MacFarlane and two staff officers (including

Templer) from the intelligence branch at GHQ, which was left behind at Arras. Thereafter information received at Arras often failed to pass from the intelligence staff at the command post to formations forward in time for them to act on it, while much of the information sent in to the command post by divisions in contact was never passed back to the GHQ at Arras. Depleting the intelligence staff at the command post by removing Mason-MacFarlane and Templer aggravated the problem (which had already manifested itself) of co-ordinating information received there with that received by the intelligence staff at GHQ. Other branches of the staff experienced the same difficulty. The apportioning of responsibility between GHQ and the command post was not well planned, and the difficulties of maintaining communications between them were accentuated by the need for the command post to move frequently as the battle flowed westwards at speed.

As the growing threat to the British lines of communication and rear areas became apparent, two steps were taken. First, GHQ at Arras organized a garrison for the defence of the city under command of Lieutenant Colonel Copland-Griffiths, CO 1st Welsh Guards, consisting of his battalion, less one company detailed to guard Gort's command post. Some light tanks drawn from the ordnance depot, and manned by men from the 2nd Reconnaissance Brigade Headquarters (who called themselves Cooke's Light Tanks after their commander), and sappers and gunners provided support to the garrison.

It was decided to entrust control of part of the rear-defence organization to the General Officer commanding (GOC) 12th Division, Major General Petre. Leaving his divisional headquarters at Fressenville, south of Abbeville, and accompanied by his GSO 2, Major Haddock, Petre reached Arras at 1300 hours on 18 May, thinking he had just come for a conference, after which he would return to his division. He now learned that he was to remain there, as a sort of poor man's corps headquarters, taking command of the 23rd Division, his own 36th Brigade (but not the rest of his division) and the Arras garrison. For this purpose he was provided with a rear-link radio set, and the loan of the assistant military secretary from GHQ, Lieutenant Colonel Simpson, as his GSO 1. It was a pitifully small staff for a corps headquarters, even a miniature one. It was called Petreforce.

Second, the three territorial divisions, the 12th, 23rd and 46th, that had been working on the lines of communication were to redeploy, to Amiens, the Canal du Nord and Seclin respectively. At the same time, the chief engineer, Major General Pakenham-Walsh, was told to organize all the sappers employed on the lines of communication and at GHQ into battalions; and the provost (military police) marshal, Colonel Kennedy, was to concentrate all available provost (military police) and concentrate them as a reserve too. All branches of GHQ that could be spared were to be transferred to Boulogne, while GHQ itself was to pull back to Hazebrouck on 19 May.

In short, the BEF was gearing itself up for the unpleasant prospect of a German breakthrough, which looked increasingly likely. The seven panzer divisions of Army Group A had poured through the fifty-mile gap in the French defences, and with the bit between their teeth brushed aside pockets of resistance, overtaking and disarming hordes of demoralized, fugitive French soldiers. Only lack of fuel threatened to stop them, but they seized ample supplies from the French. By the evening of 19 May they were breasting up to the Canal du Nord, 110 miles as the crow flies from the Meuse, and 170 miles from their start lines on 10 May.

3

BACK TO THE ESCAUT AND DISASTER
ON THE BEF'S SOUTHERN FLANK

By the time the rest of II Corps started footslogging back to the Senne on the 16 May, the 4th Division had already established a layback position there (a temporary defence-line), and was awaiting the arrival of the 3rd Division. The 11th Brigade was established on the canalized line of the Senne running through the western half of Brussels, and the 12th Brigade was five miles further north opposite Vilvorde. There were twenty-three bridges and one tunnel in the divisional sector, and all had to be blown. The time for demolition was set for 1400 hours, but one bridge had to be kept open longer to allow the 15th/19th Hussars to bring along some very tired infantrymen and locate a lost carrier of their own. There was no time to waste; the main bridge at Vilvorde was blown as German motorcyclists came roaring up to cross. German infantry were not far behind, and the 2nd Royal Fusiliers on the left of the 12th Brigade soon found themselves in the same circumstances as the 1st Coldstream of the 3rd Division the previous day – with their flank turned thanks to the early departure of the Belgians on their left fleeing ahead of the enemy. The Fusiliers held on until nightfall, making good use of their carriers to protect their flanks with fire from Brens and from their two 3-inch mortars. The latter kept up a high rate of fire for some hours before both were destroyed.

The 1st Division, in I Corps sector, took up position on the right of 4th Division. Its sector included Hal, where two brigades of the 5th Division were establishing themselves. This division had been part of the War Office reserve located at Amiens and released to Gort's command on 16 May. It had completed an exhausting journey, partly in transport and partly on foot against a stream of refugees, with many interruptions caused by Luftwaffe attacks on the road.

The other divisions kept marching back to the rear. The infantry of the 3rd Division found transport waiting for them in the western out-skirts of Brussels, behind the layback positions established by the 4th Division. The infantry of the 48th Division had marched back and forth to support the 'crumbling' right flank, only to find that it was not crumbling, at least in the sectors to which they had been directed. Now they slogged back to an intermediary line west of the Senne. Large parts of the 2nd Division also had to march, although it had been intended to transport them to the Dendre. Some were lifted by dint of dumping stores from trucks, while others, having waited, marched off muttering. The 6th Brigade, after marching forty miles from the Lasne as already related, staggered in at around 0300 hours, tumbling wearily into houses in the villages short of Grammont, their intended destination. They had made the first contact with the enemy on the night of 13/14 May, spent the whole of 15 May fighting, withdrew at very short notice that night, spent 16 May working on new positions under fire, and began their forty-mile march as soon as it was dark.

The 12th Lancers (an armoured car regiment, the only one in the BEF) had been moved to the right flank to cover the crossings over the River Haine, which runs from west to east towards the Dyle, on the boundary between the BEF and the French First Army. They blew the bridges in the early hours of 17 May, the enemy snapping at the heels of the long, plodding, horsed transport column of the French 2nd North African Division. The Lancers held the Germans at bay until 1030 hours, giving the 48th Division time to fall back through positions prepared by the 13th Brigade of 5th Division at Hal.

The fact that all was now well on this flank should have been known to I Corps HQ, because the Lancers had maintained touch meticulously by radio. But Barker, the corps commander, was showing early signs of cracking under the strain. This was very evident to his fellow corps commander, Brooke, who wrote, 'he is so overwrought with work and the present situation that he sees dangers where they don't exist and cannot make his mind up on any points'.[1] Barker issued a series of orders followed by counter-orders. For example, the 4th and 7th Royal Tanks, but not their brigade headquarters for some reason, were ordered to move at once to Hal to stem a breakthrough by German armour. At that moment they were attempting to load their tanks on to a train at Enghien in the middle of an air raid on the station. Having set off, and driven most of the nine miles to Hal, they encountered Brigadier Miles Dempsey, the newly appointed commander of the 13th Brigade. He told them he had not asked for any tanks and had no knowledge of any German armour in the vicinity. It was now too late to entrain the tanks before the next stage of the withdrawal, and in addition to the unnecessary eighteen miles they had just driven, they had a long drive ahead, bad enough for the drivers and crews, but an unwelcome strain on the tank tracks.

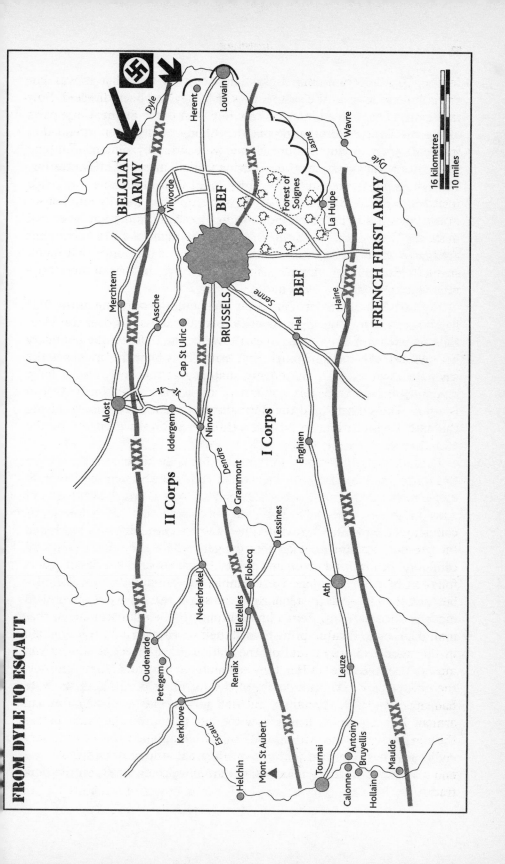

FROM DYLE TO ESCAUT

BELGIAN ARMY

Dyle

Herent

Louvain

Wavre

Lasne

Dyle

Vilvorde

BEF

Forest of Soignes

La Hulpe

Merchtem

Assche

Cap St Ulric

BEF

FRENCH FIRST ARMY

Senne

Haine

BRUSSELS

Hal

Alost

Iddergem

Ninove

I Corps

Enghien

II Corps

Dendre

Grammont

Lessines

Oudenarde

Petegem

Nederbrakel

Ellezelles

Flobecq

Ath

Kerkhove

Renaix

Leuze

Escaut

Mont St Aubert

Tournai

Calonne

Antoiny

Bruyellis

Maulde

Hollain

Helchin

16 kilometres

10 miles

The alarm had been caused by a report that the 2nd North African Division was in trouble again. In fact it had restored the position without assistance by putting in a counter-attack. But as far as Gort was concerned it was not to be trusted, any more than the rest of his allies. Disillusion set in on 17 May when the extent of the German breakthrough became clear, and Gort was worried, with good cause, that the enemy would cut in behind his right flank, across the Scarpe at Douai. This led to the formation of Macforce, mentioned earlier. The inadequate co-ordination and conflicting orders from Billotte and Georges were a source of exasperation to Gort. His lack of faith in Georges was not improved when a confusing message was received from him, postponing the withdrawal from the Senne to the night of 18/19 May. Gort sent Eastwood to Billotte's HQ to establish what was happening. Eastwood found that Billotte indeed intended to postpone the withdrawal, because Blanchard's French First Army was too exhausted to move. In spite of this, Eastwood managed to persuade Billotte to agree to stick to the original plan. Having previously pleaded for a delay, Blanchard suddenly changed his mind and had to be persuaded not to abandon his position too precipitately.

As a consequence of this late reversion to the original plan, the Belgians asked for protection of their right flank next morning, because they anticipated that there might be some delay in completing their move, and they did not want their flank left in the air. This was a reasonable request and the British Official History comments that an order to this effect was presumably issued to II Corps. But there is no note of its issue in the command-post records, nor of its receipt in II Corps documents. So a costly mistake was made. GHQ sent a report to the War Office that night in effect saying that both the British and Belgian armies were withdrawing to the Dendre on the night of 17/18 May, and that a flank guard would be maintained for the Belgians as far forward as Assche until eight o'clock in the morning of the 18th. But the II Corps order for the formation of the flank guard states that the Belgians were not retiring from the Senne until the night of the 18th and their open flank between the Senne and the Dendre was to be guarded *throughout* the 18th.[2]

The Belgians did retire during the night of 17/18 May, and by 0900 hours on the 18th they were back on the Dendre–Escaut line on the British left. The flank-guard task for the Belgians was given to the 2nd Light Armoured Reconnaissance Brigade, which also had responsibility for providing the rearguard for the British 4th Division. This reconnaissance brigade, consisting of the 5th Inniskilling Dragoon Guards and the 15th/19th Hussars, carried out the II Corps orders and maintained its position instead of falling back at 0800 hours. Attached to it for the withdrawal were the 32nd Army Field Regiment and 14th Anti-Tank Regiment, Royal Artillery (RA); and the 4th Division's machine-gun battalion, the 4th Gordon Highlanders. The Reconnaissance Brigade failed to find the Belgians, which was not surprising as they were already behind them on the Dendre. Earlier that night patrols from the brigade north of Vilvorde encountered some Belgian stragglers, who expressed doubts that the Belgian 5th Division, to which they claimed to belong, existed any more.

The British 4th Division had some trouble making a clean break during the night of 17/18 May. The enemy started attacking at last light to secure crossings at Vilvorde and elsewhere in the Belgian sector. The 10th and 11th Brigades had to fight hard to hold off the Germans, and got away with difficulty in the early hours of the 18th. Soon after first light the whole division was on the move westwards, protected by the 2nd Light Armoured Reconnaissance Brigade, whose two armoured cavalry regiments were deployed across the western outskirts of Brussels waiting for the GOC 4th Division, Major General Johnson, to give them permission to withdraw to an intermediate line running north–south through Assche and Merchtem, the latter inside the Belgian area of responsibility. German light aircraft came over, and the Reconnaissance Brigade found its radios being jammed, forcing its commander, Brigadier Clifton, to relay messages to the 15th/19th through the 5th Inniskillings. Meanwhile on the right flank of the BEF the 13th/18th Hussars and 12th Lancers covered the withdrawal of the 1st and 5th Divisions.

At 0845 hours, Clifton received the order to pull back on the Assche line. At the same time he sent a liaison officer to find the Belgians, who, on his return, reported that they had gone. By now, Johnson was also aware of this and sent the information to Clifton by despatch rider, who never found him – a situation that was to become all too familiar as the days went by. The 4th Gordons, who, together with the 14th Anti-Tank Regiment and 32nd Army Field Regiment, were to come under Clifton's command as soon as the withdrawal started, had been posted on high ground around Assche. Clifton had not been consulted about the siting of these units, and in some cases never even saw them. During the withdrawal to Assche, the 15th/19th had two tentative contacts that revealed the proximity of the Germans. One involved the sound of firing from a distance, followed by loss of radio contact with a subaltern who had, it was discovered later, been killed. At 1100 hours it became clear just how far the Germans had penetrated, using the route allotted for the Belgian withdrawal running through Merchtem. As the 15th/19th approached the village, they saw soldiers, horse-drawn artillery and tracked vehicles, and quickly realized these were not Belgians. Artillery fire was requested, but the gunners said the target was outside their arc – a specious answer, since any field gun can easily be swung round by lifting the trail and training it round.

Also at 1100 hours, the 5th Inniskillings saw that the 13th/18th on their right, covering the 1st Division, were withdrawing. The 13th/18th sent an officer over to the 5th Inniskillings to convey his colonel's apologies, but he had received strict orders to withdraw from his divisional commander, Alexander, under command of I Corps. Two corps pulling back from the same line would have problems synchronizing the movement of the line of rearguards to ensure that withdrawing one did not expose its neighbour to the danger of being outflanked. Lack of synchronization at army group level was also causing problems, and the staff at Gort's GHQ fumed at the failure of co-ordination by Billotte.

Soon afterwards the 5th Inniskillings were attacked, on their left rather than on the open right flank. German armoured cars, motorcyclists and a self-propelled anti-tank gun sped in between two of the Inniskilling tank troops and gained the road behind them, losing an armoured car in the process. The tanks charged the anti-tank gun, machine guns chattering, and all swept past, except the troop leader's tank, which crashed into a telegraph pole. The squadron regrouped in Capelle-Saint-Ulric, continuing to exchange fire with the German mobile troops. But there was now a wide gap between them and the 15th/19th on their left. A patrol from the reserve squadron of the 5th Inniskillings discovered that the Germans now held Assche in strength.

The 15th/19th were also having a hard time beset by infantry with anti-tank guns and armoured cars. The mechanized cavalrymen destroyed three armoured cars and a horde of motorcyclists, as well as some infantry who had dismounted from their trucks out in the open, well within range. But other German infantry, using the cover afforded by stream beds, took a steady toll of the 15th/19th with anti-tank guns and, by lobbing mortar bombs among the tanks, forced commanders to close down their hatches, thereby restricting their vision. But most serious were the Germans in Assche. One of the 15th/19th squadrons tried to barge through from the east and lost their squadron leader killed, the second-in-command and squadron sergeant major wounded, and four of their six troops wiped out. The town of Assche was soon a mass of 'brewed-up' tanks (i.e. in flames), with long oily columns of smoke marking the path of destruction.

Clifton decided to extricate his brigade, whether or not the 4th Division had got back across the Dendre. He motored over to the Inniskillings, and while talking to their CO he picked up a distorted message from the 15th/19th that indicated that the enemy now held the routes to both bridges on the withdrawal route south of Alost. The Inniskillings accordingly raced for the bridge opposite Iddergem, further south, and secured a bridgehead there. The supporting gunners and the Gordons were told to get across quickly. The 32nd Field Regiment crossed complete. The 14th Anti-Tank Regiment was isolated, and had to leave seven guns behind. The 4th Gordons also got back, except for one company supporting the 15th/19th with their Vickers medium machine guns deployed between Assche and Merchtem; the machine-gunners resisted until overrun section by section.

Clifton searched for the 15th/19th, unable to contact them by radio. He found one squadron still in good order, although it had suffered some losses at the hands of the enemy, who had attempted to get across its intended withdrawal route. Clifton sent this squadron back over the bridge held by the Inniskillings, and it was clear by 1400 hours. Some time later, a message was heard on the radio from the regimental second-in-command saying that the squadron he was with was bogged down and surrounded as it tried to reach the river. The third squadron had been destroyed at Assche. Clifton, with a heavy heart, ordered the Inniskillings to pull back, and the bridge to be blown.

The second-in-command of the 15th/19th, Major 'Loony' Hinde, ordered his party to split up and break out in groups. Although wounded in the neck and arm, he himself evaded the enemy. As he swam the Dendre the British 3rd Division opened fire on him, but missed. Two other officers and several soldiers also reached the Dendre. The next day the Germans caught the CO, his intelligence officer and French liaison officer, who had set off from further away. The 15th/19th had lost seventeen officers, of whom seven were killed, one on a ship bombed at Ostend, which he had reached in civilian clothes. About 140 soldiers were lost, and only a weak squadron remained.

On the BEF's right flank, the 5th Division's 13th Brigade, around Hal, came under attack late in the afternoon of 17 May, and the 2nd Royal Inniskilling Fusiliers and 2nd Wiltshires had their first experience of action repelling the Germans. Two companies of the Inniskilling Fusiliers went astray and got caught up in the human flotsam of refugees for two days. The 12th Lancers had their work cut out covering the withdrawal, with enemy motorcyclists and armoured cars continually trying to out-flank them, while tanks could be discerned not far off. Lieutenant Colonel Lumsden, the CO, fought his regiment brilliantly, but was called upon to hold on far longer than planned, not crossing the Dendre until 2000 hours on 18 May.

Headquarters I Corps had considerable difficulty locating its two divisions, despite sending out numerous despatch riders and liaison officers. One suspects poor staff work under the direction of a commander who was fast losing his grip. The GOCs of both 1st and 5th Divisions only learned of the planned withdrawal from the Senne to the Dendre by consulting each other. For lack of firm orders the 5th Division withdrew too far and its place on the right of I Corps between Ath and Lessines had to be filled by the 48th Division, earmarked as corps reserve. The 2nd and 1st Divisions were on their left. The II Corps line was held by Montgomery's 3rd Division, with the 25th Brigade of the 50th Division under command.

At 1000 hours on 18 May, Gort gave orders at headquarters I Corps for the final stage of the withdrawal. Barker of I Corps seemed obsessed by the memory of Lieutenant General Smith-Dorrien's stand at Le Cateau in 1914, and said his troops could not withdraw from the Dendre until the following night, 19/20 May. In harking back to Le Cateau, where Smith-Dorrien had stayed to fight because his troops were, in his opinion, too tired to continue marching, Barker was showing his lack of appreciation of how armour and mobile troops had changed the game for ever. Brooke was horrified, being all too aware of the need to secure the Escaut Line without delay. He succeeded in getting agreement that the Dendre should be held only until midday on 19 May, and in having the 1st Division, which alone had defended each successive line, transferred to his corps. Later he heard that Barker, on receiving a report of armour on his right flank, had decided to start his withdrawal at dawn after all. Alexander and Montgomery of 1st and 3rd Divisions were told to comply with this change of timing as best they could.

It turned out that the soldiers of the 2nd and 48th Divisions were perfectly capable of marching, and their last sub-units left their positions at first light. The infantry battalion Bren carriers and Vickers machine-gunners of the 4th Cheshires and 2nd Manchesters provided the rearguard along with the 4th/7th Dragoon Guards, the 12th Lancers and the newly committed 1st Armoured Reconnaissance Brigade. This last consisted of the 1st Fife and Forfar Yeomanry and the 1st East Riding Yeomanry. Although new to armoured warfare, and inadequately equipped with light tanks, they were posted on the right flank to guard against the tanks of XVI Panzer Corps that had so alarmed Barker.

The marching infantry of 2nd and 48th Divisions were delighted to find transport to lift them back over the Dendre. However, the Luftwaffe was about to cause havoc in the bright May sunshine. The 2nd Division, by using side roads, had greater choice of routes, but there were many confusing junctions and maps were in short supply, so wrong turnings were taken which caused delays. The 48th Division route passed through

Tournai, and every road was crammed with traffic, smart civilian cars and creaking wagons loaded with refugees, intermixed with armour, trucks and staff cars. The Luftwaffe hit Tournai, setting the town ablaze, before turning its attention to the traffic. Among the toiling refugees on the roads was a travelling circus, and the horrified troops were treated to the sight of elephants with gaping wounds in their sides going berserk, and four white horses bolting with the corpse of a girl caught in their traces.

The 48th Division's greatest moment of trial was at Leuze, ten miles east of Tournai. Here a sapper major took it upon himself to marshal the vehicles carrying the 145th Brigade and ordered them to close up. No sooner had this officious idiot departed than nine Heinkel bombers appeared overhead and unleashed their load on the cramped vehicles. The 2nd Gloucestershires lost 194 men, and the 2nd Oxford and Buckinghamshire Light Infantry 48, together with many vehicles. This was the worst blow struck from the air against British troops on the move in the whole campaign.

The I Corps rearguards kept the enemy back from the Dendre until midday. Although pressed hard, they inflicted a great deal of damage on the enemy. The 4th/7th in particular had a tough fight, ordered to hold a crossing over the Dendre at Ath until the 48th Division had got over. There were so many bridges across the river that all three squadrons had to be brought up into line, but gradually the bridges were blown and the 48th Division came back, very tired but in good order. There was some confusion about what the regiment was to do next; it was supposed to come under the command of the 50th Division, but nobody knew where this was. The colonel went to corps headquarters where he found an atmosphere of great tension, and was told to hold a 12,000-yard front on the River Dendre from midnight to noon the following day (19 May).

Two anti-tank batteries and a machine-gun battalion were to be placed under the regiment's command, but by dark none of these had turned up, and the three squadrons took up positions on their own. During the night some of the supporting troops arrived, and were in position by first light, except for one anti-tank battery that never materialized.

B Squadron on the right of the regiment learned at 0700 hours that enemy tanks and infantry had crossed the river further to its right. By 0900 hours the enemy were beginning to approach B Squadron from the other side of the river, and soon the Squadron was engaged along its complete frontage. Troop leaders had chosen their positions with skill, and the light tanks were camouflaged and dug in, making them difficult to locate. Furthermore the tanks were so sited that they were able to engage the enemy by crossfire, hitting them in the flank, rather than directly across the river, and this made it more difficult for the enemy to locate the source of the fire. The Germans kept approaching the far bank of the river in parties of about twelve, and attempting to inflate and launch rubber pontoons. As the battle progressed, the 4th/7th held their fire until the pontoons were launched, and not one got across.

All troops were still heavily engaged some thirty-five minutes after the planned time for retirement, and eventually the order to pull back was given. Unfortunately the right-hand troop took a wrong turning and ran into a strong force of enemy who had crossed lower down, and the troop was never seen again. But B Squadron was well pleased with its work, and full of confidence.

Major Frink's A Squadron in the centre had a similar story to tell of inflicting heavy casualties on the enemy as they repeatedly tried to cross. The Germans were first seen at dawn on the far side of the Canal. The squadron diary recorded:

> We had an excellent field of fire – some excellent targets of which we took full advantage. One company of Cheshires MG [machine-gunners] had arrived to reinforce me, also a battery of anti-tank guns. Heavy casualties were inflicted on the enemy. Among targets were infantry, cavalry patrols, artillery, rubber boats. Had orders to hold on till midday. At 1000 hours things became very warm – all troops under artillery and mortar fire – moved headquarters three times. Still getting good targets and doing a lot of damage.

On the left of the regiment, C Squadron also had a good shoot, but the troop in Lessines had difficulties with Germans trying to enter the town by a bridge that was only partly blown and working round its left flank. The troop held the enemy, and destroyed an anti-tank gun. By 1045 hours it was being heavily shelled, and only four members of the troop were unwounded, but it held on until relieved by another troop. As the pressure on the regiment grew, the colonel sent a reconnaissance party back to see how far the infantry had got, and the party reported that all roads to the west were clear for at least twelve miles. Having been told by corps HQ over the radio, 'Infantry withdrawal most satisfactory', the colonel ordered all squadrons to pull back. Pulling out was tricky because the enemy had crossed in strength both above and below the regimental front, and some enemy had infiltrated between squadrons. With all three squadrons deployed the colonel had no reserve to provide a layback position through which the regiment could withdraw. But they skilfully made a clean break, and the regiment moved back some twenty miles, crossing the Scarpe at Antoing, just south of Tournai.

But the move of the 4th/7th was not made without loss. Major Frink's

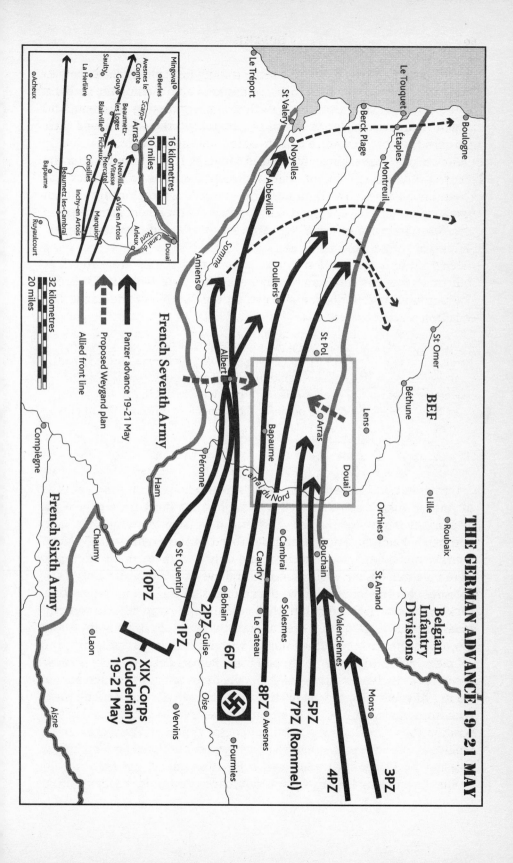

THE GERMAN ADVANCE 19–21 MAY

Panzer advance 19–21 May

Proposed Weygand plan

Allied front line

32 kilometres
20 miles

16 kilometres
10 miles

French Seventh Army

French Sixth Army

BEF

Belgian
Infantry
Divisions

XIX Corps
(Guderian)
19–21 May

1PZ
2PZ
10PZ
6PZ
8PZ
7PZ (Rommel)
5PZ
4PZ
3PZ

Boulogne
Le Touquet
Étaples
Berck Plage
Montreuil
St Valéry
Noyelles
Abbeville
Le Tréport
Mingoval
Amiens
Somme
Doullens
St Pol
St Omer
Béthune
Lens
Arras
Douai
Bapaume
Albert
Péronne
Ham
St Quentin
Bohain
Guise
Le Cateau
Cambrai
Caudry
Solesmes
Bouchain
Valenciennes
Orchies
Lille
Roubaix
St Amand
Mons
Avesnes
Fourmies
Vervins
Oise
Laon
Chaumy
Compiègne
Aisne

Canal du Nord
Canal du Nord

Acheux
Berles
Avesnes le Comte
Sauthy
La Herlière
Gouy
les Loges
Beaumetz-
Blairville
Ficheux
Croisilles
Mercatel
Vitasse
Neuville
Vis en Artois
Marquion
Incy-en-Artois
Beaumetz les-Cambrai
Ruyaulcourt
Bapaume
Arleux
Douai
Scarpe
Canal du Nord
Arras

A Squadron had started to thin out at 1200 hours under heavy fire. The anti-tank battery got away safely; the company of the Cheshires had some transport captured but got its machine-guns out on the 4th/7th tanks. A despatch rider was lost, probably captured, but the squadron was clear of the position by 1245 hours. The enemy were following up, however, and some probably crossed when the first tank troop pulled out – the position was too wide to cover completely. Both Lieutenant Stevens's 3 Troop and Troop Sergeant Major Lashmore's 4 Troop had a 'sticky get out'. But 3 Troop's withdrawal was greatly assisted by Lashmore remaining in position after the time to pull out had passed. Major Frink was relieved to see the squadron through the squadron checkpoint having crossed the canal at Tournai. Two carriers had been blown up, but the crews escaped. Trooper Harrison, lost the day before, had spent the night with C Squadron; after being blown up in a carrier, he had climbed on to a tank and was blown off that. He subsequently got hold of some civilian clothes and a bicycle, swam the Tournai Canal and turned up at A Squadron the next day.

The colonel stopped to watch the regiment go by at a place where all the squadron withdrawal routes converged. The Germans had been checked and did not pursue across the Dendre.

Up to now the 1st Division had had the hardest time of any formation in the BEF for marching, and 19 May was no exception. For the infantry it was march, dig, march, dig and, very occasionally, halt for a meal. For example the 1st Loyals, of Alexander's 2nd Brigade, had begun with a twelve-mile march back from the Dyle, which was then extended by a further twelve miles to bring them beyond the Senne at 1400 on 17 May. Being in reserve here they had been able to enjoy a hot meal, but at 1700 hours they were told to start marching again at 2300 hours. Having marched eight miles, they dug in at dawn on the intermediate line through Assche, only to be moved on at 0800 hours after being relieved by the armoured reconnaissance taking up a new layback position. They now had a march of twelve miles in great heat over pavé roads, bringing them to the Dendre, south-west of Ninove, where they dug slit trenches in the cornfields. The Loyals learned of their next move at 0200 hours on 19 May. Detailed as rearguard, they abandoned the position at 1000 hours and endured some fierce shelling, though without losing anybody. They reached the main road at the same time as 1st Guards Brigade, and marched in single file down each side of the road. Grey with fatigue, clammy with sweat and coated in dust, none of the soldiers knew where it would end or when they would stop marching.

Once troops stopped marching, it was an effort to get them moving again. The troop-carrying truck drivers, who had been on the go since

10 May, were equally tired, and every time they stopped, even for a moment, they fell asleep. Sometimes the convoy would move on without them, and in the darkness especially it was easy for a convoy to split, with the part behind a dozing driver becoming lost or badly delayed.

After a march of some ten miles, the Loyals embussed in trucks at 1300 hours, but there was insufficient transport to lift all the marching personnel in the battalion. They had eighteen miles to go before reaching the bridge over the Escaut at Kerkhove; the last man was over at 2000 hours. Now they had to dig, and were somewhat sceptical at being told that this was where they were to stay. They had marched at least fifty-four miles, had prepared for battle four times over three days, and now were making ready again.

The experience of the 1st Loyals was typical, but that of the 3rd Brigade in 1st Division was even more exhausting. The speedy with-drawal of the I Corps screen threatened Alexander's right flank. So he ordered the 3rd Brigade to hold the high ground east of Renaix, using radio to pass his orders. Familiar as it may seem to us now, this was novel at the time. The 2nd Sherwood Foresters marched into Renaix to be met by the burgomaster in full regalia. He said he had come to offer them the town's surrender, and was mortified when he discovered they were not Germans. However, the battalion was able to reassure him that the Germans were not far behind. The carrier platoons of the three battalions in the 3rd Brigade made up the rearguard, for the 13th/18th Hussars had pulled back on 1 Corps orders when Barker initiated the precipitate withdrawal. Alexander managed to hijack four troops of their rear squadron as they were on their way back, and doubled the size of his carrier rearguard. The rearguard fought some brisk encounters on the high ground round Ellezelles, Flobecq and Ogy, buying time for the footsoldiers to meet their transport and drive to the Escaut at Kerkhove. As before, there were insufficient trucks, and some had to walk. For example, 300 Foresters under Major Temple fought their way back on foot, and on arrival found all the bridges blown, so had to be ferried across the river. Like other parties that had marched all the way, they had covered some seventy miles on their feet.

There were instances of bridges being blown before all troops were on the 'home' bank. The 2nd Division rearguard was cut off when an officer was sent from I Corps headquarters to order the bridge at Tournai demolished. The 1st East Lancashires holding the town disputed the need to be so precipitate, but to their surprise the bridge was blown at 1900 hours, leaving the 2nd Division's rearguard cut off. The rearguard burned its vehicles or ran them into the river, and managed to get across by swimming or finding boats to use. All succeeded except the gallant

Captain Lewis of the 1st Royal Welch Fusiliers, who on hearing, wrongly, that two battalions were cut off on the enemy bank, swam across and fixed a lifeline. On moving forward to make contact with the 'cut off' men, he was shot by the Germans.

The BEF was now behind the Escaut river line, and by midnight on 19/ 20 May the withdrawal was complete. At 1600 hours on 19 May, Germans quickly following up had got across the river, and the 1st Buckingham- shires had to counter-attack to drive them back over it. In the northern sector German artillery began to register the British positions. This and heavy bombing of Audenarde seemed to presage a serious attack in the near future. All three corps were up, and seven divisions held a thirty- mile front. On average each forward battalion held a mile of riverbank. Company and platoon positions were sited to give mutual support and all-round defence. It was impossible to keep every yard of river frontage under constant observation, so there were places where the enemy could cross and penetrate for a little distance, especially in darkness or morning mist.

The terrain also gave scope for some bold patrolling, if COs were so minded. The CO of the 1st/6th East Surrey personally led a patrol along the banks of the Escaut in broad daylight and captured a prisoner. This was where the battalion was first 'blooded', in the opinion of the adjutant Captain White, and the CO's action did a lot to enhance the battalion's morale. The battalion was enthusiastic but lacked expertise, and if the CO could lead a patrol and defeat the Boche, reasoned the soldiers, so could they. The CO had been a prisoner in the First World War, and, according to White, his one aim was to kill the Boche.

The Escaut is normally a sizeable obstacle, and in stretches it still was. However, thanks to a long period of dry weather and the closing of sluices in the local dykes, the water level had fallen considerably and so in places was fordable by infantry. Most of the ground on the enemy side overlooked the BEF's forward positions, granting a view well to the west, as far as the French frontier. The question in Gort's mind must have been how long he could stay here. For the strength or otherwise of the Escaut position was not the deciding factor in how long the BEF could hold on. What was happening to the south was going to determine that, and indeed possibly threaten the continuing existence of the BEF altogether.

In the early hours of 19 May, Billotte paid his first visit to Gort at his command post, which had just moved from Renaix to Wahagnies. In the car on the way he kept repeating to Major Archdale, the British liaison officer, 'Je creve de fatigue – et contre les panzers je ne peux rien faire' (I am bursting with fatigue, and against the panzers I can do nothing). That must have been encouraging for Archdale to hear. Billotte had some reason to be gloomy: Giraud, who had been summoned to take over from Corap and bring his Seventh Army to prop up the crumbling Ninth, was missing. His headquarters had been overrun, and he was a fugitive, to be taken prisoner later that day.

Billotte showed Gort a map on which nine or ten German armoured divisions were marked. Their leading elements had approached Cambrai and reached Péronne that day, and there were no French troops between them and the sea. Gort, having at last heard the true situation from Billotte, realized that it was even worse than he had feared. In his despatch, he wrote that as he saw it there were now three courses of action open to the French. It is plain that he did not discuss them with Billotte. The first option was a counter-attack, and he had no idea what resources, if any, the French had to carry this out. The second was to pivot back on to the Somme, in order to preserve the lines of communication. The French lines of communication naturally ran back to France – as did the BEF's, to Le Havre, Cherbourg and Brittany. But whether pivoting back on a flank that had already been torn open was feasible is open to question. The third option was to fall back on the Channel ports as a precursor to evacuation. It was not an option that could be discussed with the French or Belgians, who would see it as British treachery. It is clear, however, that in Gort's mind evacuation was becoming the best, and indeed the only, option. In retrospect he was right. The GHQ staff immediately began to plan a withdrawal to Dunkirk. Brooke, when he heard of this, suggested that the BEF should swing back its right flank on to the River Lys, up the canal to Ypres, and thence by the Ypres canal to the sea. This was turned down for fear of what the Belgian reaction would be to hearing that the British planned a withdrawal, and Dunkirk offered better facilities. Major General Martel, the commander of the 50th Division, was ordered to act as a flank guard along the waterway between La Bassée and Béthune. This waterway flows past Aire into the canalized River Aa, which reaches the sea at Gravelines, between Calais and Dunkirk. A glance at the map on p. 66 shows that this is the one continuous water barrier flanking the route to Dunkirk, and was to become known as the 'canal line'. To cater for the extensive demolition of bridges and other key points that a further withdrawal would involve, the chief engineer, Major General Pakenham-Walsh, asked for 200 tons of explosive to be delivered from England immediately.

Pownall telephoned the War Office twice to discuss withdrawal, explaining the undertaking in guarded terms, but emphasizing that it was the failure of the French to repulse the armoured flood that had caused the trouble. Even at this stage, neither Gort nor Pownall had any faith in the French ability to mount a counter-attack sufficiently powerful

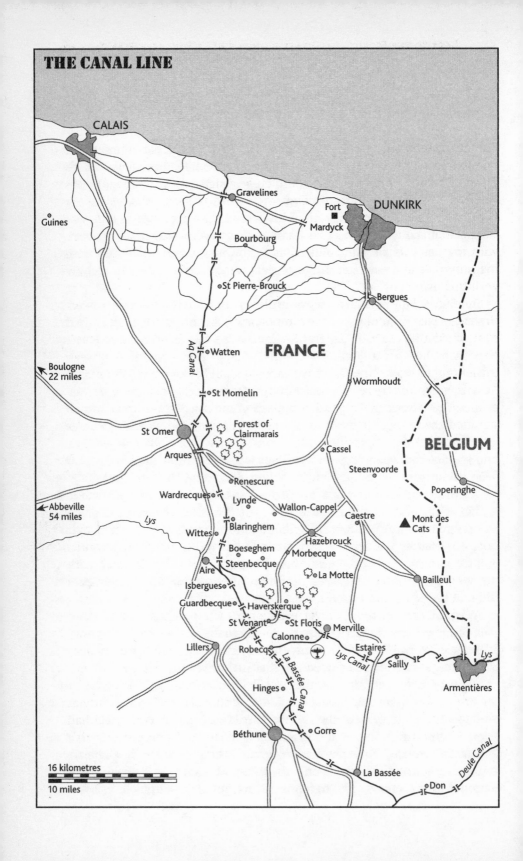

THE CANAL LINE

CALAIS

Guines

Gravelines

Fort
Mardyck

DUNKIRK

Bourbourg

St Pierre-Brouck

Bergues

Aa Canal

Watten

FRANCE

Boulogne
22 miles

St Momelin

Forest of
Clairmarais

St Omer

Arques

Cassel

BELGIUM

Steenvoorde

Renescure

Wardrecques

Lynde

Poperinghe

Abbeville
54 miles

Lys

Wallon-Cappel

Caestre

Mont des
Cats

Blaringhem

Wittes

Hazebrouck

Boeseghem

Morbecque

Bailleul

Steenbecque

Aire

La Motte

Isbergues

Guardbecque

Haverskerque

St Venant

St Floris

Merville

Lillers

Robecq

Calonne

Estaires

Lys Canal

Sailly

La Bassée Canal

Armentières

Lys

Hinges

Béthune

Gorre

Lys

La Bassée

Deule Canal

Don

16 kilometres

10 miles

to stem the German armour, let alone defeat it completely. Pownall spoke with the director of operations, Major General Dewing, who seemed taken aback by this news to the point of obtuseness. General Ironside, the CIGS, was so appalled that he managed to have the War Cabinet assembled by the afternoon. He told them that it might be possible to supply the BEF for a limited time through a bridgehead based on the Channel ports, but that complete evacuation was impossible. His solution was for the BEF to move south-west, towards Amiens, to get back on its line of communication. In making this suggestion, which was the most amazing nonsense, he was showing that he was as out of touch with events as his French counterparts. However, Churchill agreed with his proposals and told him to go to Belgium and order Gort to comply with this plan.

Sunday 19 May was also an eventful day for Gamelin: he was sacked. He had played absolutely no part in restoring the situation, and his final contribution was to visit General Georges at his headquarters at La Ferté. Here he called for an offensive, which had it been mounted a week earlier and in strength might have succeeded. But it was far too late now. At this juncture, he received a message from his headquarters at Vincennes that General Weygand had been summoned from Syria, which signified the end of the road for Gamelin. A 'quick lunch' with Georges followed. It turned out to be a substantial repast, which Gamelin tucked into with evident pleasure, and perhaps with relief that the burden had been lifted from his shoulders. After lunch, General Dill, the Vice Chief of the Imperial General Staff (VCIGS), arrived from London bearing the tidings that the BEF would do everything possible to co-operate. Georges was called away to speak on the telephone to Billotte, who told him that Gort was contemplating withdrawing to Calais and Dunkirk. Apparently, Billotte had gleaned this news by tapping Pownall's conversation with the War Office. Gamelin, after reminding Georges of the reassurances Dill had brought from London, left.

Weygand arrived to take over early on 20 May, ending the career of Gamelin, perhaps one of the most ineffectual generals in the history of France. Weygand was seventy-three years old, small and dapper with a foxy face, and reminded one British officer of 'an aged jockey'. At the very beginning of the First World War, he had been selected by the French commander Marshal Foch as his chief of staff, apparently at random. Weygand remained with him until after the Armistice. He had never commanded troops in battle. As Major General Spears (British Liaison Officer at GQG) remarked of him, commanding troops in battle and being a chief of staff were 'as different as riding in the Grand National from taking photographs of its jumps'. Weygand was an ambitious officer, who on arriving and being shown a map of the German advance exclaimed, 'If I had known the situation was so bad, I would not have come.' Spears commented, 'It meant he was thinking of his reputation.' Weygand learned all too soon how serious the situation was. Between 10 and 19 May the French had lost fifteen divisions. In the north a further forty-five were in danger of being cut off or hurled back into the sea. There were no reserves; the arsenals were empty. Between Valenciennes and Montmédy the gap measured nearly one hundred miles. The time for a counter-offensive had passed.

On that Monday, 20 May, Guderian's corps headed for Amiens and Abbeville. He told his soldiers that there were no Allied formations ahead of the armour and, having already crossed the Canal du Nord, there was no barrier between them and the coast. Gort's task was to hold the thirty-mile sector of the Escaut Line. Against Army Group B this was a big enough job in itself. The fate of the Belgian Army on his left and the French First Army on his right lay in his hands. But, given that the French First Army was bent back in a bow from Valenciennes to Douai, not only were his communications with his bases in distant Normandy threatened, but he was in danger of encirclement. He was not responsible for the threatened territory; it lay well beyond his boundary. The British 23rd Division had already been deployed on the Canal du Nord at Georges' request, to hold the sector from Douai to Péronne. Gort knew that this division could do little to stop the German armour. The British 12th Division had been ordered to cover Albert, Doullens, Amiens and Abbeville, all important traffic centres. The 12th and 23rd Divisions were, in the words of the British Official History, 'alone interspersed between the oncoming German armies and the sea'.[3]

An unequal struggle was about to be fought out on a thirty-mile-wide belt of country between the Scarpe, just north of Arras, and the Somme. The German spearhead consisted of seven armoured divisions – the armoured sickle of Army Group A. From north to south, they were 5th and 7th, of XV Panzer Corps (Hoth), 6th and 8th of XLI Panzer Corps (Reinhardt), and 1st, 2nd and 10th of XIX Panzer Corps (Guderian). In addition to their seventeen tank battalions, this force had fifteen battalions of motorized infantry, five motorcycle battalions and twelve batteries of field and medium guns, as well as anti-tank and anti-aircraft guns. Facing them were two British infantry divisions, both Territorial sent out for labour duties and to continue their training. The strength of each was little more than half a division. They had engineers but no divisional artillery. The 23rd Division had two brigades instead of the normal three. The 12th Division was provided with an improvised troop of four field guns manned by soldiers from a Royal Artillery school of instruction. The 23rd Division was luckier, having eleven field guns and two 4.5-inch howitzers from the same school. But they had no artillery instruments; eleven of the guns could fire only over open sights, the others had no sights at all. Both divisions had one Bren per platoon, instead of three, one anti-tank rifle per company, two carriers, and one 3-inch mortar. About a quarter of the men had not completed their war course with the rifle, and less than half had fired the Bren. The panzer divisions had fought in Poland and had just inflicted a crushing defeat on the French. Neither of the British divisions had fired a shot in anger.

As the British divisions were deploying on 18 May, the 37th Brigade of the 23rd Division was caught sitting in trains at Amiens by a heavy bombing attack by the Luftwaffe. That evening the leading troops of the German 1st Panzer Division reached the Canal du Nord and occupied Péronne. On pushing out of town the other side, the Germans encountered the 7th Royal West Kents and the four field guns. The leading motorcyclist was shot. He was followed by three tanks, which engaged the British with machine guns and were peppered back with anti-tank rifle rounds, pepper being the right expression as it was discovered that the Royal West Kents had been issued with training ammunition with half-charges. The field guns firing over open sights set one of the tanks on fire. Fighting continued until dark, and the Germans, having made no headway, pulled back into Péronne. The Royal West Kents and their field guns were ordered to retire to Albert, and moved without interference. The German reluctance to fight at night, even against weaker opponents, proved a blessing.

The next day the Germans closed up to the Canal du Nord in force, having outflanked Péronne to the south in a sector that was supposed to have been held by the French but was not. Soon five panzer divisions were over the canal, with two more echeloned behind. The 23rd Division was ordered to fall back. The 69th Brigade was to withdraw to the River Scarpe to the east of Arras, and completed the move during the night without enemy interference. The 70th Brigade was to deploy west of Arras and cover the Arras–Doullens road as far south as Saulty. The only continuous obstacle, and not much of one at that, was the railway line running near the main road, and there were no anti-tank guns to cover the crossings. The 7th Royal West Kents arrived in Albert at 0600 hours on 20 May and were greeted by a Stuka raid. Two companies rushed to cover the approaches to the town. They soon heard the sound of engines and the clatter of tracks, and saw the enemy armour accompanied by motorcyclists and armoured personnel carriers converging on Albert on more roads than the battalion had troops to cover. These were the leading troops of the 1st Panzer Division. The Germans encircled the town and burst in. As the two companies out on a limb started to embus, the armour caught them, massacring them in the trucks and by the roadside. Within a few minutes they were wiped out.

Lieutenant Brown, the acting adjutant of the battalion, determined to inform brigade headquarters of the disaster, stopped a civilian motor-cyclist at pistol-point and made him take him on the pillion. As they turned a corner, they ran into Germans rounding up some troops of battalion headquarters. The civilian braked and gave himself up. Brown slid on to the driver's saddle and shot off, with bullets pinging around him. He ran out of petrol a mile further on. A gunner officer who escaped in a car eventually took the news of the fate of the 7th Royal West Kents to brigade headquarters. The Germans found the four guns still in the main square with a quantity of training ammunition.

The infantry of the 70th Brigade were tired after several days of marching, so their commander, Brigadier Kirkup, decided to ferry as many soldiers as possible in the transport the brigade had managed to rustle up over the preceding days. The brigade marched to Neuville-Vitasse during the night of 19/20 May and rested there until daybreak – possibly a mistake. A British fault, the counterpart to the German reluctance to fight at night, was a lack of ruthlessness that sometimes manifested itself when troops were tired, both in withdrawal and in attack. On occasions, throughout the war, lives would have been saved had commanders pushed their soldiers harder.

In the early hours the brigade headquarters and advance parties from battalions were transported to their new locations: the headquarters to Gouy and the remainder to Saulty and Beaumetz-les-Loges on the Arras – Doullens road. The transport began ferrying the battalions, picking up a load of men and taking them to the new position while the rest marched on; the trucks would then return to collect the next load. With daylight came the Luftwaffe, so the men marched in open formation at wide intervals. The first lift consisted of about half of the 11th Durham Light Infantry. The other half had halted when the armour of Rommel's 7th Panzer Division appeared and surrounded them, killing or capturing them all. The SS Totenkopf (Death's Head) Division came up on the left flank of Rommel's division and also hit the 70th Brigade.

The Tyneside Scottish (Black Watch) were resting at Neuville-Vitasse when reports of enemy approaching at about 0700 hours got them moving again. The leading company marched about five miles and ran into an ambush near Ficheux, and efforts to work round the ambush ran into tanks. The rear company was trapped in Neuville, and attempts to fight from the houses were stymied when the tanks set fire to them with tracer and high-explosive rounds. At Mercatel, more Tynesiders and two companies of 10th DLI were surprised resting and cut to pieces.

Other Tynesiders were caught embussed in trucks along with a large body of Ordnance Corps soldiers and some pioneers, mostly unarmed, who had attached themselves to the brigade. As the trucks began their westward journey they ran into the leading elements of the 8th Panzer Division, while the tanks of the division attacked the marching troops. The panzer division had waited until daybreak to start. The marching infantry fought back, but against the armour, with light weapons, it was a hopeless task. A running fight took place over about five miles of road. The provost sergeant, Chambers of the Tynesiders, was last seen alive standing on a tank trying to lever open the commander's hatch with his bayonet. A few got away, and made for brigade headquarters. The enemy armour followed up and brigade headquarters was forced to flee to Houdain, on the road fifteen miles north-west of Arras. The remnants of the brigade joined them there, totalling some fourteen officers and 219 soldiers. The Tynesiders alone had lost over a hundred dead.

The 7th Panzer Division, under Rommel, spent an unsuccessful day attacking Arras, stoutly resisted by 1st Welsh Guards well established in their defences, and reinforced by the 9th West Yorks taken from airfield defence. Rommel went forward to see what the trouble was, and on his way back to rejoin his division, protected by one tank and an armoured car, encountered what his war diary describes as heavy tanks at Vis-en-Artois. They were probably French cavalry patrolling south of the Scarpe. They surrounded him and put his tank out of action. Regrettably they did not realize who they had netted, and he managed to get away. Had they taken him, much future trouble might have been avoided.

The 36th Brigade, less the 7th Royal West Kents, was able to take up its positions without interference. The 5th Buffs covered a frontage of six and a half miles from Pommera to La Herlière. They managed to scrape out some slit trenches forward of the railway line and set up flimsy roadblocks. On their right, the 6th Royal West Kents covered the approaches to Doullens, where Gort had intended to establish his headquarters when, as planned, his command expanded to an army group with the BEF split into two armies. In anticipation of this, it was well provided with a network of telephone lines, as well as containing the main map depot of the BEF. Unfortunately the maps had not been removed to a place of safety, which was to have serious consequences later. Brigadier Roupell warned the battalion commanders that if further withdrawal was necessary they should make for Frevent. At 0930 hours the gunner officer arrived bearing the news of the catastrophe at Albert.

A few truckloads of men escaped, but the Germans caught the quarter-master of the 6th Royal West Kents as he was distributing rations. A throng of French soldiers started coming back through the positions held by the 5th Buffs, ignoring suggestions to join in the defence. At La Herlière, on the left of the line, a woman enraged by this behaviour was seen to tear down a propaganda poster that read, 'Nous vaincrons parce que nous sommes les plus forts' (We will overcome because we are the strongest).

It was at La Herlière that Private Lungley of the 5th Buffs refused to surrender to overwhelming force, firing his Bren to the end and ignoring demands for surrender. A round from a tank gun killed him, and he was buried in the slit trench he had defended so stoutly. The villagers laid flowers on his grave each night, and when he was reburied in the village cemetery they attended in such numbers that the Germans stopped the ceremony. He was buried clandestinely at night.

One column of the 6th Panzer Division advanced rapidly on the 6th Royal West Kents, supported by artillery and machine guns, while the other column headed for the divisional objective, Le Boisle. By 1230 hours the whole of the brigade forward line was being engaged. Commanders at all levels could communicate only by runner, many of whom never got back, being cut off by infiltrating enemy infantry and armour. A despatch rider from the Buffs' left flank did, however, manage the ten-mile journey to Doullens, having two motorbikes shot from under him, experiencing several close shaves evading enemy tanks, and shooting two Germans with his pistol on the way. At 1300 hours the 5th Buffs were ordered to withdraw. None of the messages reached the forward companies. Afterwards it became clear that some of the Buffs had held out for up to two hours, and had knocked out at least two tanks with their Boyes anti-tank rifles, of which they had one to each two miles of front.

The 6th Royal West Kents were far less stretched out and so could put up a tougher resistance. The battalion kept the Germans out of Doullens until late in the afternoon, which allowed the administrative transport to get away, and a sapper officer to set fire to all the petrol in various dumps all over town. The Germans, having been denied access on the main road, came in from a flank and pumped shells into the houses, reducing them one by one. By 1700 hours about a hundred defenders were holed up in a building in the centre of town, and held out until 2000 hours. Black smoke curled up from destroyed petrol and devastated houses.

The headquarters and reserve company of the 5th Buffs joined brigade headquarters in Lucheux to find the only street through the village blocked by a German armoured car disabled by a Boyes rifle. At dusk, Brigadier Roupell led this party north but at 0400 hours, with enemy all around him, he ordered them to disperse and make their escape in small parties. Cut off from brigade headquarters, the remnants of three companies of the 6th Royal West Kents did the same, after holding out until last light in the north of the town. Most of these parties made their way south heading for the Somme. Here there were fewer enemy, and some parties of Buffs and West Kents crossed the Somme and reached safety. Brigadier Roupell hid in a farm, where he remained trapped for two years, before escaping home through Spain. All three battalion commanders were taken prisoner. Vehicle parties of the 5th Buffs and 6th and 7th Royal West Kents, with the 262nd Field Company, Royal Engineers (RE), forced their way through the teeming refugees, dodged the German armour and reached Saint-Pol. From here they were directed to Boulogne to reinforce the garrison. This party consisted of some 300 men, of whom about half were sappers. Only one officer, a captain of the 262nd Field Company, was able to report to Petre, his divisional commander, in Arras on 23 May, having spent the intervening days dodging German armoured columns.

Other battalions of the 12th Division were also involved in the mayhem in the path of the panzer divisions. These battalions had started out by train from Rouen on the night of 17/18 May, heading for Abbeville. But GHQ decided that the 37th Brigade should go to Amiens, and two trains were diverted while en route by Movement Control. The first contained the 7th Royal Sussex and the 263rd Field Company RE, and the second the 6th Royal Sussex with the 264th Field Company. The headquarters of 37th Brigade remained with the trains heading for Abbeville, and the third battalion, the 2nd/6th East Surrey, was detached on duty elsewhere. The leading train arrived on the outskirts of Amiens on the afternoon of 18 May and was pulverized by a bombing raid. Lieutenant Colonel Gethen of the 7th Royal Sussex found he had a hundred casualties including eight officers. He took his battalion into the cover of a wood, while awaiting a new engine to continue his journey. He had been told, wrongly, that his destination had been changed to Béthune, some fifteen miles on the other side of Arras from Amiens. The train carrying the 6th Royal Sussex was stopped by attacking aircraft further down the line, and the troops took shelter in woods near Ailly-sur-Noye, ten miles south-east of Amiens. Both battalions were cut off from their brigade headquarters and each other.

Still without a train, Gethen found a French headquarters in Amiens, and there was assured by a facile staff officer that the German advance had been halted at Sedan. There was no defence plan as far as Gethen could make out, and no sign of any other troops. The streams of refugees and continual appearances by the Luftwaffe made nonsense of the staff officer's assurances. Gethen decided to take up a defensive position on high ground south-west of Amiens, astride the road to Poix and Rouen.

The 1st Panzer Division arrived in the early afternoon of 20 May, and engaged the 7th Royal Sussex with its tank guns, sitting out of range of the forward companies. After drenching the positions with fire, the tanks clattered forward and overran the forward companies. The reserve companies held on, resisting until dark, long after battalion headquarters had been overrun. Gethen was captured, and his second-in-command shot for not putting up his hands speedily enough. One company commander, Lieutenant Jackson, wounded four times, was congratulated by his captor on the fight his men had put up, and was offered the German's car to convey him to hospital. Jackson preferred to remain with his soldiers.

A mere 200 of the 7th Royal Sussex survived, and the Royal Sussex, alone of all the regiments in the British Army, were awarded the battle honour 'Amiens 1940'.[4] Their sister battalion, the 6th Royal Sussex, commandeered an engine and train, and made a long journey via Rouen and Le Mans, back to Nantes, one of the British bases.

Headquarters 12th Division was at Fressenneville, well south of the Somme, eleven miles south-west of Abbeville. It was from here that the GOC Petre had left for Arras on 18 May, expecting to return, only to be detained to command Petreforce. Back at his own headquarters at Fressenneville, he spent Sunday 19 May in search of information, the whereabouts of the GOC and of missing units, and indeed any scrap of news that would throw some light on an increasingly obscure picture.

Because the 35th Brigade, the last brigade in Petre's 12th Division to be deployed, had been ordered to go to Abbeville, initially only the 2nd/5th Queen's reached the town. The other two battalions in the brigade (2nd/6th and 2nd/7th Queen's) were mistaken by Movement Control for the 46th Division and routed to Béthune. Eventually the 2nd/6th and 2nd/7th Queen's arrived at Abbeville station, after a hair-raising journey which had included a halt at Arras, where they were advised to try and return to Abbeville. The journey took thirteen hours, and, with only biscuits to eat, they were fed up with all this order and counter-order, and very hungry. They marched to billets in villages to the north and east of Abbeville: Drucat and Vauchelles. It was intended not that they should defend these localities, but that they should eventually deploy from them.

Earlier, Brigadier Wyatt of the 37th Brigade had had the 6th and 7th Royal Sussex arbitrarily, and in error, removed from him by Movement

Control, and the 2nd/6th East Surreys had been sent on lines-of-communication duty. Consequently, he had nothing to do until 20 May, when the GSO 1 of the division, the senior operations staff officer and de-facto chief of staff, decided that Petre's two-day absence might become permanent and that Wyatt should take command of the division, or what was left of it. At 1400 hours the Luftwaffe mounted several heavy raids on Abbeville, and there were spurious reports of paratroops landing. Headquarters 12th Division was still totally in the dark as to the situation. At this juncture Northern District at Rouen said that the division had been transferred to the direct command of GHQ and that the Germans were attacking Amiens. At 1700 hours a staff officer on return from a reconnaissance reported that the Germans had cut the road to Arras and reached the outskirts of Doullens at midday.

The 12th Division had been sent to Abbeville as a reserve, not to defend the town, and it was decided that the wisest course in view of the continued air attacks was to withdraw the three battalions of the Queen's in 35th Brigade back across the Somme rather than risk them being cut off. At 1715 hours Brigadier Cordova, standing in as brigade commander for Wyatt, sent a despatch rider to his battalions summoning the commanding officers and reconnaissance parties to implement the withdrawal. Abbeville was in a state of mayhem. Clouds of smoke and dust hung over the town; many roads were blocked with rubble and littered with corpses. Panic-stricken refugees crammed every passable road, fleeing hither and thither uncertain in which direction lay safety. Mixed with the civilians were equally agitated French soldiers in an assortment of army and civilian vehicles struggling to get over the Somme.

The Queen's battalions, being outside the town, survived the bombing without casualties. But the withdrawal message reached only the battalion nearest the river, the 2nd/5th. The tanks of 2nd Panzer Division had already penetrated between the centre battalion, the 2nd/7th, and the left-hand and most northerly, the 2nd/6th. The battalions had only had time to construct a few rudimentary roadblocks and some emergency slit trenches for local defence near their billets; they had not expected to defend the location against a panzer division. The 2nd/7th Queen's covering the Doullens road were hit first. The tanks sat back and pumped shells and sprayed machine guns at the exposed positions. The battalion responded with the six rounds of anti-tank ammunition per Boyes rifle, which was all it had. The commanding officer now sent a despatch rider with a message to all his companies to withdraw behind the Somme. Although he had not received Cordova's message ordering withdrawal, he had been warned earlier that moving back across the river was an option if the situation demanded it – now it did. He saw his two forward companies fall back and, thinking that his message had been received, he went to find the best crossing place. The order had in fact reached only one company; the others were withdrawing to the village of Vau- chelles, in the belief that the buildings there would offer better cover than the meagre slits they had dug in the open. Vauchelles lies off the main road, and the Germans poured past, without spotting the 250 soldiers hiding in the houses. After a quiet night, however, they found themselves surrounded by German tanks and infantry, and were forced to surrender. An exfiltration in small parties by night might have proved their salvation, but possibly they lacked the necessary leadership, or they were not well trained enough to think of it, or to carry out such an operation. Their commanding officer managed to lead about a hundred of his men over the Somme crossing on the debris of a bombed railway bridge.

The 2nd/6th Queen's sat tight and unmolested in Drucat, north of Abbeville. Lieutenant Colonel Bolton, the CO, waited until nightfall, having put his transport out of action. Marching by compass in bright moonlight, he led his men westwards until he reached the bridge he was heading for, and found no Germans there. This battalion returned intact, except for the platoon covering the rear.

Brigadier Cordova planned that the 2nd/5th Queen's, sited astride the Amiens road and nearer the river than the other two, should form the layback position through which the other two battalions would with- draw. He had to dispense with this scheme when he saw that the other battalions were now in contact and had no hope of withdrawing to the south-east or even of getting his orders. An order was sent to the 2nd/5th to cross the bridge at Epagne, but it was too late. The Germans advancing down the road from Amiens had already pinned down all four companies of the 2nd/5th in Bellancourt, two miles north of the Somme. A corporal at great risk got through with the order to pull out. But only five parties, totalling around a hundred men, made it past the Germans around Bellancourt. The first, a platoon unwisely travelling in trucks, encoun- tered tanks on a minor road to the bridge; they tried surrendering but were cut down. After this, more circuitous routes were attempted using the cover of darkness. Most who crossed the river did so by swimming, the CO among them. Some drowned in the attempt. A lifeline made of rifle slings broke and men were swept away by the strong current.

Unbeknown to the 35th Brigade they were not the only British troops in Abbeville. Two lines-of-communication battalions, the 4th Buffs and 2nd/6th East Surreys, as well as the 137th Brigade of the 46th Division, along with a battalion of the 138th Brigade, were caught up in the chaos caused by the great German breakthrough. The majority got clear on foot or in trains, usually displaying considerable initiative and resourcefulness.

The Germans' stunning advance had cut the Allied armies in two with stupefying speed, completely severing the BEF's lines of communication to its bases in Normandy, Brittany and further south. They had almost wiped out nine British battalions, and had captured Amiens, Albert, Doullens and Abbeville before the Allies could put together a plan for their defence. The way to the Channel ports was open. The 12th and 23rd Divisions had ceased to exist. What did they achieve? The war diary of the German XXXXI Corps says of the 6th and 8th Panzer Divisions that 'from about 1300 hours onwards they were only able to gain ground slowly and with continual fighting against an enemy who defended himself stubbornly'. This is praise indeed of the fighting quality of the Territorial infantry who, though widely dispersed, fought armoured divisions far stronger numerically and incomparably better armed.[5] One of these battalions claimed afterwards that it had delayed the German advance for five hours. Whether or not this modest claim is an accurate assessment, it has to be borne in mind that a delay of even one hour was of huge benefit to the British forces in France. But one cannot resist the thought that these battalions might have been used better, instead of being sprayed out over the countryside, to confront armour out in the open or on the edges of villages. The British Army had simply not given enough thought to how infantry should fight armour. This had to wait until later when the invasion of Britain looked likely; and by then troops were taught to hold the rear half of built-up areas, entice the armour in and destroy it at close range. Even that tactic was susceptible to the village or town in question being bypassed by armour, while enemy infantry remained behind to mop up the defenders. But the trick would have been to pick key points which the enemy could not afford to bypass, at least for long, such as Amiens and Abbeville.

The fundamental problem was that neither the French nor the British could match their thinking and planning to the speed of the German armour's progress. In modern terminology the Germans frequently got inside the Allies' Observation Orientation Decision Action loop, or OODA for short. Too often by the time the Allies had *observed* the enemy, worked out what they were about to do (*orientation*), *decided* what to do, and taken *action*, including giving the necessary orders, the game had moved on, with the result that the action taken did not fit what was actually happening on the ground. If Allied commanders ignored what air reconnaissance was telling them, as happened at the Meuse crossings, the OODA process could not even begin.

The RAF played an insignificant part in these momentous days. On

20 May, reconnaissance Hurricanes had reported the German armour crossing the Canal du Nord, and produced other sighting reports. Unfortunately at that very moment plans were being made to withdraw the RAF Air Component back to England because the German advance threatened its airfields. At the same time the Advanced Air Striking Force, situated south of the German breakthrough, and intended not to collaborate with land forces but to bring the aircraft nearer to military targets in Germany, had difficulty communicating with the BEF on the other side of the gap torn in the Allied lines. Co-ordinating what were effectively three air forces, the Air Component with the BEF, the Advanced Air Striking Force, and the rest of the RAF in the United Kingdom, was becoming impossible for the Air Ministry. So all squadrons were in the process of pulling back to Britain.

Nevertheless two squadrons of bombers with fighter protection were ordered to attack the armoured columns on the Canal du Nord. By the time the bombers arrived the columns were no longer there, and the panzer divisions were moving rapidly, widely dispersed, across country between Arras and the Somme (the Germans had got inside the OODA loop, yet again). On the critical day when the Germans were in full cry, the air force took no effective part in the fighting. Although some 130 bombers of Bomber Command and the Advance Air Striking Force attacked a variety of targets in support of ground forces, or 'collaboration targets' in the jargon of the day, 'it is impossible to conclude that their action had any very significant effect on the course of the battle', to quote the British Official History.[6]

By 21 May the only British fighter squadrons still in France were Nos 1, 73 and 501, very much reduced in serviceable aircraft. Thereafter, all air support for the BEF and neighbouring Allied forces would have to come from England. As the Germans advanced and the Allies retreated towards the Channel, the air umbrella from south-east England became increasingly effective. But it was never totally sufficient. In just twelve days, starting on 10 May, the German advance had put the BEF in peril of its existence and at the same time had almost completely stripped it of its close air support. This close air support, moreover, was never as good as that which the Germans enjoyed, for a number of reasons, not least lack of organization and the means to communicate with the supporting aircraft. In addition, it has to be said, at senior level in the air force there was a less than can-do attitude towards support for the army – an attitude, it must be emphasized, that was not to be found among the air crew.

Air Marshal Barratt, the commander of the Advanced Air Striking

Force, remarked, 'the RAF could not win the war if the French infantry [sic] lost it'. This was an interesting admission on the part of a senior RAF officer when one bears in mind that the British Air Staff policy before the war had in effect maintained that any future war would be decided by air strikes before ground operations became pressing. Barratt's eyes had been opened to the reality that air power alone does not win wars, a principle that holds good to this day. Whether any other RAF officer would have admitted this is quite another matter. There were some RAF senior commanders who would not see it almost to the end of the Second World War; and a handful of airmen who still do not perceive this fact over sixty years later. The RAF had spent the inter-war years planning to fight a very different war from that which it found itself fighting in May 1940. The blame does not lie entirely with the Air Staff, but must be shared with successive British governments who shied away from the continental commitment until too late. By that time the RAF's doctrine, operational concepts and force structure were unsuitable for this assignment in France and Belgium, sprung upon them almost at the last moment.

One bright spot in the gloom of Monday 20 May was that Arras still held out, although more than half encircled. In order to check the enemy at this important place, Gort ordered the 1st Army Tank Brigade and Major General Franklyn's 5th Division to join the 50th Division in the Vimy area, north of Arras, and to prepare for offensive action. The force was to be called Frankforce, after the GOC of the 5th Division.

Also on this day, General Ironside, the CIGS, descended on Gort's headquarters at 0800 hours. With him he bore an order from the War Cabinet resulting from his discussions with them the previous day, known as Order A. This read:

1. The Cabinet decided that the CIGS was to direct the C-in-C BEF to move southwards upon Amiens attacking all enemy forces encountered and to take station on the left of the French Army.
2. The CIGS will inform General Billotte and the Belgian Command making it clear to the Belgians that their best chance is to move tonight between the BEF and the coast.
3. The War Office will inform General Georges in this sense.[7]

This intervention by the War Cabinet was the result of the conversation Pownall had had with the War Office the previous day. Order A was based on an appreciation by the War Office of 19 May which in summary argued that:

1. Unless, therefore, the French are in a position to launch an organised
   counter-offensive on a large scale, the chances of preventing the
   German thrust reaching the sea are receding.
2. If a counter-offensive is considered impossible the only alternative
   would be to endeavour to hold the general line Ham–Péronne–Douai
   for sufficient time to enable the Allied left wing to withdraw to the
   line Péronne–Amiens–the sea.
3. The Germans cannot yet be in great strength and must be considerably
   disorganised by demolitions, the distance they have marched, and
   above all by air action. The present appears a favourable moment with
   the German mechanised forces tired and main bodies strung out.[8]

By the time Ironside arrived at Gort's headquarters, Condition 1 of the
War Office appreciation had already been realized because the French
were not in a position to launch a counter-offensive. The 'only alternative' outlined in Condition 2 was nonsense. By the evening of 19 May
the Germans already held most of the line Ham–Péronne–Douai on the
Canal du Nord, and by the evening of Ironside's visit the following day
would hold Amiens, Abbeville, Le Boisle and Hesdin as well. Although
the second sentence of Condition 3 was accurate, the first sentence was
wishful thinking on a grand scale, especially the reference to the Germans being considerably disorganized by air action. The effect of air
action on the Germans was negligible; the only significant damage was
to the RAF.

What the War Office was seeking in Condition 3 would come to pass
four and a half years hence. In December 1944, in a replay of the
Ardennes offensive, as German armour with their tails up headed for
the coast, the US Army's General Patton could pronounce with glee,
'they've stuck their heads in the meat grinder, and I've got my hand
on the handle'. But in 1940 the Allies had neither air supremacy nor
battle-practised armoured divisions; the French Army's performance in
1940 bore no resemblance to the dogged resistance by the Americans
in 1944 that contained the thrust; they did not have a Patton, and in
1940 Montgomery was only a divisional commander.

Gort was perfectly well aware that everything the War Office proposed
was impracticable. His right flank was already turned, and he had to do
all he could to prevent his left flank from being turned as well. If the
French could not close the gap, he would have to withdraw northwards.
He had heard nothing from the man who was supposed to be commanding him, Billotte, or from Georges, under whose command the British
government had placed him. He explained this to General Ironside and
told him that he intended mounting a limited offensive south of Arras.

The last entry in the German Army Group A war diary for 20 May says: 'Now that we have reached the coast at Abbeville the first stage of the offensive has been achieved . . . The possibility of an encirclement of the Allied armies' northern group is beginning to take shape.'⁹ Gort was right. Although Order A was a fantasy of *Alice in Wonderland* proportions, Pownall's conversation had one good outcome. It goaded the War Office into initiating discussions with the Admiralty that very day on the practicability of evacuation from Dunkirk.

Despite the outward signs of confidence evinced by the war diary entry above, the German command had become alarmed by the speed of their own advance. Hitler had an attack of nerves, as did Rundstedt, who had an over-inflated respect for Gamelin. This was based on Gamelin's performance as Commander in Chief General Joffre's operations officer, and especially his successful plan for the celebrated flank attack on the German Army on the Marne in September 1914, which had brought the whole scheme of manoeuvre of the German invasion of France in the First World War crashing down. Worried about his flanks, Rundstedt ordered a halt on 16 May. When Kleist came forward to order Guderian to comply, the latter threatened to resign, and kept moving. There was of course some activity by the Allies that understandably caused the odd wobble of confidence among German commanders – for example, the attack by Brigadier General de Gaulle's improvised 4th Armoured Division at Montcornet on 17 May in an attempt to cut Guderian's line of communication. More of an armoured raid than an attack, it fizzled out within twenty-four hours and did not achieve its objective. De Gaulle's next attack at Crécy-sur-Serre on 19 May was equally unsuccessful. However, despite the confidence displayed by press-on types like Guderian, anxiety within the German high command about exposed flanks and consequent differences of opinion over the right course to follow were to surface again. What Gort was cooking up at Arras was to feed some of these fears.

4

COUNTER-STROKE AT ARRAS

The limited offensive south of Arras that Gort had mentioned to Ironside, the CIGS, during his visit on 20 May was just that – limited. Gort's original intention as expressed in his orders to General Franklyn early on the 20th was to 'support the garrison in Arras and to block the roads south of Arras, thus cutting off the German communications [via Arras] from the east.' He was to 'occupy the line of the Scarpe east of Arras' and establish 'touch by patrols' with the French. Gort did not mention a counter-attack or any more ambitious aim, nor was there any suggestion that the French would take part.

Gort convinced Ironside that the gap had to be closed if disaster was to be averted, but the French would have to undertake this task. All the BEF divisions except two committed to Arras were fully engaged on the Escaut Line. Ironside, taking Pownall with him, went to see Billotte at his headquarters at Lens, and found him with Blanchard, the commander of the French First Army. Both gave Ironside the impression of being totally defeated, and with no idea what to do next. Ironside lost his temper. At six foot four, and like many large men in the British Army nicknamed 'Tiny', he towered over the two French generals. He shook Billotte by the button on his tunic, writing later in his dairy, 'the man is completely beaten'. Ironside having bludgeoned him into attacking towards Amiens, Billotte snapped to attention and said that he would make an immediate plan to do so. It was agreed with Billotte and Blanchard that the BEF and the French First Army would both attack on 21 May with two divisions.

Ironside took the opportunity to telephone Weygand and tell him that there was neither resolution nor co-ordination at Billotte's headquarters, adding that Billotte should be sacked. It was plain that the French were only agreeing to attack under the pressure of Ironside's unnerving presence. When Ironside called at Gort's headquarters on his way back to England, Gort convinced him that the French would never attack. Ironside's visit had one positive outcome: it opened his eyes to the true state of affairs in France. The scale of the defeat of the French Army was now much clearer in his mind – as was, consequently, the desperate situation

1. *Left*. General Lord Gort, C-in-C of the BEF, left, with General Gamelin, Supreme Commander French Land Forces, right.
2. *Right*. General Maxim Weyg, left, after being appointed Supreme Commander French Land Forces in Gamelin's place. Centre, with briefcase, French Prime Minister Paul Reynaud, examining papers proffered by an official. Lurking in the background, Marshal Pétain.

3. Hitler at his headquarters at Bruly-de-Pêche in the Belgian Ardennes during the campaign in France and Flanders 1940. On Hitler's left, Field Marshal von Brauchitsch, Commander-in-Chief of the German Army, and on his right General Jodl, Chief of the Operations Staff of the German armed forces (Wehrmacht). Far right, Admiral of the Fleet Raeder, Commander-in-Chief of the German Navy.

4. A sergeant of the Royal Ulster Rifles in 1940s-style battle order (minus haversack), with First World War vintage steel helmet, .303 in Lee Enfield bolt-action rifle slung, gas mask between his ammunition pouches, and eighteen-inch long bayonet slung on his left hip.

He is wearing battledress, only recently issued to the British Army, based on contemporary ski fashion, not a clever design for a fighting soldier. The blouse had insufficient pockets, provided no cover for the nether regions, and after a few minutes' crawling about often parted company with the trousers. The map pocket on the front of the trousers, instead of the side, made extracting maps difficult when lying down taking cover.

5. British soldiers in the ubiquitous 15 cwt truck. These soldiers are wearing the old-style 1914 tunic, and haversacks on their backs in place of the large pack.

6. Left to right:
Major General B. L. Montgomery
(GOC 3rd Division),
Lieutenant General A. F. Brooke
(GOC II Corps), and
Major General D. G. Johnson
(GOC 4th Division).

7. Major General the
Hon. Harold Alexander,
GOC 1st Division
in the BEF (left) with
Lieutenant General Sir John
Dill who commanded I Corps
in the BEF until April 1940
when he was appointed
Vice Chief of the Imperial
General Staff. Dill handed
command of I Corps to
Lieutenant General Barker.
Taken at an exercise at
Aldershot in May 1939.

8. General Heinz Guderian standing in his command vehicle. An Enigma for encrypting and decrypting radio messages is in the bottom left-hand corner of the picture.

9. 'Phoney War': The King's Company 1st Battalion Grenadier Guards practising 'going over the top' in 1914–1918 War style, 8 April 1940; one month before the German invasion of Holland, Belgium and France.

10. Light tanks of the 4th/7th Royal Dragoon Guards on exercise, winter 1939–1940.

11. Soldiers of the 4th Battalion Royal Northumberland Fusiliers on their motorcycle/side-car combinations. The British dispensed with these vehicles as a means of transporting infantry to battle after the 1940 France and Flanders campaign.

12. 'Phoney War': a Bren gunner and his number two in a 1914–1918 style trench in the winter of 1939–40.

13. Matilda Mk I tanks exercising with the 2nd Battalion North Staffs in January 1940.

14. (Left to right) General 'Tiny' Ironside, Chief of the British Imperial General Staff; General Georges, Commander-in-Chief of the French North-Eastern Front; Winston Churchill, then First Lord of the Admiralty; General Gamelin, Supreme Commander French Land Forces; General Lord Gort, Commander-in-Chief of the BEF; pictured in France in January 1940, before the German offensive in the West.

15. A British cruiser tank on a training exercise.

16. Bren-gun carriers on a training exercise in France before May 1940.

17. A French Char B tank on a training scheme.

18. A British Bren-gun carrier crossing the border into Belgium, 10 May 1940.

faced by the BEF. He began to wonder if it would ever be able to fight its way to the Channel coast. In his diary he wrote: 'God help the BEF, brought to this state by the incompetence of the French command.' Believing that only a minute portion of the BEF could escape, he was disturbed to find that Churchill 'persists in thinking the position no worse'.

Although Gort may have remained personally unconvinced that the French would attack to close the gap, the British Official History claims that Franklyn's operation was beginning to be seen at Gort's command post as part of a bigger push. Franklyn, however, was not told that his operation was now regarded as being part of a larger counter-attack in which the French would participate.[1] He visited General Prioux commanding the French (mechanized) Cavalry Corps, whose patrols were on the Scarpe. There he found Blanchard and Billotte. The French were discussing the possibility of an attack southwards towards Bapaume and Cambrai. They asked if Franklyn could co-operate by attacking towards Bapaume the next day, 21 May. Franklyn replied that he could not do more than the operation he had already been ordered to undertake. For this operation he suggested that Frankforce should 'occupy the line of the Scarpe on the east of Arras' and be responsible for its defence between Arras and Biache, and that the French mechanized cavalry, on being relieved, should move to the west of Arras and watch that flank. Prioux, one of the few French generals to maintain an offensive spirit, offered more; he would order part of a mechanized cavalry division (3rd DLM) to operate on the outer flank of the British force on 21 May. This promise would be fulfilled.

Billotte and Blanchard had tried to arrange for General René Altmayer's French V Corps to attack with two divisions east of Arras in the direction of Cambrai, as they had promised Ironside they would. Blanchard had sent a liaison officer to Altmayer to impress upon him the importance of this attack. The liaison officer reported back that Altmayer had wept silently on his bed, saying that his troops had 'buggered off' and refused to carry out the attack.

That evening Blanchard despatched a letter to Gort saying that, because of congestion on the roads, Altmayer could not mount his attack towards Cambrai before 22 May. Franklyn had already been told. He was in no way put out. As far as he was concerned his plans were not affected at all, and he would be able to carry out the limited tasks he had been given. In Gort's headquarters, where the notion had taken hold that the British and French operations were part of a major counter-attack, there was a feeling of being let down by the French.

What has been known ever since as the British 'counter-attack' at Arras was not intended as a counter-attack, but was designed as a large-scale mopping-up operation to support the Arras garrison by blocking German communications from the east. This is why the major part of two divisions was used to bolster the defence of Arras on the River Scarpe, and a minor part, all that could be spared, was employed to clear the country to the south of the town. The two infantry divisions (5th and 50th) totalled only four brigades, instead of the usual six. The 13th Brigade from the 5th Division had been detached to relieve Prioux's cavalry on the Scarpe so that the latter could take part in the attack. Franklyn decided to keep the other brigade (the 17th) in reserve until the first phase of the operation was complete. One of the brigades of the 50th Division (the 150th) was sent to reinforce the Arras garrison and to hold the Scarpe to the immediate east of the town. Only the 151st Brigade of the 50th Division was to take part in the clearing-up action, and, of its three battalions, one was kept back in support of the attacking troops. Thus, although Ironside and Pownall had told Billotte when they visited his headquarters that the British were mounting an operation with two divisions, the assaulting infantry on 21 May were in fact two battalions. Most of the infantry in what were already under-strength divisions were going to be holding ground, not attacking.

The attacking force consisted of what we would now call two battle groups of infantry, armour and artillery. The 1st Army Tank Brigade provided the armour. This brigade had covered long distances by road, so tracks and engines were worn, and there had been little time for maintenance. Of a total of seventy-seven Mk I tanks and twenty-three Mk IIs, fifty-eight Mk I and sixteen Mk II tanks were still runners, and many of these were badly in need of a good overhaul.

Franklyn ordered that the Arras–Doullens road should be the start line for the operation: the line which the attacking force crosses at the designated time for the attack to begin, shaken out in formation. The road fulfilled most of the requirements of a start line – or, in modern parlance, a line of departure. It was easily identifiable, and it lay at approximately 90 degrees to the axis of attack. The most important requirement it did not meet was that a start line should be secure, that is not held by the enemy. Franklyn was aware that the 70th Brigade of the 23rd Division had been sent to secure the road on 19 May. Perhaps the news of the disaster that overcame this brigade while it was on its way to its positions (covered in the previous chapter) had not reached Franklyn. The 12th Lancers had reported enemy south and west of Arras, but possibly Franklyn did not realize that they were already far beyond the Doullens road.

Indeed the strength of the enemy in the area was grossly underestimated. Air reconnaissance from the RAF was not available as all the

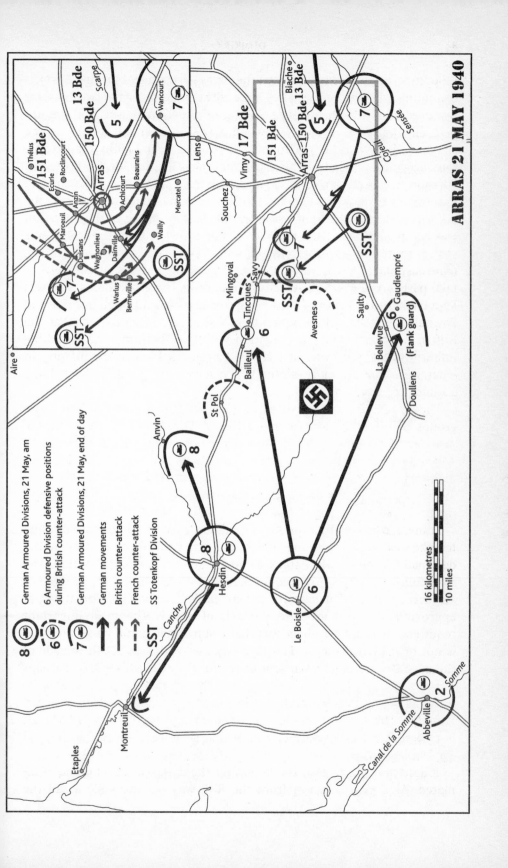

ARRAS 21 MAY 1940

Map legend:

- German Armoured Divisions, 21 May, am
- 6 Armoured Division defensive positions during British counter-attack
- German Armoured Divisions, 21 May, end of day
- German movements
- British counter-attack
- French counter-attack
- SST   SS Totenkopf Division

Scale: 16 kilometres / 10 miles

Places (inset, Arras detail): Aire, Thélus, 151 Bde, Ecurie, Roclincourt, 13 Bde, 150 Bde, Scarpe, Anzin, Arras, Achicourt, Beaurains, Wancourt, 7, 5, Maroeuil, Duisans, Wagnonlieu, Dainville, Wailly, Mercatel, Warlus, Berneville, SST, 7, SST

Places (main map): Lens, Vimy, 17 Bde, Souchez, Biache, 13 Bde, Arras-150 Bde, 151 Bde, 5, 7, Coeul, Scarpe, Sensée, SST, SST, SST, Mingoval, Savy, Tincques, Avesnes, Saulty, Gaudiempré, 6 (Flank guard), La Bellevue, Bailleul, 6, St Pol, Doullens, Anvin, 8, Hesdin, 8, Canche, Le Boisle, 6, Montreuil, Etaples, Canal de la Somme, Abbeville, 2, Somme

squadrons were still in the process of moving back to Britain. The commander of the attacking troops, Major General Martel, had been ordered to clear and capture a swathe of ground about five miles wide from the Doullens road to the Arras–Bapaume road. If one imagines Arras as the centre of a clock, this involved a piece of terrain from eight o'clock anti-clockwise all the way round to five o'clock. This meant clearing of enemy and capturing a piece of ground that covered an area of over forty square miles – fine if only light enemy forces were present, but still a big enough task for two battle groups, and a very different proposition if strongly held.

During the inter-war doldrums that affected the British Army, Martel had been one of the most enthusiastic proponents of the use of armour, and thus was an excellent choice to command the first-ever British armoured attack in the Second World War. He decided that the advance would be carried out by two mobile columns, or battle groups, thus:

Right column

7th Royal Tank Regiment (7th RTR)[2]

8th Durham Light Infantry (8th DLI)

360th Battery, 92nd Field Regiment RA

260th Battery, 65th Anti-Tank Regiment RA (2-pounder anti-tank guns)

One platoon, 151st Brigade Anti-Tank Company (Boyes 25mm anti-tank rifles)

One scout platoon, 4th Royal Northumberland Fusiliers (4th RNF) (motorcycle)

Left column

4th Royal Tank Regiment (4th RTR)

6th Durham Light Infantry (6th DLI)

368th Battery, 92nd Field Regiment RA

206th Battery, 52nd Anti-Tank Regiment RA (2-pounder anti-tank guns)

One platoon, 151st Brigade Anti-Tank Company (Boyes 25mm anti-tank rifles)

One company and one scout platoon, 4th Royal Northumberland Fusiliers (4th RNF) (motorcycle)

It should be emphasized that neither column bore much similarity to an armoured battle group in today's British Army, nor, for that matter, in the 1940 German Army. For example, the infantry were on foot, not travelling in armoured personnel carriers. The artillery was towed, not self-propelled, and the anti-tank guns likewise. The only truly 'mobile' elements in each column were the tanks and the motorcycles.

Both columns were ordered to cross the start line (the Arras–Doullens Road) at 1400 hours. The infantry, having debussed from their trucks on the Vimy Ridge (the old First World War battlefield), had an eight-mile march to reach their forming-up positions, the place where an attacking force marries up with its support and shakes out into assault formation, before advancing to the start line. As the force approached the forming-up position, they crossed the roads radiating out northwards from Arras, jammed with refugees, so the troops were late arriving. The second-in-command of 8th DLI bringing up the rear of the battalion reported that enemy aircraft had appeared and attacked with machine guns only, possibly because they had already dropped their bombs. The air attack caused no casualties among the battalion, merely some punctured tyres or radiators among the vehicles moving with them. The infantry of the 50th Division were trained as 'lorried infantry'. In theory, and sometimes in practice, they would be taken close to, or even right up to, the forming-up position in trucks, or lorries as they were called at the time. They did not fight from the lorries, which being 'soft-skinned' vehicles were in no sense armoured fighting vehicles, such as the contemporary German half-track. But, having trained to carry out all their moves in transport, the 50th Division, a TA formation, had not spent much time marching, so the Geordies of the DLI were not march fit and now their feet were soft and badly blistered from a twenty-five-mile move three days earlier, carried out without benefit of transport.

For lack of time there was no reconnaissance, and orders were hurriedly passed down the chain of command. The process could have been speeded up, and some misconceptions ironed out, if Martel had given orders to the infantry and tank commanders all together at one orders group (O Group). Instead he adopted the more conventional method of briefing just the commanders of the tank brigade and the infantry brigade. These commanders then held their own O Groups independently of each other, at which they briefed their own commanding officers, who in turn briefed their company commanders, and so on down, ending with section commanders briefing each section of eight to ten men. The most serious misconception concerned the command relationship between armour and infantry. The infantry COs, commanding each column, thought the tanks were under their command, whereas the tank COs thought they were merely in support, and not bound to follow the column commander's orders. This was not a happy state of affairs.

The British Army still had a great deal to learn about infantry–tank co-operation, and the DLI battalions and the 4th and 7th RTR had not even begun the process. Furthermore, the infantry had no means of communicating with the tanks other than by runner or motorcycle despatch rider. Nor, it must be borne in mind, did battalions have any wireless contact with their companies, a crippling disadvantage in a mobile battle, such as this was intended to be. The tank commanders also had communication problems caused by lack of time to tune and net in their wireless sets. In 1940 and throughout the Second World War, and for years afterwards on all but the smallest sets, this was a tedious procedure involving twiddling knobs to set pointers on dials, tuning the aerial, followed by laborious and often time-consuming netting-in calls to all stations on one's own net (all the radio stations on the same frequency belong to a net). Command tanks would be on at least two separate nets, thus increasing the complexity of the process.

Operating was probably the most difficult in the Mk I tank, which had a crew of only two, commander and driver. A section commander, like Lieutenant Hunt of C Company 4th RTR, had to navigate his tank, fire the gun and command the other two tanks of his section. There was no intercommunication (intercom) system between commander and driver, so directions from commander to driver were given by kicking him using an agreed set of signals (kick on left shoulder = go left, and so forth) or by shouting. The Mk II tanks with a crew of four were better, but had no intercom at this stage in the war.

By 1100 hours the infantry column commanders had sorted out who was supposed to be in their columns and were ready to set off for the start line. Unfortunately, the 8th DLI right-hand column had to move off without their motorcycle reconnaissance platoon and their field gun battery, which had both been held up on the gridlocked roads in rear. This was a pity, because this column was on the exposed right flank, and being on the outer edge of a wheeling manoeuvre had further to go. To assist co-operation the CO of 7th RTR left a liaison officer in a scout car with the CO of 8th DLI. But the RTR liaison officer lost wireless communication with his own CO early on, and 8th DLI had no contact with 7th RTR for the rest of the day.

For the first three miles there was no opposition. The tanks clattered off ahead, steadily drawing ahead of the infantry slogging through the dust churned up by the armour. The tanks of the left-hand column were preceded by a posse of 4th RNF motorcyclists, as well as ten of their own. Behind the infantry rode Martel in his staff car, followed by his reserve, the 9th DLI. In rear the artillery bumped along behind the gun towers. The tanks crossed the River Scarpe by the small road bridges, and as the right-hand column crossed the Arras–Saint-Pol road, the soldiers were cheered by the sight of the smouldering wreckage of a German mechanized 150mm howitzer battery, caught and pulverized by the 12th Lancers. No one seems to have wondered what an enemy medium battery was doing so far north.

A few minutes later, 8th DLI came under fire from the village of Duisans to their right front. The tanks of 7th RTR and the French 3rd DLM, which as promised was on the right of the British advance, swiftly retaliated. For a moment there was a danger of them shooting each other up, but once identities were established the misunderstanding was quickly resolved. A and D Companies of 8th DLI pushed on through Duisans while B Company picked up prisoners in the grounds round the château. Major McLaren found that the Germans had no fight left in them. The commander of B Company took twelve prisoners single-handed in the village cemetery. But the Germans reoccupied the cemetery, and had to be cleared out by C Company supported by French tanks. In the process eighteen more prisoners were taken, all wounded, and according to McLaren the tanks killed about a hundred Germans.

At this juncture, the CO of 8th DLI, Lieutenant Colonel Beart, decided to leave B and C Companies at Duisans as a flank guard, under the command of McLaren, while A and D Companies, the carrier platoon, mortars and battalion headquarters went on to Warlus. The 8th DLI advance reached Warlus at about 1630 hours and were ordered to press on. The carrier platoon commander, Lieutenant English, and A Company could see the Arras–Doullens road ahead, but as soon as they left Berneville they came under heavy fire. This, as far as English could tell, was mainly from mortars from German positions in the vicinity of the road. It stopped the two DLI companies in their tracks. The solution now would have been to call down fire from their own artillery on the German mortars and guns, but the battery of field guns supporting 8th DLI was miles away still trying to get into position through roads jammed with refugees. The advance by 8th DLI ground to a halt.

Meanwhile, at Dainville, on the start line, Y Company, 4th RNF, put in the first and only attack ever mounted by a British motorcyclist unit. Major Clarke, the company commander, attacked with one platoon dismounted, supported by a section of 4th RTR.[3] A column of German half-tracks towing anti-tank guns had been seen motoring between the right flank of 4th RTR and the left flank of 7th RTR, the boundary between the two at that point being a railway line. Lieutenant Hunt of C Company, 4th RTR, took part in this action, ambushing the Germans in a section of sunken road, which led to an archway under the railway line. He sited one of his tanks so that even if it was damaged or destroyed it would plug the route under the railway line. Most of the German vehicles brewed up, some forty prisoners were taken, and Dainville was secured. As a result of this successful little action, one of Hunt's tank commanders, Corporal Beetham, was awarded the MM. On completion, Hunt's section was ordered back on to the original axis.

The rest of 4th RTR swept on, crossing the start line on time at around 1400 hours. As they moved down into the valley, a few gouts of earth were thrown up around them by enemy shellfire. The tanks crossed the railway line, some gleefully barging through the closed level-crossing gates. Breasting the tree-lined Orinchon stream between Achicourt and Agny, 4th RTR saw streams of German lorried infantry trundling south across their front. This was almost too good to be true, and the machine guns on the Mk Is and Matildas ripped into the trucks, the tracer setting fire to the vehicles and cutting down the German soldiers as they jumped down and scuttled for cover. The German 37mm anti-tank guns speedily came into action, but to the horror of their gunners the solid, armour-piercing shot bounced off the armour of both the Mk I tanks and the Matildas. One of the latter with its 70mm of armour shrugged off no fewer than fourteen hits by German anti-tank guns. The tank crews were jubilant at the sight of the hitherto invincible enemy fleeing in disorder.

Continuing up the slope to Beaurains and beyond to Wancourt, still firing at enemy troops legging it, 4th RTR suddenly ran into trouble. German medium guns, firing direct, smashed into the tanks, brewing up at least twenty, including the CO's light tank. Lieutenant Colonel Fitz-maurice was killed. The adjutant, Captain Cracroft, seeing a battery at point-blank range, charged the guns, annihilating the crews. But more distant, concealed guns continued firing, wreaking havoc among 4th RTR. Cracroft ordered a speedy withdrawal, as black smoke poured from wrecked tanks, bodies hung half out of turrets and hatches, and wounded men dragged their torn bodies through the grass.

Plodding on behind 4th RTR, the 6th DLI had entered Achicourt and Agny, and mopped up large numbers of shaken Germans. The CO, Lieutenant Colonel Miller, sent two companies on to Beaurains, taking more prisoners to bring the battalion's total up to 400. The news that 4th RTR had run into trouble coincided with a message that the Germans were bringing tanks along the road from Cambrai.

Meanwhile the right-hand column had split, with 8th DLI advancing on Warlus, and 7th RTR, not realizing that Warlus was one of the objectives, swinging left towards Wailly. At that moment communications in 7th RTR broke down, and the CO, Lieutenant Colonel Heyland, was shot when he got out of his tank to re-form the regiment using hand signals. His adjutant, trying the same, was also cut down by machine-gun fire. Some tanks headed for Wailly, others on to Mercatel. Here two Matildas commanded by Major King and Sergeant Doyle knocked out four tanks, overran two anti-tank batteries and crashed through a road-block. Their headlong advance was eventually brought to a stop by some 88mm anti-aircraft guns firing in the ground role, possibly the first recorded instance of their being employed in this capacity. These guns were to cause British, Russian and American tank crews much grief right up to the last day of the Second World War. On this occasion, King and Doyle knocked one out before King's tank caught fire, leaving Doyle to press on until hit by another 88 and brewed up.

During the attack on Wailly, a lone British tank caught another German infantry column on the move, and shot up a howitzer battery, putting it out of action by killing, wounding and putting to flight all the gun crews. General Rommel, who had been leading his tanks to the south and west of Arras through Warlus, was greeted by scenes of chaos when he returned to bring up his two infantry regiments. He found that they had been shot to pieces by the two British tank regiments. He personally redeployed a number of 88mm and 20mm anti-aircraft guns, as well as some anti-tank guns and howitzers of his divisional artillery in the Wailly area, and ordered them to open fire on British tanks deployed near by. Although the shells from the 20mms could not penetrate the British tanks' armour, their crews' habit of lashing their kits on the outside was to prove unwise. The incendiary rounds set these alight, and the fire spread to the engine. The howitzers were lethal, even against the Matildas, as were the 88s. This was the fire that brought 7th RTR's advance to a dead stop. As the surviving tanks withdrew, their final burst of fire killed Rommel's ADC.

Both 4th and 7th RTR, having rushed ahead of the infantry and out of range of their supporting artillery, were caught by guns and brought to a halt. It would take British armoured commanders plenty more such unpleasant shocks in the years to come, many at the hands of Rommel in the desert, before the penny dropped that tanks on their own charging well-sited anti-tank guns and 88s were dead meat. You needed your own artillery to deal with the enemy guns, and infantry working with the tanks to winkle out the anti-tank guns from their covered positions. Unfortunately, the teaching of Liddell Hart had affected British thinking on armoured warfare, and led to armoured commanders deluding them-selves that tanks could swan about the battlefield like ships at sea, and need take little or no account of what the infantry and artillery could do for them.

The crews of tanks out on their own, beset by enemies, often found the battlefield a lonely place. Sergeant Hepple was the commander of a light tank, 'Guinevere', five-and-a-half tons, with 14.4mm of armour, two machine guns in the turret, a .303 and a 5.5, a maximum road speed of

35mph, and a crew of three. His task was reconnaissance for the Mk I tanks of B Company, 7th RTR.[4] As he motored forward, having crossed the start line, his tank was hit three times by anti-tank fire, probably on the tracks, because the effect was like hitting a large stone at speed, and he could see the right-hand track a couple of yards in front of the tank. None of the crew was hurt. Two more shots followed, but missed. The guns that had fired on him were silenced either by him or by the Mk Is that went on past him without stopping. Hepple's tank was subjected to small-arms fire for some minutes, but this stopped in his opinion because the enemy thought the crew was dead. Whatever the reason, about fifty Germans appeared and stood around in groups in the road near by. Hepple opened fire on them and despatched those who did not run off or take cover immediately. The Germans tried to bring an abandoned anti-tank gun into action, but Hepple put a stop to them as well. His attempts to get in touch with B Company by wireless proved fruitless, as the aerial had been damaged by small-arms fire.

The appearance of a second wave of British Mk I and Mk II tanks, followed by infantry, persuaded Hepple that it was safe to dismount and inspect the damage. Although he and his crew, Troopers Tansley and Mackay, attempted to repair the damage to the tracks, and to the radiator, it became clear that the tank was beyond local repair. As they worked they were subjected to shellfire and air attacks. Hepple investigated a Mk II stopped near by, but its right track was off, and the commander, Sergeant Temple, and a crew member lay dead beside it.

By this time dusk was approaching. The infantry had withdrawn, and Hepple decided to abandon 'Guinevere'. He set fire to her, and she was soon burning fiercely. He also set fire to three German motorcycles abandoned in the vicinity. He found a map in one, which he later handed over to one of his officers. He then came upon an abandoned British Bren carrier, which he managed to start, and piling on to it all removable kit, including his two machine guns, he headed for Achicourt, where he found some of 4th RTR.

General Franklyn had spent much of the day in fruitless attempts to get the RAF to provide some support. But the only aircraft that appeared in the sky over the Arras area were German Stukas. At around 1800 hours, they hit 8th DLI on the ridge between Warlus and Berneville, and kept up the attacks for approximately ninety minutes, according to Major McLaren, the second-in-command, who tried to get in touch by motorcycle with the half of the battalion that had gone forward with the CO. This proved impossible because of German tanks between him at Duisans and the rest of the battalion. The effect of the Stukas' screaming sirens, the crash of bombs and streams of bullets directed at men lying in the open was shattering. Few were hit, but Lieutenant English had to kick dazed men to their feet.

When the noise of the last attack died away it was replaced by the sound of approaching enemy tanks. Fortunately there were three tanks from the 3rd DLM close by and, while these held off the Germans, 8th DLI withdrew to the cover of Warlus. The two companies took up positions of all-round defence in the village, which Lieutenant English found took some time because of the shock of the air attack. Despite the terrifying noise the total casualties inflicted on 8th DLI caught out in the open were ten men wounded and three trucks destroyed. It was a useful lesson, that troops well spread out in the open, rather than in a village or town, were hard to hit, and the air-to-ground weapons carried by the Stuka were nothing like as lethal as those borne by other aircraft later in the war and after it. On subsequent occasions when the battalion was dive-bombed, they took cover, and carried on as normal after it was over.

Back in Warlus, the two 8th DLI companies started taking casualties from German artillery. The CO was among those wounded, but carried on. The German attacks were not pressed home, which was fortunate as the front half of the battalion was out of touch with the rear half back at Duisans. The CO sent the mortar platoon commander back to brigade headquarters, and after giving him a situation report the brigade commander ordered the battalion to withdraw.

Meanwhile at Duisans, some soldiers of B Company, 8th DLI, came running back to McLaren saying they were under attack from enemy tanks. McLaren had to take the men forward to their positions himself, while an anti-tank gun destroyed enough of the enemy to persuade them to withdraw. But the anti-tank gun was damaged and two of the crew were wounded in this exchange. A Matilda coming back through Duisans went out and sat in front of the anti-tank gun to shield it from enemy fire, while a new crew dashed forward and moved the gun to a less exposed position. McLaren judged that B Company's nerve was 'bad', but C Company was steady.

The Stukas also dived on 6th DLI at Agny, Achicourt and Beaurains, causing far more casualties than 8th DLI suffered. With reports of German armour approaching from several directions, Franklyn authorized Martel to withdraw his columns back to the River Scarpe west of Arras. During the day the 150th Brigade had raided across the Scarpe and caused some mayhem among the enemy. The 13th Brigade had established a bridgehead further east in preparation for the second phase of the operation. But Franklyn realized that with the enemy continuing to work round his right flank no further attacks could be made, and his main concern must be to stave off the threatened envelopment of his whole force.

The 6th DLI pulled back at last light on Achicourt, leaving Y Company, 4 RNF, and scout cars as a rearguard between Achicourt and Beaurains. A German tank approached from Beaurains as the last of 6th DLI were passing through the rearguard, and was knocked out by Y Company with an anti-tank gun. The Germans took some time to react, and the next attack by infantry with artillery support, which came in at dusk, was repulsed. German tanks followed and outflanked the Y Company position, setting fire to the houses with high explosive and flame throwers. Although surrounded, the Northumberland Fusiliers fought on, buying time for the rest of the column to get clear. The 5th Panzer Division, which had been responsible for the attacks on the rearguard, took the survivors prisoner.

Captain Cracroft, the adjutant of 4th RTR, stationed himself near Achicourt, assembling what was left of the regiment. When a tank approached, he waved his map in the driver's face as he peered out of the hatch, only for an unmistakeably German head to pop up out of the turret. Cracroft ran for his tank, chased by a burst of machine-gun fire. After an exchange of fire, both sides withdrew. The weary British were lucky that the Germans were not more aggressive in following up. The soldiers of 6th DLI were so bone-tired that they kept flopping down in the road at every halt, and had to be kicked to their feet by officers and NCOs.

Lieutenant Hunt of 4th RTR never reached the objective, but met the battalion coming back. One tank commanded by Sergeant Strickland was escorting about fifty Germans with their hands on top of their heads. Although the Germans did not know it, he had run out of ammunition, and did not even have one round 'up the spout'. During the withdrawal, Hunt's tank threw a track in soft ground, a fault to which the Mk I was prone. Unable to replace the damaged track, Hunt and his driver were rescued by the company second-in-command in a staff car, after first destroying the wireless set in the tank.

Sergeant Hepple of 7th RTR, having arrived at Achicourt after abandoning 'Guinevere', drove out in the carrier he had found, but this broke down. Trooper Nichol, also of 7th RTR, and an infantry straggler tagged themselves on to his party, which now numbered five. They managed to find two Bren guns and some water bottles, and set off across country, arriving at Arras the next morning. On reporting to the area headquarters, they were sent to join the remnants of their units at Vimy.

The rearguard for the Right Column was also found by the scout platoon from 4th RNF. They were attacked by Rommel's 7th Panzer Division and all killed or taken prisoner. But the 2-pounders of the 260th Battery of the 65th Anti-Tank Regiment did good work covering the withdrawal of 8th DLI, as did the French tanks of the 3rd DLM. Three battalions of the 25th Panzer Regiment had to fight their way back to the rest of the division against what Rommel judged, incorrectly, to be a superior force. They made it after nightfall, with a loss of twenty tanks, but they claimed to have destroyed seven heavy tanks, French Somuas, and six anti-tank guns – difficult to substantiate in the chaos of a battle fought in the gloom of approaching night.

With the 7th Panzer Division on the Arras–Hesdin road, 8th DLI were cut off, with two companies in Duisans and the rest of the battalion in Warlus. After dark an officer from A Company turned up at Duisans and told McLaren that he with four others on a Northumberland Fusiliers' scout car were all that were left of A Company at Warlus. He was closely followed by four men of D Company, who told the same story about their company. At that juncture, another four men, including the orderly-room clerk, arrived in the CO's car, with a similar account concerning battalion headquarters. At around 2300 hours, McLaren sent an officer to their brigade headquarters in Maroeuil, north-west of Arras, to apprise it of the situation. The officer was not seen again until he turned up in England, having arrived there via Boulogne with other flotsam and jetsam from the Arras battle (see Chapter 6).

McLaren tried to contact the CO, but could not do so because burning vehicles on the road gave enough light for German tanks to shoot up anything that moved towards Warlus. C Company reported German tanks at the rear of Duisans, and this was confirmed by French cars arriving to pick up their wounded, with news of panzers between Duisans and Maroeuil, north of the Arras–Hesdin road. At midnight, McLaren sent back the battery commander from 92nd Field Regiment, who was with rear battalion headquarters, with a message to his battery asking for defensive fire on the north end of Duisans. Sending messages by runner, in this case an officer, was an indication of how poor wireless communications were in the BEF. The fire fell short, wounding soldiers in both B and C Companies.

At about 0100 hours, McLaren, having heard absolutely nothing from brigade headquarters, sent off Captain Potts to find out if there were any orders. By now everyone at Duisans was saying that they should withdraw, but McLaren refused to do so without orders. He was sitting in the château at about 0230 hours when he heard the sound of transport starting up, and discovered that the anti-tank gunners had gone, and B and C Companies were preparing to do so. The motor transport platoon had also gone, leaving four vehicles without drivers. McLaren could not find anyone to drive them. In 1940, unlike today, few soldiers and not all officers and NCOs could drive. The wounded in the château were left behind because the doctor would not move them. McLaren decided that as the anti-tank gunners and motor transport had 'fled', the remainder might as well go too. Leaving the wounded in the care of the doctor, McLaren sent an officer to catch the motor transport in Maroeuil and hold them there, which he managed to do. McLaren then marched with the remainder, encountering French tanks but no Germans. He arrived in Maroeuil at about 0315 hours, finding most of 9th DLI in the village, and Captain Potts, who said that the brigade commander had instructed him to tell McLaren to withdraw. McLaren was 'much relieved' that the withdrawal had been authorized. Some accounts mention that an officer on a motorcycle from brigade headquarters managed to bring orders to the two companies at Duisans to withdraw. It may be that in the confusion whoever took the message failed to tell McLaren, hence the precipitate withdrawal without his knowledge.

The CO of 9th DLI told McLaren to defend the west side of the village. After McLaren had moved his men into the houses, they all fell asleep. At dawn, he was told to withdraw, and had a very hard time waking the exhausted soldiers and getting them on the move in transport to the battalion rendezvous, a road junction north of Maroeuil. The company sergeant major of HQ Company overshot the rendezvous and was never seen again. McLaren took the men from the road junction back to Vimy, where they lay up in woods on the north-east side.

At approximately 0600 hours, Lieutenant Colonel Beart with three officers, including Lieutenant English, and some thirty men joined McLaren in the woods; he had believed them all to be dead. They had abandoned Warlus, where they had been shelled, bombed by Stukas and obliged to fight off attacks. At around 0300 hours tanks had been heard approaching. They turned out to be six French tanks and two armoured troop carriers. Lieutenant Colonel Beart, who had himself been injured, got all his wounded loaded on to the French vehicles, and they set off to traverse some four miles of German-held territory. They were shot at but only sporadically. They found Duisans empty and pressed on to Vimy. Beart was sent to hospital with a flesh wound in the thigh, and McLaren took over command. So by 0600 hours what was left of 8th DLI was back at the point from which it had started twenty-four hours before, Vimy Ridge. Here McLaren deployed the battalion, using woods for cover where possible, as German aircraft were very numerous overhead, and (as he put it) 'by now no English [sic] aeroplanes were ever seen'. The next day, more survivors of A and D Company came in to rejoin the battalion.

Lieutenant England's carrier platoon was down to six carriers out of an original strength of thirteen. Everybody was very tired.

Although now temporarily out of contact with German ground forces, the units on Vimy Ridge came under frequent air attacks as McLaren's remark indicates. The 2nd Light Anti-Aircraft Battery with its 40mm Bofors was sited on the ridge in an effort to give some protection from the Luftwaffe. Second Lieutenant McSwiney's 2 Troop was in action pretty well throughout the Arras counter-attack and until the withdrawal from the ridge. Most of the enemy bombers cruised overhead just out of range of the Bofors and, because there were no heavy anti-aircraft guns on the ridge, were untouched. McSwiney moved his headquarters from a wood, which he felt was distinctly unhealthy after a visit by enemy reconnaissance aircraft, to a brick kiln. The reconnaissance aircraft had been fired on by French troops with every light automatic available, reminding McSwiney of the continental habit of shooting at anything that flies, including sparrows. His intuition was right – the wood was dive-bombed a few hours later and went up in flames. But he was not to escape the Luftwaffe's attentions. As he and his battery commander, Major du Vallon, arrived at one of his gun sites, the air sentry spotted three sections of dive-bombers starting on the circular flight that normally preceded an attack, and sure enough they were the target. Attacked from three angles at once and regrettably out of support range from the other guns, he and du Vallon took shelter in the shallow gun pit. One gunner lay outside with his back exposed, and had his right shoulder almost ripped off by a bomb splinter.

When the last aircraft made off, McSwiney jumped into the driving seat of a French ambulance, whose driver was still shivering with fright in a nearby ditch. Before setting off he opened the back and discovered five French corpses, which he and some of the gunners removed, before taking their own casualty to the nearest dressing station.

Early in the afternoon of the next day, three Dornier bombers crept very low up the valley between Souchez and Vimy Ridge, clearly with the object of eliminating McSwiney's guns. One of these was positioned behind a haystack. The leading aircraft dropped a stick of bombs as it approached this gun, four of which failed to explode, but the fifth landed just the other side of the haystack, lifting it completely off the ground and dumping it on top of the gun and its crew. Watching from a respectably safe distance, McSwiney could not help laughing first at the spectacle of the erupting haystack itself, and then at its aftermath as faces and bodies emerged from the hay. The last man to struggle clear was the Bren-gunner who had been firing until the last moment; he now ran yelling down the cart track. When McSwiney picked him up in his truck, he explained that the strap of his steel helmet had been under his chin, and the blast had forced the hat upwards carrying him with it to a height of three or four feet, until the descending haystack brought him back to earth. Apart from stretching his neck and spine, he suffered no other ill effects. Two of the three Dorniers were destroyed by the battery. An hour later, the battery was ordered to withdraw

Thus ended the Arras 'counter-attack'. It was a foolhardy undertaking. Two regiments of tanks and two battalions of infantry formed into two weak battle groups, plus a battalion in reserve and part of a French DLM, had encroached on the territory of three panzer divisions. The spearhead of this attack thus comprised about 1,400 infantry and 74 tanks, against around 7,000 infantry and 740 tanks, not to mention the discrepancy in artillery, and the total lack of air support for the British.

The question remains why the attack was launched in the first place. When Billotte had warned Gort and Pownall that nine panzer divisions were racing west with nothing to stop them, someone at GHQ or Gort's command post should surely have worked out that some at least of these formations – in fact six – would be somewhere south of Arras. The factors contributing to this failure of comprehension were threefold. First, by now the British high command were thoroughly sceptical of anything the French told them in general, and of their ability to fight in particular. Consequently, by extension, it was assumed that the French must be exaggerating enemy strengths as a way of explaining their panic and defeat. So, one properly asks, what about intelligence? The answer lies in the second factor: the handling of intelligence was never particularly efficient at either GHQ or Gort's command post, and, as we have noted, sending Mason-MacFarlane, the chief of intelligence, to command Mac-force had made the situation worse. When Pownall wrote in his diary, 'we haven't yet encountered the real German Army; this is only their armoured cavalry that is sending us reeling', there was no intelligence staff with sufficient authority and knowledge to correct this misconception. Third, the British, along with the French, failed to appreciate the fighting power and tempo in attack that panzer divisions supported by aircraft could generate.

The price of this venture was the loss of all but two Matilda Mk II tanks and twenty-six Mk Is, out of a total of seventy-four Mk Is and Mk IIs with which the two tank regiments had gone into battle. That was the bad news.

The good news was that the Arras counter-attack gave the Germans a very nasty fright. Why? To a German looking at a map, the panzer corridor was a tentacle about 30 miles wide and 200 miles long vulnerable to attack from either flank, and there were British and French divisions well placed both north and south. Nor was this 'tentacle' uninterrupted, a solid obstacle. On the march in peacetime conditions, a panzer division occupied fifty miles of road. In operations there were traffic jams that caused a concertina effect in some places, while in others the columns were strung out, with long gaps between the armour, the infantry, the supply train and the artillery. The motor infantry, towed artillery and unarmoured supply vehicles stretched along the road were especially susceptible to air attack along the line of the road or to ground assault from a flank. Only French paralysis, a flawed operational concept and inept command-and-control arrangements (to the point of there being hardly any) precluded the mounting of a counter-attack that would have inflicted a massive defeat on the Germans.

In the event, the Arras action was the only Allied counter-stroke singled out for special mention in the German propaganda film *Sieg im West* (Victory in the West). This is a measure of the psychological effect that these two weak British battle groups had on the Germans. They had advanced up to ten miles at the furthest point and had captured more than 400 prisoners, more than in any other action against the Germans since 10 May. They and the 3rd DLM had destroyed a large number of tanks and trucks. The 7th Panzer Division war diary speaks of 'hundreds of enemy tanks and following infantry'. The situation map marked in Rommel's own hand shows arrows suggesting a counter-attack by five enemy divisions. It certainly cost Rommel's division more tanks than any other operation so far, and 89 killed (including seven officers), 116 wounded and 173 missing (mostly captured) – four times the number suffered during the breakthrough into France. The remainder of the prisoners bagged by the 50th Division were from the SS Totenkopf Panzer Division, of whom Guderian was to write they 'showed signs of panic' – a damning indictment of Hitler's SS elite.

Rommel's angst reverberated up the German chain of command. General von Kluge, commanding the German Fourth Army, wrote that 21 May was 'the first day on which the enemy had met with any real success'. He wanted to halt any further advance westward from Arras until the situation had been stabilized. In Kleist's Panzer Group, the 6th and 8th Panzer Divisions were ordered to swing back from Hesdin and Le Boisle to take up defensive positions on the flank of the supposed five enemy divisions. At the Nuremberg Tribunal after the war Rundstedt said:

A critical moment in the drive came just as my forces had reached the Channel. It was caused by a British counter-stroke southwards from Arras on 21 May. For a short time it was feared that our armoured divisions would be cut off before the infantry divisions could come up to support them. None of the French counter-attacks carried any serious threat as this one did.[5]

General Halder, the chief of staff to Brauchitsch at Supreme Command of the German Army (Oberkommando des Heeres, or OKH), expressed concern in his diary, and the shock transmitted itself all the way to Hitler. It was to contribute to decisions he made later which were to be of immense importance to the BEF.

The action at Arras, or rather its failure, had another beneficial effect. It persuaded Gort to question very carefully the notion of trying to bulldoze a way south to join up with the French Army, as envisaged by Churchill. He was coming round to the view that the BEF might have to move in another direction.

5

FIGHTING ON TWO FRONTS

As the Arras 'counter-attack' began, General von Bock's Army Group B attacked the BEF on the Escaut. Gort's sector on the Escaut from north of Oudenarde to Maulde on the French frontier was about thirty-two miles long. He deployed seven divisions along it, having sent his other two as well as his tank brigade to the Arras sector in the attempt to plug the gap torn in the French Army. Every division had to take its place in the Escaut Line, and in some places there was very little depth to the defence. The complete river line had to be covered, for failing to do so would have been a tactical error; an obstacle is no bar to the enemy's progress unless it is covered by fire, a principle as old as warfare itself and drummed into every young officer and NCO at an early stage in his training.

On the extreme left of the British line was the 44th Division, abutting the Belgian Army. This junction point with the increasingly ineffective Belgians was a potential weak spot, and the Germans were all too aware of it. The 44th Division was deployed in greater depth than any other British division on the Escaut. But to achieve it the division was deployed with four battalions forward and five back, which meant that its fire-power in the 'shop window' was not perhaps as strong as it might have been had the GOC chosen a different defensive layout. The commander, Major General Osborne, was a former Royal Signals officer, the only non-infantry divisional commander in the BEF, which might explain his choice of deployment. A key piece of ground, the Anseghem–Knok ridge, lay in the 44th Division's sector. If the Germans seized it, they might well turn the whole Escaut position.

The other division in Adam's III Corps, the 4th, had five battalions forward on a frontage of five miles, somewhat shorter than that held by its left-hand neighbour, the 44th. The 1st East Surreys of 11th Brigade were responsible for the bridge at Kerkhove. While the BEF was still withdrawing to the Escaut, the battalion had two companies (C and D) on the east bank and two (A and B) on the west. When the order to blow the bridge was given, C and D Companies under Major Bousfield were withdrawn. 'Bouser', as he was known in the battalion, had served in the First World War, first as a private soldier, then as a lance-sergeant, and

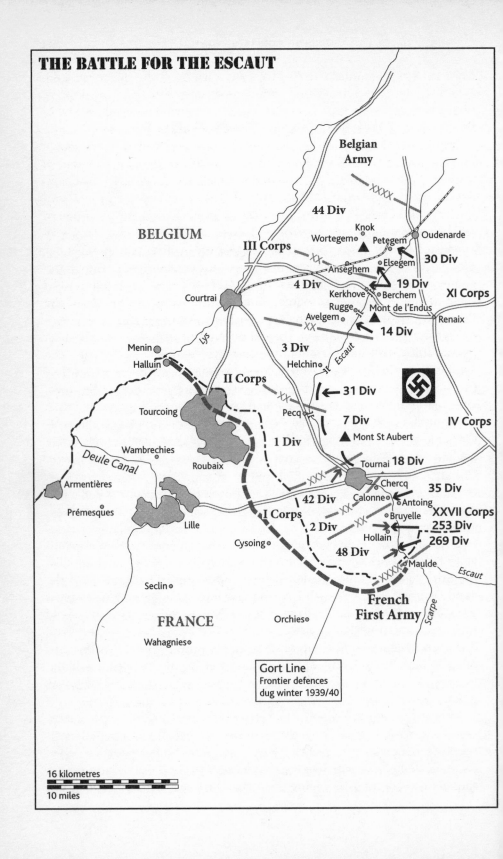

THE BATTLE FOR THE ESCAUT

Belgian
Army

BELGIUM

44 Div

Knok
Wortegem   Petegem   Oudenarde
III Corps
Anseghem   Elsegem   30 Div
4 Div   Kerkhove   19 Div
Courtrai   Berchem   XI Corps
Rugge   Mont de l'Endus
Avelgem   Renaix
14 Div
Menin   3 Div
Halluin   Helchin   Escaut
Lys
II Corps
31 Div
Tourcoing   Pecq
1 Div   7 Div   IV Corps
Wambrechies   Mont St Aubert
Deule Canal
Roubaix   Tournai   18 Div
Armentières   Chercq   35 Div
42 Div   Calonne   Antoing   XXVII Corps
Prémesques   Bruyelle   253 Div
Lille   I Corps   2 Div   269 Div
Cysoing   Hollain
48 Div
Maulde   Escaut
French
First Army
Seclin   Scarpe
FRANCE   Orchies
Wahagnies

Gort Line
Frontier defences
dug winter 1939/40

16 kilometres

10 miles

from 1915 as a commissioned officer. He was now forty-seven years old. When the 1st East Surreys first came out to France in 1939, in common with many other battalions every company commander had fought in the First World War, but by May 1940 some of these had been replaced.

Brooke's II Corps held the face of the shallow salient the river made into the British front. No major road entered this sector from the east, so it seemed the least likely to come under attack. It was however the worst-developed section of the BEF's area of responsibility, because Montgomery's 3rd Division, on the left, had not arrived until the afternoon of 19 May. Alexander's 1st Division had moved in even later, and was pretty exhausted for the reasons described in Chapter 3. The corps commander (Brooke) and the two divisional commanders (Alexander and Montgomery) in II Corps were the best in the BEF, and they deployed most of their firepower on the river line. Mont Saint-Aubert, to the east of the Escaut, overlooked much of the 1st Division's sector.

To the right of 1st Division, the 42nd Division, with one brigade short (it was still with Macforce), held the river line each side of Tournai. The 1st Battalion the East Lancashires covered demolition parties responsible for blowing the main bridge over the river that ran through the town. During the night the Germans could be heard approaching, and in broad daylight the next morning, 20 May, one of them approached the river and shouted in English, 'Heil Hitler, you democratic swine.' A Lancastrian soldier responded, 'You square-headed bastard,' and shot him dead. Some of the Germans approaching the Escaut were clearly full of confidence, or perhaps alcohol, because a party of six in a staff car and on a motorcycle drove up as bold as brass to another part of the riverbank and were wiped out.

The deployment of I Corps reflected the less than exemplary staff work that had characterized Barker's command since day one. Originally, the 6th Brigade of 2nd Division had been put in under command of the 42nd Division, with the 48th Division continuing the line right on down to Maulde. When Barker realized that the Escaut was supposed to be held for some time, the 2nd Division was shoehorned in between the 42nd and 48th Divisions, and some readjustments were planned for the night of 20/21 May. The 6th and 143rd Brigades were to be relieved by 4th and 5th Brigades respectively. But, before this could happen, the Germans struck.

During the late afternoon, the German artillery rained down shells, especially on the 1st/8th Royal Warwicks, the right forward battalion of the 143rd Brigade. Part of their front included the village of Calonne. Factories and cottages on the water's edge on the British bank prevented the rear companies from seeing the forward companies sited among, and in some cases on the other side of, these buildings. The spires and turrets in buildings in Antoing, under a mile from Calonne, provided the Germans with excellent observation posts overlooking the riverbank. The Germans also infiltrated soldiers into a factory building on the Warwicks' side of the river, allegedly dressed in civilian clothes. However they got there, they caused considerable trouble to the inexperienced Warwicks. As the German bombardment intensified, it spread to the 1st/7th Royal Warwicks, the left forward battalion of the brigade. The British artillery fired back, but not as effectively as on the Dyle, because there had been less time to register targets, and there was less ammunition.

This activity disrupted the relief plan, so that eventually – despite a certain amount of order, counter-order, disorder – two battalions of the 4th Brigade (2nd Royal Norfolks and 8th Lancashire Fusiliers) took over from the 6th Brigade, while the third battalion in the brigade, the 1st Royal Scots, relieved the 1st/7th Royal Warwicks. The relief was completed just before first light on 21 May, amid bursting enemy shells, and some instances of 'friendly fire' in the confusion. The 1st Queen's Own Cameron Highlanders of the 5th Brigade assembled for a counter-attack, which was then cancelled. The 1st/8th Royal Warwicks waited for relief, while trying to keep the Germans out of Calonne.

Just after first light on 21 May, the Germans assaulted in strength, preceded by a heavy bombardment. But before this, in the 2nd Royal Norfolk's sector, Captain Barclay commanding A Company saw some Germans on the far bank, apparently totally oblivious of being under observation. Barclay told his company to hold their fire until he sounded his hunting horn. A German officer appeared, got out a map and seemed to be holding a briefing with his senior warrant officers. After this they withdrew into a plantation, followed by sounds of chopping, and young trees falling. Eventually they emerged from the plantation carrying a number of long hurdles constructed from the trunks of saplings, and started to lay these across the rubble and concrete blocks that were all that remained of a bridge across the canal in the A Company sector. It was clear that the Germans had no idea that the British were so close and watching with interest. As they started to cross, Barclay decided to wait until there were enough to make a good target on the home bank, but not so many that they could not be disposed of quickly. When about twenty-five had crossed and were milling about, he blew a blast on his horn and his company cut down all on the home bank and most on the other side too.

The outcome was a storm of artillery and mortar fire. The battalion headquarters of the 2nd Royal Norfolks was hit, wounding the CO, adjutant and intelligence officer. Major Ryder took command of the battalion. Captain Barclay was wounded in the stomach, back and arm, and had a field dressing put on each wound. As by then the company had suffered several casualties, there were no more stretchers. But his batman, with great presence of mind, ripped a door off its hinges, and in spite of Barclay's orders to the contrary tied him to it. Barclay then told his batman to carry him round the position so he could visit his men. The door was so heavy that it took four men to carry him.

At this moment, the Germans opened fire on A Company from the home side of the canal. Barclay sent his sergeant major, Gristock, in charge of a small force of about ten men from company headquarters, including a wireless operator, to deal with this new menace. Barclay told Gristock not only to hold the company's right flank, but to eliminate a German machine-gun post that had set up just off to the right of the company. Gristock sent some of the party to attack the post, and they succeeded in wiping it out. While this was in progress, another group of Germans opened up on the company. Gristock, spotting where they were, ordered two men to give him covering fire while he went forward to deal with this new threat, which consisted of a group of men behind a pile of stones on the canal bank. He got to within about twenty yards of them without being spotted when a machine gun opened up on him from the far bank, smashing both his knees. In spite of this he dragged himself until he was within grenade-throwing range of the pile of stones, lobbed a grenade over the top and finished off the survivors with his rifle.

The fighting went on. Private Leggett of A Company was manning a Bren on the upstairs verandah of a cottage and 'killed a lot of Germans'. Although they reached the far bank of the canal several times, they were unable to cross, but retaliated with mortar and artillery fire. Leggett was hit; first his left leg went numb, then his back from the waist down. He had multiple minor wounds, but more seriously a shard of shrapnel about three inches long had ripped through his left buttock and exited via his groin, tearing a huge hole out of which blood was pouring. His comrades took all the field dressings they could find, plugged the entry and exit wounds, bound on two more to hold these in place and used a piece of rope to tie a tourniquet. They carried him downstairs, dragged him outside and returned to their posts as they had to, leaving Leggett to crawl to company headquarters. They had taken his trousers off and in his underpants and battledress top he inched forward, showered with earth from exploding mortar bombs and shells. He had some hundred yards to cover, and his hands bled as he dragged himself along. He was almost at his last gasp when a mortar bomb exploded very close, knocking him unconscious and showering him with earth. When he came to he found himself being tugged along by his arms, and looked up into the faces of two bandsmen carrying out the duties of stretcher bearers. He heard them say, 'Bloody hell, he's had it.' He, Gristock and Barclay were evacuated with severe wounds. Gristock died of his wounds in England before he knew that he had been awarded the Victoria Cross.

The 1st Royal Scots were still sorting themselves out after relieving the 1st/7th Royal Warwicks when the Germans came surging up the banks of the river. The Royal Scots went for them with bayonets fixed and, supported by their carriers, drove them back some 300 yards to the outskirts of Calonne. At that moment they were hit by a great weight of shellfire. The 'Jocks' went to ground, and eight of their ten carriers were smashed. Nearby, the forward companies of 1st/8th Royal Warwicks were in serious trouble, cut off in a small area on the edge of the village. Their CO, Lieutenant Colonel Baker, tried to break through to assist them with a platoon and a couple of carriers. The party was cut to pieces by heavy fire on an open slope. One survivor came back after dark bearing the news that the CO and the officers with him, all members of battalion headquarters, were dead. The second-in-command was killed by a mortar bomb within half an hour of assuming command of the battalion.

The 1st Cameron Highlanders, having spent a fruitless night marching to mount a counter-attack and marching back again, set off once more at mid-morning to launch an attack at Calonne, through positions held by the 5th Gloucestershires at Bruyelles. At 1300 hours they attacked, gaining a ridge from which they could see Antoing, but short of the riverbank. At last light they put in another attack in an attempt to clear the bank. The right-hand company succeeded for a few moments, but the left-hand company could make little progress against machine-gun fire from enemy firmly established in Calonne. The Camerons had to be content with forming blocking positions to check further gains by the enemy. Their presence eased the pressure on the Royal Scots and allowed survivors of 1st/8th Royal Warwicks to pull back in the night. The 2nd Dorsets provided a back-stop while this was in progress.

During the day's fighting Gort sent out a message, referring to the Arras counter-attack: 'News from the south reassuring. We stand and fight. Tell your men.' His aim was probably to tell them that there would be no more retreating – laudable enough, but perhaps a bit premature in view of the situation unfolding to the south. It is unlikely that many of the BEF, some engaged in fighting for the first time and others dog-tired, actually received the message.

To the south of Calonne, the 144th Brigade fought off repeated attacks by the German 253rd Infantry Division throughout the afternoon of 20 May, but by daybreak on the 21st the enemy had gained the wood north of Hollain, driving a wedge between the 2nd Warwicks and 5th Gloucesters.

Major General 'Bulgy' Thorne, GOC of 48th Division, summoned the reserve battalion of the 143rd Brigade, the 1st Oxfordshire and Buckinghamshire Light Infantry, or 43rd Light Infantry as they preferred to be called, to regain the wood. The battalion had spent most of the night marching hither and thither in response to orders to counter-attack that were subsequently cancelled. The CO of the 43rd was both shocked and irritated to be told by Thorne to remember Nonneboschen. In the same way that General Barker had earlier likened the Dendre Line to Le Cateau, Thorne was harking back to the First World War, but rather tactlessly. The charge at Nonneboschen during the First Battle of Ypres in 1914 had been carried out by the 2nd Battalion the Oxfordshire and Buckinghamshire Light Infantry, or 52nd Light Infantry for short. There was little love lost between the 43rd and 52nd.[1] The 43rd were desperately tired after marching for twenty-four hours, following a week with less than two hours' sleep in any twenty-four. But they set to and attacked the wood, driving the Germans out of this foothold that threatened the whole of the sector. The Germans also threatened the I Corps left flank north of Tournai, but a series of brisk counter-attacks ejected the infantry groups that had infiltrated across the canal.

The 1st Division had no German attacks to contend with during the whole of 20 May, and the exhausted soldiers were able to catch a modicum of sleep. But the next day, after a heavy bombardment, German infantry under the cover of morning mist crossed the river and secured a foothold between the two forward battalions of the 1st Guards Brigade, 3rd Grenadiers on the right and 2nd Coldstream on the left. Following speedy reinforcement by rubber boat, the Germans swung to their left and overran the Grenadiers' left-hand company, killing the company commander and his one officer. The attack threatened the flank of the whole battalion. The Grenadiers quickly mounted a counter-attack, which was thrown back with the loss of three more officers. The Germans had now penetrated so far that they threatened the 2nd North Staffs on the Grenadiers' right, who in turn quickly sent a reserve company to counter-attack. But this too failed.

The Grenadiers now put in a more deliberate counter-attack using their reserve company, supported by the carrier platoon and two 3-inch mortars. The attack began well, but soon communications problems with the poor wireless sets issued to the British Army made it so difficult to direct the mortar fire that they stopped firing. Passing through waist-high corn as they advanced towards their objective some 300 yards away, the right-hand group of Grenadiers were lashed by machine-gun fire, killing three more officers, including Lieutenant the Duke of Northumberland and the carrier platoon commander, Lieutenant Reynall-Pack, who had attempted to use his carriers as tanks. At close range, machine-gun bullets ripped through the thin armour. The group went to ground, and any attempt to rise drew a hail of bullets.

All now depended on the left-hand platoon. Lance-Corporal Nicholls, the regimental heavyweight boxing champion, was commanding a section. At the start of the counter-attack he was wounded in the arm by shrapnel, but continued to lead his section. As the platoon moved over a small ridge, they came under heavy machine-gun fire. Nicholls grabbed the Bren, and followed by Guardsman Nash carrying spare magazines, charged forward and killed the crew of one machine gun, followed by two others. Although hit by a splinter in the head, he crawled up on to a slight ridge with Nash and continued to engage the German trenches near the river. He was hit for a third and fourth time, but continued firing until he ran out of ammunition. He was seen to collapse at his gun. The Germans rallied and gained the ridge from which Nicholls had so gallantly engaged them, and despite every effort the Grenadiers were unable to turf them out. With help from the 2nd Hampshires, the third battalion in their brigade, the battalion did, however, seize back most of the ground lost.

At dusk a Grenadier patrol approached the ridge and found it abandoned except for thirty German corpses below it and on the riverbank. Guardsmen taken prisoner had buried other bodies. The enemy had relinquished the position, thanks mainly to the efforts of Nicholls. He was awarded the Victoria Cross, at first posthumously, until it was learned some four months later that he was recovering in a German hospital.

In the 3rd Division sector, it was another battalion of the 1st Regiment of Foot Guards that bore the brunt of the first attack, this time the 2nd Grenadiers at Helchin. The enemy approached with an engineer bridging 'train', waving maps and shouting. This party was soon despatched. More serious was a party of German snipers who infiltrated into Helchin in civilian clothes. The Grenadiers, who had had quite enough of being sniped at from behind both on the Dyle and the Dendre, rounded up seventeen of this crew and executed them on the spot. As an aside, one wonders what the outcome would be to this entirely understandable piece of summary justice in today's politically correct society.

The Germans put in another attack on the 3rd Division, in the 8th Brigade sector, but Montgomery had the waterline well covered and it was repulsed. By first light on 22 May the II Corps front was still intact.

In the III Corps defensive zone, the 4th Division rebuffed all German attempts to cross the river. Especially good work was done by the 2nd Royal Northumberland Fusiliers, whose well-sited Vickers medium machine guns, firing along the length of the river, carved up no fewer than seven attempts to cross by boat. German shelling inevitably caused a number of casualties; for instance in the 1st East Surrey sector, the cottage containing the RAP took a direct hit, killing several wounded men, the drum major and the NCO in charge of the stretcher bearers. The medical officer (MO) Captain Bird was lucky not to be hit. Battalion headquarters near by also suffered, with signallers killed and the signal officer and sergeant both wounded. The second-in-command was hit by shrapnel in the same part of his body as he had been in 1917. During this very unpleasant time the CO, Lieutenant Colonel Boxshall, sitting in a shallow trench behind battalion headquarters, with splinters and clods of earth flying, saw Regimental Serjeant Major (RSM) Adams standing up calmly shaving, which was 'very good for everybody's morale'. The dead were buried, the wounded evacuated and the battalion waited for the enemy to attack.

The situation on the left flank of III Corps, held by the 44th Division, was more serious. The attacks started at 1530 hours on 20 May against the 1st/6th Queen's of the 131st Brigade, astride the village of Elsegem. The brigade commander Utterson-Kelso, a four-times-wounded and highly decorated officer in the previous war, reacted robustly. The Germans were hurled back by means of carriers and the use of the brigade's reserves, the 1st/5th Queen's and a company of 1st/6th, but at some cost including the life of the company commander. In order to bolster this flank Utterson-Kelso took the reserve company of the 2nd Buffs, his left-hand battalion, to take over from the 1st/6th Queen's company. The 2nd Buffs had joined the division in the first week of May, having been employed on pioneer duties for the previous eight months with only a short period of training – a curious way to use a regular battalion. They had not had the opportunity to shake down and learn the skills necessary to face a ruthless and well-trained opponent. Second Lieutenant Blaxland, a recently commissioned platoon commander, described his company commander as 'having no views on how his company should be deployed in battle', and the company second-in-command, 'a veteran of the First World War, [had] little notion of subsequent developments'.

The 2nd Buffs were deployed in an area where the river took a right-angled bend, which exposed the battalion to an attack from two directions. Just before dusk the enemy hit them, having crossed where woods grew right down to the riverbank. They overran a platoon and came in behind the Buffs' centre company, now left unprotected by the brigade commander's removal of the reserve company. Before he could stop them, the company commander, Major Bruce, saw two platoons of the centre company begin to edge away to the flank in the face of this unexpected attack from the rear.

The brigade commander sent the Buffs' reserve company back as well as the 1st/5th Queen's carrier platoon with orders to restore the situation. A confused night followed. At first no artillery support was used by the Buffs, for fear of hitting their own men. Repeated attacks followed, all without artillery support, although it had been promised after the first abortive attack. Meanwhile Major Bruce tried to get the remnants of his own company forward by resorting to short rushes and hurling grenades. After being wounded for the third time, he passed out, to wake at dawn on a stretcher with Germans all around him. At that moment a salvo of shells whistled in – the promised artillery support at last. The Germans ran off, leaving Bruce behind. The Buffs were shaken and not in the best position to receive the next attack, which came in the morning. The Germans penetrated the centre of the battalion position and levered open a passage between their two flank companies. Counter-attacks failed to eject the Germans. This infiltration alarmed the divisional commander, Major General Osborne, to the extent of persuading him to issue the order that the artillery was not to withdraw but should stay and fight it out over open sights if necessary.

The battle swayed back and forth, as each counter-attack was followed by further German attacks. The German penetration of the 44th Division's sector reached Petegem, two miles south-west of Audenarde and a mile from the river. Eventually the town was retaken and cleared of the enemy, but the Germans still retained a bridgehead on the western bank as a result of the long day's fighting on 21 May.

The experience of Second Lieutenant Blaxland and his platoon of the 2nd Buffs, during the fighting on the BEF's left flank in the 44th Division sector, gives a flavour of the chaos of war, especially to men in battle for the first time, and after inadequate preparation. Blaxland's company were thinly spread, as was the rest of the battalion. He was a long way from company headquarters and the other platoons, and for much of the time he had not the slightest idea what was happening. Without wireless sets within battalions, the only way to pass and receive information was by runner or by visits of the company commander. The first attack by a Stuka in the vicinity of Blaxland's platoon position found the Bren that had been mounted for anti-aircraft protection standing alone and unattended. Blaxland felt he could hardly arrest the soldier who should have manned it and who had instead precipitately taken cover, when he, the man's platoon commander, had dived into his slit trench with equal speed. Despite being told that Stukas were designed to spread fear rather than destruction, it was hard to remember this advice the first time one was subjected to a dive-bombing attack, the shriek of the aircraft's sirens mounting to a frenzy as they plunged vertically to attack.

The second evening after their arrival on the Escaut, the right-hand part of the battalion position came under heavy attack. Blaxland could hear bursts of heavy fire and streams of tracer. The latter was especially significant to him because it proved that the Germans were in breach of the Geneva Convention, which forbade the use of tracer – a rule which the British quixotically observed at this stage in the war, to the extent of allowing tracer to be loaded in Bren magazines at a rate of only one round to every eight of ball, but only if engaging enemy aircraft.[2] The discovery that the Germans were prepared to flout international conventions with such ruthlessness merely increased Blaxland's awe of the enemy.

A flurry of Verey lights (flares) during this battle on their flanks led to an altercation between Blaxland and one of his section commanders, Corporal Pilling, who claimed that a red Verey light followed by a green signified withdrawal, as stated in standing orders at Aldershot. Although Blaxland said it did not apply here – the meanings of the colour combinations changed frequently to avoid the enemy using the flares to cause confusion – doubt had been sowed in his mind. He wished he could discuss it with his company commander, sited a long way off. He found that his platoon sergeant, Skippings, was not being as supportive as platoon sergeants should be and had become silent and withdrawn, offering no help or advice.

During the night, one of the section commanders hurled a grenade into the darkness, followed by a long burst from one of his Brens and a spatter of rifle fire from the rest of the section. Blaxland could see nothing. Two words were heard from the gloom: 'Fookin' 'ell.' Clearly these were not Germans, and on being questioned the strangers turned out to be from a South Staffordshire pioneer battalion. 'Pass, friend, hope no one was hit,' called out Blaxland, at which an officer and sergeant stepped forward, both equally elderly. 'You weren't good enough to hit any of us,' observed the sergeant drily. They were on their way to reinforce Petegem, which to Blaxland seemed ominous.

Blaxland sensed from firing and other activity that a counter-attack had been mounted by members of his own battalion somewhere in his vicinity, but had not the slightest idea where or with what purpose. Their first sight of enemy was an attempt at infiltrating the position by some infantry, who took up a position in a nearby cottage and fired on the platoon. A burst of Bren fired by Blaxland seemed to quieten them down. Some wounded men passed through the position, including C Company's cook, bringing bad tidings that A Company, which had indeed been counter-attacking, had been wiped out, and C Company on Blaxland's left had had an entire platoon captured by German soldiers disguised as Belgians.

By now well over twenty-four hours had passed since Blaxland had been visited by his company commander, and there were prolonged sounds of fighting from where he thought the other two platoons in his company were located. He began to think that perhaps a withdrawal was now called for. Some time later a platoon of C Company appeared, marching to the rear. The platoon sergeant major knelt by Blaxland's trench and told him that C Company had been badly mauled and that he was taking his platoon to the rear to regroup before returning to the battle, adding that they were all that was left.

At this point, Blaxland, who lacked the experience to challenge the unlikely assertion by the platoon sergeant major that he was going to return to the battle, having apparently pulled out with no authority, decided to withdraw his own platoon too. Doubt assailed him after he had retreated about 400 yards, but sheeplike he followed the retreating backs of the C Company platoon. Utterly ashamed, he continued, eventually to stumble upon a barn held by a company of Royal West Kents. Here he and his platoon were given tea and sympathetically treated by the Royal West Kents, who had heard that the Buffs had been roughly handled.

After spending the best part of a day with the Royal West Kents, and being sent off to hold part of their perimeter, Blaxland was astonished to see a carrier coming up the road containing the adjutant of the 2nd Buffs. Having felt the rough edge of the adjutant's tongue on more than one occasion, Blaxland was surprised to be greeted warmly. He told his story of being abandoned without orders during the battalion's withdrawal and extricating his platoon without loss, thus in his words 'enrolling himself into an army of sole survivors who are to be found roaming every battlefield'. He was taken aback when the adjutant said this was the first he had heard of withdrawal and that the Buffs had not fallen back on Courtrai as Blaxland appeared to imagine. The battalion was still defending Petegem, was having a hard fight and would be glad of Blaxland's help. He could join them by marching his platoon back up the road and turning left at the first T-junction. His little party was comprehensively shelled as it advanced up what was clearly a main axis road and therefore likely to be a prime target. Their heads splitting with concussion from the shelling, but with no other form of damage, his platoon encountered some soldiers obviously retreating, not Buffs but 1st/5th Queen's, being harangued by a brigadier whom he did not recognize shouting, 'We can't let this beastly Hitler fellow win the war – we've got to stop him somewhere, why not here?' The retreating soldiers ignored him. Blaxland pressed on, reaching the T-junction with the adjutant's words ringing in his ears: 'Turn left for the battle being fought by the Buffs.' At that point Blaxland collapsed and was taken to the RAP of the reserve battalion of his brigade, where he was diagnosed as suffering from battle exhaustion. Here he met his company commander with a badly wounded leg. In the ambulance some lines of Latin learned at his preparatory school ran through his head: 'Alii pungent, alii fugunt' (Some fought, others fled). He passed out.

In the 4th Division sector, the enemy succeeded in forcing a crossing of the Escaut in a number of places. In some cases inexperience led to overreaction. The first intimation of trouble in 1st East Surreys' position was a breathless sergeant waving a revolver as he arrived at Captain Ricketts's C Company, saying that A Company was surrounded and needed the reserve company to help. Ricketts had been the RSM of the battalion on arrival in France in 1939, and had subsequently been commissioned. Normally he would have been appointed quartermaster, but he asked for a combatant commission instead. He took the sergeant to battalion headquarters, where he repeated the story to Major Bousfield – the CO was out visiting the companies at the time. Bousfield told Ricketts to go in with his company, drive the enemy back across the river and extricate A Company.

Ricketts advanced to A Company's assistance, two platoons up and one back. The only enemy they encountered was a small party in a house. These were quickly despatched by Ricketts with a Bren and Platoon Sergeant Major Gibson bowling a couple of grenades. On arrival at A Company's headquarters, it appeared that the situation was not as bad as the sergeant had painted, although in the words of the company commander, 'the company was taking a belting and could do with some help'. Ricketts left his riflemen with A Company, but took his Brens back. On his return he encountered a small group of Germans and, in the exchange of fire, both he and his only officer were wounded. It was an unnecessary sortie, sparked off by a sergeant in a panic, but Bousfield – based on what he had learned from this NCO – was probably right to order a counter-attack. In fact the CO had only recently been with A Company and had assessed that there was no cause for concern.

The main threat to the battalion was actually from its left flank, which was in danger of being turned as a result of penetration of the 44th Division's front. Captain Buchanan of B Company maintained contact with the 5th Northamptons, the left forward battalion of their own brigade, and had seen several groups of Queen's coming back through

them and into his own position. It was when he went to visit the
Northamptons, found them gone and Germans there instead that he
realized that the East Surreys' flank had been turned.

High-Level Decisions

While his soldiers were fighting hard on two fronts, some sixty-five air
miles apart, Gort held a corps commanders' conference at Brooke's
headquarters. After remarking that the picture looked gloomy, Brooke
commented in his diary, 'Decided that we should have to come back to
the line of the frontier defences tomorrow evening [22/23 May]. Namely
to occupy the defences we spent the winter preparing. Unfortunately we
are too thin on the ground and forced to hold too wide a front.'³ Gort
undertook to get the agreement of his Belgian and French allies to the
withdrawal. He was bitter about the 'complete lack of effort by Billotte
and Blanchard', and described sending his only reserves to Arras as a
'desperate remedy to put heart into the French'. From Brooke's corps
headquarters at Wambrechies, Gort moved to the new location of his
command post, which had just opened at 1800 hours at Prémesques,
between Lille and Armentières.

While Gort had been conferring with his corps commanders a great
deal had been happening at Ypres, much of it epitomizing the chaos that
was descending on the French and Belgian armies. General Weygand, the
new French Army C-in-C who, whatever his manifold faults, did not lack
personal courage, had eventually arrived at Ypres at 1500 hours, after a
nightmare flight from Paris during which his escorting fighters successfully beat off attacking Messerschmitts. He had stopped at his planned
destination, Norrent-Fontes, north-west of Béthune, where he had hoped
to meet Billotte, the purpose of the trip. Here there was no transport to
meet him, the driver having gone to Abbeville, only to find the town in
flames and narrowly escaping being put in the bag (taken prisoner) by
the 2nd Panzer Division. Eventually by flying on to Calais Weygand
learned that King Leopold, who was C-in-C of the Belgian Army, was at
Ypres town hall, waiting for him and Billotte. When he arrived Billotte
was not there. Three separate meetings took place. The accounts of what
happened are confused and vary greatly. What follows is merely a
summary.

At the first meeting attended by Weygand, Leopold and his malevolent
ADC, General van Overstraeten, Weygand said that the Belgian Army
should now withdraw as soon as possible from the Escaut to the line of
the Yser. This would shorten the left flank and allow the BEF to strike

south at full strength. Overstraeten said that the Belgian Army was disintegrating. Leopold said he would think about it, but gave Weygand the strong impression that the position was hopeless and that he was expecting defeat.

At this juncture Billotte arrived. But two key commanders were still missing: Gort, who had been invited (of which more later), and Blanchard, whose opinions on the matters being discussed were equally important, but who had *not* been invited. Billotte was not able to record his impressions of what occurred at this meeting, and opinions of its outcome differ. Weygand outlined his plan, involving a simultaneous offensive, south from Cambrai and north from the Somme, meeting near Bapaume. Although Billotte did say that the French First Army was very tired, he did not make it clear that Weygand's plan was in the realms of cloud-cuckoo land. He failed to tell Weygand that Blanchard had said that he was unable to launch a two-division attack until 22 or 23 May, nor did he reveal that Gort's 'counter-attack' consisted of a mere two battle groups, with some additional elements. If Gort and Blanchard had been present, they might have been able to disabuse Weygand of the supposed virtues of his plan, which he was to present to Churchill and Reynaud in Paris the next day.

Weygand waited for Gort until 1900 hours, and was contemplating remaining at Ypres until he could be found, when Admiral Abrial, French commander of the Naval Forces of the North, told him that flying back to Paris was now out of the question thanks to the air situation. He offered a passage in the French torpedo-boat the *Flore*, then alongside at Dunkirk. Weygand accepted and departed. After another action-packed journey, which included being bombed as he left Dunkirk, and calling at Dover to top up with fuel, Weygand disembarked at Cherbourg after first light on 22 May. He reached Paris at 1000 hours showing no signs of wear and tear. One has to admire the man's stamina, if nothing else.

Gort arrived at Ypres about an hour after Weygand had left. Very reasonably both Overstraeten and Leopold had urged that he be brought to Ypres, because without him much of the discussion would be academic. Eventually Overstraeten, with Admiral Sir Roger Keyes, Churchill's representative at Leopold's HQ, unearthed Gort in his new command post, having first driven to the old location at Wahagnies. All Gort knew about Weygand's visit was a message from Churchill to Keyes, copied to him, saying, 'Weygand is coming up your way tomorrow to concert action of all forces.' The message from the British Mission at French GQG warning Gort that Weygand would land at Norrent-Fontes was never received either at BEF GHQ or at Gort's command post. Not using the laid-down procedure for ensuring that important messages get through was bad staff work on the sender's part. In short, one should finish the signal with the word 'acknowledge'; then if the addressee does not acknowledge receipt, there is a chance it has not arrived, in which case it should be transmitted again or sent by other means. Gort had spent the whole day wondering where Weygand was, without, it must be said, doing very much about finding out. Until Overstraeten went on his personal hunt for Gort, neither Billotte nor Weygand thought of sending people out looking for him.

From then on Weygand believed that Gort had deliberately played truant in order to avoid falling in with his attack plans. To this day, the Anglo-haters in France believe that Gort's absence is proof that all along he intended pulling out the BEF (which he did not *begin* contemplating until 22 May when the Arras operation failed). To be fair, many French historians have criticized Weygand for not waiting for Gort.

At the third Ypres meeting, the Belgians were persuaded to withdraw to the Lys, to release British formations for the counter-stroke offensive. This was nothing like as satisfactory as pulling back to the Yser; as a glance at the map on p. 119 shows, it actually makes the Belgian line longer and the Allied position more dangerous. The British and Belgian lines would be at right angles. The Germans would attack the hinge and drive the Belgians back to the north, thus separating them from the Allies and leaving them no option but surrender. In saying that the Belgian Army could not withdraw to the Yser, Leopold and Overstraeten were in effect accepting defeat.

It was agreed that the BEF should withdraw to its old position on the French frontier between Maulde and Halluin, and in order to free British divisions the Belgian Army would relieve one and the French two. Neither could do this until the night of 23/24 May, and the relieved divisions would not be ready to attack until 26 May at the earliest. Gort reported that the progress of the Arras operation was not very encouraging and that he had committed all his reserves. He, and the French commanders present, believed that sooner or later, and preferably sooner, the Belgians would have to swing back to the Yser. But, when the matter was raised, all Leopold would agree was that if forced to withdraw from the Lys no alternative to the Yser existed. Beyond this he would not commit himself. It was a depressing meeting.

The failure of Gort and Weygand to meet on 21 May had disastrous consequences. Weygand returned to Paris mistrusting Gort, but determined to carry out a plan that Gort could have told him had not the remotest chance of success – as indeed Billotte could have confirmed had he had the guts to do so.

Soon after leaving the conference, Billotte, on his way to brief Blanchard, was mortally injured when his car rammed the back of a refugee truck. He died without regaining consciousness. Some writers have suggested that Billotte was the most outstanding of all the French commanders; if so, based on his performance so far, the standard was pretty low. The contention by General d'Astier that Billotte was the only one who could have staved off disaster is also questionable, given his condition as early as 18 May, especially the incident related in Chapter 3 ('I am bursting with fatigue ... and against these panzers I cannot do anything'), which was hardly the conduct one would look for in the potential saviour of the French Army.[4]

What is beyond doubt is that because the French command dithered while Billotte lay in a coma, instead of appointing his successor straight away, three days passed without a guiding hand to co-ordinate the French, British and Belgian Armies to execute the Weygand Plan, if indeed the plan as envisaged was achievable. The successor appointed was Blanchard, already a broken reed. Brooke visited him on 24 May before he was to step into Billotte's shoes. In an afternote in his diary Brooke wrote:

> He [Blanchard] was standing studying the map as I looked at him carefully and I soon gathered the impression that he might as well have been staring at a blank wall for all the benefit he gained out of it! He gave me the impression of a man whose brain had ceased to function, he was merely existing and hardly aware of what was going on around him. The blows that had fallen on us in quick succession had left him 'punch drunk' and unable to register events. I was badly shaken and felt that if he was to take the tiller in the current storm it would not be long before we were on the rocks![5]

At his headquarters at Vincennes on the outskirts of Paris, on 22 May, Weygand briefed Churchill and Reynaud on the plan, which he said he had thoroughly explained to Leopold and Billotte the day before, giving the impression that everybody who would have to implement it had been present and concurred. But he had not seen Gort, and Billotte was dying. Churchill was immensely impressed by Weygand, as was Reynaud. The latter made much of the fact that Weygand had been Foch's right-hand man, responsible for restoring the situation when the Germans threatened to break through in 1918. Having received approval for the plan, Weygand drafted his General Operation Order No. 1, which can be summarized as follows:

(I) The group of forces being co-ordinated by the General Commanding the First Group of Armies (the Belgian Army, the BEF, and the French First

Army) has the imperative task of preventing the German attack from making its way to the sea, in order to maintain contact between the armies, to restore contact with the main body of French forces, and to regain control of the British lines of communication through Amiens.

(II)   The only way to hold, and beat, the Germans is by counter-attacks.

(III)   The forces necessary for these counter-attacks already exist in the group, which is moreover much too thick on the ground, namely:
    certain infantry divisions of the First Army;
    the cavalry corps;
    the BEF, which could with advantage be moved in its entirety to right
        of the disposition by accentuating the movements already begun,
        and by extending the Belgian Army's front.
These counter-attacks will be supported by the entire strength of the British air forces based in Britain.

(IV)   This offensive movement in a southerly direction should be protected on the east by the Belgian forces retiring in successive bounds on to the line of the Yser.
    The German Panzer Divisions must be hemmed in within the area to which they have so rashly advanced.

(V)   Enemy mobile detachments which, supported by bombing of aero-dromes and ports, are trying to spread confusion and panic in our rear between the frontier and the Somme have taken a chance and should be wiped out locally.[6]

This order was fantasy and bore little relation to the reality on the ground. The Germans had already reached the sea two days earlier. There was no sector where the Allies were 'too thick on the ground'. What would Bock be doing with Army Group B while all this redeployment was taking place on his doorstep? Certainly not passively leaving the Allies unmolested. The BEF was having enough difficulty holding off the Germans on the Escaut, and certainly could not mount an offensive off to the south. The Belgians had *not* agreed to withdraw to the Yser, and even if they changed their minds, they would have their hands full enough retiring in good order and staving off a headlong rout, and so could not even contemplate extending their line and covering the BEF's movement to the south. To dismiss seven panzer divisions as 'enemy mobile detachments' indicates that Weygand was, to put it unkindly, away with the fairies. Finally, until a successor to Billotte was appointed, there was no one to plan and co-ordinate this crackpot scheme.

Churchill followed with a message to Gort that was if anything even more fantastic than Weygand's order. Having told Gort that he had met with Reynaud and Weygand, he said that it was agreed:

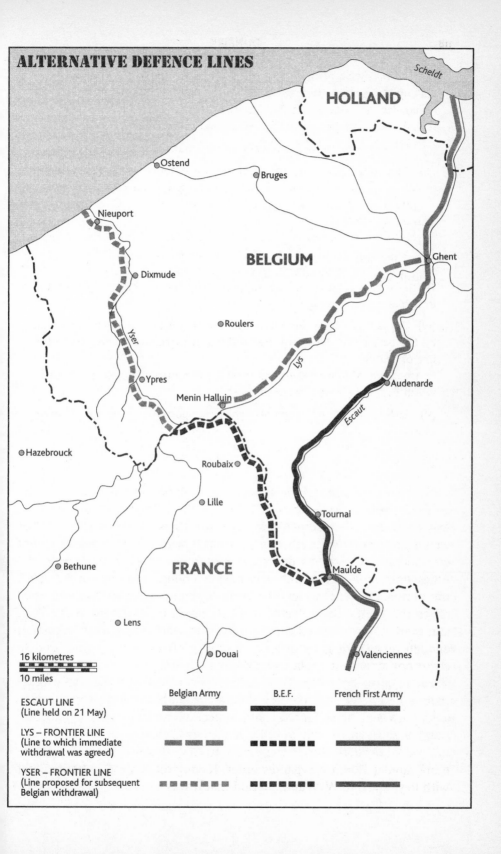

ALTERNATIVE DEFENCE LINES

HOLLAND

Scheldt

Ostend

Bruges

Nieuport

BELGIUM

Ghent

Dixmude

Yser

Roulers

Lys

Ypres

Audenarde

Menin Halluin

Escaut

Hazebrouck

Roubaix

Lille

Tournai

FRANCE

Maulde

Bethune

Lens

16 kilometres

10 miles

Douai

Valenciennes

	Belgian Army	B.E.F.	French First Army
ESCAUT LINE (Line held on 21 May)			
LYS – FRONTIER LINE (Line to which immediate withdrawal was agreed)			
YSER – FRONTIER LINE (Line proposed for subsequent Belgian withdrawal)			

1. That the Belgian Army should withdraw to the line of the Yser and stand there, the sluices being opened [to flood the terrain, as the Belgians had done in 1914].
2. That the British Army and French First Army should attack south-west towards Bapaume and Cambrai at the earliest moment – certainly tomorrow with about eight divisions – and with the Belgian Cavalry Corps to the right of the British.
3. That as this battle is vital to both Armies and the British communications depend upon freeing Amiens, the British Air Force should give the utmost help both by day and by night while it is going on.
4. That the new French Army Group which is advancing upon Amiens and forming a line along the Somme should strike northwards and join hands with the British divisions who are attacking southwards in the general direction of Bapaume.[7]

Churchill repeats the mistaken belief that the Belgians had agreed to withdraw to the Yser. Perhaps he was unconsciously harking back to what the Belgians had done in the First World War, as possibly was Weygand. Next, there was absolutely no chance that eight divisions, some 100,000 men, facing east and locked in battle with the enemy, could turn their backs on them and march away to attack south-westwards at such short notice. Weygand several times made much of his association with Foch, the implication being that the great man's mantle had descended on his shoulders. Foch, however, had always known the strength and fighting power of forces he could commit to battle. Weygand clearly did not. He had gone north the day before to meet Billotte having already fixed in his mind that a counter-attack from the north would sort out the mess, and seemed to be in a state which psychologists call perseveration: an inclination to allow judgements made in the early stages of a developing situation to affect later assessments, without revising them in the light of new evidence. Or in the vernacular, 'Don't confuse me with the facts, my mind is already made up.' It did not of course help that Billotte never told him the facts, and that he did not meet Gort, who one assumes would have put him in the picture.

There was no new French army group advancing upon Amiens, and Weygand must, or should, have known this. South of the Somme in a ninety-mile swathe of country between the coast and the Crozat Canal were five divisions in General Frère's newly cobbled-together Seventh Army. In addition the 2nd and 5th Light Cavalry Divisions (DLC), which had been savaged in the Ardennes battle, and the newly arrived British 1st Armoured Division were deployed to the left of Frère, under command of General Robert Altmayer.[8]

Finally, the big gap behind the advancing panzer divisions, and the many spaces between them, into which a properly co-ordinated counter-attack in sufficient force would have been so devastating, would be filled by German infantry divisions by 23 May, which would steadily advance to cover the southern flank of the 'panzer corridor' and reinforce the bridgeheads over the Somme at Abbeville, Amiens and Péronne.

Reality

By the evening of the conference at Vincennes, the Allied position was considerably worse. It was to be the last day on the Escaut. The southern and central sectors were comparatively quiet, mainly because German preparations for attacks here were broken up by artillery fire, and attempts at crossing were beaten off. That night, 22/23 May, the withdrawal to the old Gort line was carried out, the carrier platoons and machine-gun battalions doing sterling work as rearguards.

It was a different story in the north of the BEF sector on the Escaut. Here Bock's attempts to break through were renewed, and at 0700 hours the 44th Division was under severe pressure, which by the afternoon extended to the 4th Division on its right. The enemy pushed out from the small foothold they had acquired the previous day and overran many positions. The fighting was bitter and confused, and, uncharacteristically for the Germans, continued unabated into the night. Withdrawal for the 4th and 44th Divisions while in contact and fighting was a hazardous and difficult business.

When orders for the withdrawal reached the 1st East Surreys, it was still daylight. The CO sent his written orders to the companies by runners. Line communication had been repeatedly cut by shellfire, and there was, of course, no wireless below battalion level. Because of the intensity of enemy shelling and mortaring and the possibility of some or all of the runners being knocked out before they could deliver their messages, the CO decided to send his adjutant, Captain Bruce, in a carrier to D and B Companies, and Lieutenant Lindsay, his anti-tank platoon commander, on foot to C and A Companies. Captain Bruce reached D Company, but on his way to B Company his carrier was hit by shellfire and overturned in a ditch. Captain Bruce crawled out and resumed his journey on foot. He had not gone far when another salvo of shells fell all around him, wounding him and knocking him unconscious. He came round to see a German soldier standing over him with a sub-machine gun. He spent the next five years as a prisoner of war.

Lieutenant Lindsay got close enough to B Company headquarters to shout the message about withdrawal to the company commander, Captain Buchanan, but could not get through to A Company. After seeing B, C and D Companies on the move, the CO set out in a carrier towards A Company, which was still, as far as he knew, in position. The carrier was first hit by an armour-piercing round, the shock of which gave the CO a bruised backside, and was then assailed by shells falling so close that the steering failed. The CO, now at the tail of the withdrawing battalion, dismounted and followed his three companies up the slope as they moved well spread out away from the river. In addition to enemy machine-gun, mortar and artillery fire, low-flying German aircraft now appeared bombing and machine-gunning and causing further mayhem and casualties.

The CO had left a small rearguard consisting of the RSM and the intelligence section under Lieutenant Bocquet to cover the withdrawal of battalion headquarters. The enemy followed up so closely that Lieutenant Bocquet flung his empty pistol at them as they overran his position. He was lucky to get away, and was later awarded the MC.

Meanwhile, Captain Finch-White's A Company on the right of the battalion position still had not received the order to withdraw. One platoon under Lieutenant Faulkner was in touch with the 2nd Lancashire Fusiliers on A Company's right, the left-hand platoon was on the riverbank, and the reserve platoon with company headquarters was in a village. The village was being subjected to heavy artillery bombardment and low-level bombing, which caused several casualties. During the afternoon, the company quartermaster sergeant, Clarke, pointed out to Finch-White that the Germans were advancing unopposed across positions previously held by the Lancashire Fusiliers and would soon be behind A Company. Finch-White went to the riverbank and withdrew his left-hand platoon. By then the Germans had crossed the river on both flanks. Finch-White withdrew the company, less Faulkner's platoon, to a crossroads in rear of the village, and headed for battalion headquarters to report the situation. He had only gone a short way when he was fired on from what had been the position occupied by battalion headquarters, and he decided to get his company out quickly. By this time the Germans were in between the main body of the company and Lieutenant Faulkner's platoon, and most of the platoon were taken prisoner, except for one section that managed to get away and join the main body. For a while, A Company withdrew with Germans advancing parallel to it on either flank. Either they mistook A Company for friends or were too preoccupied to fire on them. Whatever the reason, the company next came under fire from its own brigade rearguard, not its own battalion, as Finch-White was subsequently swift to point out. The company went to ground, and after a time it was recognized and allowed through. The soldiers were able to get a lift in some transport and rejoin the battalion.

Thus the battalion, withdrawing under fire, succeeded in breaking off the engagement and, marching through the night, crossed the French frontier near Halluin, where it had been stationed during the Phoney War. Everyone was now completely exhausted, and on one occasion when giving out orders at battalion headquarters the CO himself fell asleep. The French, with memories of the previous war, were not pleased to see them: the enemy were at the gates, and the British had failed to defend them. There were the familiar rumours and reports of fifth columnists and collaborators engaging in spying, signalling the enemy and other clandestine activity, and the intelligence officer of the 1st East Surreys, Lieutenant Bocquet, was present when one suspect was summarily shot in the garden at brigade headquarters.

Other units also had to fight their way out. A company of the 1st Royal West Kents in the 44th Division had to mount a hasty counter-attack at 2200 hours to allow the rest of its battalion to disengage. Only good discipline and steady troops can carry out such a disengagement without it unravelling and becoming a debacle. Casualties were heavy. For example, the 1st/6th Queen's in Utterson-Kelso's brigade suffered 400 casualties in two days, mostly in the four rifle companies, which were down to platoon strength. The field guns of the 44th Division had been told by Osborne to stay and fight it out, and when the order arrived for them to withdraw, the enemy were almost upon them. The gun towers were some way back, the road was choked by refugees, and in the confusion thirty-four field guns were lost or destroyed, over half the divisional artillery of seventy-two guns. But Bock did not break through. His army group situation report states that 'the enemy is offering stubborn resistance, supported by strong artillery'.

During the night the withdrawal was completed, and by 23 May the BEF was back where it had started on 10 May. Brooke wrote in his diary on 23 May:

> Nothing but a miracle can save the BEF now and the end cannot be very far off!
>
> We carried out our withdrawal successfully last night back to the old frontier defences, and by this evening were established in the defences we spent the winter preparing. But the danger lies on our right rear; the German armoured divisions have penetrated to the coast, Abbeville, Boulogne and Calais have been rendered useless. We are therefore cut off from our sea communications, beginning to be short of ammunition,

supplies still all right for 3 days but after that scanty. This evening the Germans are reported to be pushing onto Béthune and on from St-Omer namely right in our rear. If only we now had the armoured division, and at least two of them, to clear our rear![9]

In contrast to Weygand, Gort, Brooke and indeed all the British corps commanders were absolutely clear what the Allied situation was north of the Somme. To the right rear of the BEF on the Maulde–Halluin line, the Arras garrison still held off the enemy, as they had been doing for four days. To the west of Arras, the Germans were beginning to press the British back from the line of the River Scarpe. But the Allied forces north of the Somme were now threatened from three sides. The Belgians, the BEF and French First Army were engaged with German Army Group B on the east. Arras still held, and from there a meagre line of defence was spread along the line of canals towards Gravelines and the sea. Boulogne and Calais were still held, and between these ports and the BEF were the advancing Germans.

The Belgian and French armies had been fighting and withdrawing, and had suffered heavy casualties. Until 20 May, the main weight of the enemy armour had fallen on the French. For the British, who also had been fighting hard and marching long distances, and were back where they had started, on the frontier, things were different in that they had not been leaving large parts of their own country, along with most of its population, in enemy hands. But they were in danger of being cut off from escape, and their lines of communication and supply had already been severed. On 23 May the BEF was put on half-rations. The airfields from which air support should have come were in enemy hands, and all but one flight of Lysanders of the Air Component were back in England. Without fighter protection, this flight was unable to perform reconnaissance and liaison duties for the BEF. On 22 May, the RAF sent 198 fighter sorties from England, mainly over Boulogne and Calais, where, as will be related later, there was to be much fighting. There was little RAF activity over the main battlefront, and the Luftwaffe was able to carry out reconnaissance and interdiction on the BEF unhindered.

Bad as the situation was for the BEF, it would have been worse had not Gort, foreseeing the possibility that the French might not be able to close the hole torn in their line by the panzer divisions, made provision to protect his southern flank by some of the measures already described – such as setting up Macforce, and then creating Polforce to extend the line along the canals from Saint-Omer to La Bassée via Béthune, the Canal Line. Polforce was commanded by Major General Curtis, the commander of the 46th Division, and so named because St Pol was the

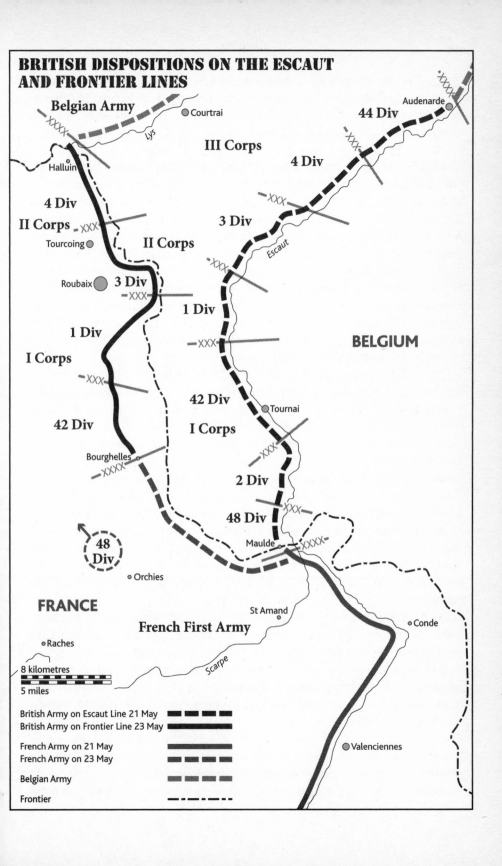

BRITISH DISPOSITIONS ON THE ESCAUT AND FRONTIER LINES

Belgian Army

Courtrai

Audenarde

44 Div

Lys

III Corps

4 Div

Halluin

4 Div

II Corps — XXX

3 Div

Tourcoing

II Corps

Escaut

Roubaix 3 Div

1 Div

— XXX —

BELGIUM

1 Div

— XXX

I Corps

42 Div

— XXX —

Tournai

42 Div

I Corps

Bourghelles

— XXXX —

2 Div

— XXX

48 Div

Maulde

— XXXX —

48 Div

Orchies

FRANCE

St Amand

French First Army

Conde

Raches

8 kilometres

Scarpe

5 miles

British Army on Escaut Line 21 May
British Army on Frontier Line 23 May

French Army on 21 May
French Army on 23 May

Valenciennes

Belgian Army

Frontier

biggest town in his sector. Some of his units had already been sent to Macforce and he acquired engineers and gunners in lieu. With this ad hoc force amounting to the equivalent of seven battalions he was required to hold some 48 miles of front.

Although the German high command and army group commanders had recovered from the temporary fright they had experienced at Arras, and fears of an Allied breakthrough from the north had subsided, they now had another matter to occupy their minds. They, and Rundstedt especially, were turning their minds to the next phase in the campaign, the forthcoming operations to be undertaken after the Allies in the north had been disposed of – the culmination of Operation Yellow (the sickle-cut) – which could only be a matter of days. They were preoccupied by the need to refurbish their armour and all the myriad preparations for the second phase, swinging through 90 degrees and smashing the French armies south of the Somme – Operation Red. Increasing preoccupation with Operation Red explains much of the German conduct of the campaign in the north from 23 May onwards.

The BEF's deployment on the frontier involved four divisions: I Corps on the right with 1st and 42nd Divisions, and II Corps on the left with 3rd and 4th Divisions (Brooke had handed back 1st Division to I Corps, and reassumed command of 4th Division on 23 May). Meanwhile the 2nd and 48th Divisions were to be prepared to defend the Canal Line and assemble south-west of Lille for this purpose. The 44th Division was to be held in General Headquarters reserve, while the 5th and 50th were, as Frankforce, holding the Arras salient. As the threat to the Canal Line increased, the 2nd and 48th Divisions were each ordered to pro-vide a small force consisting of artillery, machine guns and infantry to move in advance of the divisional main bodies to hold the threatened sectors. These were X Force commanded by Brigadier Lawson CRA 48th Division, and Y Force commanded by Brigadier Findlay CRA 2nd Division.

Since Weygand's visit to the north, followed by the Vincennes meet-ing, the issue of Weygand's Order No. 1 and Churchill's directive, Gort had experienced a mounting sense of frustration. He simply could not see how the northern armies could mount a counter-attack by eight divisions by 23 May. The whole of French First Army totalled eight divisions, plus elements of the Cavalry Corps. The Belgians could produce nothing. His own reserve of two divisions was fighting hard around Arras. By the morning of 23 May, the day set for Weygand's great counter-attack, Gort had not received any orders, and there was no sign of co-ordination. So he sent a telegram to the Secretary of State for War, Anthony Eden, saying that co-ordination was essential, and asking that

General Dill, the VCIGS, be sent out to assess the situation on the ground. He added, 'my view is that any advance by us will be in the nature of a sortie and relief must come from the south as we have not, repeat not, ammunition for a serious attack'.

Blanchard turned up at Gort's HQ that morning and agreed with this judgement. But Gort, without knowing what the plans were for the attack from the south, suggested that the northern attack should be by two British divisions (where these were to come from at the time he said it is a mystery), plus one French division and what remained of the French Cavalry Corps, and that it should be mounted on 26 May. This was the earliest possible date given of moves and reliefs currently being carried out by formations of the BEF.

Churchill's reaction to Gort's telegram to Eden was to demand that Reynaud issue orders to French commanders in the north and south and to the Belgians to carry out the counter-stroke immediately; time was vital and supplies were short. Although not responding in full to Gort's request, Churchill was beginning to have his doubts about Weygand's grandiose schemes in particular, and about the French ability in general to pull off any sort of counter-blow. By the evening of 23 May, as no orders had been received by Gort, Churchill fired off another telegram to Reynaud, in effect asking him to lean on Weygand to produce some action, and repeating Gort's view that the main effort had to come from the south, because the BEF had insufficient ammunition for a major attack. He added that Gort was still obliged to implement the agreed plan.

Far more encouraging was the telegram Gort received from Eden, also on 23 May:

> Should, however, situation on your [line of] communications make this [Weygand Plan] at any time impossible you should inform us so we can inform the French and make naval and air arrangements to assist you should you have to withdraw on the northern coast.

It was a welcome indication that the British government was at last beginning to realize how desperate the situation was, and was coming to terms with reality. This, as Gort saw it, gave him the opportunity to act on his own initiative. He was absolutely clear that the Weygand Plan would never come off, that the French would never attack, and that if he was to save the BEF he would have to fall back on Dunkirk without delay. It was fortunate that he came to these conclusions, for Weygand's signals and orders over the next two days displayed an increasing descent into a world of fantasy. Weygand persisted in the view that the French First Army could attack southwards with five or six divisions. The orders

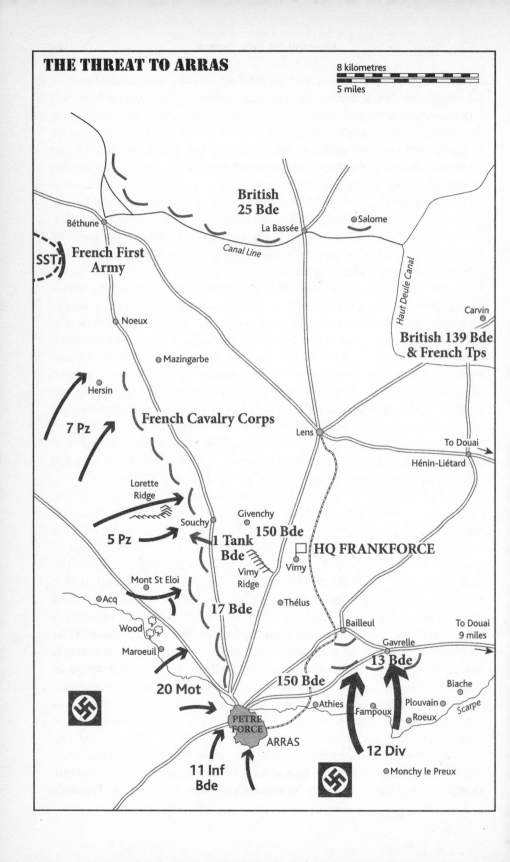

THE THREAT TO ARRAS

8 kilometres
5 miles

British
25 Bde

Salome

Béthune

La Bassée

Canal Line

SST

French First
Army

Noeux

Mazingarbe

Haut Deule Canal

Carvin

British 139 Bde
& French Tps

Hersin

7 Pz

French Cavalry Corps

Lens

To Douai

Hénin-Liétard

Lorette
Ridge

Souchy

Givenchy

150 Bde

5 Pz

1 Tank
Bde

Vimy
Ridge

Vimy

HQ FRANKFORCE

Mont St Eloi

Acq

17 Bde

Thélus

Wood

Bailleul

To Douai
9 miles

Maroeuil

Gavrelle

13 Bde

20 Mot

150 Bde

Biache

Athies

Fampoux

Plouvain

Roeux

Scarpe

PETRE
FORCE

ARRAS

12 Div

11 Inf
Bde

Monchy le Preux

issued by General Georges, C-in-C North-East Front, were equally fanciful. Weygand deluded himself that the manoeuvre to join up the First and Third Army Groups and close the gap was in 'good shape', as he believed that the French Seventh Army, south of the Somme, had already recaptured Péronne, Albert and Amiens. In fact it had not even reached the Somme, where the Germans were strongly established with numerous bridgeheads held by infantry divisions.

While this high-level discussion was in progress, the situation in Arras was becoming increasingly dangerous. With three German panzer divisions (SS Totenkopf, 5th and 7th) and 20th Motorized Division pressing in from the south-west and within striking distance of the road on the line Arras–Béthune, the German 11th Infantry Brigade investing the town from the south, and 12th Infantry Division advancing on Bailleul northwards from the Scarpe, Frankforce and the Arras garrison were in danger of being cut off at the end of a long sack. The bottom of the sack was about 40 miles wide and some 70 miles inland from the coast. The neck of the sack was very much wider than the bottom, and stretched some 90 miles from Gravelines to the Belgian positions on the left of the BEF. Boulogne and Calais were still in Allied hands but not for much longer.

The Canal Line was also under attack. As matters stood on the evening of 23 May, it looked highly likely that the sack would eventually be bounded along its whole south-western side by nine panzer divisions and on the eastern side by Army Group B, and not only the Arras garrison but the whole BEF and French First Army would be in the bag.

The night of the Arras 'counter-attack', Franklyn decided he would have to commit his reserve, the 17th Brigade, to prolong the defences of Arras along the Scarpe to the north-west. The leading troops of the brigade did not arrive until 1300 hours on 22 May. Half a mile to the right rear of the right-hand battalion, the 2nd Northamptonshires, the remains of the abbey of Saint-Eloi stood on the summit of the sharp little hill of that name. As a key piece of ground it attracted the attention of Rommel, who proceeded to attack it, driving off troops of the 1st DLM, who regained it with a swift counter-attack. Although the Northamptons were not directly involved in this part of the battle, the woods in which they had hastily dug shell-scrapes were comprehensively shelled. The rounds bursting in the trees acted like airbursts, spraying shrapnel down on the soldiers, whose first experience of battle this was. Their morale was not helped by the sight of a company commander breaking down and having to be relieved of command.

Petreforce, garrisoning Arras, consisted of the 1st Welsh Guards holding the south and eastern sectors (their CO, Lieutenant Colonel Copland-Griffiths, was the garrison commander); the 5th Green Howards (detached from 150th Brigade) holding the Citadel and western sector; the 8th Royal Fusiliers (from the 23rd Division) on the northern side of the town; a company of 25mm guns and a battery of 25-pounders; Cooke's Light Tanks; the 61st Chemical Warfare Company RE; detachments of the 9th West Yorkshires (originally on airfield defence), some Military Police and Pioneer Corps troops; a collection of unattached troops known as the Station Rifles; and a veteran French officer and nine Zouaves who had refused to leave when other French troops had pulled out.

In an atmosphere of increasing chaos, the Luftwaffe subjected the town to Stuka raids, their sirens screaming. The BBC added to the mayhem by broadcasting on 21 May that the town had been captured by the Germans, only to announce that it had been recaptured by the French. The two remaining battalions of the 150th Brigade, the 4th East Yorkshires and 4th Green Howards, posted along the Scarpe to the east of Arras, were having a quiet time until an order arrived telling them to withdraw that night (22 May). This order, whose origins were never established, was also passed to Petreforce. The battalions' transport came forward in daylight to remove ammunition and equipment that could not be carried on the men, and this movement attracted heavy shellfire. On the heels of the bombardment, the Germans began crossing the river in the Green Howards' sector. Luckily the battalion was still in its defensive positions, so was not caught withdrawing. The Germans pulled back across the river, at which point the battalion learned that the withdrawal had been cancelled.

The 13th Brigade held some four miles of river line on the Scarpe between Biache and Fampoux, placed there to relieve the French Cavalry Corps to enable it to participate in the Arras attack on 21 May. In contrast to the rearward movement being planned by the 150th Brigade on its right, the 13th Brigade was planning an advance that night (22/23 May). Whether this was on the orders of Franklyn or Brigadier Dempsey is not clear. The 2nd Wiltshires, holding the deserted villages of Roeux and Fampoux, covered a frontage of about two miles which meant that all four rifle companies were in forward positions. On arrival the battalion had been cheered to see that there were numerous French tanks in their area, but no sooner had the Wiltshires started to dig in than the tanks moved off, never to be seen again. The enemy occupied the high ground on the other side of the river, giving them good observation over the British positions and restricting movement by day in forward localities. About twenty-four hours after occupying the position, the Wiltshires along with other battalions of the 13th Brigade could hear the sounds of battle to their west, where the Arras 'counter-attack' was going in, before eventually being driven back to its start point.

As a prelude to the move forward on the night of 22/23 May, the 2nd Wiltshires sent a company across just before first light on a pontoon bridge to establish a bridgehead opposite Roeux, from where the 2nd Cameronians were to push on to Monchy-le-Preux. The Germans had been waiting in carefully prepared positions, and at daybreak the Wiltshire company came under heavy mortar and machine-gun fire from either flank, causing casualties and mayhem. With no wireless, and thanks to heavy German fire unable to use the pontoon bridge, one of the platoon commanders, Second Lieutenant Chivers, swam the river and, having been given permission to withdraw, swam back. Only Chivers, his company commander and thirty soldiers made it back to the home bank.

On the evening of 22 May, Franklyn was warned by the 12th Lancers that two columns of enemy armour were moving round his right flank. By first light the next day it became clear that the greatest threat was on this flank. The battle ebbed to and fro, ending in the Germans seizing Mont Saint-Eloi and endangering the vital ground of Vimy Ridge to the north of Arras. Franklyn was not allowed to move the 25th Brigade from the Canal Line, some sixteen miles to the north, and so had to resort to stripping the 13th Brigade of its anti-tank battery and the 2nd Cameronians to reinforce the battered and under-strength 151st Brigade on the ridge whence it had withdrawn after the counter-stroke two days earlier. With the 2nd Northamptons in dire straits and the whole of his 17th Brigade in imminent danger of being cut off by the 5th Panzer Division and under attack by 20th Motorized Division, Brigadier Stopford was allowed to fall back to the line of the Arras–Béthune road. The battalions succeeded in bringing off that most difficult of movements, a daylight withdrawal in contact. But the Stukas dived in, sirens howling, as the soldiers occupied their new positions. The most casualties following this attack were suffered by the 6th Seaforth Highlanders. The battle cost the Northamptons 352 casualties, including the CO, Lieutenant Colonel Hinchcliffe, his second-in-command, adjutant and RSM. As darkness fell, the exhausted soldiers dug in on the rolling chalk down, without the cover they and their fellow formations had enjoyed on the river line, where copses, villages and tree lines had provided some camouflage and cover from view from the Luftwaffe.

The withdrawal of the 17th Brigade had been greatly assisted by the 7th Royal Tank Regiment. Making good use of ground, the few Matildas remaining from the battle on the 21st caught the German armour in the flank as they rolled down the forward slopes towards Souchez, threatening to cut the Arras–Béthune road. All the while the bombing and shelling of Arras continued unabated. At 1600 hours, preceded by a two-hour bombardment, the German 12th Infantry Division began to put in an attack in strength on the Scarpe line east of Arras, now held by only four battalions. As the German infantry and engineers moved forward with their assault boats down the open slopes from Monchy-le-Preux in front of the 13th Brigade, they were comprehensively malleted by the 25-pounders of the 91st Field Regiment and the Vickers of the 9th Manchesters, and the attack ground to a halt. The enemy shelling continued, and at 2000 hours an attack in greater strength came in on the 4th Green Howards, the left-hand battalion of the 150th Brigade, east of Athies. The attack curled round and cut off the right-hand Green Howard company. The characteristic, slow 'bagga-bagga-bagga' sound of the Brens, easily distinguishable from the higher-pitched, faster chatter of the German MG 34s, died away as the company was overrun. The remainder of the battalion, after vainly trying to break through to the cut-off company, pulled back to high ground astride the Arras–Gavrelle road.

The 2nd Wiltshires, the right-hand battalion of the 13th Brigade, took the brunt of the German attacks crossing the river west of Roeux, and one company was overrun. The battalion was ordered to withdraw. The experiences of Sergeant Giblett of the Wiltshires provide a vivid example of the hazards of a night withdrawal in contact, especially if the enemy has the initiative. By the time the withdrawal began it was almost dark, but being early summer the darkness was not intense, except where buildings, high hedgerows or trees cast deep shadows. All the battalion transport was well back, the exception being that each company's 15-hundredweight truck had been sent to a pick-up point some way in rear of the position, to collect digging tools, spare ammunition and other bulky company stores. Wearing greatcoats and battle order, carrying gas masks, rifles or Brens, and encumbered with picks and shovels, spare ammunition and grenades, the men of Giblett's company started trudging back to the rendezvous.

The sections withdrew one at a time, formed into their platoons at the platoon rendezvous and moved off towards company headquarters, before setting out again, making for the rendezvous, where they would pick up the rear platoons and head for the rear. The company moved as quietly as heavily encumbered men could, with a section acting as rearguard in the expectation of trouble from that direction. The route was planned to take them through Roeux to a crossroads where the company 15-hundredweight truck would relieve them of much of their impedimenta.

As they neared the crossroads and were emerging from the village, a burst of sub-machine-gun fire rattled out ahead and from a flank; several men fell to the ground. For a second there was utter confusion, followed by everyone dropping their loads of spare kit and diving for cover. The German fire came from several directions and was accompanied by a shower of stick grenades. Some men were hit as they dived through gateways or over low walls. Giblett, having hurled himself over a garden wall, lay panting, straining eyes and ears to try to locate the enemy. The sound of heavier machine-gun fire joined the clatter of the sub-machine guns as the fighting spread along the area where the company had gone to ground. The company fired back. But the Wiltshires were scattered, making control impossible, and uncertain of the location of the enemy, so only a spatter of fire was returned, mostly from bolt-action rifles, which could not compete with the streams of automatic fire from sub-machine guns at close range, let alone the MG 34s. The enemy in concealed positions knew where their fellows were, whereas the Wiltshires found it difficult to distinguish friend from foe, so that any movement was likely to draw fire from comrades as well as enemies. After a while many Wiltshires lay still, not wishing to draw attention to themselves, as the Germans continued to douse the road with fire.

Giblett, having lain low briefly, rolled over a low garden wall and joined two other soldiers. They wondered what, if anything, would be done to gather the company together and restore the situation. As time passed and nothing seemed to be happening, Giblett crawled out from cover. Hearing the sound of movement almost at once, he froze in the shadow of a wall, and saw Germans with British prisoners walking along the road about forty yards away. Clearly the enemy were rounding up prisoners, and getting away was preferable to joining them. He crawled back to the other two men, who were still so shaken that initially they were reluctant to move. He proposed withdrawing through the gardens behind the houses and back through the village to see if they could link up with what remained of the company. Unknown to Giblett at the time, some of the company had been extracted, but the majority being so scattered could not be gathered up.

Giblett and his two companions crept through one of the gardens and were just approaching a wall when a burst of sub-machine-gun fire and bullets striking the ground near them showed that they had been spotted. Shouting 'Come on!' Giblett dashed to the wall, rolled over and landed in a shallow ditch. He paused, waiting for his companions, but they did not materialize. Hearing Germans shouting in the garden behind him, he ran crouching along the ditch, over another garden wall, through gardens and eventually into a field, where he paused for breath by a convenient haystack. There was no sign of the other two, and he conjectured that perhaps the enemy had been too preoccupied with taking them prisoner to follow him up. He could hear considerable activity in the village, and to avoid being scooped up by enemy clearing the area he worked his way round the village, through the fields, using shadow as much as possible, until he struck a road leading in a direction which he hoped would take him back to British troops.

Pausing in the ditch alongside the road to get his bearings, he heard the sound of a vehicle coming from the direction of the village and therefore likely to be German. Peering carefully over the rim of the ditch, he saw as the vehicle passed that it was a British 15-hundredweight; from the troops packed in the back he heard the unmistakable sound of English voices, and he made out the outline of British steel helmets. Jumping to his feet, he shouted and waved his arms, breaking into a run as the truck accelerated away. He raced up the road after it, whereupon it slowed and stopped. On reaching it he found himself covered by several rifles bristling from the back. 'You're lucky,' the soldiers told him. 'We nearly shot you thinking you were German – they're every-where. Jump on.' With the back of the truck crammed full, and three men in the front as well as the driver, Giblett perched on the front mudguard, grasping a bracket in one hand and his rifle in the other. They set off.

There was no one at the battalion rendezvous designated in the orders they had all received, so they pushed on, until after a mile or so they heard the sound of a tracked vehicle. The two vehicles stopped about fifty yards from each other, while the men in the 15-hundredweight debussed and crouched behind it, straining their eyes to see who the occupants of the tracked vehicle were. It looked like a British carrier, but they could not be too sure. Slowly the tracked vehicle edged towards them, and a faint British challenge was called out. Giblett and his companions were quick to answer it, before standing up and walking towards what transpired to be a carrier from their own battalion, whose crew they recognized. They were part of a group of carriers sent forward to establish a patrol line while the battalion regrouped further back.

Giblett and his companions were directed back to battalion head-quarters and from there sent to rejoin their company. They were to find that, not counting their own party, a mere thirty had escaped from the village, more than half the company being dead or prisoners of war. Most of those who got away did so thanks to the usual German reluctance to attack or follow up in strength at night.

The German 12th Infantry Division fanned out, having crossed the Scarpe, and initially forced the Wiltshires back to a position of all-round defence with brigade headquarters at Gavrelle. The 2nd Royal Inniskilling Fusiliers were also in danger of being outflanked, and only got away by charging with their carriers and wheeled transport over a ploughed field and over any Germans who happened to be in the way. Eventually the whole of 13th Brigade was repositioned on the line of the Biache–Gavrelle road, with a dangerous salient forced by the German 12th Division between them and the neighbouring 150th Brigade.

Franklyn's first request, at 1800 hours, to evacuate Arras, now in danger of being completely surrounded by the following morning, was refused by Gort. At 2200 hours Franklyn telephoned again to warn Gort's command post that if he did not get out that night it would be too late by morning. To his surprise he was told that the order to withdraw had been given an hour previously, and the instruction was being brought by a liaison officer. It seems strange that it was not passed over the telephone. It later transpired that the decision had been made by Gort at 1900 hours based on a report that the Germans were attacking near Béthune and had destroyed many Somua tanks. Gort took this to mean that the Cavalry Corps was shattered. Since Frankforce's line of communication depended wholly on the Cavalry Corps, it is highly likely that this news persuaded him that he had to pull the force out without delay. In fact his deduction was incorrect, and in the morning the French Cavalry Corps found to their consternation that the British had gone.

Franklyn's orders took some time to reach the formations under his command – two hours in the case of the 13th Brigade. The orders to General Petre in Arras nearly failed to get through. The officer carrying them in a car found the road to Arras blocked by a German tank. He continued on foot, but the British soldiers guarding the perimeter would not let him in and greeted any attempts to approach with a fusillade of bullets. Eventually the order was passed by wireless, reaching Petre in cipher at 0130 hours on 24 May. By the time it had been decoded, time was running so short that it was passed to the Welsh Guards as 'wake up, get up, pack up'.

The designated withdrawal route was the Douai road via Bailleul and Hénin-Liétard, and most of the transport used this. Fortunately the French railway engineers had blown the bridge over the railway on the Gavrelle road, the most direct way for some units to take to get to the Douai road, so most of the transport avoided running into German forces that had penetrated as far as Gavrelle. The 5th Green Howards and 8th Royal Northumberland Fusiliers were not so lucky. The Green Howards forced their way through, but the Northumberlands had 125 all ranks taken prisoner, including their CO.

The main body of the Welsh Guards made a wide sweep to the north out of Arras and, apart from being shelled, avoided contact with the enemy. For some reason the transport of the Welsh Guards and Cooke's Light Tanks took the 'scenic' route through Athies, where they ran into the enemy. Forty soft-skinned vehicles under the command of the quartermaster were jammed nose to tail in a narrow lane. The carrier platoon commander, Lieutenant the Hon. Christopher Furness of the Welsh Guards, said he would occupy the Germans while the vehicles were turned round. He set off with three carriers, supported by Major Cooke and six light tanks. The Germans were well established in a heavily wired strongpoint with machine guns and anti-tank guns. Although they attacked with great gusto, all six light tanks were soon brewed up. The carriers, by virtue of being smaller and by keeping moving and racing around the position, survived for longer. But in the end all three were hit and stopped. Furness, with his driver and Bren-gunner dead beside him, carried on fighting from the wrecked carrier, until he too was killed. All the surviving British witnesses were wounded and captured, so Furness was not awarded a posthumous Victoria Cross until after the war.

The quartermaster managed to turn all his vehicles round and get back on the correct route, before heading for Carvin eighteen miles from Arras where the 139th Brigade was holding the Canal Line. On the morning of 24 May, General Franklyn sat by the roadside as the men and vehicles of the two divisions of Frankforce marched, staggered or drove up the road. Lieutenant General Adam of III Corps found him there, and told him that he was taking the 5th and 50th Divisions under command to mount a counter-attack on Cambrai in conjunction with the French V Corps, whose commander General René Altmayer would be in overall command. This was the attack that Gort had discussed with Blanchard in response to Weygand's Operation Order No. 1, that the BEF and French First Army should attack south-west with eight divisions. It would never take place, and indeed the 5th Division, within an hour of reaching its concentration area, was ordered to defensive positions along the Deule Canal. The Arras salient, with the enemy pressing in from two sides, was no place from which to mount a counter-attack.

To keep his force intact, Gort very properly ordered the withdrawal from Arras before it was too late. His action, however, gave the French, humiliated by an unrelieved succession of thrashings, the perfect excuse to shift the blame for their ultimate defeat on to Gort. The recriminations started immediately with a telegram on 24 May from Reynaud to Churchill which, having reminded him that he had ordered Gort to take part in Weygand's plan, included this passage:

> General Weygand however informs me, according to a telegram from General Blanchard, and contrary to formal orders confirmed this morning by General Weygand, that the British Army had carried out, on its own initiative, a withdrawal forty kilometres towards the ports at a time when our forces from the south are gaining ground towards the north, to join up with the Allied Armies of the North. This withdrawal has naturally obliged General Weygand to modify his plan. He is now compelled to give up his attempt to close the breach and establish a continuous front.[10]

Reynaud's assertion that the unilateral action by the British had scuppered Weygand's plan and forced him to give up any idea of closing the gap and restoring a continuous front was complete nonsense and indicative of the cockeyed world inhabited by Weygand; but Reynaud depended upon the French commanders to give him the true picture, and cannot be blamed if almost everything they told him was eyewash.

The southern forces were not 'gaining ground towards the north'. The BEF had not 'carried out a withdrawal forty kilometres towards the ports'. Only two divisions had been withdrawn from the Arras salient to the Canal Line some twenty-five miles away. The withdrawal was not 'contrary to formal orders', for Gort had never been ordered to hold at Arras. By early on 25 May, Weygand knew from Blanchard's liaison officer the true state of the French First Army, and that the attack from the south was a dead duck (although he had not told Gort yet). General Besson, assigned to command the southern attack, had leaped on the Arras withdrawal as a perfect excuse for his inability to deploy the requisite forces. He lied to Weygand, telling him that the First Group of Armies had had to withdraw to the north, and that the enemy in front of him had been reinforced, adding that the offensive could not now proceed. The First Group of Armies had not withdrawn. The French front between Douai and Valenciennes had not moved. The distance between the Allied forces north and south of the Somme had not changed. Only Frankforce had withdrawn from Arras, and its two divisions were now preparing to attack to the south on 26 May.

But, as Major General Spears, the British liaison officer at GQG, observed, 'Gort's inevitable withdrawal is being seized upon as an excuse for the fact that no French forces have advanced from the south.' As early as 23 May it was actually too late for a counter-attack from the north; any attempt by the Allies to break out from that direction would itself have come under attack on both flanks by more mobile forces. The Weygand Plan was on its last legs, although it lingered on for two more days.

During 24 May, the tempo of the German advance slackened, albeit temporarily. German Army Group B, following up the withdrawal from the Escaut, had made contact with the four divisions of BEF on the old frontier line facing east, but was not yet in sufficient strength to put in a full-blooded attack on the British. Four German divisions attacked the Belgian line on the Lys, forcing the Belgians back and beginning the process of opening a gap between them and the BEF. This came as no surprise to the British, who saw this as the inevitable outcome of the Belgians' refusal to withdraw to the Yser. The British reaction was to strengthen the left flank by moving up a machine-gun battalion and an anti-tank battery. The second front, the Canal Line facing south-west, was coming under increasing pressure. Calais was besieged and Boulogne was about to fall (the story will be told in the next chapter). A series of engagements took place, fought in many cases by scratch mixed forces. At Gravelines, the 6th Green Howards and detachments of the 3rd Searchlight Regiment guarded all the bridges for three miles to the south of the town and resisted all attempts by the 1st Panzer Division to take the bridges. During the day they were relieved by French troops. At Saint-Pierre-Brouck, a detachment of the 1st Super-Heavy Regiment fought as infantry, and held off elements of 1st Panzer Division for several hours until forced back. Similarly some of the 3rd Super-Heavy Regiment held the crossing at Watten against a German panzer reconnaissance battalion until relieved by the French. The 52nd Heavy Regiment fought as infantry at Saint-Momelin, until French troops relieved them on the night of 25 May. The most dangerous development occurred between Saint-Omer and south of the River Aire. Here elements of two panzer divisions and an SS motorized division gained a foothold on the east bank of the canal. Counter-attacks by the 5th Inniskilling Dragoon Guards, and defence of the area by the 4th/7th Dragoon Guards, a squadron of the 13th/18th Hussars and miscellaneous infantry from a reinforcement camp, as well as machine guns of the 9th Royal Northumberland Fusiliers, managed to contain the enemy penetration but not drive it back. The enemy now held key ground between the Forêt de Clairmarais and the Forêt de Nieppe. South of this elements of the SS Verfügungs Division had also crossed the canal, and been contained by the 2nd/5th West Yorkshires. From here south through Béthune to La Bassée and as far as the junction with the French First Army at Raches, all enemy attempts to cross the canal were repulsed.

Why was there no large-scale attempt by the Germans to break through the Canal Line? It is clear from the German war diaries that on 23 May Rundstedt believed that there was a possibility of concerted action by the Allied forces north and south of the Somme. In addition there was a need to close up their mobile formations and consolidate the German northern flank. The British and French attacks at Arras and Cambrai had underlined the importance of this. Because the German XIX Corps had so far failed to take Boulogne and Calais, and because the defence of the Somme flank was not yet secure, the advanced units of the Kleist and Hoth Groups were instructed to deny the Canal Line to the enemy but not cross it. Orders to the two groups to this effect were given on the evening of 23 May: 'in the main Hoth Group will halt tomorrow; Kleist Group will also halt, thereby clarifying the situation and closing up'. At this stage the corps grouped under General von Kleist and General Hoth were as follows:

> XIX Corps, General Guderian: 1st, 2nd and 10th Panzer Divisions, and smaller motorized units
>
> XLI Corps, Lieutenant General Reinhardt: 6th and 8th Panzer Divisions, and the Motorized SS Verfügungs Division
>
> XVI Corps, General Hoepner: 3rd and 4th Panzer Divisions, and the Motorized SS Totenkopf Division
>
> XXXIX Corps, General Schmidt: 5th and 7th Panzer Divisions, and the 20th Motorized Division
>
> The 9th Panzer Division was in reserve at this time.

Eighteen hours after the issue of this order, Hitler visited Rundstedt at his headquarters, at around 1130 hours on 24 May. The Führer agreed completely with the view that east of Arras the attack must be made with infantry, while mobile forces could be halted on the line Lens–Béthune–Air–Saint-Omer–Gravelines in order to intercept the enemy under pressure from Army Group B. He insisted that it was necessary to conserve the armoured forces for future operations, and that any compression of the ring encircling the enemy would have the undesirable effect of restricting the activities of the Luftwaffe.[10] It is clear from these extracts from the German war diaries that the decision to halt the armour on the Canal Line was taken by Rundstedt and subsequently endorsed by Hitler. But, after Hitler had left, Rundstedt issued a directive which stated, 'By the Führer's orders . . . the general line Lens–Béthune–Air–Saint-Omer–Gravelines (Canal Line) will not be passed'. The panzer divisions were to close up to the canal and use this day for repairs and maintenance. After the war, the German commanders were to quote this interference by Hitler as the reason why the British were able to escape at Dunkirk. The inference was that, if the upstart ex-corporal Hitler had not stuck his oar in on this and other occasions, the brilliant German generals would have won the war instead of losing it. Although his decisions on many occasions contributed to that eventual outcome, this was not one of them.

Gort took advantage of the comparative lack of activity on 24 May to make a number of adjustments in the deployment of the BEF. From 0300 hours on 25 May, Frankforce, Petreforce, Polforce and Macforce were abolished. The British sector of the frontier line facing east would continue to be held by I and II Corps. The defence of the Canal Line would be the responsibility of III Corps. Almost immediately the instruction was modified: III Corps (5th and 50th Divisions, and 1st Army Tank Brigade) was relieved of responsibility for the Canal Line and ordered to prepare for the Anglo-French counter-attack planned for 26 May. The defence of the Canal Line was now assigned to the 2nd, 44th and 46th Divisions under Major General Eastwood, vice chief of general staff at GHQ BEF. The 48th Division, less one brigade, was ordered to the Dunkirk area. Other tidying-up moves were also made, including the allotment of artillery and armoured cavalry units.

The long sack containing the BEF and French First Army stretching from the coast was now seventy miles long and twenty-five miles wide, narrowing to thirteen. To the north-east, in an appendix to the sack some thirty-one miles by twenty, stood the Belgian Army. The roads were jammed with refugees trying to escape the German armies pressing in on three sides of the sack. Mixed with the hordes of refugees were men separated from their units in the chaos of fighting, and trying to find their new location. The lines of communication to the BEF and French First Army were totally disrupted by the panzer corridor, and the supply situation was dire. Amazingly in the light of the actual situation, planning for the counter-attack on the objectives Plouvain–Marquion–Cambrai was still grinding on and was to be completed by early on 25 May. According to this plan, the following day General Adam with three divisions (two British and one French) was to advance east of the Canal du Nord, and General Altmayer with two divisions was to advance to the west of the Canal du Nord, his right covered by the French Cavalry Corps. No one can accuse Gort of not loyally doing everything possible to fall in with Weygand's plan.

At 0700 hours on 25 May General Dill arrived at Gort's headquarters from England. They were joined by Blanchard, and together they discussed the plans for the Franco-British attack to the south. Blanchard confirmed that two or three French divisions with some 200 tanks would co-operate with Adam's two divisions. He did not regard the withdrawal

THE SACK

BELGIUM

Ostend
Bruges

Dunkirk
Bergues
Thielt

Gravelines
St Pierre Brouch
Misc French Troops
Watten
French Troops
Cassel
48
Wormhoudt
Roulers
Belgian Army
X
XI
IV
Documents captured here
Ypres
St Omer
Hazebrouck
Wytschaete
Menin
XXXX
Courtrai
Lys
Warnaton
Halluin
Escaut
44
Armentières
Comines
4
II
Roubaix
XXX
3
XX
Rusty Force
GHQ
Prémesques
143 Bde
Lille
1
Gort Line
Aire
I
50 5
XX
42
Tournai
Robecq
2
La Bassée
23
Cysoing
XXX
Béthune
Sealin
Attiches
Maulde
Carvin
46 &
French First Army
Deule Canal
French V
French III
Escaut
FRANCE
French V
Scarpe
Douai
French IV
Arras
Valenciennes
Sensée
Cambrai

32 kilometres
20 miles

from Arras as rendering the operation impossible, nor the difficulties he had reported to Weygand as insurmountable. However, he made it clear that the attack from the south was the principal offensive. He evidently had not been told that Weygand had given up the idea of the attack *the day before.*

All that day, 25 May, Brooke, commanding British II Corps, urged that his left flank, and that of the BEF, be strengthened, for the Belgians were being pushed back and the gap between the Belgian right and British left was now some eight miles wide, screened only by armoured cars of the 12th Lancers. Early that morning the Germans began probing west from Menin along the north bank of the Lys, which raised fears that Army Group B was about to attack across the rear of the BEF and link up with the panzer corridor, cutting the British off from the sea. Prisoners taken by the 1st/6th East Surreys at around this time were very 'cocky', in the opinion of Captain White, the adjutant. Their attitude was that 'this isn't going to last for long. We'll soon be back with our units.'

Brooke ordered the 4th Division to extend its left flank to cover his own left flank, while sending two machine-gun battalions (1st/7th Middlesex and 6th Black Watch) with a battery of 20th Anti-Tank Regiment to cover the southern bank of the Lys from Menin to Comines. Machine-gun battalions with their carriers and Vickers were again proving invaluable as mobile firepower with a modicum of protection. At 0200 hours on 25 May, Brooke persuaded Gort over the telephone to send the 143rd Brigade, the BEF's last reserve, to cover the gap between Ypres and Comines. He had already sent another machine-gun battalion, the 4th Gordon Highlanders, there.

The liaison officer from the 4th Division sent to make contact with the Belgians found their soldiers drinking in cafés, unconcerned about who, if anybody, was holding their front a bare mile away. The British liaison officer with the Belgian III Corps, despite the lies he was being told, gained the strong impression that, far from withdrawing to the Yser, the Belgian Army was swinging back to Bruges. These and other reports built up the picture in Gort's HQ of a Belgian Army falling apart in disarray, and exposing the BEF to an attack on its rear.

Perhaps the most compelling evidence of the impending threat to the BEF came in later that day. Sergeant Burford of the 1st/7th Middlesex, transferred that morning from the 3rd to the 4th Division, was told to patrol across the Lys from the battalion reconnaissance line on the southern bank. He took his section in a collapsible boat to a village between Comines and Menin, where he learned from an English-speaking Belgian woman that Germans had been seen. A few moments later, his Bren group covering him came under fire and suffered two casualties, one dead. Almost immediately, to his astonishment, a large blue staff car with two German officers came up the village street. Burford had only a .38-in revolver, but he emptied it at the car, killing the driver, and it crashed into a house. The surviving officer leaped out and scuttled off, leaving a briefcase behind. Grabbing it, Burford gathered his patrol, and carrying his wounded man evaded the Germans, eventually reporting back to his battalion. The briefcase was sent to the 3rd Division head-quarters, because until earlier that morning the Middlesex had been attached to it. Here Brooke, visiting the division, found the staff poring over the contents, and ordered that they be sent to GHQ without delay.

The escaped passenger was Lieutenant Colonel Kinzel, a liaison officer with Colonel General von Reichenau's German Sixth Army. In the brief-case there were two documents. One, of which only four had been issued for taking forward, was of the very highest security classification. It contained a detailed picture of the whole German order of battle, right down to divisional commanders and their chiefs of staff. It gave the British the first true picture of the German Army, and was the stepping-stone for all assessments thereafter. However, the other document was even more important for the information it provided about the immedi-ate future, as it gave the German Sixth Army's orders for the attack that had begun that morning. It showed that the German XI Corps was to attack towards Ypres, and the VI Corps towards the Wytschaete or Messines ridge, round the BEF's left flank. The IX Corps was to assault Thielt, north of Courtrai, pushing the Belgians even further away from the BEF.

Gort was now faced with a dreadful dilemma: keep his promise to attack south, and face the prospect of the destruction of the BEF; or save the BEF by breaking faith with his Allies and heading for the coast. Lieutenant Colonel Templer, on his way to brief Pownall, had to pass through Gort's office in his temporary headquarters at Prémesques. Gort was standing gazing at a map of northern France, and Templer sensed that he was deeply troubled, although he did not know why. Rather than disturb him on his way out, Templer left Pownall's office by the window. Gort unburdened himself to Major Archdale, his liaison officer with the French First Army. He castigated the Belgians for letting him down, and for retreating to the Scheldt instead of keeping in line with the BEF.

At 1730 hours, Adam telephoned to say that despite Blanchard's promise, made that very day, of three divisions and 200 tanks, he could provide only one division for the attack the next day. At 1800 hours, Gort decided that he would extract the BEF. It was a brave judgement and the right one. By now he had totally lost faith in the ability of the senior French commanders to keep abreast of the swiftly changing situation and arrive at the correct decision; they were always trailing well behind events, with the result that their orders bore little relevance to what was actually happening.

Gort ordered the 5th and 50th Divisions to abandon preparations for the attack southwards and to move immediately to close the dangerous gap between the BEF and the Belgians. He made the decision in the nick of time, for had these two divisions arrived a few hours later the BEF would have been surrounded. He then told French First Army of his intentions.

6

BOULOGNE AND CALAIS

To tell the stories of Boulogne and Calais, we must rewind to 20 May, and the German Army Group A war diary entry on that date, quoted in Chapter 3, which began, 'Now that we have reached the coast at Abbeville'. The German advance cut off the BEF from its main line of supply, which fed forward from various ports south of the Somme at Abbeville: Dieppe, Fécamp, Le Havre, Cherbourg, Saint-Malo, Brest and Saint-Nazaire. This system had been deliberately designed in an attempt to keep the flow of stores and equipment as free as possible from the attentions of the Luftwaffe while the BEF engaged the enemy in Belgium. Although Dunkirk, Boulogne and Calais were the nearest to the BEF's intended area of operation, and also played a part in the supply chain, they were by no means the major ports in the system. Now, however, Boulogne and Calais were the *only* ports, other than Dunkirk, available to supply the BEF. Gort had no troops to spare for their defence. So the War Office ordered the 20th Guards Brigade to Boulogne, and for the defence of Calais they sent the 30th Brigade and the 3rd Royal Tank Regiment. The 30th Brigade and 3rd RTR were actually part of the 1st Armoured Division, which itself was about to leave England for Cherbourg. As these units and formations left England, the Germans began to swing their armour north from the Somme.

Although the fighting at Boulogne and Calais was carried out at the same time, there was no tie-in between them, so it will be convenient to tell each story separately.

Boulogne

The Germans had bombed Boulogne on the night of 19/20 May, causing some damage and inflicting a few casualties, some of them officers and soldiers of Rear GHQ located in the Imperial Hotel. So Gort's adjutant general, Lieutenant General Sir Douglas Brownrigg, ordered Rear GHQ to move to Wimereux, some three miles north of Boulogne. He had already evacuated many of the 'useless mouths' from Boulogne, Calais and

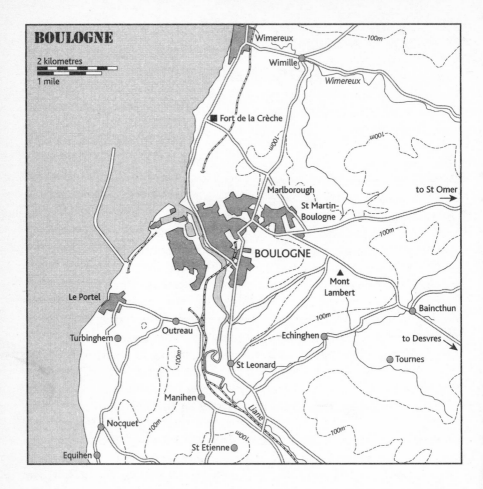

Dunkirk, including patients and convalescents from the various medical units that acted as satellites for the main casualty reception area around Dieppe. Although the news received by Rear GHQ of the German armoured advance was sketchy, it soon became apparent to Brownrigg that something was amiss, as hordes of terrified refugees poured in, full of stories of panzers supported by swarms of aircraft. Boulogne lay open for the taking.

There was no British garrison at Boulogne. The only British contribution to its defence, hurriedly provided on 20 May, consisted of eight 3.7-inch guns of the 2nd Heavy Anti-Aircraft Regiment, eight Bofors 40mm guns of the 58th Light Anti-Aircraft Regiment and one battery of the 2nd Searchlight Regiment. The French had two ancient 75mm guns two 25mm anti-tank guns and two tanks, one of which was broken down and immobile. There was an assortment of Allied troops at Boulogne.

These included French and Belgian recruits who had not completed their training and were totally unfit to fight. The largest British contingent consisted of 1,500 men of No. 5 Group Auxiliary Pioneer Corps. Some of their veteran officers and NCOs had experienced military service, but the vast majority of the soldiers were either elderly men who had volunteered for employment after years on the dole during the depression, or low-category conscripts (graded unfit for any other military employment being mentally or physically inadequate, sometimes both).

Since their arrival in France, No. 5 Group had been engaged on labour duties to the detriment of any training, which would have been difficult in any case since only a quarter of them had been issued with rifles, and of these only a handful had actually fired them. The youngest officer in the group was the CO, Lieutenant Colonel Dean, who had won the VC fighting with the 8th Royal West Kents in the First World War. The group had been working in the Doullens area, and on being ordered to evacuate in the face of the advancing German armour, Dean had extracted them by bribing the stationmaster and requisitioning a train at Saint-Pol. Here they had a brisk engagement with the first Germans to arrive, before reaching Wimereux early on 21 May. Leaving most of the group there, a large, unarmed party was sent to Boulogne as dock labourers (one of the roles of the Auxiliary Pioneer Corps). Other British troops also turned up, mainly the survivors of units and sub-units bundled out of their deployment locations by the advancing enemy or cast aside in the backwash of *Blitzkrieg*. These included most of 262nd Field Company, seventy of the 7th Royal West Kents (the survivors of the encounter at Albert with 1st Panzer Division – see Chapter 3) and fifty of the 5th Buffs, as well as some soldiers of the Durham Light Infantry separated from their battalions during the fighting at Arras.

The 20th Guards Brigade comprised the 2nd Irish Guards and 2nd Welsh Guards (the 2nd Loyals, the third battalion of the brigade, still in the process of training, was left behind in England), although, in the opinion of the brigade commander, Brigadier Fox-Pitt, the two Guards battalions still lacked much training. Support for the brigade was provided by the Brigade Anti-Tank Company and the 275th Battery of the 69th Anti-Tank Regiment (less one troop). The brigade had been recalled from a night exercise and embarked at Dover, arriving at Boulogne early on 22 May. The Guards battalions had been transported in two cross-Channel ferries which could embark carriers and motorcycles but no trucks. One Irish Guards company had to be left behind to follow on in the *Mona's Isle*, a small ferry converted to an armed boarding vessel. Before leaving England, Brigadier Fox-Pitt spoke by telephone to General Dill at the War Office and was just told to defend Boulogne while Rear

GHQ was evacuated. Fox-Pitt's staff consisted merely of the brigade major, as the staff captain and the intelligence officer had crossed to France in the destroyer *Whitshed*. When he reported to General Brownrigg at Wimereux, Fox-Pitt discovered that no one at Rear GHQ knew very much about the situation, other than that enemy transport had been seen at Etaples, sixteen miles south-east of Boulogne, and that armour had been reported in the Forest of Crécy. He was also told that General Lanquetot's French 21st Division was arriving by train to hold a line Samer–Desvres about ten miles east of Boulogne; three of its battalions were already in position. Brownrigg reiterated that Fox-Pitt's task was to hold Boulogne, and that he would be reinforced by 3rd RTR and the 1st Queen Victoria's Rifles (one of the battalions of the 30th Brigade), who would arrive from Calais the following day. With the promise of these additions to his brigade, Fox-Pitt set off in requisitioned or, as Fox-Pitt put it, 'pinched' cars and motorcycles to carry out his reconnaissance and make his dispositions. The two battalions also 'pinched' cars for their reconnaissances. (See the map on p. 146.)

Boulogne lies at the mouth of the River Liane, which flows to the sea through high, rounded hills. There is a small built-up area of level ground round the harbour. From here the town climbs the steep hill to the old walled town known as the Haute Ville or Citadel. The river and harbour cut the lower town in half. The Irish Guards held the sector between the river west of Saint-Léonard and the coast north of Le Portel. The Welsh Guards were allocated the ground north-east of the river, from the reverse slopes of Mont Lambert and the high ground through to Saint Martin-Boulogne, a sector about three miles long. Fox-Pitt intended that the area on the Welsh Guards's left, Saint Martin-Boulogne/Marlborough/ the coast, should be occupied by 3rd RTR and the 1st Queen Victoria's Rifles from Calais. The Welsh Guards in particular were thinly spread to hold what was the vital ground, as Mont Lambert dominates the town and the harbour. The rolling country lent itself to armoured action, and there were plenty of covered approaches. There was very little depth to any of the positions held by the brigade, and Fox-Pitt had no troops to spare for a reserve. The deployment of his battalions was not made any easier by the lack of maps. When Lieutenant Colonel Sir Alexander Stanier Bt, CO 2nd Welsh Guards, and Lieutenant Colonel Charles Haydon, CO 2nd Irish Guards, reported for orders, the maps issued before leaving England were unrolled. Except for five 1-inch maps of the Boulogne area which had to suffice for the whole brigade, all the maps were of England not of France, although on one set Boulogne was shown in one corner. There were two of these particular maps in the brigade, one per battalion.

General Lanquetot of the French 21st Division dropped in to see Fox-Pitt, and had a few words with him, most of which Fox-Pitt found difficult to understand. But Lanquetot finished by saying that his, Lanquetot's, troops were *pliés*, 'folded up', which Fox-Pitt understood as the equivalent of the English slang they had 'had it'. This was hardly encouraging. Lanquetot left abruptly, without saying where he was going. It transpired that he was off to command a miscellany of French troops in the Haute Ville.

There were some lighter moments. Stanier put his headquarters in the office of the local water board. After a while the adjutant came to Stanier to say that the head of the water board wanted to see him. When Stanier appeared, the official said, 'I won't have your soldiers walking across my flower beds.' At that moment there was a huge explosion.

> I thought it was a shell. Actually it was a primus stove cooking my supper, which had blown up. My quartermaster with great presence of mind threw a French mattress stuffed with feathers on the stove, it made a most awful stench, so we put on our gas masks. I was delighted that the head of the water board did not have one and had to leave immediately.

Lieutenant Colonel Dean of the Auxiliary Pioneer Corps brought Fox-Pitt the first firm news of the enemy. He had been sent on a somewhat bullish task to hold the River Canche some seventeen miles to the south with a company of men. On his way there he had run into enemy motorcyclists, but had returned with little loss.

The panzer divisions, whose advance had been slowed by the British 'counter-attack' at Arras on 21 May, had by now begun to resume their advance northwards. The war diary of Guderian's XIX Corps (1st, 2nd and 10th Panzer Divisions) has two entries on 22 May relevant to the forthcoming battle in Boulogne. The first, timed 1240: '2nd Panzer Division will advance direct to Boulogne via the line Bainethun–Samer; 1st Panzer Division via Desvres to Marquise in order to protect on this line 2nd Panzer Division's flank against attack from Calais.' At the end of the day's entries it was recorded that, recognizing the need for quick action, 'the corps commander sent 2nd Panzer Division towards Boulogne at noon without waiting for orders from [Kleist] Group. In consequence the division succeeded in penetrating to the town.'[1]

This division had difficulty overcoming French resistance at Samer, but reached the outskirts of Boulogne, making first contact with the Irish Guards in mid-afternoon on 22 May. No. 1 Company of the Irish Guards, arriving last on the *Mona's Isle*, had been put in to hold the left of the battalion sector to cover the Etaples road near Outreau, and had just begun to dig in when the Germans started to shell them. The 'Micks' dug faster.

A German Mk II tank came up the Etaples road accompanied by infantry. The Irish Guards knocked out the tank with seven rounds from a 25mm Hotchkiss anti-tank gun. This was an almost useless weapon, but somehow worked on this occasion. The infantry were beaten off. Another attack was similarly dealt with, followed by a third, on each occasion accompanied by armour. The third attack was more successful, overrunning most of a platoon and two anti-tank guns. The Irish Guards blocked the road with their carriers, while the battalion's despatch riders tried to find brigade headquarters to alert them of this dangerous situation. It is difficult to know what the brigade commander could have done about it since he had no reserve. With the onset of darkness, the German attacks died away and they failed to exploit the penetration they had achieved so far on this flank.

Meanwhile the Welsh Guards had also been under attack, but on each occasion the enemy were driven off. The German armour was starting to curl round and envelop Boulogne from the north-east, threatening Wimereux in the process. This persuaded Brownrigg that Rear GHQ should leave that night, which it did, Brownrigg departing in the destroyer *Vimy* at 0300 hours on 23 May.

With the departure of Brownrigg, Fox-Pitt was now the senior British officer left in the area. The only communications he had with England after Rear GHQ left were through whichever destroyer happened to be in Boulogne harbour. The message would be signalled by wireless-telegraphy (using a morse key, not radio-telegraphy, that is voice) to Dover, transmitted to the War Office via the Admiralty, and the reply would come back down to Fox-Pitt by the same convoluted route. Within the 20th Guards Brigade, there were no radios at all, even between brigade headquarters and battalions. Communication was by liaison officers on bicycles or motorcycles, all 'borrowed', or field telephone, which was useless once the battle began.

During the night Major General Lloyd, temporarily employed in Rear GHQ having been sacked as GOC of the 2nd Division, visited Fox-Pitt on his way to embark for England. He told Fox-Pitt that the 1st Queen Victoria's Rifles and 3rd RTR would arrive from Calais that morning. Unfortunately this was nonsense, as we shall see. Elements of the French 21st Division did manage to delay the 1st Panzer Division at Desvres throughout 22 May and well into the next day. But the Germans caught the bulk of the French 21st Division sitting in the trains in which it had arrived. The division was scattered to the four winds, and unable to form a stop line south of Boulogne as originally envisaged.

Fox-Pitt would have to defend Boulogne with the two battalions of the 20th Guards Brigade, the assorted French troops and what else he could scrape together. The appearance of German armour to the north of the town with the coming of daylight on 23 May was a sign that no reinforcements would be arriving from Calais. Fox-Pitt decided to plug the three-mile gap between the Welsh Guards and the coast with the Auxiliary Pioneers. About 800 of these, mostly elderly, warriors established roadblocks in the built-up areas of north Boulogne. They had all been equipped with rifles by stripping weapons off soldiers about to embark. A further 150 armed Pioneers were sent to reinforce the Welsh Guards along with the 262nd Field Company RE.

The Germans completed the encirclement of Boulogne an hour after first light by seizing Fort de la Crèche and its French garrison. A troop of the 2nd Heavy Anti-Aircraft Regiment was overrun, but managed to knock out two tanks with their 3.7-inch AA guns first. As an aside it was a pity that the British did not see fit to employ these guns in this role more often, and failed to do so throughout the war – unlike the Germans, whose use of their equivalent, the 88mm AA gun, as an anti-tank gun has already been noted.

The Germans mounted a two-pronged attack on the defences of Boulogne, starting with an assault on the Welsh Guards' positions, followed shortly afterwards by an attack on the Irish Guards. Two Guards battalions with no artillery support and no radio communications faced a full-blooded attack by the experienced 2nd Panzer Division with numerous armoured fighting vehicles supported by artillery and the Luftwaffe. The open slopes around the town soon became untenable, and the two battalions fell back among the houses. The Welsh Guards had one platoon cut off, but still fighting, and the 'Micks' left a platoon in Outreau. Around noon, the two battalions pulled in to tight defensive positions, the Welsh Guards being allocated defence of the two bridges connecting the town with the harbour. The French still held the Haute Ville.

Throughout the fighting on the outskirts of town, Royal Navy destroyers provided support and continued evacuating troops. Lieutenant Lumsden was the navigator of the *Keith*, which with the *Vimy* was ordered into Boulogne. Both were alongside the quay and had begun to embark a mass of waiting troops into the two ships, who were blocking gangways and ladders on board, when at this critical moment the town and harbour were attacked by a wave of enemy aircraft. Thirty Stukas in a single line wheeled to a point about 2,000 feet above the harbour and poured down to attack the crowded quay and the two destroyers. The only opposition was some scattered rifle fire and light machine-gun fire, mostly from soldiers ashore, and from the single-barrelled 2-pounder pom-poms in each destroyer.

The captain of the *Keith* ordered the crews of the 4.7-inch guns below because they were useless against aircraft. He also ordered the bridge cleared. The bridge was just above quay level and was exposed to splinters from bombs bursting there. Lumsden stood back to allow his captain down the ladder to the wheelhouse, as seniority and courtesy demanded, but was invited to precede him; no captain likes to leave his bridge while under attack. Lumsden had taken only a couple of steps down when the captain fell on top of him, shot in the chest. The doctor arrived and pronounced him dead. The first lieutenant, now in command, was shot in the leg. He ordered everyone in the bridge structure to lie down, because German small-arms fire and splinters from mortar bombs fired from weapons sited in houses overlooking the destroyer's berth were piercing the sides of the wheelhouse and hitting frightened men struggling to get down the steep ship's ladders to the mess decks below.

It seemed a miracle that neither *Keith* nor *Vimy* suffered a direct hit by any bombs. But both ships, lying alongside one another, were open to further air attack and their bridges and upper decks were swept by small-arms fire from positions thought to be occupied by British troops but plainly already held by the enemy. Able Seaman Harris on the *Vimy*'s bridge noticed the captain, Lieutenant Commander Donald, train his binoculars on a hotel diagonally opposite but quite close to the ship. Another burst of fire from the hotel struck the captain down. He was choking on his own blood, so Harris moved him on to his side. His final order was 'get the first lieutenant to the bridge urgently'. As Harris rose to his feet, more shots from the hotel swept the bridge, and the ship's sub-lieutenant fell at his feet with four bullet holes across his chest.

The *Vimy*'s first lieutenant took her out to sea followed by *Keith*, also under command of her first lieutenant. Lumsden navigated the *Keith* out of Boulogne harbour stern first, conning the ship from the chart house looking out of a small porthole. No communication was possible with men on the upper deck to slip the wires, so after ringing on main engines Lumsden shouted orders to the signal officer and chief yeoman who were manning the engine telegraphs to make the ship surge ahead and part the wires. This achieved, it was not too difficult to swing her stern off the quay and start her moving astern. He rushed up to the bridge more than once to increase his view astern, but soon clattered down again when bullets whistled past as he showed his head. Keeping as close as he dared to the stone pier on the northern side of the channel, he was mightily grateful to round the corner successfully. Knowing that the rudder would be more effective at higher speed, he increased shaft revolutions to give 14 knots, still going astern. Outside the harbours, the bridge was manned and the ship's company sorted out the load of disorderly refugees. Captain Simson and some dozen others were quietly buried at sea as the crew scanned the skies for enemy aircraft. The *Keith* returned to Dover to land evacuees and wounded.

Meanwhile other destroyers in the harbour and offshore from Boulogne shelled enemy gun positions and machine-gun nests, which gave much encouragement to the British troops still fighting in the town. At about 1500 hours Fox-Pitt decided to pull back his brigade to new positions, and moved his headquarters to a location by the quay to make communication to London via the destroyers easier. When the Irish Guards received the message by despatch rider it was to evacuate, rather than withdraw further back. The battalion pulled back to the docks area where they barricaded the approaches with vehicles and barrels, taking cover in warehouses. The order was premature as embarkation was still in progress, and the enemy were doing all they could to make it as difficult as possible by machine-gun fire. The Irish Guards were given close support by the destroyer *Whitshed* firing at point-blank range with a 4.7-inch gun, on one occasion stopping an enemy penetration almost in the middle of the battalion position.

Fox-Pitt sent the message to London, 'Situation grave'. With messages being transmitted to Dover and passed on to the War Office via the Admiralty, and back again, as already described, the response took a while to get through. Eventually the order to evacuate immediately was received by a destroyer at 1730 hours, by which time she had left the harbour loaded with wounded. An hour elapsed before the message reached Fox-Pitt. At this point some fifty German aircraft bombed the harbour. The attack had been asked for by the German commander on the spot, concerned at the lack of progress being made by 2nd Panzer Division. The German bombers ran into a mass of anti-aircraft fire both from the ships and from the guns ashore. They also encountered RAF fighters, who accounted for eight bombers, for the loss of three fighters.

It was now time to withdraw the 20th Guards Brigade, which had held off the enemy all day. The Royal Engineers demolished the bridges, while naval parties covered by Royal Marines sent in for the purpose destroyed dock installations. The whole harbour was under enemy fire, *Whitshed* and *Vimeira* were loaded with brigade headquarters and the Welsh Guards, and the Irish Guards stood by to board the next two, *Wild Swan* and *Venomous*. A third destroyer, the *Venetia*, was ordered in, although the tide was low. As she slipped in through the entrance, German gunners engaged her from positions north of the town, and were joined by tanks shooting at her from just across the harbour. She was hit hard and seemed to be about to block the harbour entrance. But she went hard astern, clearing the harbour behind a great cloud of smoke generated by fires on deck and escaping back out to sea.

The Germans now switched their attentions to the destroyers berthed alongside, but as the tide was low the dock walls masked them and rendered them hard to hit. The Irish Guards and rearguards of the Welsh Guards embarked, and these last two destroyers engaged enemy armour at point-blank range with their 4.7-inch guns – absolutely devastating against even the heaviest tank of the period (the equivalent of a 120mm and far bigger than any tank gun of the Second World War). One German tank was seen to be blown into the air and somersault. Soon after 2100 hours the last Bren teams scrambled on to the decks of the two destroyers, and they slipped their moorings and steamed out of the harbour.

The Irish Guards came back some 600 strong out of the 700 who had arrived at Boulogne. The Welsh Guards were somewhat weaker – almost three companies were left behind. This was thanks to the complete lack of radio communication and the chaos of the withdrawal, including blowing the bridges connecting the harbour with the town while the Welsh Guards companies in question were still on the wrong side of the river. By the time some managed to cross on the wreckage, the ships had gone.

The Pioneers were also left behind, after fierce fighting at their roadblocks, where they notched up at least one successful tank kill by setting light to the petrol tank of an overturned truck while a tank was grinding its way over the top of it. Lieutenant Colonel Stanier had passed the order to Lietenant Colonel Dean to withdraw to the docks, but Dean was away from his headquarters, and before pulling out had first to extricate two of his posts surrounded by enemy. Taking his reserve company with him, he went to the relief of his men. The fighting was savage but brief, some of the Glaswegians in the reserve company resorting to what was then a favourite Glasgow gang weapon, cut-throat razors, in preference to rifles, with which they were less well acquainted. Four other posts were withdrawn, the remaining two having already been overrun. Dean and his men reached the harbour with some sappers of 262nd Field Company just after the Guards completed their embarkation.

At about 2230 hours the destroyer *Windsor* arrived and took off 600 men, including most Pioneers and demolition parties. The last ship to arrive was the *Vimeira*, making her second trip, at about 0140 hours on 24 May, entering the harbour in eerie silence. She stayed for over an hour, embarking 1,400 men, and in a dangerously overloaded condition made England safely. The *Wessex* had also been ordered to Boulogne, and had she arrived she might have taken off the 300 or so remaining Welsh

Guards. But she was diverted to Calais, and no further ships were sent to Boulogne.

All that now remained were the wounded, looked after by a doctor and the padre of the Pioneers, who had volunteered to stay, and three companies of Welsh Guards, plus a few Pioneers and some sappers. Two of the Welsh Guards companies set off in groups to try to make their way to an unoccupied part of the coast. No. 3 Company under Major Windsor Lewis withdrew to the harbour at daybreak just after *Vimeira* had gone. Windsor Lewis took about a hundred French soldiers, some sappers and unarmed Pioneers under his command. He began by defending some sheds, until German fire made this location too hot. So under the cover of parked railway wagons, he moved his party to the burned-out railway station, the Gare Maritime, which had some underground shelter for the refugees who had joined him. Here he held out until 1300 hours the following day, blasted by tank shells, pounded by artillery and mortars, and running short of food and ammunition. At last he decided to surrender. Just before this General Lanquetot surrendered at the Haute Ville under German threat to destroy the town if he continued to resist. By early afternoon on 25 May, the Germans could report that Boulogne had fallen.

General Lanquetot was bitter about the British withdrawal, and blamed them for the fall of Boulogne. The British Official History comments, 'it shows how easily misunderstandings may arise between allies in such a confused situation'.[2] The point is that the 20th Guards Brigade, in Fox-Pitt's words a half-trained brigade with no communications, was ordered to Boulogne at short notice by the British government for purely national reasons to defend a port through which the BEF was supplied. When it became apparent that two battalions could not hold the town they were, reasonably enough, ordered out, again by the British government. When Fox-Pitt was ordered to evacuate his brigade, he was unable to communicate with Lanquetot as the Germans were between him and the Haute Ville. So the latter was totally unaware that the British had gone. For his part, he had been ordered to hold Boulogne with his 21st Division. Arriving ahead of his division, and subsequently learning that most of them were cut off and could not join him, he deployed what French troops he had, taking into account the 20th Guards Brigade dispositions. Having done this he seems to have made no effort to find out what was happening to Fox-Pitt's brigade. Rather than visiting his subordinates, as the British were accustomed to do, Lanquetot sat in his command post in accordance with French practice, totally out of touch and unable to communicate with anybody. When he discovered on the morning of 24 May that the British had left for England without telling him, it is easy to see why he might have been somewhat annoyed; but in view of his passive command style, one does not feel all that sympathetic. As the French in the Haute Ville held out for a further twenty-four hours, and of the British only Windsor Lewis's party remained to do likewise, it seems rational in French eyes to regard the defence of Boulogne as primarily a French effort. In truth, French *and* British action was responsible for holding up the 2nd Panzer Division at Boulogne for three days.

Calais

At 2000 hours on 21 May, a group of sergeants of 3rd RTR drinking in a pub at Fordingbridge, Hampshire, were told to report back to camp immediately – their regiment was moving in two hours. It came as no surprise because a few days earlier all the battalion's tanks had been taken by rail to Southampton and loaded on the cross-Channel steamer the *City of Christchurch*. The twenty-seven 14-ton cruisers and twenty-one 6-ton Mk VI light tanks had been stowed in the hold, with the battalion's wheeled transport on the deck and hatches. The battalion was under orders to join the 1st Armoured Division south of the Somme, and now it seemed the call had come.

After boarding a train at Fordingbridge, the battalion expected a swift journey to Southampton and were puzzled by an all-night trundle through Sussex and Kent, before arriving at Dover the next morning. There was no sign of the *City of Christchurch* with all their tanks. The CO, Lieutenant Colonel Keller, was summoned for orders and reappeared looking distinctly gloomy and clutching a letter. Meanwhile the battalion embarked on the *Maid of Orleans*. About halfway across the Channel the battalion was paraded by squadrons and told that the destination was Calais.[3] This order followed swiftly by counter-order was a foretaste of what 3rd RTR, and indeed everyone else involved with the action at Calais, were to experience repeatedly. It is a fairly common feature of all wars, but Calais was to provide an extreme version. The British Official History of the campaign, after commenting on the devotion to duty of all units that fought at Calais, remarks, 'Unfortunately the conditions under which they were required to fight show some of the failings which have been matched too often in the conduct of our military excursions.'[4]

Calais is an ancient port, and much fought over in its long history. It lies in flat country seamed with drainage ditches and canals. These confine any approach by vehicle to the roads, except in the south-west and west where high ground stretches across northern France to the sea between Calais and Boulogne. Here the high ground is only three miles

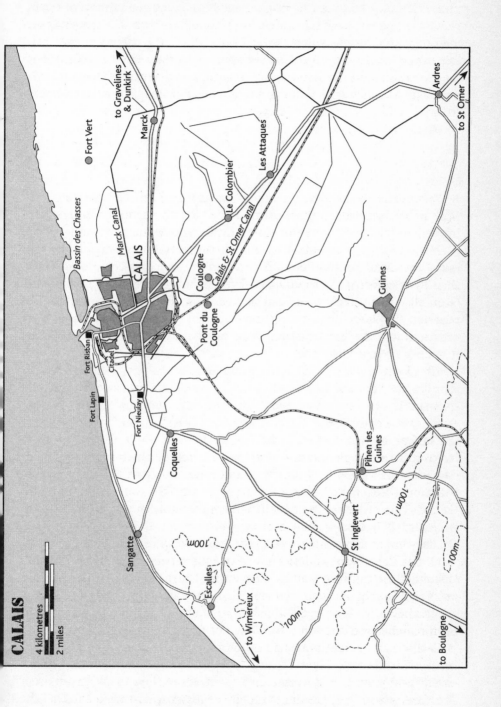

CALAIS

4 kilometres
2 miles

to Gravelines & Dunkirk

Fort Vert

Marck

Bassin des Chasses

Marck Canal

CALAIS

Le Colombier

Les Attaques

Calais & St Omer Canal

Coulogne

Ardres

to St Omer

Guines

Fort Risban

Citadel

Pont du Coulogne

Fort Lapin

Fort Nieulay

Coquelles

Pihen les Guines

100m

Sangatte

100m

St Inglevert

100m

Escalles

to Wimereux

100m

to Boulogne

from Calais, providing observation over the town and hence the opportunity of good shooting by artillery. Much of Vauban's seventeenth-century fortifications still surrounded the town. The Citadel shielded the old town, which is almost surrounded by water. Eight of the eleven bastions still stood in the angles of the ramparts (see the map on p. 157).

On 19 May, Colonel Holland had been appointed to command British troops in Calais, which then consisted of one platoon of the Argyll & Sutherland Highlanders and some AA gunners. The Argyll platoon was ordered to set up a roadblock on the Dunkirk road. Two batteries of the 1st Searchlight Regiment were deployed in Forts Risban and Vert and in some outposts out of town. A battery of the 2nd Anti-Aircraft Regiment (3.7-inch guns) sited four guns near Sangatte and three near Fort Vert. Part of a battery of 58th Light Anti-Aircraft Regiment (40mm Bofors) sited their two guns to protect the lock gates in the harbour. French troops in Calais consisted of coastal gunners and elements of units driven ahead of the German advance.

The first British troops sent to reinforce Calais arrived in the personnel ship *City of Canterbury* on 22 May, as the 2nd Panzer Division was approaching Boulogne and 1st Panzer Division was motoring north from the Somme. The leading British unit was the 1st Queen Victoria's Rifles (QVR), a TA motorcycle battalion, but without their 142 motorcycles (99 with side-cars), without trucks, without 3-inch mortars, with only smoke bombs for their 2-inch mortars, without their forty-three Brens, and with two-thirds of the men armed with rifles, the remainder with pistols. When they had been ordered to move to Dover by train to embark, the embarkation staff told the battalion that there was no space for their transport, although in fact there was room for their motorcycles. At Dover, one of the porters at the station said to Corporal Day, a signaller with 1st QVR, 'I don't know what you blokes are going over there for. Everybody else is coming back.' This was the first anyone in 1st QVR had heard of the retreat.

They were deployed to block the main roads into Calais, guard the undersea telephone cable terminal at Sangatte, and patrol the beaches on either side of the harbour. Without any form of transport they took a while to deploy, carrying as much as they could of their stores and ammunition.

Next on the scene were 3rd RTR. The CO, Lieutenant Colonel Keller, was the only one to go ashore at this stage, because there had not been time to issue BEF identity cards to 3rd RTR. Reacting to the usual overblown fears of fifth columnists, a feature of this campaign, an order had been issued that anyone without identity papers would be shot. The CO, however, was determined to find out what 3rd RTR was supposed to do. He accosted a British colonel on the dockside who had not the slightest idea what was going on and was bent on obeying his own orders to return to England. Keller requisitioned the British colonel's staff car, dumping the kit with which it was loaded on the dockside, and drove off to the Hôtel de Ville (the town hall). Here the gendarmes did not shoot him for being without a BEF identity card, but told him he could not enter without it and directed him to the Boulevard Léon Gambetta, where the British headquarters might be found. Here Keller found the addressee of the letter he had been given at Dover, Colonel Holland, an ex-gunner and, like most of his generation, a veteran of the First World War.

Holland told Keller that he would receive his orders from GHQ at Hazebrouck, forty miles away. He added that, as the Germans had already bombed Calais and were likely to do so again, the sooner he unloaded his tanks the better. Keller replied that the ship carrying the tanks had not arrived and, until it did, his battalion had only pistols with which to engage the enemy. On returning to the docks, he found that his battalion had disembarked without being shot for lack of identity cards, so he deployed them among the dunes to the side of the harbour entrance.

At around 1600 hours the *City of Christchurch* docked and 3rd RTR were astonished to see her decks covered with wooden crates. These turned out to be full of four-gallon petrol cans. The tanks were in the holds below. The French dockers were already exhausted, and were chary of being cremated alive if a bomb hit the ship or even landed close by. Every time a siren sounded they bolted into shelters. The ship' crew were equally nervous and an armed guard had to be posted to stop them leaving in a body. The electricity supply to the cranes was frequently cut, and the ship's derricks had to be used instead. Fortunately some sappers had travelled out with 3rd RTR and thanks to them the unloading continued, albeit very slowly.

With the deck cargo removed, the tank crews could descend to the gloom of the holds to locate their vehicles. The lighting in the holds was feeble, and it did not help that the internal lights in some of the cruiser tanks were not working, despite being fresh from the factory. Before loading, the tanks had all been prepared for the sea voyage in accordance with the manuals. This involved the liberal application of mineral jelly to gun barrels, breech blocks and other metal working parts to protect them from the salt-laden air. The heaviest tanks, the cruisers, were at the bottom of the hold, light tanks on the level above and scout cars on the top level. The ammunition, spares and radio accessories had been distributed around the holds to a stowage plan that suited the ship's first mate, and without regard for ease of access. There was an acute shortage of cotton waste to clean off the mineral jelly, which consequently took hours.

To cap it all the .5-inch ammunition for the light tanks had been packed loose. Machine-gun ammunition has to be tightly held in the loops in the belt, otherwise the rounds fall out as the belt snakes up into the gun, causing stoppages. Loading is normally done by machine, forcing each round in, but there was no belt-loading machine on the ship. Loading belts by hand is a laborious process, very much second best, and the result is inevitably a rash of stoppages – inconvenient in action.

At 1700 hours that afternoon the adjutant general at GHQ, Lieutenant General Brownrigg, passing through Calais en route to Dover from Wimereux, ordered 3rd RTR to proceed *south-westwards* as soon as unloading was completed to join the 20th Guards Brigade in the defence of Boulogne. Six hours later a liaison officer brought orders from GHQ; 3rd RTR was to motor as soon as possible *south-eastwards* to Saint-Omer and Hazebrouck, and make contact with GHQ. During the night, Keller had received a signal from Brownrigg, sent from Dover, repeating the order for 3rd RTR to go to Boulogne. Keller debated with Holland which way he should take his battalion, and opted to obey the orders of the adjutant general, but send three light tanks off to Saint-Omer to see if the road was clear, while the rest of 3rd RTR headed for Coquelles, from where they could drive either to Boulogne or to Saint-Omer via Guines and Ardres.

Unloading the vehicles began in the early hours of 23 May. Each tank had to be hoisted out from the hold through the hatch and swung ashore. The ten Dingo armoured cars of the Reconnaissance Troop commanded by Lieutenant Morgan were out first. Sergeant Close was troop sergeant, and described the Dingo as 'one of the few vehicles I encountered (on our side) during the war which was ideal for the job it had to do'.[5] It is a biting comment on the poor design of British tanks and armoured vehicles throughout the Second World War, only put right with the advent of the Comet in late 1944. And Close was in a position to know. As the war progressed – he fought in France, the western desert, Greece and north-west Europe, from May 1940 right to the end in May 1945 – he had to bale out of eleven tanks destroyed by the enemy. The Dingo, less than five feet high and with a crew of two (driver and commander), open-topped, weighed 2.8 tons, could motor at 55mph forwards or backwards, and was armed with a Bren light machine gun.

The Reconnaissance Troop was the first away, in two groups of five Dingos each; one led by Lieutenant Morgan drove towards Gravelines up the coast, while Sergeant Close's group headed in a south-westerly direction to reconnoitre the area around Guines. As they left the battalion, 'men were sitting in the dunes painfully forcing rounds into ammunition belts, blistering their hands and breaking their nails'.[6]

After motoring for about five miles, Close spotted vehicles parked under some poplar trees. Scanning them with his binoculars, he saw a line of trucks and soldiers cooking over small fires. A few seconds later a couple of high-velocity shells screeched over his head from anti-tank guns sited to cover the troops at breakfast: the vehicles were German. Close told his driver to 'get out of it quick'. His driver backed, swung the Dingo off the road, expertly crossed the ditch at right-angles and bounced away over a field of half-grown crops. Two other Dingos, either hit or by bad driving, tipped over and ended upside down in the ditch with their wheels spinning; no one got out. Of the other Dingos there was no sign. Close's Dingo raced off pursued by streams of machine-gun bullets, until he encountered a shallow valley, which led in the right direction back the way he had come and offered cover from view and direct fire. With no radio, he drove back and reported to the CO at Coquelles that the light forces he had been sent to locate were far from light.

The CO was not best pleased at losing two, possibly four, of his Reconnaissance Troop, and told Close to follow his tank when the battalion moved off. By now the light tanks sent to reconnoitre the Saint-Omer road had returned without incident, so Keller sent the GHQ liaison officer back to Saint-Omer escorted by three light tanks. The liaison officer returned, his staff car riddled with bullet holes, having driven into a mass of German motorcyclists from which he was lucky to escape with a light wound. Of the light tanks there was no sign.

The nearest enemy, as far as Keller knew, were somewhere in the vicinity of Guines and Saint-Omer, and it was there that he decided to take his battalion. At about midday, led by the light tanks of B Squadron in lieu of the missing Dingos of the Reconnaissance Troop, 3rd RTR set off to engage the enemy. The battalion was deployed with C Squadron on the left of the road, B Squadron on the right and headquarters on the centre line down the road. In the scramble to unload its vehicles and get them battle-ready, the battalion had not netted in its wirelesses properly.

Between Coquelles and Guines, Sergeant Cornwell of B Squadron spotted vehicle movement ahead. The road was clogged with refugees fleeing north, and it was difficult to make out whether the vehicles were enemy or refugees. He tried to pass a message back that he was investigating a possible enemy contact, but failed to get through. Annoyed at his slow progress, and unaware of the reason, Keller sent his adjutant forward in his cruiser tank to ginger up the reconnaissance. Muzzle flashes pricked the hedgerows and the adjutant's tank brewed up. Cornwell looked round and saw the battalion withdrawing to better fire positions. From here it engaged the enemy to good effect. The cruisers with 2-pounder high-velocity guns were getting the better of the Germans, who were armed mainly with low-velocity guns firing HE, which had little effect on the cruisers' armour. Before long the Germans brought up anti-tank guns and artillery, and the boot was on the other foot. 3rd RTR learned for the first time a lesson British formations were to learn on many occasions, that, as already noted, armour on its own is unlikely to prevail against a combination of tanks, anti-tank guns and artillery such as the 1st Panzer Division was able to deploy. As Close moved his Dingo behind the CO's tank for shelter, a shell exploded on the turret jamming the gun, although the tank was still a runner. More of 3rd RTR's tanks were hit and reduced to flaming hulks, with ammunition cooking off inside. The intelligence officer of 3rd RTR, Lieutentant Ironside, moving with the headquarters, reported columns of German tanks as far as the eye could see. Keller withdrew his battalion by bounds to a spur of high ground south of Coquilles.

In the late afternoon a British staff car appeared in the wood where Keller had sited his tank. Out stepped an officer who introduced himself as Brigadier Nicholson. He had tried to contact Keller by wireless but had been told, 'Get off the air, I'm trying to fight a bloody battle.'[7] Nicholson said he commanded the 30th Brigade and had been sent from England to take command at Calais. He had with him the 2nd King's Royal Rifle Corps (KRRC) and 1st Rifle Brigade (RB), and was taking 3rd RTR and 1st QVR under command.[8] He ordered Keller to withdraw to Calais after dark, replenish with fuel and ammunition and concentrate in the Parc Saint-Pierre near the Hôtel de Ville. Sergeant Close was told to follow Nicholson back to town in his Dingo for the brigadier's use as an armoured battle taxi. There was room for only two people in the Dingo, so Close dropped his driver at the battalion concentration area, and after filling up with petrol and collecting ammunition for the Bren drove to brigade HQ in the Boulevard Léon Gambetta, which Colonel Holland had used as his headquarters.

Through no fault of its own, the 30th Brigade arrived without many of its weapons, and without much of its ammunition and equipment. The two infantry battalions were motor battalions intended to operate with the 1st Armoured Division, and their COs were exceptional officers with considerable battle experience. At 1800 hours on 21 May they had received orders to move, and by 2300 hours were loaded and motoring from Suffolk to Southampton. They had no idea where they were bound. As the battalions arrived, most of the maps were taken away from them and over-excited staff officers took charge of the vehicles. The COs were not allowed to arrange anything. Weapons and equipment

19. German parachute troops dropping on The Hague, Holland.

20. General von Rundstedt.

21. A German assault gun driving through Belgium on 29 May 1940. Equipped with a 75mm gun, it is an armoured self-propelled artillery piece designed to support infantry in a panzer division, not a tank.

22. German armour, including Mk III tanks, entering Sedan.

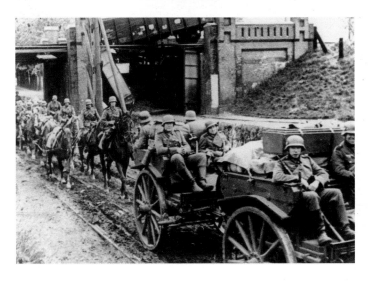

23. German horse-drawn artillery in Holland.

24. German troops and horse-drawn transport crossing a pontoon bridge over a Belgian river on 11 May 1940.

25. British carriers withdrawing from Louvain, 14 May 1940.

26. German panzer-grenadiers assaulting a farmhouse having dismounted from their half-tracks. This is very likely to be a posed propaganda photograph.

27. A British sapper takes cover round the side of a building while blowing a bridge in Louvain before retreating.

28. A rubber boat camouflaged with a bush lands infantrymen after crossing a river in Belgium. The horse has waded across with them. The German Army used vast numbers of horses throughout the Second World War.

29. Two German Mk IV tanks with short-barrelled 75mm guns wading a river in Belgium.

30. *Above*. Contrasting styles of transport in the German Army: a mounted German officer, possibly artillery or infantry, watches German armour moving up a road in Belgium.

31. *Above, right*. German troops and transport crossing a pontoon bridge over a canal near Nieuport in Belgium. German formations were well equipped with these bridges, and their engineers were adept at throwing them across water obstacles quickly.

32. *Right*. A battery of French 75mm guns of pre-1914 vintage with solid wheels deployed under token efforts to camouflage them.

33. A German half-track towing an 88mm gun. Originally designed as an anti-aircraft gun, the 88 first demonstrated its devastating effect on armour in 1940; a reputation which endured for the whole of the Second World War.

34. Major General Rommel, in cap with map board on his knees, and his staff of the 7th Panzer Division plotting the next move during the armoured advance through northern France.

needed by men on the personnel ships were loaded on the vehicle ships, and everything was loaded in a muddle. The confusion caused by officious embarkation staff was to lead to difficulties the following day when the battalions disembarked at Calais with the enemy about three miles away. Eventually with vehicles loaded in the *Kohistan* and *City of Canterbury*, and men, including brigade headquarters, in the *Royal Daffodil* and *Archangel*, the ships sailed in convoy from Southampton to Dover. Here they joined up with *Autocarrier* carrying the 229th Anti-Tank Battery and sailed for Calais. The *Autocarrier* was also loaded with six wireless trucks intended for another unit, so the anti-tank battery had to leave four of its twelve guns on the dockside; they never arrived at Calais. There was no field or medium artillery with the brigade.

By the time the 30th Brigade convoy docked at Calais on the afternoon of 23 May, the 1st Panzer Division was closing in on the town. Leading elements had reached but not yet taken Le Colombier, and had driven 3rd RTR almost back to Coquelles. Unbeknown to Nicholson, the 1st Panzer Division was ordered not to push on towards Calais, but to bypass it and head for Dunkirk, leaving the 10th Panzer Division to take Calais. The 10th Panzer Division had actually been pulled out of Guderian's XIX Panzer Corps to refit, leaving him with two divisions: the 1st Panzer Division which, in Guderian's opinion, should make short work of such a lightly defended town as Calais before heading off for Dunkirk; and the 2nd Panzer Division already attacking at Boulogne. But when the British unexpectedly reinforced Calais, the 10th Panzer Division was hastily hauled back from refitting to deal with this new threat, while the 1st Panzer Division was told to make straight for Gravelines and Dunkirk.

But, although Nicholson was not privy to this reasoning at high level in the German camp, he was absolutely clear that there was no question of moving to Boulogne or to Saint-Omer. His most urgent task was to defend Calais. He ordered the 1st RB to hold the outer ramparts on the east side of town, and the 2nd KRRC to do the same on the west side. Advanced posts of the Queen Victoria's Rifles and anti-aircraft units were deployed forward of the ramparts. Having just given his orders, Nicholson was instructed by the War Office to take some 350,000 rations for the BEF to Dunkirk, and was told that this task was to be treated as 'over-riding all other considerations'.[9] Calais contained one of the biggest ration dumps in France, and these orders came direct from General Ironside, the CIGS. Although, as related in Chapter 5, Gort did not made his decision to withdraw through Ypres to Dunkirk until 25 May (two days hence), Ironside on assessing the situation had come to the conclusion that the BEF might have to resort to retreating in this direction. If the ration convoy was to get through it had to go as soon as possible

with tanks and carriers to clear the way before the 1st Panzer Division
blocked the Calais–Dunkirk road at Marck.

Nicholson took some infantry from the perimeter defence and sent
them to picket the first part of the road to Dunkirk twenty miles away,
while the convoy was being formed. A patrol of one cruiser and three
light tanks of B Squadron, 3rd RTR, under Major Reeves was sent ahead
of the infantry. The 10th Panzer Division had by now come up from the
south, occupied the high ground overlooking Calais and started shelling
the town.

It took hours to load the rations into ten 10-ton trucks. As this was
being done, the ships that had transported the 30th Brigade vehicles
were being unloaded. This also took a very long time. Whenever shelling
started up, the stevedores, who were already exhausted after working
non-stop for thirty-six hours, took cover.

Meanwhile since midnight on 23/24 May, a composite company of the
Rifle Brigade under Major Hamilton-Russell had sat in its trucks waiting
for news of Major Reeves's reconnaissance. By 0400 hours Reeves had not
returned, and the convoy moved off. Reeves's patrol had an amazing
adventure. Not far out of Calais they lost wireless contact with Keller
and the tanks that were to follow up. They continued through three
unguarded roadblocks set up by the 1st Panzer Division and through
numerous other positions lightly held by Germans, who thought they
were their own tanks. The patrol reached Gravelines without a scratch.
They fought in the town the next morning, knocking out five German
tanks and two troop carriers.

Hamilton-Russell's force, which was accompanied by Nicholson, a
curious decision, moved with five tanks leading, followed by three
carriers, three platoons in trucks, the ration trucks and two platoons
bringing up the rear. About three miles east of Calais, between Le Beau
Marais and Marck, the column ran into a strong German roadblock with
anti-tank guns sited among the houses. The British tanks were forced to
stop, and although the platoons of the Rifle Brigade managed to outflank
the Germans it was clear by daybreak that the convoy and escorts would
be cut off if they did not pull back. Hamilton-Russell reluctantly ordered
a withdrawal, leaving two dead and taking several wounded with him.
3rd RTR was reduced to nine cruisers and twelve light tanks.

By now Calais was under heavy shellfire, for at dawn on 24 May the
artillery and mortar preparation for the 10th Panzer Division's attack on
Calais from the west started. Guderian had told Major General Schaal,
commanding the 10th, to advance carefully, so as to avoid excessive
casualties. He had ordered heavy artillery units up from Boulogne in
support. It should be borne in mind that only three days had elapsed

since the British counter-stroke at Arras that had caused such dispropor-
tionate dismay within the German high command. Kleist's staff were still
talking about 'the crisis at Arras' late on 23 May.

In Calais docks the *Kohistan* (brigade headquarters and KRRC vehicles
and stores) had been unloaded by 0400 hours on 24 May, but the *City of
Canterbury* (1st RB vehicles and stores) took much longer. At 0730 hours,
a sea transport officer, claiming that he had Nicholson's permission, gave
orders that the latter's holds were to be closed, although the ship was
still full of vehicles and ammunition. Wounded were unloaded from a
hospital train in the docks and placed in their stretchers on top of the
hatches, under which still sat most of the Rifle Brigade's vehicles and
ammunition. The *City of Canterbury* and other ships then sailed, taking
the stevedores and other non-fighting troops back to England.

It is possible that Nicholson had given permission for unloading to
stop, for early that morning, 24 May, he had been told by the War
Office that evacuation had been agreed 'in principle'. Although fighting
personnel had to stay to cover the final evacuation, non-fighting personnel had to begin embarking at once. It therefore made sense not to
unload equipment that would subsequently have to be restowed or more
probably abandoned. But, as the Official History comments, 'it was
unfortunate that the fighting troops were thus deprived of weapons and
equipment which they sorely needed'.[10]

During the afternoon of 24 May, the Germans attacked Calais on three
sides, using all of 10th Panzer Division's rifle battalions and a battalion
of tanks supported by 150mm guns. The French garrison of Fort Nieulay
west of Calais surrendered, along with a small detachment of the Queen
Victoria's Rifles which had taken refuge in the fort. The French Marines
in Fort Lapin disabled their coastal guns and escaped. By now the
surviving Queen Victoria's Rifles had been distributed between the two
regular battalions and the QVR ceased to function as a separate battalion.
In the south, the Germans made some gains in the town and could not
be dislodged. Ammunition on the ramparts was running short, and all
but two of the 229th Battery's anti-tank guns had been put out of action.
But the Germans were by no means having it all their own way, and the
entry in the 10th Panzer Division war diary for 1600 hours on 24 May
reflects this: 'Enemy resistance from scarcely perceptible positions was
however so strong that it was only possible to achieve quite local success.'
And three hours later XIX Panzer Corps headquarters was told that a
third of the German equipment, vehicles and personnel and a 'good half
of the tanks' were casualties; the troops were 'tired out'.[11]

Brigadier Nicholson was clear that he could not hold the outer perimeter for much longer, for he had no reserve with which to plug gaps

or to counter penetration. He received another message from the War Office confirming the decision to evacuate, but saying that final pull-out of the fighting troops was not to take place until 0700 hours the next day, 25 May. Responding to this order, Nicholson withdrew his infantry to the line of the Boulevard Léon Gambetta and Marck Canal. After more fighting, he ordered a further withdrawal, to take place at 2100 hours, to the old town and the area to the east enclosed by the outer ramparts. The weak points in this defence line were the bridges. The French had not prepared them for demolition, and the British had no explosives with them. Only two out of the eight anti-tank guns remained.

With the onset of darkness, the German assault petered out – the usual form. But as the British troops were withdrawing Brigadier Nicholson received a message from the CIGS in Whitehall telling him that the French commander in the north 'forbids evacuation'. By moving his headquarters from the Boulevard Léon Gambetta to underneath the Gare Maritime, Nicholson lost the use of the telephone cable to London. He was visited in his new headquarters at 2323 hours by Vice Admiral Sir James Somerville, who had just landed from the destroyer *Wolfhound*. Somerville had been commanding a destroyer force engaging enemy batteries all day, as well as battling with the Luftwaffe. He handed Nicholson a message which read: 'In spite of policy of evacuation given you this morning, fact that British forces in your area now under Fagalde who has ordered no, repeat no, evacuation, means that you must comply for sake of Allied solidarity.' Nicholson's role, he was told, was to hold on, and as the harbour 'was now of no importance to the BEF' he was to select a position in which to fight to the end. Ammunition was being sent, but no reinforcements. He was also told that a brigade of the 48th Division was marching to his assistance that morning. This information was nonsense: the 48th Division was never told to send a brigade to Calais, as it was fully engaged elsewhere.[12] Had it attempted to break through the panzer divisions between the main body of the BEF and Calais it would have been destroyed. The War Office order forbidding evacuation and talking nonsense about a brigade marching to Nicholson's relief reveals a state of unreality in Whitehall about the actual situation almost on a par with that pervading Paris. According to Somerville, Nicholson took the news in good heart and, although he appeared to be tired, was 'in no way windy'.

The appointment of General Fagalde to command troops in the three Channel ports is covered in Chapter 9. He had forbidden evacuation from Calais, as well as placing the French commander there under British command. The French commander in question had complained about the British intention to leave. Since the British risked losing more troops of far greater value than the French stationed in Calais, it is questionable that Fagalde's order would have been heeded had Churchill not been feeling aggrieved by Reynaud's complaint about the British withdrawing from Arras. Believing that British honour was at stake, Churchill supported the stay-and-fight order. This is hard to justify in the light of hindsight, given that the mess the BEF found itself in was entirely of French making. But at the time it made complete sense to Churchill: almost anything that would buttress the sagging morale of the French would have seemed absolutely crucial and had to be seized upon if they were not to throw in the towel and abandon the war. However, the phrase 'for sake of Allied solidarity' he thought 'very lukewarm', saying 'this is no way to encourage men to fight to the end'.

One unfortunate outcome of the earlier instruction to evacuate the British was the loss of more of 3rd RTR's tanks. Orders had been passed to the battalion that nothing of value was to fall into enemy hands. It started burning its tanks and ammunition near the Gare Maritime, to the accompaniment of black pillars of smoke and loud explosions. By the time it was ordered to stop, five more cruiser tanks had gone up in smoke, leaving only nine.

Faced with the stark stay-and-fight order, it is arguable that Nicholson should have concentrated immediately behind the water barrier of canals and basins that surrounded the old town. But he decided to make the enemy pay for every inch of ground, and it is easy to be critical six decades later when one is not weighed down by responsibility and fatigue. Noting that the Germans, as usual, had not followed up his withdrawal during the night, he sent mobile patrols into the town, and finding it clear he ordered some of his troops forward. But at daylight on 25 May the 10th Panzer Division resumed the assault with its customary ferocity, and by 0800 hours the swastika was flying over the town hall. A little later the mayor walked forward under escort to discuss surrender terms. Nicholson detained him and sent the escort back.

In the Rifle Brigade's sector the Germans had penetrated at several points. Counter-attacks by platoons, all that could be spared, failed with heavy losses. The brigade lost five officers and two platoon sergeant majors killed in one hour.[13] The CO, Lieutenant Colonel Hoskyns, was mortally wounded.

The KRRC found that the town hall afforded the Germans excellent observation over their sector and they took advantage of it to shell the approaches to the forward houses held by the battalion. The KRRC sector included three bridges into the old town from the new, and guarding these took three companies. Their task was not made easier by the hordes of refugees, including 1,000 or more unarmed French and Belgian soldiers. These added to the chaos by spreading rumours of fifth columnists. Although there were undoubtedly some fifth columnists in Calais (as elsewhere), they, like snipers, were not so pervasive as so often reported. As Lieutenant Davies Scourfield, a platoon commander in B Company, 2nd KRRC, discovered, the 'snipers' were more often than not single riflemen who had infiltrated into forward positions and climbed up on to the roofs of tall buildings. It is common in war for the so-called 'sniper' to be just a lone rifleman, not a specialist equipped with a high-performance rifle fitted with sophisticated optics.

The KRRC's fourth company was sited forward of the Citadel, itself garrisoned by around 200 French soldiers, two 75mm guns and a detachment of Royal Marines. Here the commander of French troops in Calais, Commandant (Major) Le Tellier, had his headquarters. Nicholson moved his forward brigade headquarters into the Citadel to enable him to keep in touch with Le Tellier. The Citadel was an immensely strong fort built by Vauban in 1680, and despite its age was able to withstand considerable battering even from the modern medium guns of 1940.

Sergeant Close benefited from the move to the Citadel. Nicholson told him that he had no further use for the Dingo, nor did Lieutenant Colonel Keller, so he could now return to England. Close knew nothing of the 'fight on' message, a good indication that few heard it, or subsequent such messages, because as the brigade commander's driver he would have been one of the first to learn about it, if only by overhearing conversations. He drove to the Gare Maritime, and before leaving the Dingo took a grenade from the box of six on the vehicle, pulled the pin and slipped it under the bonnet where it exploded. Arriving at the docks he saw a small naval vessel about to leave, and rushed down the gangplank just before it was pulled inboard. To the end of his life, Close never knew the name of the vessel or what she was doing there. But she might have been carrying a message for the naval detachment at the Gare Maritime. Once she was clear of the smoke in the harbour, Close could see the flashes of German batteries on the ridge above Coquelles shelling Calais. Offshore destroyers were engaging the enemy batteries, and zigzagging to avoid the Stukas. Ships would be engulfed in spray and columns of water and would emerge with pom-poms blazing at the enemy aircraft. Arriving at Dover, he was shoved on to a train for Aldershot, still wearing the revolver he had never drawn.

At about 1400 hours on 25 May Nicholson received a wireless message from the Secretary of State for War in London, Anthony Eden, who had served in the KRRC in the First World War. It had been generated by Churchill, who had been so unimpressed by the term 'Allied solidarity' in the earlier message. This one read:

Defence of Calais to the utmost is of the highest importance to our country as symbolising our continuing cooperation with France. The eyes of the Empire are upon the defence of Calais, and HM Government are confident you and your gallant regiments will perform an exploit worthy of the British name.[14]

The message was copied to unit headquarters, but it is doubtful that it was sent further forward. Indeed it may not even have got to some unit headquarters. Lieutenant Ironside, intelligence officer at 3rd RTR headquarters, did not know of it at the time. Even if it had been distributed down the chain of command, the impact on the fighting troops would have been minimal. In battle such exhortations usually have a derisory effect; soldiers fight for each other, their 'mates', not for some higher cause, however worthy.

An hour later, the German shelling stopped, and an officer approached with a flag of truce, accompanied by a French captain and a Belgian soldier. The German officer was taken to Nicholson and belligerently demanded surrender, threatening that the garrison would be given a pounding if it did not immediately lay down its arms. Nicholson's reply was entered in the war diary of the 10th Panzer Division, where it was recorded in English:

1. The answer is no as it is the British Army's duty to fight as well as it is the German's.
2. The French captain and the Belgian soldier having not been blindfolded cannot be sent back. The Allied Commander gives his word that they will be put under guard and will not be allowed to fight against the Germans.[15]

Just before sending in the flag of truce, the Germans dropped leaflets giving the garrison one hour to surrender. Along with many others, Lieutenant Davies Scourfield's platoon used this hour to bring up food and ammunition. The attack was not renewed until 1830 hours, starting with a massive artillery programme thickened up by mortar fire. The bridges were attacked at 1900 hours. At two of them the leading German tanks were knocked out on the bridges themselves, blocking access; at the third a tank got across, but was forced back by a vigorous counter-attack by the KRRC. At dusk the German assaults died away, because, according to the 10th Panzer Division war diary, 'the Infantry Brigade Commander considers further attacks pointless, as the enemy resistance is not yet crushed and there is not enough time before the fall of darkness'.[16]

During the night the Royal Navy brought in more ammunition and evacuated some of the wounded. Food was not a problem, as there was a huge stock of undelivered rations. Also during that night a boat brought in a message from the War Office:

> Every hour you continue to exist is of greatest help to the BEF. Government has therefore decided you must continue to fight. Have great admiration for your splendid stand.[17]

Few of the defenders would have seen this message. The KRRC and Rifle Brigade fought on because they were the best-trained battalions in the British Army. As the first of the motor battalions they had been treated as 'experimental' since 1937, had been given every opportunity to train and were supplied with the means to do so – unlike the rest of the BEF. With the cohesion that follows good training, these well-led battalions did not need pronouncements from on high to persuade them to do their duty. The only people who mattered, other than their families, were those around them. This sustained them in the darkest moments.

The men of 3rd RTR also gave the enemy a bloody nose during the battle. They claimed six enemy tanks knocked out, and their light tanks had been invaluable in supporting the Rifle Brigade. With very little scope for further fighting, Keller decided to break out of Calais. He ordered his three surviving cruisers to make their way along the beach to Gravelines, and followed in a light tank. He and one of his squadron commanders, Major Simpson, were the only ones to reach their destination. Along the way the 3rd RTR tanks were engaged by the Germans, who had spotted them from the road running parallel to the beach, and others ran out of fuel. Keller's tank broke down. He completed the journey on foot, collecting a crew that had baled out of another tank. On reaching the Aa river at Gravelines, the party found the Germans holding the port, and although Keller and Simpson managed to swim the wide, fast-flowing river, the others refused to do so. On the morning of 26 May, Keller and Simpson walked into Petit Fort Philippe held by the French, were sent to Dunkirk and thence taken to Dover in a trawler. As they passed Calais they could see the cruiser *Galatea* firing into the town.

At 0700 hours the attacks on Calais resumed, and, assisted by a mass Stuka attack at 0930 hours, the Germans broke through on the west and isolated the Citadel. Lieutenant Colonel Miller reorganized his battalion into a tighter perimeter in the dock area. Around 1600 hours the Germans burst into the Citadel and ran into Nicholson, who had come up from the cellar. He was surrounded and had to surrender. It was a bitter moment. He was to die in prison camp, tortured by totally unjustified feelings that he could have done better.

The Rifle Brigade was driven back to the area of the Gare Maritime, fighting on until it ran out of ammunition, with many dead and even more wounded. Lieutenant Davies Scourfield, having temporarily taken command of his company during his commander's absence at battalion headquarters, walked back to where his platoon was sited to find the whole place a shambles with bodies lying everywhere. As he moved around, he 'walked straight into a German machine gun'. He was hit in the arm and then in the ribs, and finally knocked senseless by a grazing round on the side of his helmet. He came round lying in a gutter, hearing Germans driving up and down the street shouting, 'Come out, Tommies! It's all finished.' But it seemed it was not over, as he heard shots being fired at the Germans. He passed out again to find a German standing over him with a knife in his hand, who proceeded to cut away Davies Scourfield's clothing and applied both the Briton's field dressing and his own.

The last organized resistance was by a company of the Queen Victoria's Rifles, cornered by tanks and infantry. It surrendered at 1700 hours.

Lieutenant Colonel Miller of the KRRC ordered his men to split up, go into hiding and escape after dark. Nearly all were rounded up, and the only ones to escape were some wounded and unwounded men who got away in the Royal Navy yacht *Conidaw*. She had come in with ammunition and had been lying grounded on the mud by the low tide most of the afternoon. While attempts were being made to refloat her, two bombs dropped near by and the blast wave floated her off. Sergeant Mitchell of the Royal Marines and a small party of Marines and soldiers who had been cut off from their units, a total of 165 in all, waded out to her and were taken off. Sergeant East RM, who had similarly been cut off, joined up with a party of others evading capture and hid from the Germans under the jetty. As a small motor yacht, the *Gulvar*, passed close inshore that night looking for survivors, East signalled with a torch. The *Gulvar*'s captain, concerned about German guns on the jetty, shouted through his loud hailer that he could not stop but would make one close pass and the men would have to swim for it. Four officers and forty-seven Marines and soldiers, including East, made it to the yacht.

Lieutenant Ironside, along with Captain Moss the adjutant and some of 3rd RTR headquarters, tried making their way on foot to Dunkirk along the beach. Their mental alertness was dulled by exhaustion. At daybreak, instead of finding somewhere to lie up for the day, they kept going and walked straight into a German armoured car. Ironside and Moss stood looking across at the white cliffs of Dover lit up by the early-morning sun. The armoured-car commander, who had been to Oxford and spoke perfect English, said, 'I wonder when you'll see those again.' Ironside replied, 'I suppose you'll have a go at getting over there next.' 'Oh no, our next task is Russia.' In retrospect that was an extraordinary remark to make, bearing in mind that another year was to pass before Hitler invaded the Soviet Union.

Most of the Calais garrison spent the rest of the war, another five years, in prison camps. Some were to escape later. Captain Williams, the adjutant of the KRRC, and three staff officers from brigade headquarters slipped away from the prisoner column as it marched through France, as did several others. Only Williams, a fluent French-speaker, and the staff officers made it back to England. Airey Neave, who fought at Calais as a second lieutenant in the 2nd Searchlight Battery, escaped from Colditz Castle in January 1942, arriving in England four months later.

It was Churchill who had decided to order the garrison to fight on to the end. It is clear from his own account that the option to evacuate was still open for discussion in Whitehall until 2100 hours on the evening of 26 May, some five hours after Nicholson's surrender, which was unknown to Churchill at the time. In the belief that the garrison was still resisting, a sortie was made by the RAF on the morning of 27 May to drop water and ammunition, all of it into German hands, for the loss of three aircraft out of twenty-one. Having made the decision, Churchill wrote later, 'I could not help feeling physically sick as we afterwards sat silent at the table.'[18]

Opinions are at variance over whether the epic stand at Calais contributed to the escape of the BEF at Dunkirk. Churchill certainly thought so, writing after the war:

> Calais was the crux. Many other causes might have prevented the deliverance of Dunkirk, but it is certain that the three days gained by the defence of Calais enabled the Gravelines waterline to be held, and that without this, even in spite of Hitler's vacillations and Rundstedt's orders, all would have been cut off and lost.[19]

Those who fought at Calais and spent five years as prisoners of war drew much solace from this. Yet Guderian, again writing after the war, says that the defence of Calais made no difference to the effort he put into the attack on Dunkirk. That is an exaggeration. For what is beyond question is that the 30th Brigade at Calais tied up the 10th Panzer Division for three days, inflicted large casualties on the division's infantry and diverted all Guderian's heavy artillery from his main effort, which was to cut off the BEF heading for Dunkirk. If that is not 'making a difference', one has to ask what is. When added to the delay imposed on the 2nd Panzer Division at Boulogne, one has to concede that the holding up of two panzer divisions, two-thirds of Guderian's XIX Panzer Corps, by two under-strength brigades (one without any armour and one with only one battalion of armour) was no mean feat.

But did the 30th Brigade have to fight to the bitter end to achieve this aim, if indeed that was the aim seen for them at the time? They could have been evacuated on the night of 25/26 May, as the 20th Guards Brigade had been from Boulogne earlier, and the ultimate effect on the 10th Panzer Division would have been little different. Given the customary German supineness at night, many, if not most, of the brigade could have been got away. Was the purpose of sending the 30th Brigade to Calais as clear cut in minds in Whitehall as Churchill implied – that is, to slow down the German armour advancing on Dunkirk? The rain of contradictory orders that descended on Nicholson's head before and after his arrival at Calais suggests not; and that the reason for despatching the brigade had not been properly thought through (understandable in the chaos of the moment). It leads one to suspect that Churchill is justifying the decision he took. One could argue that writing after the war (the second volume of his war memoirs was published in 1949) Churchill realized that the 'Allied solidarity' argument would not wash. By then his British readers would have been well aware that the 'allies' in question had been almost entirely responsible for the plight in which the BEF found itself in May and June 1940, and they would also have been familiar with the subsequent woeful performance by the French that led to their capitulation. In the vernacular of the time, the French had made a horlicks of it, and although there was sympathy for the French people, there was none for their leaders, who had mismanaged the campaign and signed an armistice with the Germans. If this was Churchill's reasoning, the only line left to him to take was that the defence of Calais had delayed the German armour advancing on Dunkirk. It certainly had, but, for the reasons given above, the 30th Brigade could have done that *and* been evacuated. One is left with the view that maintaining Allied solidarity was the reason that the brigade was abandoned to its fate – a decision which may have seemed right at the time, but which would not appear so in the light of subsequent events.

7

THE WITHDRAWAL:

II CORPS ON THE EASTERN FLANK

Having told the story of Boulogne and Calais, and thereby gone ahead of the narrative of the main body of the BEF, it is time to turn the clock back to the evening of 25 May. Gort's instructions to his corps commanders that evening included orders to Adam to relinquish command of III Corps and prepare a defensive perimeter around Dunkirk; and to Brooke to build up a defensive line along the line of the Ypres–Comines Canal, extending it northwards along the Yser Canal to the River Yser. With this as a shield, the BEF would withdraw to Dunkirk, starting with I Corps. For this task, Brooke was allocated the 5th and 50th Divisions in addition to his own 3rd and 4th Divisions, and as the fighting withdrawal progressed he would take other formations under command as required.

The 5th Division was ordered to move to the Ypres–Comines line that evening. Franklyn's division was only two brigades strong, one being detached in Norway, so Brooke told him to take under command the 143rd Brigade that had already been sent to the Ypres–Comines Line. By midday on 26 May the 5th Division started digging in. The 50th Division had to disengage its 151st Brigade from the Canal Line first, and this, followed by problems with traffic congestion, resulted in the division arriving at Ypres on 27 May to extend the line to the north. Until its arrival, the section of front was held by the French 2nd DLM, which remained under II Corps command for the time being.

Brooke's task would demand some complex manoeuvring. First he had to form his eastwards-facing shield and protect the BEF against the assaults of two or more enemy corps. All the while, as the BEF withdrew, he had to sidestep his formations progressively northwards. North-west of his 'shield', in succession he had to create three south-facing defensive layback positions, through which formations could withdraw as they peeled away from the right flank of the defence. The first layback line would be along the north bank of the Lys. The second was planned to be along the line Poperinghe–Ypres, although this might be changed if circumstances demanded. The third would be the Yser river, and Brooke's

II Corps would withdraw through this layback to the Dunkirk perimeter, having shielded the BEF from Bock's Army Group B throughout.

Although Montgomery and others subsequently criticized the perform-ance of the 1940 BEF, citing its lack of training for modern war and other inadequacies in both skill and equipment, most of the blame for these deficiencies can be laid at the door of the politicians, as is neatly summed up in the quotation at the head of Chapter 1. In his memoirs, Mont-gomery wrote: 'the campaign in France and Flanders in 1940 was lost in Whitehall in the years before it ever began, and this cannot be stated too clearly or too often. One might add after Whitehall the words "and in Paris".'[1] What one cannot belittle is the steadfastness of the soldiers of the BEF, their discipline and morale under the most testing circum-stances – of retreat, uncertainty and the ever present scourge of the Luftwaffe. Of course there were cases of ill discipline, of men losing their nerve, and indeed of cowardice, but these were the exception. The BEF was fortunate in many of its senior commanders. They had been tem-pered in the fires and shocks of the First World War, and most, especially Brooke, Alexander, Montgomery and the much maligned Gort, remained calm in the face of the utmost danger, and their skilful handling of the withdrawal is testimony to their professionalism. Their performance shines forth compared with that of their allies, many of whose command-ers were prone to breaking down in tears at stressful moments.

Second Lieutenant Martin's platoon of Cheshires were amazed when they were told that they were going to Dunkirk to be evacuated, as they thought they were 'doing all right' and could not see the reason for it. The performance of the BEF also says much about the leadership at junior level. In any army, the kind of discipline required is different from that required in the navy, where, as Captain White of the 1st/6th East Surreys wrote, 'they are all in the same ship, and when father says turn, they all turn. In the army on a dark and dreary night, they can hide behind boulders, or take Private Bloggins to the Regimental Aid Post and disappear.'

High morale and discipline is needed to withstand the shocks and surprises of war, including last-minute changes of orders and unpredict-ability. Lieutenant Robin Dunn of the 7th Field Regiment spent most of 26 May in the OP, and at 1900 hours handed over to another officer, his mind dwelling on thoughts of dinner and bed on return to his troop in their gun position. As he arrived he was told to report to regimental headquarters for the commanding officer's conference. Here he found all the troop commanders of the regiment with all battery commanders. The CO walked in with a 1/250,000 map of France, put it up against the wall, turned to the assembled officers and said; 'Gentlemen, the

Commander-in-Chief has decided that the BEF's position is untenable. We are to move to the coast and re-embark for England. Personnel only can be moved. All equipment is to be rendered useless and left.' There was more in the same vein. The officers listened in horror. It was impossible to believe that what the CO had said could be true. He continued, 'The Belgians have bolted on our left. The French counter-attack to close the gap has failed.' Looking round at faces he knew so well, Dunn saw that they all had the same air of bewildered depression. He thought of all their high hopes, their training, their confidence in their men.

The CO continued addressing them: 'Robin, you will take your troop back at once to beyond Wambrechies and will remain in action there to cover the withdrawal. John, you will stay in action here under command 8th Infantry Brigade. You will all remain in action until the last possible moment, when you will disable your guns and get away as best you can. On your way back you will shoot anyone on sight who tries to stop you.' Dunn drove back to his troop, his mind in a turmoil. After warning his troop to expect a move, he ate dinner. When the troop was ready, he told them what was to happen and why. There was dead silence for about a minute, before a gunner stepped forward and asked, 'It's not our fault, sir, is it?' Dunn reassured him that it was not their fault, but as he thought it over, he concluded that that made it worse. It was not their fault, but they had to go.

Just as he was about to give the order 'cease firing', which would bring the guns out of action, an order came down the telephone, 'Stand fast. No move until further orders.' The men slept in the vehicles, Dunn by the telephone.

The next day, Dunn was summoned again to regimental headquarters. He learned that the retreat was to be an orderly rearguard action, not a race to the sea as they had originally been told. A bridgehead was to be formed round Dunkirk, at first of substantial size but becoming progressively smaller. The 3rd Division was to hold the northern part of the Ypres Canal, to the north of Ypres. A mobile force consisting of some anti-tank guns, machine guns and two gunner troops was to go back to this line. The rest of the division was to move that night. In half an hour the two troops were limbered up and away.

Dunn's troop moved north through Messines and along the Messines Ridge. Everywhere there were war cemeteries and memorials to the 'war to end all wars'. And there they were doing the same thing against the same people over the same ground, only twenty-five years later. As he drove along the ridge, Dunn thought of the refugees, the desolate homes, the ruined towns and the wounded, and wondered how to make sure that twenty-five years hence his son would not drive along the Messines

Ridge leading his troop into action in the same area against the same enemy.

His daydreaming was cut short by shelling as they drove through Wytschaete. British batteries were firing on the left of the road, which was full of infantry all looking east. They all seemed very tired and were caked with dust and sweat. They waved as the guns drove by.

Dunn had been ordered to go via Messines, Wytschaete and Saint-Eloi. Approaching Saint-Eloi, he found some infantry, so he halted and spoke to an officer. The infantry was from the 1st Division, which was holding the canal south of Ypres. The Belgians had retreated more quickly than expected, and contact had been made with the enemy, who were in Ypres and over the canal at Hazebrouck, although only in small numbers. Dunn told the officer where he wanted to go, and the officer laughed, saying that they had just sent a patrol there, and there's the answer: he pointed at a tall German smoking a cigarette. Apparently this soldier had been part of a machine-gun detachment. He looked very like a guardsman, tall, slim, holding himself well. He seemed tired but fit, burned a good colour by the sun.

Dunn looked at his map to find a detour. At that moment two traffic-control policemen arrived to mark the route for the main body of the 3rd Division. He told them what the position was, and offered to take them with him. Telling the guns to swing round in a conveniently wide area formed by a crossroads, he set off to retrace his steps. As the last of his ammunition trucks pulled clear, four shells fell on the crossroads, followed by four more.

He stopped in Wytschaete, went into the headquarters of a medium regiment in action there and sent a message to headquarters 3rd Division via I and II Corps to say that their route via Saint-Eloi was blocked, and suggested an alternative. He asked if anyone knew what was happening north of Ypres, as he did not want to drive into the front line again. No one seemed to know, but the impression was that the Germans were some way beyond the canal, so he drove on through Dickebusch back on to the original route. There were some new shell holes all round, but his troop got through without a round falling on them, and finally arrived in their allotted area. There, they encountered some RASC men, due to embark that night, who gave them 500,000 cigarettes they could not carry.

When the 5th Division arrived on the Ypres–Comines Line (taking under command 143rd, and with its own 13th and 17th Brigades), it found that the eight-mile-long canal was disused, dry except for some mud, and in most places a poor obstacle, although better than nothing at all in this flat landscape. A railway line ran east of the canal, for most of the way on a low embankment, giving the enemy a covered approach. There were numerous houses in the vicinity of the canal, some grouped into small hamlets, all packed with refugees who refused to budge. Three miles west of the canal lay the Messines Ridge, for which so much blood had been expended in the First World War. The ridge was the vital ground in this sector.

The 5th Division had enjoyed less than twenty-four hours of rest after their withdrawal from Arras, and, dog-tired though the soldiers were, there was not much sleep to be had sitting crammed in the jolting trucks that transported them to the position. Arriving from about 1000 hours onwards, the division deployed with the 17th Brigade on the left, in an area of low hills and woods, forward of the canal and behind the railway line which here ran about a mile to the east of the canal. The 2nd Royal Scots held Hill 60, that feature of ill fame in the First World War. The 6th Seaforths were posted behind the Zillebeke Lake a mile south of Ypres, and with an open flank within sight of the town. In the centre, the 13th Brigade held a front of two miles from inclusive Hollebeke to exclusive Houthem, with on the left the 2nd Cameronians and on the right 2nd Royal Inniskilling Fusiliers. The 143rd Brigade, originally responsible for the whole sector, concertinaed into its right to hold slightly less than three miles of the canal, with all three battalions forward – from left to right the 1st/7th Royal Warwicks, 8th Royal Warwicks, and 1st Oxfordshire and Buckinghamshire Light Infantry. Facing these three British brigades were three German infantry divisions – from north to south the 18th, 31st and 61st.

While Lieutenant Colonel Lumsden's 12th Lancers screened Ypres until the 50th Division arrived to take up its positions to the north of the town, what became known as the Battle of Wytschaete roared into life. Beginning on 25 May and continuing until the 28th, it was the toughest engagement Brooke faced in his shielding of the BEF's withdrawal. As the battle progressed, Brooke reinforced the 5th Division with the 13th/ 18th Hussars and three battalions from the 1st Division (3rd Grenadier Guards, 2nd North Staffordshires and 2nd Sherwood Foresters – one from each of Alexander's brigades, and with his happy co-operation). Alexander had sent them back to the Lys to form a layback for his own division's withdrawal. When Brooke asked for them, Barker transferred them to II Corps.

Brooke took the two machine-gun battalions covering the south bank of the Lys (1st/7th Middlesex and 6th Black Watch) and moved them to reinforce the 9th Manchesters, the 5th Division's own machine-gun battalion. The 5th Division was well served by artillery, having its own three field regiments, as well as one field regiment from the 48th

Division, and one from I Corps. In addition the guns of I and II Corps' four medium regiments were particularly effective in breaking up German attacks. In thirty-six hours these medium regiments fired 5,000 rounds, a rate of fire not to be overtaken by British artillery until the Battle of Alamein two and a half years later.

During 26 May, enemy probing patrols became more aggressive across the whole Ypres–Comines Line (see map pp. 180–1). But Brooke's main worry was that the Germans would attack Ypres and outflank the 5th Division. The 12th Lancers reported that there were no Allied troops in the area except for a party of about twenty Belgian sappers, who had failed to prepare the bridges for demolition. The 150th Brigade, the leading formation of the 50th Division headed for Ypres, had a difficult time forcing its way through the rubble in the streets of Armentières, which had been comprehensively bombed by the Luftwaffe. In the turmoil, many of the inmates had escaped from the nearby lunatic asylum, and stood by the road grinning at the British troops as they passed by, adding a grotesque touch to the proceedings.

At first light on 27 May, the enemy mounted a series of attacks by three divisions south of Ypres. First to be hit was the 143rd Brigade. Observation in this sector was difficult; there were no prominent features, but visibility was severely restricted by orchards, hedges, copses and houses. Given that there were no wirelesses within battalions at this stage of the war, once telephone lines were cut the CO, if he could not see much, had great difficulty in keeping abreast of the battle. The terrain lent itself to infiltration, a tactic the Germans were rarely slow to adopt wherever they could. In the confused fighting, the enemy worked steadily round the flanks of the battalions. Forward companies were cut off, and the 143rd Brigade held on as best it could, but – with no reserve in rear – of necessity had to concede ground. Some of the temporary stop positions held further back were actually easier to defend among the houses and copses than the more open ground just west of the canal.

The attack on the 13th Brigade in the centre of the line took longer to wind up and did less damage. But German penetration between the two forward battalions, the Cameronians and the Inniskillings, was especially worrying because the forcing back of 143rd Brigade endangered its right flank. Brigadier Dempsey, faced with the prospect of having his brigade split in half and outflanked, ordered a withdrawal to slightly higher ground in rear, but still forward of the Messines Ridge. Orders for this move reached battalions before 1600 hours, but transmitting it to companies and platoons was, for lack of wireless, undertaken by officers or runners, who had to find the company and avoid being captured or killed by parties of enemy milling around in the area. Unfortunately some of

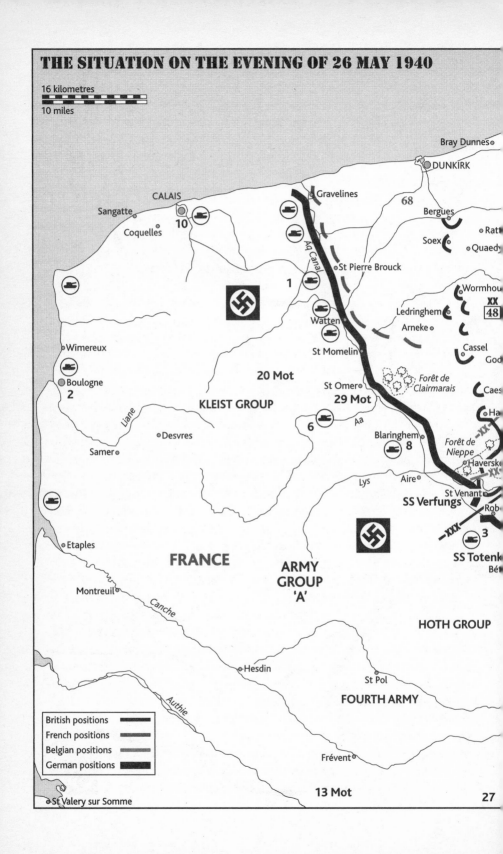

THE SITUATION ON THE EVENING OF 26 MAY 1940

16 kilometres

10 miles

Bray Dunnes

DUNKIRK

CALAIS

Gravelines

68

Sangatte

Bergues

Coquelles

10

Rat

Soex

Quaedy

St Pierre Brouck

Wormhou

XX
48

1

Ledringhem

Watten

Arneke

Wimereux

St Momelin

Cassel

God

Boulogne

20 Mot

Forêt de
Clairmarais

Caes

2

KLEIST GROUP

St Omer

29 Mot

Ha

Liane

Desvres

6

Aa

Blaringhem

Forêt de
Nieppe

Samer

8

Haversk

Lys

Aire

St Venant

Etaples

SS Verfungs

Rob

FRANCE

ARMY
GROUP
'A'

3

SS Totenk

Bé

Montreuil

Canche

HOTH GROUP

Hesdin

St Pol

FOURTH ARMY

Authie

British positions

French positions

Belgian positions

German positions

Frévent

St Valery sur Somme

13 Mot

27

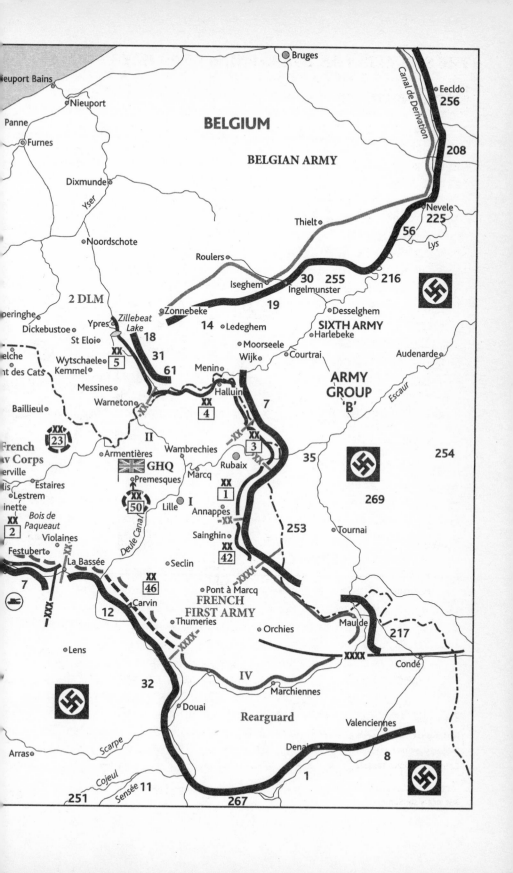

the Cameronian platoons inadvertently went too far back, and had to be taken forward again. The Germans followed up in force, whether by design or accident we shall never know. The CO of the 2nd Cameronians, Lieutenant Colonel Gilmore, took charge, and with his artillery battery commander (BC) rapidly arranged a heavy concentration to be fired by all the guns his BC could raise on the wireless. Gilmore quickly gathered all the men within sight, including clerks and other battalion head-quarters 'cooks and bottlewashers', and some of his carriers. As the Germans came on, they were malleted by the guns. When these ceased, the carriers charged followed by a line of 'Jocks' with fixed bayonets. This did the trick, and although some Germans fought back, most fled, pursued by screaming Cameronians. Gilmore was wounded by a shell splinter, but was awarded a bar to the DSO he had won in 1918.

The Inniskillings delayed their withdrawal, partly because orders took so long to get to them, but also because they were under the impression that the Cameronians were still in place. As a result the Germans followed up the Inniskillings so closely that the battalion headquarters became cut off in the confusion, and the CO, second-in-command, adjutant and RSM were all captured after a stiff but forlorn resistance. Further fighting reduced the Inniskillings to about one company strength. Dempsey decided to pull back a little further after dark to the forward edge of the Messines Ridge.

In the right of the 17th Brigade's sector the canal bent off to the north-west, widening the gap between it and the railway line to over two miles in the centre of the area. The two forward battalions (on the left the 6th Seaforths, and on the right the 2nd Royal Scots Fusiliers) were deployed on the railway line, and the rear battalion, the 2nd Northamptons, back on the canal. The pressure on the left flank threatened to overwhelm the 6th Seaforths, and when the 13th Brigade, on the right, pulled back, it exposed the 17th Brigade to envelopment on both flanks. A withdrawal to the canal was ordered, which was successfully carried out while in contact, but the 2nd Royal Scots Fusiliers lost all their fighting vehicles when the bridge over the canal was blown prematurely.

Brooke was aware from the captured German papers (see Chapter 5) that the German 7th Division's attack south of the Lys was a holding operation designed to keep the British 3rd and 4th Divisions fixed in that locality, and was less of a threat than the attacks north of the Lys. So he ordered Montgomery to extend his 3rd Division line to the left to release the 10th Brigade of the 4th Division, followed by its 11th Brigade, to come in behind the 5th Division on the Messines Ridge. This move was in the nick of time. At 2300 hours, the 10th Brigade arrived to find that the enemy had almost reached the gun positions of the 91st Field Regiment east of Wytschaete. During the second half of the night the guns were withdrawn to Kemmel Hill, two miles further back. By 0900 hours on 28 May, the 10th and 11th Brigades were firmly established east of Wytschaete, but had not covered the gap to the north of the 17th Brigade. In the south of the 5th Division line, the Germans pushed forward to within mortar range of the bridge over the River Deule at Warneton by the evening of 27 May. The Messines Ridge was now threatened by a pincer movement from the north and south.

Fortunately, Franklyn was not content merely to shore up the line and wait passively to be attacked, but reacted vigorously. He decided to use the two battalions on loan from the 1st Division, the 3rd Grenadier Guards and 2nd North Staffordshires, to attack in the 143rd Brigade's sector with the canal as their objective. If successful it would restore the situation in the most threatened part of the division's line. He was asking much of two battalions that had marched all night, had a further eight miles to march to reach the start line for the attack, and had not eaten all day. As a precursor to this attack, he arranged for the 6th Black Watch with one of its own companies, the 7th and 59th Field Companies RE, plus a few tanks and a dismounted squadron of the 13th/18th Hussars, to attack along the banks of the Lys river up to Comines. These troops actually belonged to the 4th Division and had been sent to the Lys as a flank guard for this division's withdrawal. But Franklyn reasoned that by counter-attacking in the manner desired by him they would be fulfilling that task admirably; if the road north through Warneton fell to the enemy, the 4th Division's withdrawal route would be jeopardized. This preliminary attack was launched at 1900 hours, at which time Franklyn was able to brief the COs of the 3rd Grenadiers (Major Adair) and 2nd North Staffords (Lieutenant Colonel Butterworth) and tell them he wanted them to attack at 2000 hours. He was acutely aware that he was asking them to attack over ground that neither of them had seen and was giving them very little notice to prepare and issue orders to their companies, let alone to co-ordinate their attacks.

The North Staffords crossed their start line at 2012 hours, and the Grenadiers at 2032 hours, pretty good going given the circumstances. The North Staffords, on the left, advanced with two companies up, one each side of the Messines–Kortekeer road. At first they encountered only small groups of Germans, the backwash of earlier infiltration attacks. These were soon disposed of. After a mile or so, they came under heavy mortar and artillery fire, and increasing small-arms fire in the lengthening dusk. By midnight the leading companies had reached the Kortekeer river, just under a mile from the canal, so Butterworth decided to consolidate and dig in. Both commanders of the leading companies were mortally wounded.

The Grenadiers also advanced two companies up, using the railway line on their right as an aid to maintaining direction. At the start line, the battalion intelligence officer gave the two leading company commanders the axis of the attack. Neither had had time to work out a compass bearing and as Captain Brinckman, commanding the right-hand company, recalled, 'the whole attack was taking place over ground which we had never seen in our lives'. After advancing for about half an hour against patchy resistance and in gathering darkness, they topped a low rise to see a farm building blazing to their right front, and British soldiers charging in with bayonets fixed. It was the Black Watch group rounding off their successful advance well supported by the 13th/18th Hussars' light tanks that had set the building alight with their tracer rounds. Encouraged by this spectacle, the Grenadiers pressed on against stiffening opposition, the darkness lit by bursting shells and mortar bombs, Verey lights arcing up into the sky and tracer rounds. Casualties mounted in the two leading companies, and all the officers, except the company commanders, were killed or wounded. Captain Brinckman was wounded by a shell or mortar-bomb splinter, followed by a round through the right shoulder and another through his left arm. He crawled forward in the darkness, trying to contact the platoon commander of his right forward platoon but could not find him. While lying there puzzling what to do, he saw other Grenadiers advancing near him and heard the voice of No. 1 Company commander. Brinckman hobbled across and told him that they must charge together. On the way back to his own company he was hit again. He shouted 'Charge!' to the men nearest to him, and they got up and followed him. The Germans in front immediately threw up their arms. One surrendered to Brinckman and then shot his runner in the back. Brinckman killed him with his revolver, then snatching up a rifle he bayoneted two more. This did the trick, and enemy fire ceased.

The Grenadiers were now on the canal, their objective. Captain Brinckman noticed a small cottage near by, which appeared to be full of Germans. Taking cover behind a hedge, he saw that with him he had only Sergeant Ryder and two guardsmen, and that of the four of them only one was unwounded. Brinckman sent the unwounded guardsman back to tell the CO that they were on the position but needed more men if they were to hold it. Brinckman then tossed a grenade through the cottage window, which seemed to quieten the enemy inhabitants, at which point a German fired at them point-blank through the hedge. Ryder despatched him. More enemy ran across the canal bridge, and

Brinckman threw another grenade at them. With difficulty he pulled the pin out of a third grenade, but realizing he was getting weaker and his right arm was becoming paralysed so that he would not be able to throw it, he asked Ryder to help, but the sergeant was wounded in the thigh and could not do so either. Brinckmann transferred the grenade to his left hand, still holding down the lever, and everything went quiet. The remaining guardsman was now dead, so telling Ryder that there was no point in staying, Brinckman started crawling back. By now the moon was up. They had gone about fifty yards when a bullet was fired from the cottage, wounding the captain in the leg, followed by another that hit Ryder. Brinckman threw the grenade he had been clutching, his last, underhand towards the flash of the weapon, and dragged himself on to where he thought some of his men might be hiding. But the pain was too bad and he was weak with loss of blood. Everything seemed quiet except for the sound of groaning men. He passed out and came round lying on a bed in the cottage, surrounded by dead Germans, and with a live one standing at the foot of his bed. His sergeant was next door in great pain.

The Grenadiers had found it impossible to hold the Canal Line, and Adair, with the other company commander killed, pulled back a little to the rear. But the efforts of the Grenadiers, the North Staffords and the Black Watch group had knocked the enemy off balance and, with the support of the artillery, positions east of the Saint-Eloi–Warneton road, some three miles east of Wytschaete were firmly held. All the next day, 28 May, the German attacks continued supported by mortars, guns and Stukas. But the British medium guns broke up the attacks, and the British line held. Had this section, Ypres–Comines, caved in under German attacks, the whole of Brooke's shield would have been outflanked and the BEF in all probability cut off.

The 2nd Light Anti-Aircraft Battery, in which Second Lieutenant McSwiney commanded 2 Troop, was allocated to AA duty on the roads leading north towards Dunkirk. Each troop was to take up position at key points along these routes, and wait until the main bodies of Allied units had gone through. Nothing was said about how long they were to wait before moving themselves – the timing was left to troop commanders. The battery moved with gun layers (aimers) in the seats of the Bofors guns as they were being towed along, and opened up while still on the move at any aircraft attempting to attack. This tactic worked because usually enemy aircraft sheered off when fired on by the Bofors, and went off to look for easier meat. McSwiney's troop managed to bring down a Messerschmitt 110 on 27 May, and the lieutenant was feeling pleased at this coup when he was called to a battery conference in the vicinity of

Poperinghe. He got trapped in an air raid on the town, which lasted for the best part of two hours. About 80 per cent of the vehicles caught in the ensuing vast traffic jam were destroyed or temporarily immobilized. It was the worst experience of bombing and strafing he had experienced, and he arrived at battery headquarters seven hours late. Having been allocated new tasks he had to retrace his steps to collect his troop. Had there been a system of wireless communications from battery to troop, the task would have been simple, but it took him the rest of the night to work his way back against the stream of retreating vehicles, tanks and guns. Eventually outside Poperinghe the road suddenly became clear, and remained so for the last four miles. He imagined himself running into the advancing Germans at any moment. The troop sergeant-major had given up hope of seeing him again after an absence of about eighteen hours with no news. They got the troop on the road in double-quick time and made their way to their next position using side roads wherever possible. At one point they came across a French truck parked right in the centre of the road. The driver was asleep, and was so annoyed at being woken that he refused to budge. McSwiney drew his revolver and told him he would have no alternative but to shoot him unless he removed his vehicle forthwith. Neither the Belgians nor the French had any road discipline, but later when McSwiney's troop ran into a mêlée of prancing Belgian horses trying to drag some ancient howitzers out of a ditch, the situation proved more difficult to deal with.

By the early morning of 28 May, Brooke had completed the first of his major steps sideways, by pulling out formations south of the River Lys and extending beyond Ypres northwards along the Yser Canal to Noordschote. This involved the 3rd Division leaving its positions south of the Lys and coming in on the left of the 50th. This was the move in which Lieutenant Robin Dunn had carried out the preliminaries when he moved his troop north and discovered that the enemy were in Saint-Eloi. The 2nd DLM came into reserve to the left rear of the 3rd Division, and the 12th Lancers, now under Montgomery's command, covered the eighteen-mile gap to the left of the 3rd Division, opened by the Belgian retreat to the north-west. This all sounds so simple. In reality it was difficult, and fraught with potentially dangerous consequences. In essence the 3rd Division had to break contact with the enemy in such a way that they did not immediately follow up, motor in darkness to the east of Armentières, cross the Deule and Lys rivers, then drive twenty miles on minor roads, in front of the British gun positions, and a mere 4,000 yards behind where the 50th Division was engaged with the enemy, to occupy unprepared positions in full view of the enemy in daylight along the Yser Canal.

Fortunately Montgomery had spent the months of the Phoney War training his division for night moves in transport, including fitting his vehicles with shaded tail lights that shone forward on to rear axles painted white. When Brooke visited him the evening before he found him full of confidence and treating the whole affair as if it was a 'glorious picnic'. The manoeuvre unfolded like clockwork. Montgomery decided to disable and abandon the medium guns, to reduce the weight of traffic. He sent reconnaissance parties to the new positions, expertly thinned out his positions on the old line, and led the division himself, barging his way through traffic jams. His system of guides, and route-marking drills so painstakingly practised in peace, paid dividends, as did traffic direction by the Royal Military Police, when put to the test in war over a route that consisted mainly of country lanes, in the dark and pouring rain. Brooke described it in his diary:

> There was little possibility of sleep that night, as the 3rd Division was moving past [his HQ] and I repeatedly went out to see how they were progressing. The whole movement seemed so unbearably slow, the hours of darkness were slipping by; should daylight arrive with the road crammed with vehicles the casualties from bombing might well have been disastrous. Our own guns were firing from the vicinity of Mont Kemmel, the German artillery were answering back, and the Division was literally trundling slowly along in the darkness down a pergola of artillery fire, and within 4,000 yards of a battle front which had been fluctuating all day, somewhat to our disadvantage. It was an eerie sight which I shall never forget. Before dawn came, the last vehicles had disappeared northwards into the darkness.[2]

Even so, the 3rd Division arrived at 0700 hours on 28 May to find that the 12th Lancers and 2nd DLM had been fending off enemy attacks for three hours. The Belgians had thrown in the towel while the 3rd Division was still driving through the night. To give them their due, they held out for a day longer than predicted by Brooke, and enabled him to gain the line of the Yser Canal. But from now on the security of the eastern flank of the BEF's withdrawal was completely in the hands of II Corps.

That morning the Germans dropped some leaflets, which caused much amusement, not only among the British troops but also the French of the 2nd DLM, who impressed Lieutenant Dunn by their optimism and sangfroid. The leaflets included a map with the caption:

British soldiers!
Here is your true situation!
You are completely surrounded!
Lay down your arms!

On 27 May, Gort had been warned in a message from Admiral Keyes (Churchill's representative at King Leopold's headquarters) that the Belgians were about to fold. Gort was in his new headquarters at Houtkerque. The German advance had forced the headquarters off the underground cable route, and, without the telephone, communications were restricted to wireless. In 1940, and for a long time afterwards, military wireless sets for anything other than very short-range communications were heavy, vehicle-mounted and often inefficient at night thanks to the troposphere, off which high-frequency waves are bounced, moving closer to the earth during the hours of darkness. They were not secure, so any messages containing information that one did not wish to share with the enemy had to be encrypted before transmission, and decrypted on receipt, adding unwelcome delays before the information was in the hands of those who needed it.

Having no telephone communication with Blanchard, commanding the French First Army Group, Gort went to Dunkirk, to Admiral Abrial's headquarters, in the hope of contacting him, to tie up the next stage of the withdrawal. Here Weygand's representative, General Koeltz, told Gort that the King of the Belgians was surrendering unconditionally at midnight (27/28 May). It was actually to become effective at 0400 hours on 28 May, but as the Germans had been approached on the subject of surrender at 1930 hours on 27 May they had been given plenty of time to exploit the situation and get moves under way to take advantage of Belgian reluctance to continue fighting right up to the last moment.

On return to his headquarters, Gort received a message: 'General Weygand makes a person appeal to General Gort. The British Army must participate strongly in the necessary joint counter-attacks. Situation demands hard hitting.' There were no joint counter-attacks envisaged, nor was there any prospect of any such attacks succeeding even if they had been planned. This message indicated once again how far removed from reality Weygand was. Blanchard arrived at Gort's headquarters at 2300 hours, and Gort read to him Eden's telegram ordering him to move to the coast and evacuate the BEF. Blanchard tried to dissuade him from withdrawing, but Gort was unmoved: the situation on the south-west front (see next chapter) was as dangerous as it was on the Belgian flank. He emphasized how important it was for Blanchard to conform to the BEF's withdrawal. Blanchard was adamant that he would not allow French troops to be evacuated, and seemed to take comfort in doing nothing on the grounds that it was preferable to withdrawal and that honour was thereby satisfied.

The Yser Canal, a sizeable commercial waterway north of Ypres, was a far more substantial obstacle than the Ypres–Comines Canal. Throughout

27 May the defence of the Yser Canal had been the responsibility of the 12th Lancers, later reinforced by a machine-gun company from the 2nd Middlesex, which was 3rd Division's machine-gun battalion and part of the divisional advance party. As the 50th Division starting taking up its positions in Ypres and on each side of the town during the morning of 27 May, enemy probing attacks started. But the German attacks on the Yser Canal and Ypres took longer to develop than those against the 5th Division. The German XI Corps had been drawn northwards following up the Belgians, so was unable to support the German IV Corps to its south. The IV Corps had, therefore, to extend to its right to engage the 50th Division, while also fighting the 5th Division. Only on 28 May, following the Belgian surrender, did the four divisions of XI Corps start attacking the Yser Canal, as well as mounting attacks on both sides of Ypres starting early on that day. The Germans penetrated between the 17th and 150th Brigades north of the Zillebeke Lake. The 11th Brigade had just arrived and was not in a position to counter-attack. The 150th Brigade attacked with an adhoc force of motorcycle infantry from the 4th Royal Northumberland Fusiliers, and with sappers, gunners and lancers fighting as infantry. The 8th DLI was put in to beef up the counter-attack, but contact with the 17th Brigade was still not restored. The 150th Brigade refused (that is, turned) its right flank along the line of the Dickebusch road joining up with the 10th Brigade east of Wytschaete,[3] although the left of the 17th Brigade was open and it fought hard to avoid being encircled and cut off. As the German XI Corps came into the battle, the attacks on the front of the 151st Brigade intensified. Enemy attempts to cross the Yser Canal in rubber boats and by pontoon bridge were thwarted. In the afternoon, the Germans succeeded in establishing a small toehold on the western bank, but were wiped out by the Vickers guns of the 2nd Middlesex and tanks of 2nd DLM. The fighting north of Ypres never reached the intensity it did on the Ypres–Comines Line, mainly because the latter was not much of an obstacle.

Brooke visited Montgomery on 28 May to confirm the orders for operations on the night of the 28th/29th May. The 3rd and 50th Divisions were to swing like a gate with the hinge at Lizerne on the Yser Canal back to Poperinghe. This would be the second layback position through which the 4th and 5th Divisions would withdraw to form the third layback position on the Yser river. Back at corps headquarters Brooke was greeted by reports from the 12th Lancers that the collapse of the Belgians had allowed the Germans to threaten Nieuport, the anchor point of the eastern end of the planned Dunkirk perimeter. Only light forces held the town and the bridges were not prepared for demolition. Soon afterwards, the 12th Lancers reported that the Germans were appearing in strength at Dixmude on the River Yser, Brooke's intended eastern anchor point for his third layback position. The imminent prospect of a Belgian collapse had persuaded Gort to withdraw to Dunkirk. Now his plans looked like being brought to naught by the surrender of the Belgian Army at 0400 hours on 28 May, and the swift moves by the Germans in anticipation of this event.

The 12th Lancers had been screening the eighteen-mile gap between the BEF and the Belgians, and destroying all the bridges over the River Yser north of Noordschote, selected by Brooke as the obstacle to protect his left flank. Before the main bridge at Dixmude could be demolished, a patrol of the 12th Lancers consisting of two armoured cars commanded by Second Lieutenant Mann saw a German staff car with a white flag and four German officers race across and drive up the road to Nieuport. Another Lancer patrol reported seeing an officer in the car engaged in an excited conversation with some French and Belgian officers. The car returned to Dixmude and was shot up by Mann's patrol, but it escaped. A French major came up to Mann and said that he was taking over the bridge garrison and ordered him to withdraw. When the rest of his patrol joined Mann, the French major disappeared. At this point, Lieutenant Smith of the Monmouthshire Engineers arrived, having demolished some minor bridges and barges. He discovered that the main bridge had been prepared for demolition by a party of Belgian sappers. Smith persuaded the Belgians at pistol-point to explain how the charges were set up, and blew the bridge. Ten minutes later a column of German motorcyclists roared up and skidded to a halt by the shattered bridge. Behind them appeared trucks carrying at least 250 soldiers, and several towed artillery pieces. The Lancers hosed them with machine-gun fire, driving them back to take cover among the houses. For the rest of the day, Mann frustrated all German attempts to cross the Yser, reinforced by another two armoured cars – which was all that could be spared from the thinly held 12th Lancer patrol line. His gallant efforts were recognized by the award of the DSO.

Montgomery, when apprised of the situation, sent the 59th Field Company Royal Engineers to augment the defences of Dixmude, but refused to commit his reserve brigade. He ordered the 2nd DLM to screen the Loo Canal in preparation for his own withdrawal that night, and this became the water obstacle on II Corps' left flank, in place of the eastern end of the Yser river. Soon after midnight on 29 May, the 50th Division and all but the 8th Brigade of the 3rd Division swung back to form the layback position on the Poperinghe–Lizerne–Noordschote Line. The 150th Brigade withdrew from the Yser Canal, covered by its remaining carriers and a squadron of the 4th/7th Dragoon Guards. The survivors of the 4th/7th Dragoon Guards, enough for one squadron (henceforth called the Combined Squadron), had been formed into a composite regiment with the 5th Inniskillings. The 150th Brigade was digging in east of Poperinghe by 0800 hours. The 151st Brigade, having withdrawn from the Yser Canal at 0400 hours, came in on the left of the 150th. The line from east of Poperinghe to Proven was supposed to have been the responsibility of I Corps, but was left unoccupied. So Brooke ordered the flank held by machine-gunners of the 4th Royal Northumberland Fusiliers and the 13th/18th Royal Hussars.

During the night of 28/29 May, beginning at last light, the 5th Division, the 143rd Brigade and the 10th and 11th Brigades of the 4th Division broke contact on the Ypres–Comines Line. They destroyed their heavy and medium artillery, the ammunition on the gun position being exhausted, and pulled back through the Poperinghe–Lizerne–Noordschote layback line. The 4th Division got back mostly unscathed. But the 5th Division had a much harder time disengaging. During the 28th the Germans had enveloped the left flank of the 17th Brigade, and cut off its battalions one by one. The 2nd Royal Scots Fusiliers were encircled; the CO, Lieutenant Colonel Tod, and his remaining three officers and around forty men surrendered at about 1100 hours on 28 May. Only part of one company of the 2nd Northamptons got clear, the rest, including battalion headquarters, being overrun after fighting for four hours. A small group of the 6th Seaforths escaped capture thanks to a counter-attack by carriers of the 2nd Duke of Cornwall's Light Infantry from the 10th Brigade. The 17th Brigade now consisted of 441 all ranks. Also thanks to the 10th Brigade's efforts, the 13th Brigade came away with fewer casualties than the 17th, as did the 143rd. But the overall brigade strengths do not reveal entirely how the battle on the Ypres–Comines Canal, like most battles, had taken its toll on the infantry battalions and rifle companies especially – for example the 3rd Grenadiers were left with nine officers and 270 soldiers, and the 8th Royal Warwicks were down to four officers and fifty-four men. The 4th and 5th Divisions now, as planned by Brooke, headed for the Yser river line.

The journey was far from pleasant. A major choke-point was Poperinghe, on which the main roads in the area converged. The Luftwaffe had been busy as vehicles drove nose to tail. Marching men, mainly from the 1st Division, could bypass the town across country, but the weary drivers, dismounting to take what cover they could each time enemy aircraft came over, had no option but to join the queues of transport. All along the road edges, abandoned vehicles and guns restricted movement. Here and there broken-down ambulances laden with unattended wounded were scattered among other wrecks. The Luftwaffe continued the attacks on Poperinghe by night, using flares to illuminate the target already lit by blazing fires. Most of the 5th Division was clear of the northern outskirts of the town by first light. Once out of Poperinghe, troops on the road were left untouched by enemy aircraft – the Luftwaffe was too busy bombing Dunkirk to spend much time interdicting the roads.

Now that II Corps line along the Ypres–Comines Line no longer existed, Bock's Army Group B was able to link up with the panzer divisions coming in from the south-west. The story of how these divisions had fared up to this point will be told in the next chapter. When Bock launched an attack in an attempt to outflank the right of the 50th Division at Poperinghe and against the 8th Brigade of 3rd Division, the panzer divisions were reluctant to participate. The first to be hit by Bock was the 8th Brigade of 3rd Division, which was still on the Yser Canal. Its right-hand brigade, the 9th, had swung back on to the new line; the Germans crossed the canal south of Lizerne and hit the right-flank battalion of the 8th Brigade, the 4th Royal Berkshires. The battalion was forced back, losing three company commanders and nearly being over-run in the process. The 1st Suffolks on the left of the brigade were also pushed back, but regained the ground in time to stop German sappers trying to build a pontoon bridge across the canal. By now the 7th Guards Brigade was marching back to Furnes, on the Loo Canal, as the first step in the 3rd Division's withdrawal.

At Nieuport, at 1100 hours on 28 May, an enemy motorcycle column moving unseen with a crowd of refugees had seized an intact bridge. A patrol of the 12th Lancers engaged the column, but, although they were reinforced by two tanks of the 15th/19th Royal Hussars and some hundred gunners fighting as infantry, as well as by four 18-pounders of the 76th Field Regiment, all efforts to regain or destroy the bridge were unsuccessful. The enemy lodgement grew steadily stronger. However, it is an ill wind that blows nobody anygood. The Belgian collapse that led to the decision to rest the left flank of the final layback on the Loo Canal meant that the 4th Division, which originally was to hold the eastern section of the Yser, was now free to be sent to bolster the defence of Nieuport.

By 0700 hours on 29 May the 5th Division occupied the shortened Yser Line, where it linked up with the 42nd Division to its right. The Yser Line consisted of a number of positions covering the likely crossing points; there was no time to construct a fully interlocking defensive layout. The 2nd DLM held ground to the west of the Loo Canal. The division had done quite well, but it had lost all its tanks, and according to Brooke, who spoke to its commander, the DLM:

Now consisted of a column of buses and workshops, with a certain number of men with rifles. The whole outfit was more of an encumbrance than anything else, its fighting value was practically nil, whilst its power of blocking roads with its huge vehicles was unlimited.[4]

The DLM did more than block roads. Montgomery's brilliant GSO 1 (de facto chief of staff), Lieutenant Colonel 'Marino' Brown RM, was on his way to II Corps on the night of 28/29 May when he encountered DLM vehicles blocking the road. He got out of his car and, being a man who did not suffer fools gladly, gave the French a tongue-lashing. He was shot dead.

As troops moved north there was less choice of good areas in which to deploy guns and even essential vehicles. The 7th Field Regiment's new position just north of Oostverleteren, which it occupied on 28 May, was the worst the regiment had seen tactically. Open fields and hedgerows offered little opportunity for camouflage. Lieutenant Dunn's troop wagon lines (the gunners still used this expression to describe the vehicle park), command post and administrative echelon were all crammed into a farmyard. Fortunately the enemy did not take advantage of such a tempting target for aircraft and artillery.

The following day, Lieutenant Dunn's men found a large number of abandoned Belgian rifles and ammunition in the cellar of the farm and, as soldiers will, every man acquired a souvenir. All through the morning an almost continuous stream of traffic passed Dunn's troop heading along the main Ypres–Furnes road towards the coast. At about 0800 hours Poperinghe was comprehensively bombed. Just before midday, the enemy shelled Oostverleteren, which was a prime target as it contained headquarters 3rd Division, regimental headquarters of Dunn's regiment and a medium artillery battery. The latter was not deterred from shooting back despite shells falling all around.

During the afternoon, the 7th Field Regiment received orders to move back at 1800 hours to the final bridgehead round Dunkirk. The CRA of the 3rd Division made it clear that this was not simply a 'dive for the sea', but that the division was to cover the embarkation of other divisions, and it might have to fight hard, possibly for several days.

Dunn was deeply impressed by the conduct of the infantry. The artillery had some respite and at least could drive from position to position – unlike the infantry, who more often than not walked. Yet their dogged cheerfulness and courage seemed inexhaustible. There were exceptions, and one of the officers from 7th Field Regiment witnessed a failure of resolve in a battalion they were supporting. The officer concerned shared a cellar with the headquarters of one of the infantry platoons, and the enemy were shelling heavily. Suddenly a man ran down the steps shouting that the anti-tank guns had gone. The platoon commander shouted that they should all go too, and they did. The rot was started by another subaltern who was seen leading his company out of the line without orders. Dunn's only comment: 'Fortunately for him he was killed.'

The 7th Field Regiment moving back to its final position near Coxyde, two miles north of Furnes, witnessed the only case of disorder it encountered in the campaign. Stragglers in torn uniforms shouted for lifts, and soon the vehicles, guns and limbers were overflowing with men. The road presented a chaotic scene, with ditched vehicles lining the sides, shells bursting at most crossroads, and infantry filing down the sides of the road. At one point Dunn passed the 1st Grenadiers, a single line of men on each side of the road, their equipment complete, marching, all in step, back to their final position – a fine sight. As he approached Furnes, the number of abandoned vehicles increased, and progress slowed thanks to traffic jams. At Coxyde the regiment found the artillery of the 4th Division firing hard in an attempt to stop a German attack which was in progress along the coast between Nieuport and Nieuport les Bains – the enemy were trying to cut the BEF off from this sector.

Throughout 29 May and the morning of the next day, II Corps trudged or drove into the Dunkirk perimeter. The loss of roads east of the Loo Canal, and French horse-drawn artillery and trucks crossing the roads funnelling into the perimeter to reach their sector west of Dunkirk, created huge traffic jams. The 2nd DLM's commander felt the rough edge of Brooke's tongue via Blanchard's liaison officer. When Brooke learned that Blanchard had ordered the DLM to withdraw to La Panne and embark, Brooke informed the liaison officer that if he did so he would uncover II Corps' left flank and add to the chaotic traffic jams. 'Told Liaison Officer that if the General [commanding DLM] disobeyed my order I would have him shot.'[5]

The military police ruthlessly ordered all non-essential vehicles to be driven off the roads before they entered the perimeter, and immobilized or destroyed. Anti-tank guns, 25-pounders, machine-gun and Bren-gun carriers, ambulances, water bowsers, bridging equipment, wireless vehicles and some staff cars were admitted. Sergeant Green, a platoon sergeant in the 2nd Bedfordshire & Hertfordshires, was marched with the rest of the battalion into a field where, after a meal, they were told to unload their large packs from the company B Echelon transport, take out what they wanted and throw the packs away. Some of the transport was smashed there and then. One of his soldiers came up to Green and said, 'It's going to take fifty years to live the shame of this down. It's a general scuttle.' The men then loaded into some of the transport and were driven off to the perimeter, where most of the remaining trucks were destroyed.

The 2nd Light Anti-Aircraft Battery was ordered to move to one of the transport-dumping grounds at Killem, south of the Bergues–Furnes Canal which was to form the southern boundary of the Dunkirk perimeter. Apart from guns and tractors, all stores were to be destroyed, and every personal item of kit except what the soldiers were wearing. McSwiney adapted the order to suit himself and kept his air bed, a change of underwear and his mackintosh. Tons of ammunition, stores and equipment and hundreds of vehicles were going up in smoke. It was a depressing spectacle, relieved temporarily as far as the soldiers were concerned by the 'help yourself' sign on the NAAFI food and cigarettes.

The next morning, 29 May, the battery's commander Major du Vallon rode with the guns as far as the Bergues Canal. The French had blocked the bridge which the battery hoped to use. Du Vallon, rather precipitately, and without trying to find another bridge, of which there were certainly some open still, ordered them to destroy the much needed anti-aircraft guns by throwing the barrels and breech blocks into the canal. McSwiney's troop was ordered by du Vallon to form up on the other side of the canal and march away under command of the sergeant major. McSwiney was about to accompany them when du Vallon called him back and pointed to a considerable number of wounded men abandoned in RAMC ambulances. McSwiney was told to have these casualties carried on stretchers over the canal. Volunteers for this task were hard to come by, but in the end by persuasion and coercion twelve men managed to complete the job in an hour and a half. The wounded having been taken charge of by RAMC personnel on the other side, and the rest of the battery having gone ahead, du Vallon and McSwiney marched the 'volunteers' the ten miles to La Panne. Du Vallon then left the party to seek orders. Meanwhile the beachmaster added to McSwiney's party another fifty waifs and strays who were without an officer. So McSwiney found himself responsible for a motley crew of men, who belonged to such a wide variety of units that according to him no embarkation officer 'would look at them'.

The 1st East Surreys of the 4th Division managed to evade the order to destroy all transport, which turned out to be fortunate because on 29 May the battalion was rushed forward to take up a temporary position on the Furnes–Ypres Loo Canal. This was in response to the threat posed by German formations approaching the gap between the left of the 5th Division on the River Yser and Furnes. The 1st East Surreys carried out this move just in time, using their own transport and some lent by their brigade. The fighting at Furnes amounted only to a skirmish, and a patrol sent across the canal by B Company accounted for a German sniper. It was here that a tired senior officer of the 1st East Surreys was heard to remark that he would give anything for a bottle of champagne. One was produced. On the Escaut, a Belgian had given the carrier platoon some cases of champagne rather than let them fall into the hands of the enemy – at least that was the carrier platoon version. From the Furnes position, the 1st East Surreys moved to the coast and took up a position of all-round defence in the sand dunes. Along with other units, the East Surreys had already sent all who could be spared for evacuation. These mainly consisted of B Echelon[6] personnel, cooks, clerks, storemen, drivers without vehicles, and of course the wounded. By now the battalion consisted of a small headquarters and four rifle companies, the strongest of which could muster about seventy men.

Now that the Germans held Dixmude, the 4th Division was forced to march to Nieuport via Furnes. The division's passage, held up by the scrum of refugees and all manner of units and other impedimenta on the roads, was not completed – with all three of its brigades able to take over the defence of this key point in the perimeter – until early on 30 May.

The Germans did not bother to mount a co-ordinated assault on the Yser Line, but followed up the withdrawal snapping at the heels of the retiring brigades. The rearguards were subjected to mortar and artillery fire, while main bodies on the roads were strafed by the Luftwaffe, as well as being shelled. But by noon on 30 May the formations of II Corps were manning their positions within the Dunkirk perimeter. Although, as will be related, formations on the other side of the BEF sack had fought hard and their contribution to the BEF's survival was important, II Corps' performance had been truly remarkable. The Corps had fought a continuous and sometimes fluid withdrawal battle against superior forces for five days, in the process covering a distance of over forty miles. Its tenacious defence and skilful night moves had kept it inside Bock's OODA loop at all times, a refreshing change in this campaign, and one of only a few examples of the Allies being 'quicker on the draw' tactically speaking than their opponents.

On 29 May, Gort told Brooke that he was to hand over II Corps and 'proceed home so as to be available for the task of re-forming new armies'.[7] Brooke protested, but Gort told him it was an order that had to be obeyed. He did however allow Brooke to remain until 30 May to see his corps into the perimeter. That day, Brooke went round his divisions and found:

3rd Div at 13,000 strong
4th Div at 12,000 strong
very satisfactory considering what we had been through.
    5th Div, only 2 brigades, 17th and 13th, both very weak, about 600
        per brigade, 50th Div a little stronger with 2 brigades about 1200
        each.
There is no doubt that the 5th Div in its fight on the Ypres–Comines
Canal saved the II Corps and the BEF.
I can hardly believe that I have succeeded in pulling the 4 [four]
divisions out of the mess we were in, with allies giving way on all flanks.
Now remains the task of embarking which will be a difficult one.[8]

Before leaving his corps, Brooke arranged that Montgomery should take it over, while Anderson commanding the 11th Infantry Brigade took over the 3rd Division, and Horrocks moved up to command the 11th Brigade. Before we look at how the embarkation went, we must turn our attention to the fighting on the other flank of the BEF.

8

THE WITHDRAWAL: FIGHTING THE PANZERS ON THE WESTERN FLANK

To tell the story of the fighting on the western flank, we must return to 25 May, and Gort's order (see Chapter 5) assigning the defence of the Canal Line to the 2nd, 44th and 46th Divisions. The 48th Division, originally deployed in that area, was ordered to Dunkirk, leaving one brigade behind. However, on arrival at Dunkirk, the French general in command of the local defences told Major General Thorne, the GOC 48th Division, that there were sufficient French troops in the port and its immediate surroundings to protect it.

So Thorne deployed his 144th Brigade between Cassel and Bergues, and especially in Wormhoudt, shown on a captured German map as an objective; and his 145th Brigade at Cassel and Hazebrouck (his 143rd Brigade was deployed on the east side of the BEF salient, under Brooke's command). To cover the eighteen miles of front, the 48th Division deployed in a string of strongpoints from Bergues–Wormhoudt–Cassel– Hazebrouck, with two brigades and Usherforce along the Aa Canal. The latter consisted of the 6th Green Howards holding Gravelines and two bridges on the Aa Canal to the south, the 1st Super-Heavy Battery at Saint-Pierre-Brouck, the 3rd Super-Heavy Battery at Watten, and the 52nd Heavy Regiment at Saint-Momelin. The force took its name from Colonel Usher, left behind to command the lines-of-communication sub-area when the BEF advanced into Belgium. He had spent most of the First World War in a German prison camp, and was determined to save as many British soldiers as possible from the same experience this time round. The French held the Canal Line from Gravelines to opposite Saint-Omer.

The 44th Division moved up on Thorne's left into the area of the Nieppe Forest, occupying a sector exclusive of both Hazebrouck on its right and Merville on its left. The division occupied the Nieppe Forest with the 132nd Royal West Kent Brigade (2nd Royal Sussex on loan from the 133rd Brigade, 1st, 4th and 5th Royal West Kents). The division's right flank, held by the 133rd Royal Sussex Brigade (4th and 5th Royal

Sussex), curved in a hook towards Hazebrouck. The 131st Brigade (5th and 6th Queen's, and 2nd Buffs) occupied the centre of the division's sector.

The 46th Division, less 137th and 138th Brigades, was deployed around Carvin, with its right flank on the Deule Canal, and the French First Army on its left. French armoured cavalry covered the four-mile gap between the Deule Canal and the British 2nd Division, whose left flank rested on La Bassée.

Lieutenant General Sir Ronald Adam, commander of III Corps, had been sent to organize the Dunkirk perimeter and the evacuation of the BEF, and his corps was taken over by Major General Wason, who until then had been the Major General Royal Artillery at Gort's headquarters. The Canal Line defence had originally been assigned to Major General Eastwood, while Adam with III Corps headquarters was busy preparing for the counter-attack under the Weygand Plan. Now that the plan was dead, III Corps headquarters, under Wason, was available to command the formations on the Canal Line and assumed this duty.

The next day, 26 May, found the German panzer and other divisions of Army Group A still strung out along the Canal Line from Douai north-west to Gravelines on the coast, in response to the 'Halt Order' on 24 May. As the order applied only to panzer divisions, the infantry had pressed on and in some places they had crossed the canals and held shallow bridgeheads on the eastern banks – notably the SS Verfügungs Division across the Aire Canal opposite Merville, and 12th and 32nd Infantry opposite Carvin. Before the 'Halt Order' came into effect on 23 and 24 May, the British 2nd Division's sector had come under a series of attacks and, although in places the Germans had pulled back, all three brigades in the division had already taken casualties and were tired before the German armour started moving forward again in a concerted attack all along the Canal Line.

The other two British divisions on the Canal Line, the 44th and 48th, were granted two days' respite from attack, 24 and 25 May, to prepare their positions. The 'Halt Order' was rescinded on the evening of 26 May, and by the evening of the next day the panzer, motorized and infantry divisions were across the Canal Line and pushing east to squeeze the BEF and First French Army against Army Group B advancing from the east. The Germans pushed back the advanced companies of the 48th Division and Usherforce. French troops in the Clairmarais Forest reported being overrun by tanks. Spearheads of the 1st and 8th Panzer and 29th Motorized Divisions crossed the Aa Canal, with 6th and 8th Panzer Divisions echeloned in behind them, and with just a screen of French troops opposing them.

By the evening of 26 May, Major General Osborne, GOC 44th Division, was reporting frequent dive-bombing attacks in his divisional sector at Merville, the Nieppe Forest, Estaires and Armentières. During the night the BGS (chief of staff) of III Corps arrived at Osborne's headquarters, and told him several things. First, the BEF would withdraw to Dunkirk, although Osborne was not informed of the timings for this move. Second, the 2nd and 44th Divisions were to continue to act as flank guard to the French First Army, which held the sides of a sack about twelve miles wide and over twenty miles long, stretching from the right flank of the BEF's II Corps facing east, to Maulde and Raches facing south-east and south, and right round to La Bassée facing south-west. Eventually it was intended that the two British divisions were to withdraw using routes west of and inclusive of Armentières and Poperinghe. Third, Osborne should keep in touch with the French Cavalry Corps, which would be on his right. Fourth, Lieutenant General Adam had been placed in charge of the Dunkirk defences, and Wason, the new III Corps commander, would visit him the next day, 27 May. Finally, if possible, Osborne was to 'make some advance on to the plain between Cassel and Hazebrouck to help keep back the German mechanized advance'. Much of what Osborne had been told about co-operating with the French made operational sense, but only if they responded in a way that enabled him to provide the necessary co-operation – a big 'if'. The vague instruction to advance on to the plain between Cassel and Hazebrouck with what elements could be spared from his defensive tasks (at most a couple of infantry battalions on their feet, and probably without armoured support) to head off two panzer and two motorized divisions was meaningless. Being told to advance on a place without specific objectives is open to a variety of interpretations, not least how far to advance and for how long. The instruction indicated a lack of grip at III Corps headquarters.

The British 2nd Division, holding some twenty miles of the La Bassée Canal, had been stripped of most of its anti-tank guns for the defence of Dunkirk. It came under attack by three panzer divisions (3rd, 4th and SS Totenkopf), as well as part of 5th Panzer and the right-hand formation of SS Verfügungs. The first assault by the SS Totenkopf and 4th Panzer ran into the 4th Brigade in the centre of 22nd Division's line, but spread to the 6th Brigade, on the 4th Brigade's right. Because the Germans had held a bridgehead at Robecq since 24 May, they were able to rush tanks across without any preliminary bridging operations. The 6th Brigade was deployed with the 2nd DLI in the centre, with 1st Royal Welch Fusiliers to their left and 1st Royal Berkshires on the right. The tanks attacked them first at around 0800 hours, preceded by artillery fire that was well directed on the few anti-tank guns the brigade had left. In the open country there was little cover, and soon every anti-tank gun was out of action. The tanks emerged as the artillery lifted, and turned their machine guns on defended positions, shooting in their own infantry: that is, the tanks engaging the defenders, while the German infantry closed in. Within three hours the 1st Royal Welch had lost their two forward companies, and the 2nd DLI were within a whisker of being cut off. Too late, Brigadier Furlong ordered the two battalions to fall back to the Lys Canal, about a mile in rear, covered by the Royal Welch. Unfortunately by now the German armour could flay the DLI every time they rose from their slit trenches, and shoot up the battalion headquarters in a barn. Only the right-hand company of the DLI got away. Their battalion headquarters was overrun, despite a last-ditch defence with Brens, rifles and even the CO engaging the enemy with his revolver.

A few of the Royal Welch got back over the Lys Canal to some cottages that afforded a modicum of cover. The CO, Lieutenant Colonel Harrison, was last over the pontoon bridge, carrying a wounded officer. He shouted that the bridge should be blown, but there was no one to carry out the order. A German tank approached and lurched over this bridge – which had been erected by the British. The Germans had demolished the main bridge two days earlier after withdrawing from a foray across the canal. The pontoon bridge, designed to carry only a 15-hundredweight truck, should have collapsed under the tank but unfortunately held together. Harrison was killed trying to stop the tank.

The 1st Royal Berkshires were beset on both flanks – by tanks on their left and infantry of the SS Verfügungs on their right. The Berkshire's reserve company mounted a counter-attack that allowed the battalion to keep open a withdrawal route across a little bridge, over which they fell back when ordered. The Berkshires, supported by their three remaining carriers, one anti-tank gun and some 18-pounders of the 99th Field Regiment, held Haverskerque, while the remnants of the Royal Welch and DLI took cover in the Forest of Nieppe. But the brigade transport never made it, being destroyed in the mayhem. As the Berkshires headed for the forest, two Panzer Mk IVs started to follow up, harassing them but inflicting few casualties, and were not inclined to pursue them into the forest. They may have been deterred by the prospect of fighting in the thick stuff, and some light tanks of the 4th/7th Dragoon Guards lurking in the forest possibly provided an added disincentive to a follow-up.

Along with the 6th Brigade, the 4th had already taken heavy casualties by dawn on 27 May. The 2nd Royal Norfolks had amalgamated their two right-hand companies into one sixty strong. This represented a total loss of around 180 men from these two companies alone, the equivalent of the loss of a rifle company and a half – a severe drain on the fighting strength of the battalion. The 1st Royal Scots suffered casualties mounting a successful counter-attack. The 1st/8th Lancashire Fusiliers opposite Béthune were overlooked by Germans established in slag heaps and buildings. At 0330 hours on 27 May, a series of heavy artillery concentrations fell on the 4th Brigade positions, followed by an attack on both flanks. Brigadier Warren found himself unable to do much to relieve the situation. He withdrew his headquarters to Lestrem, leaving a platoon of Lancashire Fusiliers and a machine-gun platoon of the 2nd Manchesters at Epinette to impose a delay on the enemy. These were the only fighting sub-units of the 4th Brigade that got away.

The enemy attacks on Merville intensified. The village was held by the 6th King's Own, a pioneer battalion mainly of older reservists, and although attacked on three sides it held out all day. In the course of the day, a company of machine-gunners from the 6th Argylls had rushed to reinforce the King's Own and been cut to pieces in an ambush.

Major General Irwin, the GOC of 2nd Division, was forced by these German gains to commit his reserve, the 25th Brigade (originally of the 50th Division). He sent the 2nd Essex and some guns to the north of Merville. The 1st Royal Irish Fusiliers with machine-gunners of the 2nd Manchesters, and supported by the 5th Inniskilling Dragoon Guards, were posted out as a flank guard facing west. The light tanks of the Inniskillings notched up a success when they caught some German tank crews who had dismounted for a quick smoke and, charging in, sent them flying. The third battalion of the 25th Brigade, the 1st/7th Queen's Royal Regiment, was warned for a counter-attack towards La Bassée, and so Irwin had nothing to spare to save the 4th Brigade from destruction by the 4th Panzer and SS Totenkopf divisions.

As early as 0750 hours the CO of the 1st/8th Lancashire Fusiliers reported that he was cut off from all but one of his rifle companies. At about 1430 hours, he sent a message to brigade headquarters saying that they were now surrounded, the building was on fire and they were holding on. Brigadier Warren despatched an officer with orders for the battalion to withdraw after dark, but he was never seen again, and nothing more was heard from the Lancashire Fusiliers.

The 2nd Royal Norfolks went down fighting, resisting until 1640 hours. As the German armour started to overwhelm what was left of the rifle companies, the headquarters signallers were sent out to defend the perimeter of Druries Farm, where battalion headquarters was sited, on the outskirts of Le Paradis village. Here the adjutant, Captain Lang, ordered Private Brown, who was manning the telephone switchboard, to hand over this duty to the wireless operator on the brigade net and go to keep watch for the enemy. With a Regimental Police lance-corporal, he kept lookout from one of the farm buildings and spotted a German motorcycle combination with a machine gun mounted on it coming in behind the headquarters. He and the lance-corporal opened fire and stopped the motorcyclist, but it was obvious that the enemy were surrounding them. Brown and his companion dashed back to battalion headquarters and told them the bad news, before diving into a small brick outhouse, which they converted into a little strongpoint by bashing holes in the brick walls to fire through. Others had done the same in the remaining outhouses, to provide all-round defence of the farm.

By the afternoon, all except battalion headquarters had been overrun. The acting CO, Major Ryder, went round saying that there was no chance of getting away and, with ammunition running low, canvassed opinion on whether they should surrender. To begin with everybody was for fighting on, which they did for a while. But soon Ryder said that with ammunition almost exhausted they would have to cease firing. Anyone who wished to do so could attempt to get away to save himself. The men in the stables and outbuildings tried going out through the stable door to the field outside, but were fired on and turned back. After a short while they went out again, this time with a white towel on a rifle, and were allowed out to surrender.

These men, and a few others captured near by, were marched away from Druries Farm by No. 3 Company of the 1st Battalion, 2nd SS Totenkopf Rifle Regiment, under the command of Hauptsturmführer (Captain) Fritz Knoechlein. Their subsequent behaviour towards men who had fought well was a foretaste of what SS troops would do for the rest of the war; they even adapted a slang expression for it, a *Rabatz*, meaning to have fun killing everyone in sight.

About a hundred of the Royal Norfolks were marched off the road into a meadow beside some farm buildings. Private Pooley, a signaller with A Company, saw two machine guns inside the meadow, pointing towards the head of the column. He 'felt as though an icy hand gripped his stomach' as the guns began to fire. For a few seconds the cries and screams of stricken men drowned the chatter of the guns. Men fell like grass before a scythe, and then the stream of bullets hit Pooley. 'I felt a searing pain in my left leg and wrist and pitched forward. My scream of pain mingled with the cries of my mates, but as I fell into the heap of dead and dying men, the thought flashed through my brain, "If I ever get out of here, the swine who did this will pay for it."'

Ninety-seven men were cut down. As the SS soldiers moved among the sprawling bodies they shot or bayoneted anyone who seemed to be breathing. Pooley was shot twice more in the same leg, but by a supreme act of will he kept still until the SS men left. One other man survived the massacre, Private O'Callaghan, who had lain with a shattered arm under a pile of his friends. O'Callaghan pulled Pooley out from under the dead bodies and they dragged themselves away to the safety of a farm where a farmer's wife tended their wounds. After recapture by ordinary German soldiers, Pooley was eventually repatriated because he was so severely wounded. No one would accept his story until he returned to Le Paradis after the war and found the farmer's wife. She supported his story, and this time he was believed. Both Pooley and O'Callaghan were prosecution witnesses at Knoechlein's trial at the British Military Court at Hamburg in October 1948. The former Hauptsturmführer was found guilty and hanged. Pooley had kept his promise.

Other soldiers also escaped, including Private Brown and two other privates, Hagen and Leven. When they saw the others surrender, they crept away in the opposite direction to a neighbouring ditch under cover of smoke from one of the burning outbuildings. Here they discovered the adjutant of the Norfolks, who was wounded, and the MO. But before they could put any distance between themselves and the farm buildings, they were discovered by the Germans. These were also SS, but, according to Brown, after knocking them about a bit, let them keep their wallets and otherwise treated them correctly.

There was no excuse for what the SS had done. It is true that the moment of surrender is often fraught with danger for both sides. The victor may be uncertain that the vanquished is genuine about surrendering, and the vanquished unsure that his surrender will be accepted. Leaving the moment of capitulation too late, for example to the moment when the attacker is on the lip of the trench or position, may end in the assailant taking one more pace and killing the soldier who has belatedly put his hands up. The attacker simply cannot afford to take the chance; it could be him or his adversary. Nine times out of ten a soldier who leaves it too late, especially if firing his weapon up to the last minute, ends up with a bayonet or bullet in his gizzard, or a grenade in his trench. This was not the case at Le Paradis; the killing was done in cold blood.

Of the 2nd Royal Norfolks, only the cooks, drivers and other specialists of B Echeleon survived. Under the quartermaster they headed north and joined the mass of refugees making in the direction of Dunkirk.

The 1st Royal Scots, on the right of the Norfolks, fought on with the same intensity, and inflicted severe delays on the enemy. They might have been treated likewise by the SS, but for a German staff officer passing in his car, who saw the survivors of one of their companies being lined up to be shot and ordered them to be released. Some of the battalion gathered to make their final stand around battalion head-quarters at a farm in the vicinity of Le Paradis. The command of the battalion had devolved on to Major Watson. He had, unknown to himself, been awarded the Military Cross for his service on the Escaut position and a DSO for leading a counter-attack on 24 May. He did not live to receive them in person, being killed within minutes of taking command. With the farm on fire, the remnants of the battalion managed to withdraw, covered by the officers'-mess corporal wielding a Bren to good effect. They were rounded up a couple of days later.

The 5th Brigade held a long front, about seven miles, from Gorre on the right to La Bassée on the left of the sector. The brigade defensive layout was right 2nd Dorsets, centre 7th Worcestershires, and left 1st Cameron Highlanders astride the ruins of La Bassée. The 1st DLM had some of their tanks deployed in the 5th Brigade's area. Their opponent here was Rommel with his 7th Panzer Division, who started his attack on the evening of 26 May, overrunning one of the Worcestershires' companies. A counter-attack by the Cameron Highlanders failed to dislodge the enemy, and at dawn a further attack enlarged the bridgehead and overran another Worcestershire company. The counter-attack by one company of Camerons, accompanied by six French tanks, drove the enemy away from about 300 yards of their bridgehead on the canal bank. This counter-attack momentarily put the wind up Rommel, who may have mistaken the tanks, probably Somuas, for British heavy tanks, which had caused him so much angst at Arras. But he brought down a substantial artillery concentration on them, forcing them and the Cameron company to withdraw. Only six men of this company were left unwounded when they returned to their battalion.

Rommel pushed his armour into the bridgehead with the energy which was to become familiar to many British soldiers in the desert a year or so hence. With German air support, spotting aircraft and observation posts on the slag heaps, British artillery trying to bring down fire on the enemy lodgement received short shrift. His position fast becoming untenable, Brigadier Gartlan issued a warning order for a withdrawal, to be preceded by a 'stopping' blow by the 1st/7th Queen's of the 25th Brigade, and the 1st Army Tank Brigade who were expected to arrive at any moment. This time it was the Germans who got inside the British OODA loop, which sadly was often the case. At 1425 hours Rommel sent in his tanks and infantry in three groups, carving up the Camerons' position. By 1515 hours the enemy armour was almost at the battalion headquarters at Violaines, when the codeword for immediate withdrawal was received by wireless. Private Ross roared off on his motorbike to deliver the message to the companies. He managed to get through, but all the company commanders decided to lie low and wait for the battle to die down. This was a big mistake, as in the event only one platoon got clear. The remainder of the battalion at Violaines had better fortune thanks to the carrier platoon, and the anti-tank platoon, which claimed twenty-one tanks knocked out – probably an exaggeration, but there is no doubt that it did good work enabling some men to get back. A few Worcestershires, including their headquarters, also made it out of the cauldron.

At this critical moment, the 1st Army Tank Brigade arrived, a much reduced formation after the Arras battle. All it could muster was two Mk IIs, and eight Mk Is of a composite 4th and 7th RTR. The 1st/7th Queen's were no longer available as the complete 25th Brigade was now needed for other tasks. But the ten tanks set off to try to relieve the Cameron Highlanders. Two returned.

The entire length of the 2nd Division front was overhung with clouds of smoke, stabbed by the occasional German signal flare proclaiming objectives successfully achieved. As dusk fell, Irwin sent out staff officers to muster what was left of his 4th and 5th Brigades. They found fifty of the former and twenty of the latter.

There were still pockets of the 2nd Division holding out, of which the most substantial was at Festubert, held by the 2nd Dorsets. Here they had been on the edges of attacks by two panzer divisions (7th and 4th) that had brushed past their right rear and left. They had discouraged direct attack by the German armour using their Boyes rifles and a few 25mm guns. An infantry attack was also seen off. After dark, the CO, Lieutenant Colonel Stephenson, with a gunman on either side, set off on a compass bearing, leading some 250 Dorsets and an assortment of Lancashire Fusiliers, Worcesters and Argylls. It was seven miles to the Lys Canal as the crow flies, and Stephenson kept to the fields as best he could, avoiding German soldiers and blazing farms, and expertly navigating through the maze of lanes, dykes and hamlets. He met a German NCO, whom he despatched with his revolver. The column had to lie up for what seemed like eternity while a long convoy of trucks with lights on crossed his route. Coming to a wide canal, he got his men over, except for a few who drowned. Perversely, his route took him to this waterway again as it bent round in a curve. After crossing it, Germans were encountered again, this time a patrol, which went on its way without spotting the long column of weary soldiers. At 0500 hours they crossed the bridge at Estaires, which French engineers were about to blow. The British had all gone ahead, and were now followed by the Dorsets, exhausted but triumphant, and, thanks to their CO, at 250 strong the biggest battalion left in the 2nd Division.

The question has to be asked why the 2nd Division did not withdraw to the Lys Canal earlier and in good order, as all the brigade commanders in the division had asked of Major General Irwin. There are a number of possible reasons, among them the fact that Wason, the new commander of III Corps, spent two days after he took over from Adam trying to co-ordinate plans for the withdrawal ordered by Gort with the French commander on his left, General René Altmayer, commanding the French V Corps. Thanks to breakdowns in communications, frequent moves of headquarters, and traffic congestion on the roads, Wason did not manage to gain contact with his own divisions until they reached the Dunkirk bridgehead shortly before they were evacuated. Thus the formations of III Corps on the western flank of the BEF lacked the firm hand on the helm that Brooke applied in the east. Next, Irwin, recently promoted from command of the 6th Brigade, was unaware of the decisions taken to withdraw to Dunkirk and, without a corps commander to consult, may have felt unable to order a withdrawal off his own bat, surmising that this might uncover the flanks of the divisions on his left and right. Whatever the reason, Irwin did not order a withdrawal on the night of 26/27 May. This was a pity because, had he done so, instead of suffering heavy losses, the 2nd Division would undoubtedly have been in a better position to hold off the Germans – certainly up to the morning of 28 May. But their stout defence of the La Bassée Canal assisted the French III Corps in withdrawing two of its three divisions, and probably saved the British 42nd Division, out on a limb on Brooke's right flank, until the evening of 28 May.

On 27 May the German attacks continued without let-up. Although by that evening the 48th Division strongpoints were still holding, as was the 44th Division, the 2nd Division's battering and withdrawal had left the 44th's left flank dangerously exposed. The 46th Division had by now been ordered back to the Dunkirk perimeter, which increased the danger to the 44th Division. As the crisis built up, a guiding hand from III Corps commander was sorely missed, but he was stuck at General Prioux's French First Army headquarters. Here he found Prioux in a defeatist state of mind, although he did order the 1st and 3rd DLM to co-operate with the British.

Osborne, GOC 44th Division, spent most of 27 May hanging around at his headquarters waiting for Wason, who never turned up. Osborne sent a liaison officer to make contact with the French V Corps as instructed, but he did not return. It transpired that V Corps was now cut off, the French right flank south of the British 2nd Division having given way. During the day various French officers, including the commanders of IV Corps and the Cavalry Corps, and the chief of staff of First Army, turned up at Osborne's headquarters. They were apparently concerned that he, Osborne, was not aware that he was to hold the flank, the implication being that he was not doing what he had been instructed to do. As the area where the Germans had punched through with three panzer divisions and threatened to cut off large parts of French First Army was well south of Osborne's sector, there was nothing he could do about it – a fact that may have been lost on the French staffs, whose information was usually so out of date as to be useless. The chief of staff of French First Army rudely emphasized that Osborne was under command of First Army, which Osborne acknowledged with mental reservations.

All the while, the 44th Division was under attack but holding, although the 2nd Royal Sussex on the left of the 132nd Brigade were having a tough time. From the time the BGS of III Corps had left the previous night, Osborne had heard nothing from III Corps, except three messages, all of which had been so delayed as to be out of date by the time he received them. He spent some of the day attempting to mount a counter-attack as ordered. Eventually he decided, wisely, that without tank support from the French, which was not available, the operation was not possible. During the afternoon, Major General Irwin's headquarters moved into a field close to Osborne's. Irwin told Osborne that his division was fought out, and the remnants were coming back across the River Lys at Estaires. Osborne and Irwin agreed that the 2nd Division could do no more and should start north the next morning, having handed over rearguard duties to the French. Osborne gave orders that his own headquarters was to move north during the night to a position from where it could more readily control the forthcoming withdrawal.

It rained heavily on the night of 27/28 May, and, thanks to bad going, the German armour got off to a slow start the next morning. The German infantry, not so affected by terrain conditions, attacked the Nieppe Forest and Hazebrouck. The 1st Buckinghamshires (a TA battalion of the Oxfordshire and Buckinghamshire Light Infantry), part of the 145th Brigade of the 48th Division, had already been forced back into the convent at Hazebrouck by attacks the previous day. The first concentration of enemy mortar bombs hit an ammunition truck at about 0630 hours; the ensuing explosions lasted for two hours. Already short of ammunition, the Buckinghamshires were soon down to a few rounds per man as they engaged the attacking infantry that swarmed around the position. By around 1000 hours, unable to make headway against the Buckinghamshires, and after being joined by some tanks, the Germans brought up heavy guns and demolished the upper and middle floors of the convent, setting the building on fire. The remnants of the battalion, about a hundred men under Major Viney, ran out and took cover in an adjacent building. Eventually, completely surrounded and out of ammunition, they were forced to surrender. The Germans were moved to refer to their gallant resistance in a subsequent wireless broadcast as 'truly worthy of the highest traditions of the British Army'.

The 44th Division was attacked on both flanks: by the 8th Panzer Division in the north and SS Verfügungs and 3rd Panzer in the south. The fighting in the Nieppe Forest was confused and bitter. The 2nd Royal Sussex had the heaviest casualties, with few men left by the end of 28 May; the handful of survivors were cut off and rounded up. The Germans broke in behind battalions and attacked the divisional B Echelon area in rear.

By 28 May half the French First Army were surrounded in a pocket round Lille, where they held out for a further four days. There is no doubt that their stubborn resistance contributed to the BEF's escape to Dunkirk. In recognition of the garrison's gallantry, the Germans allowed them to march out with the full honours of war. But, equally certain, the fall of Lille added to the wave of anti-British sentiment in the French Army. Blanchard bellyached to Weygand that Gort had decamped north with the BEF leaving the French First Army in the lurch. As related in the previous chapter, Gort had almost pleaded with Blanchard to conform to his northwards movement – in vain, as the Frenchman preferred to do nothing.

Major General Osborne, commanding the 44th Division, was conscious that the situation on both flanks of his sector was deteriorating as 28 May wore on. He was, however, unaware of events elsewhere even on the western flank of the BEF, and unquestionably did not have the complete picture. He had received no specific orders about withdrawing, and merely knew he was to act in conjunction with the French. He was told that the French were concerned about the move of his divisional headquarters, but, by going to explain the reason to the commander of the Cavalry Corps, he managed to provide reassurance. He asked for tanks to assist the 133rd Brigade, which was having a punishing time particularly on its right, where German tanks were working round behind it. While Osborne was with the 133rd Brigade, some French tanks appeared and their presence appeared to have the effect of instilling some caution into the Germans because the tempo of their attacks abated – but only for a while, because the French soon withdrew without fighting.

Osborne's return to his headquarters was bedevilled by the increasing chaos in rear of the now disintegrating Canal Line caused by German penetration at several points, as well as French units mixed in with the residue of the British 2nd Division streaming northwards. The journey was made all the more hazardous by German aircraft machine-gunning the packed roads but not, surprisingly, dive-bombing, which was something to be thankful for. The move of Osborne's headquarters was thrown into disarray when the signals, provost and other sub-units of the divisional organization ran into German armour at the intended new location, Godewaerswelde, five miles south-west of Poperinghe. The provost company was ordered by its commander to head straight for Dunkirk, and most of two field ambulance companies were wiped out.[1] The divisional staff collected at Mont des Cats, some two miles further south, where some remained, while others came to join Osborne who was by now with the 131st Brigade. From here he headed to General Aisne's French IV Corps headquarters, arriving at about 1430 hours, to learn that the Belgians had given up the fight. Aisne said that this meant that the German divisions in the east would close in from Ypres, and that on the next day the French First Army, and by implication the British in the area, would all have to surrender. Osborne disagreed, saying that if led by the Cavalry Corps it was possible to go out to Dunkirk. Aisne concurred, but said that General Prioux and First Army would not hear of it.

Osborne's next visit was to Prioux's First Army headquarters, where he found him in conference with his staff and saying gloomily that there was nothing for it but surrender. Osborne said he preferred to fight, and contended that by doing so it was possible to escape encirclement. One or two of the staff showed by their expressions that they agreed with him. The argument continued for about twenty minutes, and Osborne's French became 'abnormally fluent'. Prioux argued that withdrawal and evacuation was not an operation of war, that it was impossible, and that if anyone got away it would be the British and they would abandon the French. Osborne riposted that a breakout would be acclaimed as a great feat of arms, that as General Adam was organizing the embarkation it would succeed, and that every Frenchman would have the same chance of evacuation as an Englishman. He urged Prioux to send a cipher message to General Blanchard at Dunkirk asking permission to march north. Eventually Prioux grudgingly assented. A 'wishy-washy' signal was drafted, which Prioux signed, shrugging and commenting, 'C'est inutile' (It is useless).

Osborne said he would stay with the Cavalry Corps (while thinking that it might have been better to have reserved freedom of action, but at the same time calculating that his division might not last long without armoured support and Prioux's DLMs would do very nicely). He left saying that he was on his way to 132nd Brigade headquarters, which was very easy to find, getting Prioux's assurance that he would send Blanchard's answer to him there.

At the 132nd Brigade headquarters, he found Brigadier Steele very hard pressed. In a fit of gloom he and Steele tore up their wives' letters, not wanting them to fall into enemy hands. Osborne told Steele that when he could hold no longer he was to withdraw behind the 1st DLM which held a line in rear, and come into divisional reserve. From the 132nd Brigade Osborne went to the 131st in the centre, where his staff were still located. He knew that by withdrawing Steele's brigade he would be weakening the flank, and thought he had better inform General Aisne of IV Corps. On arrival, Aisne told him that the French had started pulling out, and added that Osborne should see Prioux. Osborne found Prioux at about 2100 hours alone and in a dark room lit by a single candle, and here he learned that Prioux had ordered the two DLMs and II Corps to withdraw via Bailleul and Poperinghe to Dunkirk, but that he himself was remaining with IV Corps to surrender. The withdrawal was to start at 1200 hours the next day, 29 May.

Osborne asked Prioux why he had not told him and what he was expecting him, Osborne, to do since he was in contact with the enemy all along the line in the west. All Prioux could say was 'Go and see General de la Laurencie,' commander of III Corps. Osborne, spotting a copy of Prioux's orders on the table, neither addressed to nor sent to him despite his being 'under command' of First Army, picked it up and took it with him. De la Laurencie brusquely informed him that he was not waiting until noon the next day to withdraw, but was going in an hour, at 2300 hours, through Bailleul, and that he, Osborne, could do what he liked. Osborne, riposting that he considered it the grossest treachery, walked out. One of Osborne's staff extracted details of the routes the French were to follow, and Osborne returned to his division along roads packed with French troops. Just before arriving at 131st Brigade headquarters, which was doubling as divisional headquarters, Osborne met Brigadier Steele at the head of some of his 132nd Brigade. He had heard that the 1st DLM was pulling out and decided to do likewise. Orders for the withdrawal reached most of the battalions at around last light. But withdrawal was easier said than done. On the fringe of the Nieppe Forest which they still held, the 4th Royal West Kents could break contact only by counter-attacking first, which cost them dear. The 2nd Royal Sussex were surrounded and never broke out. The 1st Royal West Kents lost their headquarters and much of their F Echelon transport in a traffic jam at a level crossing.

Despite these losses, Osborne was relieved that at least part of one of his brigades had got away. At headquarters 131st Brigade, he held what he described as a 'weird conference'. By now it was too late to disengage and get back behind the screen of the French Cavalry Corps. Brigadier Utterson-Kelso wanted to wait until morning and 'form square and die fighting'. Osborne vetoed this suggestion. He ordered the two remaining brigades to disengage and make for Mont des Cats, there being a good chance of reaching the feature before daylight and it was tank proof. If they could stay there for a day, the division could go in small parties to Dunkirk the following night. The CO of the 6th Queen's asked to be allowed to go to Dunkirk direct. He did and Brigadier Utterson-Kelso went with him. They got through, but any body of troops larger than a battalion would not have made it by the direct route.

There was an officer at the conference from the 2nd Buffs, who was sent to the battalion, sited out on a limb on the left of the 131st Brigade, with orders to withdraw. He failed to get through to them, and a warrant officer whom Utterson-Kelso despatched later was also unsuccessful. The 2nd Buffs never received the orders and the battalion, less a couple of detachments, went into the bag the next day.

Osborne sent one of his staff off on a motorcycle to Dunkirk to tell headquarters III Corps what he was about to do. The officer was not seen again. Then, having destroyed some vehicles and as much of their kit as possible, Osborne and what remained of his division trudged north to Les Cats, unhindered by the Germans, who had settled down for the night.

Mont des Cats was dangerously isolated and potentially easy to cut off. The Germans had approached the feature the previous day, and tanks had shelled it but inexplicably retired. Had they seized the feature, they would have sat astride one of the main withdrawal routes to Dunkirk. The Germans also shelled and bombed Cassel on 28 May, but did not attack. Meanwhile the German panzer and motorized divisions were pressing in to the north of Cassel and between the town and Mont des Cats to its south. The 2nd Panzer Division had taken Soex, which stands on a feature overlooking Dunkirk, and Usherforce had been forced back to Bergues (now the headquarters of both Thorne and Usher). Both 2nd Panzer and 20 Motorized Divisions were in a good position to exploit the four-mile gap between Bergues and Wylder opened up by the loss of Soex. Thorne's only recourse was to take troops from Cassel to plug the gap. Accordingly Brigadier Norman of the 1st Reconnaissance Brigade was ordered to bring one of his yeomanry regiments and the 1st Welsh Guards. The East Riding Yeomanry were exhausted by their harrying of the Germans as they bypassed the town, so, led by the Fife & Forfar Yeomanry, the Welsh Guards in trucks motored north-east on minor roads, the main road having been seized by the Germans. At one point along the narrow road slow-moving French horsedrawn limbers imposed an unwelcome delay. But an attempt to block the route by leading elements of the 2nd Panzer Division, who had just reached Quaedypre, was quickly quashed when the 1st Welsh Guards smartly booted them out of the village. Norman's blocking force was beefed up by adding the 6th Green Howards removed from the vicinity of the beaches at Dunkirk.

During 28 May, the town of Wormhoudt, between Bergues and Cassel, was taken by the 20th Motorized Division. The defenders consisted of the 2nd Royal Warwicks, minus a company, and the 8th Worcesters, minus two companies, and the 4th Cheshire and Worcestershire Yeomanry. By 1800 hours, the three companies of Warwicks, holding the north and west of the town, were badly reduced by casualties and almost surrounded. About seventy-four all ranks commanded by Major Hicks fought their way out. The rest surrendered to the Leibstandarte SS Adolf Hitler, the leading troops of the 20th Motorized Division, supported by armour of the 10th Panzer Division. The SS troops murdered more than eighty of their captive Warwickshire and Yeomanry soldiers with grenades, bayonets and bullets. A few British soldiers survived the war to report yet another atrocity by the infamous SS. One of these was Gunner Fahey, a Royal Artillery anti-tank gunner, cut off from his unit and lying wounded in a ditch with some other soldiers, after their truck had been attacked by a German aircraft. A party of British soldiers being marched into captivity came by, and were told to pick up the wounded from the ditch. They were all herded into a barn, which by now contained about a hundred men. A German officer ordered the British out in groups of five to be shot. Fahey remembered hearing someone counting in German, 'Ein, zwei, drei, vier, fünf.' Eventually his turn came, and helped by another man he staggered out. At the last moment he turned round and was shot in the back. He thought he was dead, except that he felt blood bubbling in his lung and pain in his leg where he had been shot earlier in the day. During a lull, when the Germans lost interest and moved away, he managed to crawl back into the barn where there were several dead and dying men among soldiers who had survived untouched so far. At some point the Germans had stopped taking men out of the barn, and instead went in and shot them at random with rifles and sub-machine guns. The Germans left, and the British soldiers, terrified and despairing, lay there for what seemed to Fahey like all the rest of the day. The following morning, some ordinary German soldiers arrived, dressed their wounds and cared for them, before they were taken into captivity. These soldiers told them that they had been captured by the Leibstandarte SS Adolf Hitler (LSSAH).[2] One of the LSSAH battalion commanders,

SS-Sturmbanführer (Major) Wilhelm Mohnke, was believed to have been responsible. When the time came to bring him to justice he was a prisoner of the Russians. Following his release, he was never charged, and lived the remainder of his life in Germany.

The order to the rest of the 144th Brigade to pull out of the Wormhoudt area was received in good time, and the Worcesters on the southern side of the town managed to make a clean break thanks to a combination of excellent shooting by a troop of the Worcester Yeomanry and a rainstorm. The 5th Gloucesters were still holding Ledringham, about two miles south-west of Wormhoudt, when two soldiers appeared bringing the order to withdraw, having spent four hours evading the German infantry who had invested the village. The Gloucesters had given a good account of themselves in the village, using the buildings to maximum advantage, to make the enemy come to them, and destroying tanks among the houses. But they had also paid dearly themselves, and a bare 200 men were fit to fight. It took four bayonet charges to hack their way out, an officer being killed in each one. This left 143 survivors, who taking their wounded with them on two carthorses and in wheelbarrows eventually staggered into Bambecque at 1830 hours. They brought three prisoners with them, a German officer and two soldiers, surprised while asleep.

Thorne decided he should now withdraw his 145th Brigade from Cassel. A sergeant despatch rider sent with the order to pull out was told by the 144th Brigade, which he encountered en route, that he would be unable to get through on a motorbike. He transferred to an armoured car, but this crashed into a ditch. Attempts at sending wireless messages were jammed all night by the Germans. At dawn the intrepid sergeant got through and delivered his message. Brigadier Somerset, the commander of the 145th Brigade, decided to wait for the onset of night before pulling out.

By dawn on Wednesday 29 May, Cassel, itself on high ground, and Mont des Cats with its large monastery were like islands standing out in the approaching tide of German armour and motorized infantry. These were to prove a fortuitous diversion to German formations heading for the right flank of the 50th Division astride Poperinghe.

At Mont des Cats, General Osborne, having arrived at the monastery, told his CRE and CRA to organize the defences, and as his people came in they were deployed. Eventually the remnants of the division collected there consisted of the 5th Queen's, the 4th and 5th Royal Sussex, the 65th Field Regiment with guns but no ammunition, and a battery of the 5th Royal Horse Artillery (RHA) with four guns and some ammunition. The yard was crammed with vehicles, and there were many others out on the road stretching down the hill. Osborne did not expect any German attacks before about 1000 or 1100 hours – according to him, this was their usual starting hour. But at first light the 44th Division survivors could see motorized infantry and tanks coming over the plain and in a very short time the enemy were engaging Mont des Cats with mortars. The RHA battery shot up some of the trucks carrying infantry, but before long two guns were knocked out. Wounded started to be brought in to the monastery. At about 0630 hours what they had all expected to happen happened.

A mass of Stukas arrived overhead and peeling off screamed in on Mont des Cats, inflicting around a hundred casualties. Despite a brave effort, the soldiers of the 44th Division had had little time to prepare the position, and were in no state to fight off the ground attack that would surely follow this pounding by the Luftwaffe. Although Osborne, the divisional commander, had said that he would stay and fight, he was persuaded by one of the infantry battalion commanding officers to order a withdrawal. He ordered a move in two columns to Poperinghe, where the French were supposed to be halting for that day.

His soldiers did not hang around, but streamed off the Mont and trudged northwards across country. The 4th Royal Sussex were the last to go, at 1100 hours, and took a number of casualties from shelling. It seems that the enemy did not see them go, for they kept on shelling and mortaring the monastery for several hours, eventually setting it on fire. The tanks of the French Cavalry Corps did sterling work laying down covering fire, which may have discouraged the Germans from snapping at the 44th Division's heels.

Nearly all the 44th Division's vehicles were abandoned on the Mont or on the approaches to Poperinghe. The area was a scene of devastation – guns, vehicles and other equipment lay burning or broken and abandoned. Everywhere groups of soldiers plodded north, French and British. As they headed for the coast, in the distance they could see a faint streak of smoke, rising from the fires in Dunkirk still over the horizon. The rumours, or in some cases information, that there they would find ships to carry them away sustained the British soldiers. Officers and NCOs worked to keep cohesion in units, helped by the innate bloody-mindedness of the British soldier, the comradeship within units and sub-units, and the general unwillingness to let down one's mates. The late-twentieth-century soldier's expression, 'You can't crack me, I'm a rubber duck,' would have been strange to the men of 1940, but expresses precisely how they felt.

At the tail of the horde of men came the 44th Division. The eleven miles between Cassel and Poperinghe were not defended. Had the Germans taken advantage of it, they could have gobbled up the 44th Division and swung in behind the 50th and 3rd Divisions, themselves under attack by five infantry divisions. Fortunately the enemy were diverted by Cassel and, having comprehensively bombed the town, settled down to invest it.

North of Cassel, the Germans kept up the pressure on the 48th Division. Around Vyfweg and West Cappel the 1st Welsh Guards put up a staunch resistance, but the Germans continued to advance on Rex-poede and Rattekot, where Brigadier Norman of the 1st Reconnaissance Brigade had his headquarters. Four large German tanks appeared and attacked the headquarters, but were eventually driven off by 18-pounders of the 5th RHA. Fortunately the Welsh Guards held off the accompanying infantry, or tanks and infantry together would have succeeded in overrunning the headquarters. This pressure on the right wing of the BEF coincided with attacks over on the left wing, and especially on the 3rd Division, recounted in the previous chapter.

As planned by Brigadier Somerset, the men of his 145th Brigade left Cassel an hour after dark, to find that by now some German formations were five miles to the north-east and between them and the main body of the BEF. The 4th Oxfordshire & Buckinghamshires scattered the first Germans they encountered at the point of the bayonet. But the next enemy units stood firm, and the battalion was soon surrounded by tanks and infantry and forced to surrender. Brigadier Somerset, who was with the battalion, was taken prisoner, the most senior officer from the main body of the BEF to fall into German hands in the campaign. The East Riding Yeomanry lost most of their remaining armoured fighting vehicles in a minefield. The 2nd Gloucesters tried to creep down the anti-tank ditch on the Franco–Belgian frontier, but ended up in a wood surrounded by enemy tanks. All were taken prisoner, except Second Lieutenant Fane and thirteen soldiers who evaded capture and arrived at Dunkirk on 2 June, just in time to be evacuated from the beach in a semi-waterlogged boat. The last of the Gloucesters to be captured consisted of half a platoon holding an isolated blockhouse three miles north of Cassel. They held off all German attempts to seize it, even though the enemy gained the roof. On 30 May, after three days, cut off from all other British units, they tried to break out but, failing to get clear, were taken prisoner. By then, most of the units of the BEF that were going to get there were inside the Dunkirk perimeter.

The action by Brooke's II Corps on the eastern and south-eastern flank, described in the previous chapter, is often known as the manoeuvre that saved the BEF, and has tended to overshadow the fighting on the western and south-western flank. Here six panzer and three motorized divisions attacked three British divisions, of which one was short of a brigade –

whereas on the south-eastern and eastern flank there was no German armour. One is entitled to ask why the Germans on the south-western flank failed to slice through to link up with their comrades pressing in from the east much earlier than they did, destroying the BEF in the process.

The first reason is that the German armour attacked all along the line, and did not concentrate in a sickle-like thrust, as they had done after crossing the Meuse at Sedan a few days earlier. Indeed at one stage the general direction of Hoth's Group on the south wing of the attack diverged from that of Kleist's Group on the northern wing. The second reason lay in General Reinhardt's worry about Cassel, and the consequent failure of his XLI Corps to exploit the gap between there and Hazebrouck. His concern seems to have been about his flanks, and it is possible that the British counter-stroke at Arras may have made him edgy. Instead of pressing on, his 6th Panzer Division blocked Cassel, while his 8th Panzer, the SS Verfügungs and a regiment of the 29th Motorized Division were kept busy clearing Hazebrouck and the Nieppe Forest, before his corps pressed on.

It is easy to be wise after the event, pontificating from the calm of a book-lined study. But one has to remember that in war the true state of the opposition's capability is often far from clear. Even the superbly trained and astute German officers could be misled by the aggressive defence of the BEF into thinking that they were capable of more than they actually were. The BEF was dogged in defence, and could mount local counter-attacks that sometimes gained them elbow-room for a clean break. The war diary of XLI Corps sums up the German view of the British defence:

> Fighting for individual houses and villages prevents the Corps from gaining ground to the east and north-east. Losses in men and equipment are grievous. The enemy fights with determination and stays in his positions until the last moment; if he is expelled from one point he appears a little later at some other and takes up the fight again.[3]

The British soldiers certainly earned the respect of their opponents by their guts and determination, but in reality the BEF did not have any formations with sufficient mobile firepower to generate counter-attacks with enough punch and tempo and on a scale that would seriously discommode a panzer corps in full cry for long. Such puny armoured fighting assets that the BEF had possessed, the 1st Army Tank Brigade, had virtually shot their bolt at Arras. For the reasons given above, Reinhardt may have been unaware of this of course, hence his caution.

That the 6th Panzer Division failed to cut off the British 44th Division

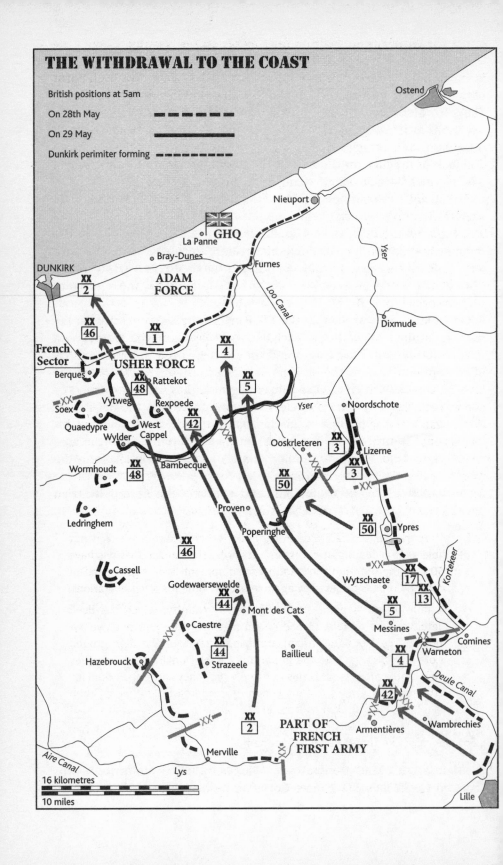

THE WITHDRAWAL TO THE COAST

British positions at 5am

On 28th May ▄▄ ▄▄ ▄▄ ▄▄

On 29 May ▬▬▬▬▬▬

Dunkirk perimiter forming ▄ ▄ ▄ ▄ ▄ ▄

Ostend

Nieuport

GHQ
La Panne
Bray-Dunes
Furnes

DUNKIRK

XX
2

ADAM
FORCE

Yser

Loo Canal

XX
46

French
Sector

XX
1

XX
4

Dixmude

Berques

USHER FORCE

XX
48
Rattekot

XX
5

Yser

Noordschote

XX
Soex

Vytweg

Rexpoede

XX
42

Ooskrleteren

XX
3

Lizerne

Quaedypre
Wylder
West
Cappel

XX
3

Wormhoudt

XX
48

Bambecque

XX
50

XX
3

Proven

Poperinghe

XX
50
Ypres

Ledringhem

XX
46

Cassell

XX
17

Wytschaete

XX
13

Godewaerswelde

XX
44
Mont des Cats

XX
5

Messines

Kortekeer

Caestre

XX
44
Strazeele

Baillieul

XX
4
Warneton

Comines

Hazebrouck

XX
42

Deule Canal

Armentières

Wambrechies

XX
2

PART OF
FRENCH
FIRST ARMY

Aire Canal

Merville

Lys

16 kilometres

10 miles

Lille

is astonishing, since by the evening of 28 May the armour was well north of the 44th, between the British and Dunkirk, and in a position to do so. The 29th Motorized Division in the Nieppe Forest clearly misread the situation, as its diary records that 'the enemy had abandoned so much equipment and vehicles that it was only possible to advance on foot'.[4] The lack of urgency on the part of the 29th Motorized also contributed to the British 44th Division getting clean away.

British anti-tank gunners also gave the Germans a nasty surprise. Well-sited anti-tank guns manned by resolute troops can cause heavy casualties to armoured formations, especially if the attacker has insufficient infantry and does not co-ordinate his artillery to best effect. The British were to learn this lesson again and again in the desert, and as late as July 1944 at the Battle of Goodwood in Normandy had still apparently not fully absorbed it.

On 28 May, the war diary of the XIX Panzer Corps commenting on the fighting around Wormhoudt included the passage: 'The Corps commander [Guderian] is not counting on any success from this attack and is of the opinion that further useless sacrifice must be avoided after the severe casualties which the 3rd Panzer Regiment has suffered during the counter-attack.'[5] The phrase 'useless sacrifice' appears in the XIX Panzer Corps war diary again after Guderian had returned from a tour of his formations, and the diary also states: 'in his [Guderian's] view the wise course is to hold positions reached and let 18 Army's attack from the east take effect'.[6] The German Eighteenth Army was part of Army Group B and had been engaged in Holland and against the Belgians. Guderian advised the chief of staff of Kleist Group as follows:

(1)   After the Belgian capitulation continuation of operations here is not desirable as it is costing unnecessary sacrifices. The panzer divisions have only 50% of their strength left and their equipment is in urgent need of repair if the Corps is to be ready again in a short time for other operations.

(2)   A tank attack is pointless in the marshy country, which has been completely soaked by rain. [It had rained heavily in the previous twenty-four hours.] The troops [German] are in possession of the high ground south of Dunkirk; they hold the important Cassel–Dunkirk road; and they have favourable artillery positions ... from which they can fire on Dunkirk.
Furthermore 18 Army [of Army Group B] is approaching [Kleist] Group from the east. The infantry forces of this army are more suitable than tanks for fighting in this kind of country, and the task of closing the gap on the coast can therefore be left to them.[7]

Kleist agreed, and General von Wietsheim's XIV Motorized Corps replaced Guderian's XIX Panzer Corps on 29 May. This change of command inevitably led to a reduction in tempo on the part of the Germans, just when the BEF was at its most vulnerable. In truth the German armoured commanders had lost interest in this battle. The infantry of Army Group B (Sixth and Eighteenth Armies) plus 9th Panzer Division reinforced and 20th Motorized Division could round up the BEF, while the bulk of the armour, eventually to consist of five panzer corps, concentrated on preparations to complete the defeat of the French.

9

COMINGS AND GOINGS AT DUNKIRK

Operation Dynamo is to commence.

Admiralty signal, 26 May 1940[1]

Dunkirk harbour in 1940 was the biggest on the Channel coast and the third largest in France. It had seven deep-water basins, four dry docks and five miles of quays. Surrounded by marshes that were easily flooded, it was the most defensible too, and although most of the fortifications around the town were old, they were capable of standing up to considerable shelling. Near the docks was the hugely strong Bastion 32, containing the headquarters of Admiral Abrial, the naval and military commander of the northern coastline, who took his orders only from Paris. The English-speaking General Fagalde, whose XVI Corps was transferred from the Belgian front, was ordered by Weygand to come under Abrial's command and take charge of the Boulogne–Calais–Dunkirk sector. So, in addition to his corps, Fagalde had three garrison battalions, two training units, three almost unarmed labour regiments, a couple of anti-tank batteries, five infantry battalions from the 21st Division and eleven batteries of artillery. By the time Fagalde arrived at Dunkirk, Boulogne and Calais were about to be invested by the Germans.

To follow the story of the forming of the bridgehead, we must wind the clock back and at times reiterate aspects of some events covered in earlier chapters. On the morning of Monday 20 May, Admiral Sir Bertram Ramsay, the Flag Officer Commanding Dover, held his first meeting at his headquarters to consider the possibility of large-scale evacuation if, 'as then seemed *unlikely*', the need should arise (emphasis in original).[2] The speed with which the situation in France and Belgium subsequently unravelled is brought home when one recalls that on the morning of Ramsay's 20 May meeting the BEF was on the Escaut Line, the Channel ports were still in Allied hands and the German panzer divisions had only just started crossing the Canal du Nord, south-east of Arras. By Sunday 26 May the whole of France north of the Somme was in German hands, except for the sack containing the BEF and the French First Army, and the Belgian 'appendix' – a sack which was being squeezed hard.

The evacuation of British troops from Dunkirk had actually started on 19 May when GHQ ordered that 'useless mouths' be sent back to England. There were plenty of these, as Dunkirk had been used as the port of entry for many non-combatant specialists. In addition there was an accumulation of wounded in casualty clearing stations in and around Bailleul, south of Poperinghe. From here the road and railway provided the safest evacuation route to Dunkirk, a route that became increasingly hazardous as the Germans closed in. Thanks to the attentions of the Luftwaffe, Dunkirk probably marked the most dangerous point in the journey. On 20 May the German bombing of the port had become so severe that all merchant ships were ordered out of port. Despite this, by midnight on 26 May 27,936 wounded and unwounded troops had been transported to England. The evacuation, codename Operation Dynamo, had begun.

There had been less than a week to plan, and furthermore no one could predict the scale of Operation Dynamo with any certainty. No one knew how many troops would reach the coast. Even if almost everyone made it, an evacuation of this magnitude was not just a matter of everyone slogging back to the coast and expecting it all to happen. To begin with, the planners in London estimated that the enemy could be held for a maximum of two days, and that around 45,000 soldiers might be brought off. Naval plans were made accordingly, and although not all the ships and craft that it was thought would be needed were yet assembled, the *Mona's Isle*, an armed boarding vessel, sailed for Dunkirk two hours after the Admiralty signal quoted at the head of this chapter was sent. She arrived in Dunkirk in the middle of an air raid, but embarked 1,420 troops. After leaving harbour to return to England, she was straddled by enemy guns on shore between Gravelines and Les Hemmes, and was then machine-gunned by enemy aircraft. Twenty-three men on board were killed and sixty wounded. She reached Dover at midday on Monday 27 May. Five transports that had sailed earlier that morning were so heavily shelled off the French coast that they could not reach Dunkirk, and turned back. A glance at the map on p. 222 shows how the fall of Calais on 26 May allowed the enemy to site guns on the coast and interdict the last leg of the most direct sea route from Dover to Dunkirk (Route Z). Accordingly an alternative route (Route Y) was swept of mines, but the diversion more than doubled the length of the passage. This longer route increased the danger of attack by surface craft, U-boats and the Luftwaffe, while doubling the turn-round time of vessels, thus halving the number of troops that could be brought off over a given period. Later, Ramsay brought Route X into operation. Against surface attack it was better protected by sandbanks and nearby British mine-

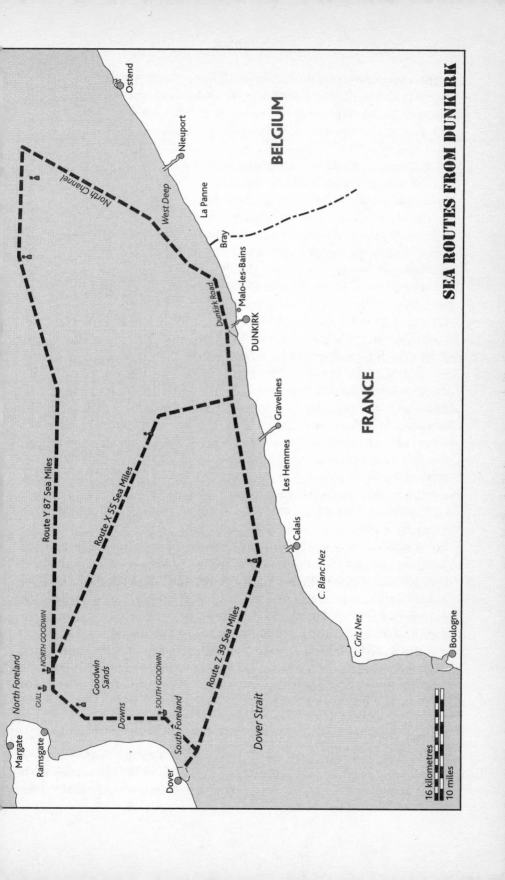

SEA ROUTES FROM DUNKIRK

Ostend

Nieuport

BELGIUM

North Channel

West Deep

La Panne

Bray

Malo-les-Bains

Dunkirk Road

DUNKIRK

FRANCE

Gravelines

Les Hemmes

Calais

C. Blanc Nez

Route Y 87 Sea Miles

Route X 55 Sea Miles

C. Griz Nez

Boulogne

Route Z 39 Sea Miles

North Foreland

Margate

Ramsgate

NORTH GOODWIN

GULL

Goodwin
Sands

Downs

SOUTH GOODWIN

South Foreland

Dover

Dover Strait

16 kilometres

10 miles

fields, and it was shorter than Route Y. But navigational difficulties posed by the sandbanks and minefields restricted this route to daylight only. These difficulties possibly explain why it took the Germans three days before they discovered that this route was in use, and provided a respite from attack by the Luftwaffe, much appreciated by the crews and passengers of the vessels ploughing back and forth.

The shipping allocated to Ramsay for Operation Dynamo was of a magnitude inconceivable today after over sixty years of erosion of British maritime power. Despite the demands of the Battle of Narvik in Norway, still in progress, the Atlantic convoys, the Mediterranean and the Far East, Ramsay had thirty-nine destroyers, including the Polish destroyer *Błyskawica* (this was one-fifth of the Royal Navy's current total), the anti-aircraft cruiser *Calcutta*, thirty-eight minesweepers, sixty-one minesweeping craft, eighteen anti-submarine trawlers, six corvettes, one sloop and seventy-nine other small craft including motor torpedo boats, gunboats and Dover flare-burning drifters. The Merchant Navy provided thirty-six passenger ferries, seven hospital ships converted from ferries, and various trawlers, barges and dredgers. In addition there were the 'little ships', civilian-owned yachts and motor cruisers. The French, Belgians and Dutch also provided shipping, including nineteen French destroyers, sixty-five French civilian craft and forty-three Dutch schuyts ('scoots' to their Royal Navy crews). In all some 848 vessels served under Ramsay for the Dunkirk evacuation, an impressive demonstration of British maritime power. Without Britain's command of the seas and the array of vessels no large-scale evacuation could have even been contemplated.

The meticulous organization by Ramsay and his staff included the issue of charts to the skippers of the mass of craft, many of whom had never crossed the Channel in their lives and whose knowledge of navigation was meagre. Lieutenant George Grandage RNR, working in the Naval Control Office at Ramsgate, had three large boxes of charts delivered to his office by London taxi. As he had not ordered them he telephoned the Hydrographic Office of the Admiralty, to be told, 'You'll need them.' There were 1,500 charts in all, 500 in each set, covering the route from Ramsgate to Dunkirk. Grandage was told by the senior operations officer at Dover over the telephone that Ramsgate Naval Control Office was responsible for despatching all the small craft from Tilbury, London, and ports on the Essex coast to Dunkirk. Grandage worked out the route, and his typist produced 500 copies – one for each craft, plus a set of three charts. Three buoys had been laid from the north of the Goodwin sands to Dunkirk, but they were not marked on the charts. Some of the craft Grandage was responsible for despatching had navigational equipment, but many did not, so he and one assistant laid off the courses and positions on about 1,000 of the charts. It took them all day and most of a night.

On Sunday 26 May, the day that Gort had been ordered to withdraw to the coast, and the Admiralty instructed to carry out Operation Dynamo, General Adam, having handed over command of III Corps, was sent to Dunkirk to organize its defence and the evacuation. He had to leave his corps staff to work for his successor, and took with him three staff officers from GHQ: the quartermaster general (QMG) Lieutenant General Lindsell; the chief engineer, Major General Pakenham-Walsh; and Lieutenant Colonel the Viscount Bridgeman, a GSO 1, who had earlier been sent to Dunkirk to start planning the perimeter defence.

The 27th of May was a crucial day in Operation Dynamo, and at 0600 hours another of the key players arrived at Dunkirk on board the destroyer *Wolfhound* – Admiral Ramsay's representative with the title Senior Naval Officer Ashore at Dunkirk, Captain W. G. Tennant RN. He brought with him a beach party of twelve officers and 150 ratings, later reinforced by another 200 officers and ratings. He found Dunkirk in the middle of an air raid, the latest in a series that had apparently been in progress for over twenty-four hours. Just before *Wolfhound* docked, Tennant saw a signal from Adam saying, 'Complete fighter protection now essential if serious disaster is to be avoided.' Tennant's reaction was to signal Ramsay at 0800 hours: 'Please send every available craft to beaches east of Dunkirk immediately. Evacuation tomorrow night problematical.'

The beaches to which Tennant had directed 'all available craft' stretched nearly twenty miles from Dunkirk to the mouth of the Yser. Behind the beaches the sand dunes dotted with clumps of grass provided good assembly areas for troops awaiting embarkation. The gently shelving sandy beaches each side of Dunkirk, one of the reasons for it being such a popular holiday resort, meant that even small craft could not get nearer than within about a hundred yards of the waterline, so soldiers had to wade out to them. There were no jetties, no little fishing harbours and no piers at the three resorts Malo-les-Bains, Bray-Dunes, and La Panne. The shoal water close in to shore meant that the larger vessels had to anchor well offshore, and the craft ferrying troops out to them had a long turn-round time. Tennant saw that the extensive inner docks at Dunkirk had been made unusable by German bombing. The outer basin was protected by two moles. The West Mole was connected to the oil terminal, which was on fire and blocking access to the mole itself. The 1,600-yard-long East Mole was connected to the beaches by a narrow causeway. Both moles were designed as breakwaters; neither was built for ships to berth alongside.

Early on the morning of 27 May, Adam met Fagalde in Cassel. Fagalde had already discussed arrangements with Bridgeman the day before, and arriving ahead of the other French generals quickly came to an agreement with Adam on the plan drawn up by Bridgeman. A perimeter was to be established between Gravelines and Nieuport-Bains, past Bourbourg, Bergues and Furnes, thirty miles long and up to seven miles deep. The French would be responsible for the sector from Gravelines to Bergues, and the British from Bergues to Nieuport-Bains. At this stage the Belgians had not surrendered, but their intentions were too vague for any of their formations to be incorporated in the plan. The perimeter ran along a series of canals around Dunkirk; small waterways and ditches seamed the marshy terrain, the sea dykes had been opened and the ground was beginning to flood. It was not good country for armour.

Soon after the plan was agreed, Abrial, Blanchard (Commander of the French First Group of Armies) and General Koeltz, representing Weygand, joined Adam and Fagalde. The new arrivals did not question the plans, but it seemed to Adam that the French saw the bridgehead as a springboard for offensive action. Koeltz said that Weygand had proclaimed that the time had come to stop the retreat and attack the Germans everywhere. Clearly Weygand had still failed to come to terms with reality. Fagalde then rose and said he would return to his headquarters and give orders for an immediate attack on Calais, 'driving the Germans before him'. British jaws dropped, as the French applauded. Adam and his party withdrew as quickly as they could.

On their way to Bergues, Adam's party was machine-gunned by some Belgian biplanes wearing German markings. Pakenham-Walsh was wounded in the shoulder. Stopping at Bergues to see Thorne (GOC 48th Division), Adam found that he could not spare any troops to man the perimeter. Thorne did however lend him his CRA, Brigadier Frederick Lawson, to provide gunner advice on the establishment of the defences. Following a reconnaissance of the perimeter, Adam set up his headquarters in the town hall at La Panne. This seaside resort had a direct telephone line to England, installed by the Belgian King Albert to enable him to keep in contact with the London Stock Exchange while in his holiday villa.

Adam went on into the Bastion at Dunkirk, where he met Fagalde and Captain Tennant RN. Fagalde announced that, thanks to German pressure, he would have to pull back from the area west of Dunkirk. Adam, tongue in cheek, remarked that in view of his, Fagalde's, intervention earlier, he had expected to find him on his way to Calais. Fagalde replied that someone had to respond to Koeltz's moving speech, and he seemed to be the only one ready. Later that day, the French withdrew from Gravelines, to a new line Mardick–Spycker–Bergues.

The British sector was split into three corps areas. II Corps was to hold the eastern end and be evacuated from the La Panne beaches; I Corps would be in the centre and be taken off from Bray-Dunes, while III Corps would be on the western end and withdraw from Malo-les-Bains. Vehicles, except those essential for fighting, would be left outside the perimeter, and supply dumps were established in each corps area.

Meanwhile, Adam was already concerned that the small number of men being taken off the beaches would result in most of the BEF being left behind. He telephoned the War Office and pointed out in forthright language that the number of craft being provided, and the number of naval beach parties, was inadequate. (Naval beach parties were responsible for calling in boats for loading, controlling the embarkation of troops, ensuring that craft were not overloaded and despatching them when full.) Adam decided to send Captain Moulton Royal Marines, a GSO 3 on Gort's staff, to see Ramsay at Dover and tell him where the troops were concentrating.

Moulton had already been down to the beaches the previous night when three small sloops arrived, with no idea where the troops were. To take them off there was one motor boat and one 27-foot whaler per sloop (six boats in all). There was a strong current, and Moulton knew enough about seamanship to realize that the boats' crews would need assistance from the shore. So he waded out with some of the soldiers, and an RNR sub-lieutenant in the stern of one of the boats fired a revolver over his head, thinking perhaps he was about to be swamped by panic-stricken troops. Moulton calmed him down and eventually went off in the boat and saw the captain of one of the sloops. He got the ships moved towards one of the corps embarkation points. But the captain was worried about the shallow water and anchored off at some distance.

Moulton immediately returned to La Panne, with water dripping from his battledress. He called on Adam and said, 'This is not going to work.' He suggested he went over to Dover and see what he could do to sort it out. At first Adam was reluctant to let him go, suspecting that he was 'windy' and wanted to escape. But in the end he agreed. Moulton crossed in one of the Royal Navy sloops, and went first to the army headquarters at Dover, whose staff had absolutely no idea what was needed, and then made for Ramsay's underground headquarters, where he saw the admiral and showed him a map with the corps embarkation points marked on it. Having done this he caught a destroyer returning to Dunkirk, only for her to be ordered back before she reached France. Nothing loath, Moulton boarded another destroyer at Dover and eventually came ashore at Bray-Dunes. He then walked to La Panne. It must be emphasized that Moulton's only task was to tell Ramsay where the corps embarkation points were. By his own admission, he had not thought of embarkation at Dunkirk, because of the risk of bombing. By this time the Luftwaffe had already bombed Dunkirk heavily, destroying part of the town and making the docks and harbour extremely dangerous.

Also starting on 27 May, the RAF began a supreme effort to keep the Luftwaffe away, an endeavour that lasted throughout the evacuation. Fighter Command provided sixteen squadrons to give continuous cover over the area from 0500 hours until nightfall, and on that first day flew 287 fighter sorties. Pilots flew two or even three sorties a day from airfields in England, nearly always being outnumbered by the enemy. Troops returning from Dunkirk claimed that the RAF was not in evidence over the beaches and town. Although the aircraft might not have been visible overhead for most of the time, the RAF's superb performance was critical in keeping the Luftwaffe from having a free run over the bridge-head, and without it only a fraction of the BEF would have been evacuated. But the troops were sceptical, and there were frequent shouts of 'Where is the RAF?' and 'We never saw a fighter.' Feelings were very bitter between the army and navy on one hand and the RAF on the other. Flight Lieutenant Deere, a Spitfire pilot of No. 54 Squadron, was shot down about fifteen miles from Dunkirk, and eventually made his way to the town. He joined a queue of soldiers on the mole and was about to board a destroyer when a major stopped him and said, 'For all the good you chaps seem to be doing, you might as well stay on the ground.' As he embarked, he was greeted with stony silence from a group of army officers, and when he asked what the RAF had done, one replied, 'That's just it, what have they done?' Altogether Coastal Command flew 171 sorties, Bomber Command 651 and Fighter Command 2,739, all directly in support of Operation Dynamo. The RAF lost 145 aircraft, of which ninety-nine were fighters, including forty-two Spitfires. The Germans lost 132 aircraft, all to Fighter Command, who were thus thirty-three 'kills' ahead by the end of the battle.

Life for the Luftwaffe over Dunkirk was made easier than it need have been thanks to a misunderstood order. The British 2nd Anti-Aircraft Brigade, consisting of the 60th Anti-Aircraft Regiment (3.7-inch heavy AA guns) and 51st and 58th Light Anti-Aircraft Regiments (40mm Bofors light AA guns), had been made responsible for the anti-aircraft protection of Dunkirk. On Monday 27 May, Lieutenant Colonel Bridgeman, the GSO 1 on Adam's staff, briefed the liaison officer of the Major General Anti-Aircraft Artillery at GHQ, Major General H. G. Martin, that all guns were to remain in action as long as possible, spare gunners were to fight as infantry, and any gunners incapable of fighting, because of wounds, lack of small arms and so on were to go to the beaches. This order filtered down to the 2nd Anti-Aircraft Brigade as requiring that *all* gunners were to go to the beaches. Martin, reasoning that if all gunners were to go to the beaches the guns must first be put out of action, issued orders accordingly. In fact the 51st Light Anti-Aircraft Regiment did not spike its guns, but the protection afforded by the heavy anti-aircraft guns was to be sorely missed.

At midnight on 27/28 May only 7,669 men had arrived in England, and about two-thirds came on ships that had loaded in Dunkirk harbour before its use was suspended. By then Tennant, having already spotted that the embarkation from the beaches was painfully slow, ordered a destroyer to come alongside the East Mole. Early the next morning, six destroyers came alongside the mole and, under the cover of the RAF, quickly filled with soldiers. Tennant's gamble succeeded, and, thanks to the skill of the captains who came alongside the flimsy structure, this would become the principal means of evacuation. Late that afternoon, 28 May, the first of the 'little ships' appeared off the beaches.

That same day, mainly because of Tennant's bold decision the night before, and possibly because of what Moulton had told him, Ramsay shifted most of the effort from the beaches to the East Mole, mainly the larger ships and destroyers. Although not designed as troop carriers, the destroyers managed to squeeze in about 900 men each and sometimes more. Despite as many as possible being ordered below, the soldiers were reluctant to comply for fear of being trapped if the ship sank, with the result that the upper decks were so tightly crammed with men that the guns could not be fought, and the destroyers were so top-heavy they heeled disconcertingly as they zigzagged sharply to avoid air attack. On 28 May, 17,804 men were brought back to England. We should remind ourselves that by the end of that day the bulk of the BEF was still fighting to hold the sack, with divisions as far south as Armentières; only a minority had reached the perimeter. During that day the Belgians surrendered, and the dangerous gap along the Loo Canal had been opened up, as related in Chapter 7.

On 28 May Gort set up his headquarters at King Albert's holiday villa in La Panne. Adam's plan for the occupation of the bridgehead was: II Corps left, I Corps centre and III Corps right. As the BEF was in the process of withdrawing to the bridgehead there were some tense moments, mainly caused by the Belgian capitulation; some of these have already been covered in Chapter 7.

Because of the way its formations had been deployed, the headquarters of III Corps had never been able to keep as tight control over its divisions as the other two. On their way back to the bridgehead the troops of III Corps were intermixed with French troops of the First French Army.

Notices were erected at road junctions, 'Français à gauche, British to the right'. General de la Laurencie, commanding the French III Corps, who had defied orders from above to surrender and marched his 12th and 32nd Divisions back to Dunkirk, now ignored these notices, marching his men to the right. He headed for Gort's headquarters and asked that his divisions should be deployed with the British.

The experience of the 4th/7th Dragoon Guards was typical of the chaos of the final days. It will be remembered from Chapter 7 that the regiment had only enough tanks to equip one Combined Squadron to work with the surviving squadrons of the 5th Inniskilling Dragoon Guards ('Skins'). The remainder of the regiment formed a 'dismounted party'. At 1700 hours an order was received ordering the Combined Squadron, commanded by Major Frink, to remain in position until 2000 hours and then proceed independently to the area of Bergues, with the intention of getting to 'the boats at Dunkirk. Vehicles and guns will be destroyed.' The A Squadron diary comments acidly, 'Such an order would have led to chaos if it had been acted on. Some units did act on it, with the result that everyone [in those units] was extremely lucky to get away.'

Major Frink's diary continues:

Squadron came out a bit after 8 pm and proceeded via POPERINGHE–DUNKIRK road. Luckily the Boche, true to form, did not advance after dark. Four lines of traffic and absolute and complete chaos – everyone pointing revolvers at each other and shouting. Williams [OC C Squadron] continually at loggerheads with all in authority but won every round. Achieved one of my ambitions i.e. running down a large ASC [Army Service Corps] officer in large staff car making for first boat.

Our B Echelon had already been lost and all kit burned. Rather a blow as no one now had anything except what they stood up in. Drivers so tired that they went to sleep every time they pulled up which was every 50 yards.

The tracked light tanks could of course drive off-road.

Wednesday, May 29th. At dawn took to the fields as the only possible means of progress – quite a good line set by Williams – several vehicles packed up under the strain – arrived eventually on the Canal NE of Dunkirk – very tired and no rations. Found our old friends the Camerons holding the bridge, only 60 of them left. Luckily orders for destruction of vehicles had not been carried out as there were many jobs ahead of us. Found RHQ [Regimental Headquarters] and joined up with them. Parked in a potato field, excellent new potatoes were much enjoyed and practically our only rations. A lot of shelling and bombing, otherwise uneventful.

The Dismounted Party of the regiment also set out for Dunkirk on foot and, having put some abandoned trucks to good use, arrived at Dunkirk on the same day as the Combined Squadron. The Dismounted Party was eventually ordered by the 2nd Division to go down to the beach and get on board a boat as best it could. The beach was packed with troops, and there was no organization. Formed bodies took their place at the end of the queue, but individuals who emerged from streets that led to the beach usually tried to take a place anywhere, opposite where they hit the queue. Eventually an order was passed down the line that everyone was to form into parties of fifty. This was done after 'a certain amount of confusion'.

The queue in which the 4th/7th found themselves was about two miles long and advanced very slowly. From to time to time the Luftwaffe dive-bombed the area, but luckily concentrated on Dunkirk, especially the ships and the harbour. If the bombers had concentrated on the beaches, the slaughter would have been widespread. The space between the water's edge and the long causeway connecting the beach with the East Mole was 'black with troops'. Although some bombs did fall on the beaches, most fell on soft sand, penetrating some distance before exploding, and with most of the blast and splinters expended upwards, the resulting casualties were remarkably light.

A wrecked French destroyer about 200 yards offshore attracted some attention from the bombers, covering the queuing men with spray each time. Whenever the queue halted, each man would scrape a little depression in the sand as cover, unless he could occupy one dug by a predecessor who had now moved further up the queue. The onset of night brought relief from the dive-bombers, and some soldiers managed to sleep. During the night little progress was made, and most found themselves only a few yards nearer the head of the queue. By 30 May the organization, according to the 4th/7th short history, seems to have improved. 'Gate crashers' were being put back in their correct places. Low cloud resulted in reduced enemy air activity, and embarkation from the mole had speeded up; in the sector in which the 4th/7th found themselves beach embarkation had ceased for the time being. The Dismounted Party slowly filed up the mole and came under the 'efficient control of the Royal Navy', and a 'big Marine gave those who had receptacles a spoonful of hot stew. One officer had only a cocktail glass, which the Marine filled with hot gravy and added, "Can I put a cherry in it, Sir?"' Most of the Dismounted Party were evacuated during the morning of 30 May in the destroyer *Malcolm* and the passenger ferry *Royal Daffodil*.

The Combined Squadron, having been told it could go, 'elected to finish the job with the "Skins"'.[3] The 4th/7th Combined Squadron took the opportunity to do some scrounging, and Lieutenant Verdin and Second Lieutenant Riley returned with two new Bedford trucks and one 8-hundredweight, twelve chickens, boxes of rations and some petrol.

Second Lieutenant Blaxland of the 2nd Buffs, who had been evacuated to hospital in the Dunkirk area from the Escaut, was discharged in time to join the remnants of his battalion, most of whom had become prisoners of war in the fighting on the western flank of the BEF's withdrawal to the sea (see Chapter 8). He found them waiting to be evacuated, and when their turn came he marched with them along the beach towards the mole. On approaching the causeway to the mole, Blaxland saw a lone Bofors 40mm AA gun lowering its barrel until it appeared to be pointing straight at him at the head of the column – it was clearly about to engage an enemy aircraft swooping low over the beach behind them. He threw himself down as with a series of deafening booms it engaged a target which he never saw, because his range of vision was restricted to the drainage ditch alongside the causeway. There were ten soldiers lying in it looking remarkably relaxed and unconcerned. Then he realized they were dead, evidently not at the hands of the Bofors, as they still had their heads. The Bofors stopped, and Blaxland saw the faces of the gunners relax. He led his party up the mole at a steady jog and was delighted to be greeted by the captain of a destroyer alongside, shouting at him to tell his men to hand over their rifles as they came on board and get below quickly. Officers were directed to the Wardroom. A steward asked him what he wanted to drink, and he asked for a whisky and ginger ale. He was in Dover by late evening that same day.

Thursday 30 May saw the final deployment within the perimeter, Adam having handed over to the three corps commanders on 29 May, his work done. The dispositions are shown on the map on pp. 246–7. This was to be the last stand by the BEF, in a campaign that had been a fight for survival from the outset. The BEF had retreated over 138 miles, with its flanks threatened throughout, and never more so than in the final stages. The Germans had nearly succeeded in breaking into the bridgehead in the gap between Nieuport and Dixmude on two occasions; the gap was held, but only just. The enemy had been held back by scratch British forces, and badly delayed by throngs of Belgian refugees on the roads. The Germans had lacked armour in this sector, and were plainly desperately tired. But the BEF could not relax, as the bridgehead could be held for a few days only. The canals along the perimeter were nothing like as formidable as those in the earlier defence lines. Flooding was widespread, though in many places only inches deep. But this was deep enough to oblige the defenders to hold the houses and farms on the bunds above the water level. This exposed them to observation and fire from the more numerous houses and villages on the German side of the canal. The British were bone weary. They had been tired enough by 27 May, but few had managed a minute of sleep in the three days of continuous movement and action that followed. Guns and ammunition were desperately short. Out of sixteen medium and heavy regiments, only the 59th Medium was operational. The remainder had abandoned their guns on orders at stages on the way back. The field artillery regiments mostly had their guns, but were short of ammunition, relying on what was still carried in the divisional column, or by scrounging from stocks discovered in the bridgehead.

On the morning of 30 May, Rear Admiral Frederic Wake-Walker arrived at Dunkirk. The previous day he had returned to the Admiralty after lunch away from his office, either in his club or in a restaurant, to be told that the Vice Chief of Naval Staff, Rear Admiral Phillips, wished to see him. Phillips asked Wake-Walker if he would like to go to Dunkirk to try to get some organization into the embarkation there. Wake-Walker replied that he would be delighted. Some discussion ensued about exactly what he should be called, because it was not the intention that he should supersede Captain Tennant who was already Senior Naval Officer Dunkirk. Eventually he was dubbed Rear Admiral Dover, and appointed to be in charge offshore at Dunkirk. Wake-Walker would command from a succession of ships offshore, feeding vessels into the beaches and Dunkirk harbour, and controlling the flow of shipping. Tennant would be responsible for embarkation and the beach and dock parties ashore. Wake-Walker and Tennant could communicate by wireless, and both had a launch at their disposal and were thus able to make personal contact with each other. This episode tells us much about the period. Now, officers of the Navy Department, the modern successor to the Admiralty, and indeed those from the other two services, however senior, and in circumstances of considerably less peril for the nation, would probably be found lunching at their desks thus projecting the politically correct image of dedication and efficiency. But, when put to the test, they would be no more effective than Wake-Walker.

On his arrival off the beaches Wake-Walker saw the long queues of men from the back of the beach stretching into the sea as deep as a man could wade. Behind each line was a large group, waiting patiently. Destroyers and other vessels lay off the beaches while small craft ferried the troops out to them. The light swell hampered the beach work, and some craft had grounded and been caught by the falling tide, to remain useless until the flood. There was plainly a need for many more small boats. These were coming from Newhaven, Portsmouth and Sheerness, but had not arrived by the morning of 30 May. In addition six tugs were chugging across from Tilbury towing twenty-three motor and forty-six rowing lifeboats. Five were coming from Gravesend, towing barges. The assortment of craft heading for Dunkirk included car ferries, cockle-boats, speedboats, seaplane tenders, pleasure boats, private yachts and a Thames fire-float. By mid-morning with troops crowding to the water's edge there was a lull in the evacuation until, at last, the first twelve motor lifeboats, the most useful in terms of capacity and speed of turn-round, arrived. These, together with a miscellany of about thirty-two other craft, started ferrying troops out to the waiting ships.

That morning the engineers of 1st Division took advantage of the low tide to drive trucks as far as they could out into the sea to form a makeshift pier at Bray, which they decked with planks. As the tide came in it proved critical for speeding up the process of embarking men into the smaller craft. A similar pier was built at La Panne. From now on the evacuation began to gain momentum, although the 30th was the only day on which more men were lifted from the beaches (29,512) than from the harbour (24,311), and the day's total of 53,823 was the largest so far. Moreover shipping losses were the smallest, only two destroyers being damaged.

Mist and poor visibility had restricted the Luftwaffe all day. Naval officers had been frustrated by the slow progress of troops along the Dunkirk mole, resulting in what they perceived as a lost opportunity to take advantage of the lack of enemy air activity. Eventually a naval officer used a loudspeaker to address the troops slowly trudging along the mole: 'Remember your pals, boys – the quicker you get on board the more of them will be saved.' At that the soldiers broke into a double, keeping it up along the whole Eastern Mole for over two hours, during which time some 15,000 were embarked.

The enemy quickly followed up as the last of the BEF divisions entered the Dunkirk perimeter. All along the perimeter the Germans pressed in and shelled and mortared. Digging in was difficult for the defenders thanks to the flooded ground. The German reports state that 'the bridge-head is held by British troops who are fighting back very stubbornly'.

At 0100 hours Lieutenant Dunn's battery commander woke him and said that the 2nd Grenadiers were asking for artillery support. Their colonel and two other officers had been killed. Would he go and see what he could do? Dunn arrived in Furnes and found some of the weariest men he had ever seen. They were having trouble with snipers on the other side of the canal, and would he quieten them? As soon as it was light, he went up to their left forward company and was shown a house from where he could see the target. It was on the canal bank, and there was still an old woman living there, almost out of her mind with terror.

Now began a most difficult task. The BEF was in an area in which no one had foreseen that it would have to operate, and consequently there were no maps. Dunn was faced with spotting for a close-in shoot with a Michelin road map. He added 500 yards for luck to his estimated range, and eventually saw one of his rounds fall, and was able to correct from that. Having hit the likely sniper positions hard, he returned to the Grenadier battalion headquarters for breakfast and a shave. To his fury he was told that the battery had now moved, and the registration would have to be done again. He returned to his house and registered two defensive-fire tasks in front of the Grenadiers. At this moment a dirty, unshaven captain of the 4th Berkshires walked in saying that they were holding the line to the left of the 2nd Grenadiers. When they were walking back from the last position, they came under heavy German shellfire and now had five officers and a hundred men left. They had no gunners allotted to them and could Dunn help? So Dunn crawled to the canal bank and registered three defensive-fire targets for them. These were to come in useful later. By this time the Germans had begun to shell the centre of Furnes with a battery of 5.9-inch guns.

Dunn had an excellent lunch with the left forward Grenadier company: pâté, bully-beef stew, hock, port and cigars in a cellar. After lunch he returned to battalion headquarters, which was being shelled hard. Uncannily, the Germans did not take long to find any headquarters and take action accordingly. The house had deep cellars and there Dunn and his OP party sat until 1800 hours. Eventually the house came down on top of them, but the rubble did not block their exit. Through it all a grandfather clock continued ticking. Dunn's admiration for the Guards, always high, became unbounded during that afternoon. They discussed everything under the sun except the war, and he thought the atmosphere of complete calm and self-control was marvellous.

At about 1800 hours the bombardment reached a climax. Major Colvin, who had taken over as CO of the 2nd Grenadiers after Lieutenant Colonel Lloyd was killed, returned from brigade headquarters saying that a smokescreen was being laid in front of the Berkshires, and an attack seemed imminent there. Dunn asked if he wanted defensive fire, to which the answer was yes. By now the telephone wires had been cut to bits, and Dunn's wireless had a splinter through it, so he got into his car and drove back to the battery. It was the most unpleasant drive he had experienced up to then. The exits from Furnes were being heavily shelled, but he got through. As soon as the SOS had been fired, he returned to the town, enduring a repeat performance of his outward journey under heavy shellfire, and entered the battalion headquarters cellar. Here reports were coming in that the attack had been beaten off. The left-hand forward company sent back a message saying, 'Intense shelling, all positions held. All platoons in good heart.'

Major Colvin said although that attack had been beaten off he expected another that night, but on the front of the Berkshires. Would Dunn make the necessary arrangements? Dunn duly returned to the guns, and collected a wireless set. He had a couple of stiff drinks and ate some bully beef. The adjutant of 7th Field told him that they would have to stay for about five days – probably guesswork on his part. Dunn returned to Furnes convinced that they would never leave.

At about 2200 hours a message came in that bridging operations were in progress at the junction between the Grenadiers and the Berkshires. Dunn brought down defensive fire for about an hour, but without definite result. Defensive fire was called for again. It transpired that some Germans had got across. The under-strength Berkshires were forced to give ground, so the 1st Coldstream Guards from the 7th Guards Brigade were called in to put in a counter-attack. After confused fighting that cost all three company commanders killed, the Coldstreams regained enough ground to enable them to overlook a newly erected enemy pontoon bridge. They called down artillery fire and smashed it.

The position having been restored, Dunn was recalled to his battery, to be told that it would be withdrawing early the next day, but that a section with three officers would remain. A coin would be tossed to decide whose troop would find the section of two guns: heads Dunn's troop, tails Lieutenant Dill's. Dunn and the others sat trying to look unconcerned, while the battery commander flicked up a ten-franc piece. It spun on the floor for what seemed an eternity and finally dropped. Tails.

In the early hours of 31 May, the 7th Field Regiment abandoned its guns, except for one section per battery. Taking with them all their optical instruments including the gun sights and what kit they could carry, the gunners marched off towards the sea with heavy hearts. They arrived at the beach as dawn was breaking, and marched down to the shore line where boats were waiting. They had to wade up to their waists to get out to them, but quietly man after man climbed in and eventually they were taken out to the vessels that would take them back to England.

As dawn broke on 31 May, the enemy shelling increased. The prospects did not look healthy for the worn-out and greatly diminished battalions along the twenty-five-mile-long perimeter. Sergeant Green, along with everyone else in the 2nd Bedfordshire & Hertfordshires, was issued with what turned out to be the last rations, one tin of bully beef and four biscuits between two men. For water they had to fend for themselves. The bridgehead was intact, but none of the officers and soldiers knew when, and indeed if, they could start withdrawing. Fortunately they also did not know that at last the Germans had got their act together and that a single commander, General von Küchler of Eighteenth Army, had been tasked with destroying the bridgehead, and had ten divisions with which to do it.

Until then there had been an uncharacteristic lack of grip within the German high command. There was no co-ordinated plan for the attack on Dunkirk, and much argument about whether Fourth or Sixth Army would undertake the task. Kleist had been told to get moving and attack on the south-western side of the perimeter, but replied that his formations were unsuitable since tanks could not be used among the canals and concrete fortifications. He was told that 'by higher orders an end must finally be made of the embarkation at Dunkirk', while the Fourth Army commander personally intervened to order all forces to the coast east of Dunkirk immediately. Kleist still dragged his feet, and reported that as the medium artillery had run out of ammunition attempts would be made to fire on Dunkirk with light artillery. It was at that point that Küchler was put in charge of operations against Dunkirk. His Eighteenth Army, which had been engaged against the Belgians, was now directed to destroy or capture all Allied troops in the bridgehead. Küchler had IX, X, XIV and XXVI Corps consisting of the 14th, 18th, 56th, 216th, 254th, 256th and 61st Infantry Divisions; two motorized brigades, the 9th and 11th, the motorized Regiment GrossDeutschland, plus the 20th Motorized Division, and the SS Adolf Hitler Regiment.

German Army Group A could now forget about attacking Dunkirk and concentrate on the next phase, attacking what Rundstedt believed was the major and undefeated portion of the French Army. He had already lost about 50 per cent of his armour, and did not want to lose more among the ditches and canals of the Dunkirk sector. To have done so would in his opinion have been bad judgement. The debate continues to this day about whether Rundstedt handled Army Group A as well as he might have done having ripped open the Allied front after crossing the Meuse. At one stage, while Gort had only the 5th and 50th Divisions in the Arras area and some scratch forces scattered thinly along the Canal Line, Rundstedt had seven armoured, six motorized and four infantry divisions in the rear of the BEF and no one to oppose him. With this potent force he contented himself with taking the lightly defended towns of Calais and Boulogne and harrying the BEF as it withdrew to Dunkirk. This was despite the fact that his Army Group alone was stronger than the BEF, and in addition he had Army Group B engaging the attention of the BEF on its other flank. What is absolutely irrefutable is that Rundstedt's 'sickle-cut' reduced the French high command to a state of paralysis so severe that they never recovered their equilibrium.

There is no evidence that Hitler interfered with Rundstedt's operations, but he certainly contributed his pennyworth to Army Group B's plan to attack Dunkirk, including suggestions for the use of artillery – an early example of the Führer's inclination to become involved in minute military detail. Hitler's helpful hints are revealed in a message from the German Commander-in-Chief, Brauchitsch, containing personal suggestions for overpowering the Allies around Dunkirk. It makes nonsense of the notion that Hitler wanted the BEF to escape.

Once in the Dunkirk bridgehead, Gort came under the command of Admiral Abrial. Weygand was no longer talking in terms of the bridgehead being used as a springboard for a counter-attack, and ordered that it should be used for evacuation, without laying down any policy for the evacuation. Gort was uncertain whether he was to get the BEF out as fast as possible or hang on with sufficient forces as long as Abrial wished him to do so. If it was to be the former, Gort told the War Office on the telephone, this should be made clear to the French. The British government response to Gort's question, received by him in the early afternoon of 30 May, was dictated by Churchill. It read:

> Continue to defend the present perimeter to the utmost to cover maximum evacuation now proceeding well. Report every three hours through La Panne. If we can still communicate we shall send you an order to return to England with such officers as you may choose at the moment when we deem your command so reduced that it can be handed over to a Corps Commander. You should now nominate this Commander. If communications are broken you are to hand over and return as specified when your effective fighting force does not exceed the equivalent of three divisions. This is in accordance with correct military procedure and no personal discretion is left to you in the matter. On political grounds it would be a needless triumph to [sic] the enemy to capture you when only a small force remained under your orders. The Corps Commander chosen by you should be ordered to carry out the defence in conjunction with the French and evacuation whether from Dunkirk or the beaches, but when in his judgement no further organised evacuation is possible and no further proportionate damage can be inflicted on the enemy he is authorised in consultation with the French Commander to capitulate formally to avoid useless slaughter.[4]

Gort's staff told the War Office by telephone that at this stage there were about 60,000 British troops remaining. Assuming that the rearguard would number about 15,000, and stay until early morning on 2 June, that left some 45,000 to lift on the nights of 30/31 May and 31 May/1 June. The position was complicated by the question of French evacuation. Large numbers of French troops were in the bridgehead, and the British government had laid down a policy of evacuation in equal numbers. But few French ships had arrived and, although Gort had allocated two ships to evacuate French troops, only a few thousand had got away so far. Churchill spoke to Gort at midnight on 30/31 May underlining the importance of evacuating French troops and requesting him to ensure that Generals Blanchard and Fagalde were evacuated.

Gort decided that II Corps, less the 50th Division, would withdraw for evacuation on the night of 31 May/1 June. At that stage, the part of the bridgehead that lay in Belgian territory would be abandoned, leaving the sector between Dunkirk and the French frontier to be defended. The 50th Division would withdraw behind the frontier and come under I Corps command. General Brooke, it will be recalled, had been told that he was to go back to England on the afternoon of 30 May, taking with him all of II Corps staff that could be spared. Montgomery was to command II Corps (his division being taken over by Brigadier Anderson).

Midnight on 30/31 May marked the fourth day of Operation Dynamo. By that time a total of 126,606 men had been shipped to England (77,412 from the harbour and 49,194 from the beaches). Gort asked permission to be the last to leave, but was told go once his command was down to the strength of one corps. On 31 May Gort issued his last operation order, extracts from which are reproduced below:

2. It is intended, after consultation with the French authorities at Dunkirk, that both Corps and Dunkirk base should continue the withdrawal of troops, maintaining the defence of Dunkirk in co-operation with our French allies, in accordance with orders already issued. It is further intended that the final withdrawal of II Corps shall be completed during the night 31st May/1st June. Shipping resources will be allotted accordingly, and action taken in the following para[graph]s. II Corps will not finally abandon the perimeter before 2300 hrs, 31 May.

3. I Corps will assume command of 5 and 50 Divs from 1800 hrs 31st May. I Corps will use those divisions to man the frontier defence and will issue orders, after consultation with II Corps, for their withdrawal to the frontier defences. 5 and 50 Div reps report HQ I Corps forthwith. An outpost line will be maintained to be selected by I Corps.

4. II Corps will be responsible for the evacuation of the beaches at La Panne.

5. When the withdrawal of II Corps is completed, GHQ will be withdrawn
   and command will pass to Command I Corps. In default of further
   instructions command will pass at 1800 hrs 31 May.[5]

The redeployment of 5th and 50th Divisions mentioned in Gort's
order was to ensure that the eastern flank of I Corps which lay along
the Franco–Belgian frontier would not be exposed by the withdrawal of
II Corps on the left. Despite Lieutenant General Barker's poor performance during the campaign, and evidence that he was on the verge of a
breakdown, Gort originally tasked him with command of the rearguard,
which would consist of I Corps. This is not mentioned in the British
Official History, which merely states that Gort appointed Major General Alexander as the commander of I Corps. Gort's original decision to
leave Barker in command is supported by Montgomery's diary entry for
30 May.

Montgomery, now commanding II Corps, had attended the meeting
of corps commanders at Gort's headquarters at 1800 hours on 30 May,
where, according to the former's diary,

C-in-C read out telegram from War Office ordering one Corps to be
surrendered to the enemy with the French at Dunkirk; Barker selected and
1 Corps, 2 Corps to be evacuated ... Barker (1st Corps) was excited and
rattled; his BGS was frightened and out of touch.... Brooke (who had
handed 2 Corps to me) was present for the first quarter hour & then left
for England; he was first class.[6]

Montgomery was even more forthright in a letter written in 1952 to
Gort's biographer J. R. Colville, in which he said that Barker was 'an
utterly useless commander, who had lost his nerve'.[7] Montgomery had
arrived early at Gort's headquarters, as his own corps headquarters was
close by in La Panne. It was obvious to him, as it would have been to any
competent soldier, that the withdrawal of the BEF would have to start by
rolling up from the left, with II Corps withdrawing through I Corps.
Gort's appearance and demeanour left a strong impression on Montgomery: 'He was incapable of grasping the military situation, and issuing
clear orders. He was incapable of instilling confidence or morale. He had
"had it" and I remember saying as much to Brooke.'

Montgomery remembered that Gort had a telegram in his hand, and
from what the C-in-C said next it is clear that this was the one dictated
by Churchill, quoted earlier. For, having outlined what he, Gort, had
been told to do, he finished by telling Barker that in his opinion I Corps
would not get away, and that Barker must stay with his corps and
surrender to the Germans. The effect on Barker, according to Mont-

gomery, was 'catastrophic'. After the conference broke up, Montgomery spoke to Gort alone and 'Told him that we could not yet say it was impossible to get 1 Corps away; but that it would never get away if Barker was in control, and that the only sound course was to get Barker out of it as soon as possible and give 1 Corps to Alexander. Gort agreed, and Barker was sent away.'[8]

It is evident from entries in the GHQ war diary that Gort believed that the rearguard would have to surrender; indeed at 0830 on 31 May Alexander, on visiting GHQ, was told to thin out his division, as it appeared probable that he would have to surrender the majority along-side the French. At this point he did not know that he was to command I Corps – indeed it took until 1300 hours that day for Gort to tell him. Alexander's reaction was to declare that it was his intention at all costs to extricate his command and not to surrender any part of it. No one at GHQ appears to have raised the matter of Gort's undertaking to Fagalde.

For General Fagalde had earlier been given the impression by Gort that the three divisions of I Corps were his to use as he thought fit, and had planned to integrate them with his own 60th and 68th Infantry Divisions, to hold the perimeter until capitulation was forced on them. Neither Abrial nor Fagalde was in favour of evacuation, even if it included French formations. Believing that the war was lost, Fagalde considered that the only honourable way out was to stand and not retreat. There was also an air of Micawberism in the French camp, a hope that something would turn up. This was based, correctly as it turned out, on their interpretation of the German deployment which indicated that the Wehrmacht aimed at driving south, rather than going straight on to invade the United Kingdom after Dunkirk fell. In that case it would be better to keep the armies intact in the hope that the enemy might make a mistake that would retrieve the situation rather than attempt an evacuation which in their view was doomed to failure amid losses so catastrophic they would be intolerable to the public. The German break-through at the Meuse had paralysed the French Army, reducing it to a state of doing nothing in the hope that the problem would go away. Little wonder that some days earlier General Dill, on hearing that Fagalde was threatening to use force against the BEF to prevent its embarkation, had suggested that he tell Weygand 'that through the failure of their Army we have lost the BEF'. Unpalatable though this was, and still is, to the French, it was nothing less than the truth. Although the BEF was not lost, this was due to the Royal Navy and the RAF, and to its own efforts, as well as to the gallant stand made by some French units. The BEF's survival owed nothing to the French high command. Indeed the sorry tale leading to the predicament in which the BEF found itself was the product of inept command at senior level in the French Army.

While Gort and Alexander were conferring, the Supreme War Council was meeting in Paris. The British team, which had flown over that day, consisted of Churchill, the Deputy Prime Minister Attlee and Generals Dill, Ismay (Chief Staff Officer to Churchill) and Spears. During the discussion on the situation at Dunkirk it became apparent that the French seemed to have very little idea what was happening to the Northern Armies.[9] When the subject of evacuation came up, Churchill, overtaken by sentiment and much to Dill's alarm, said that the British would not embark first, but 'arm in arm' with the French. Dill intervened, and it was agreed that the British would remain as long as possible under Abrial's orders, and that British and French commanders on the spot would make the decisions. After the meeting, Churchill and his party flew back to London.

While the Supreme War Council was in session in Paris, Alexander went from Gort's headquarters to Bastion 32 at Dunkirk, taking Tennant with him. Here he found Abrial and Fagalde with their staffs, and General Altmayer, commanding French V Corps. Abrial said that Alexander would now come under Fagalde's orders. The latter outlined how he proposed deploying Alexander's units. Alexander, having listened without interrupting, laughed and said that Fagalde must be joking. His orders were to evacuate his troops, not defend part of the perimeter. Fagalde riposted by reading Gort's letter to him, and then asked if Alexander was in effect saying that the French Army alone would cover the embarkation of the British, while the British would not help the French to withdraw. Alexander replied that he would like to help, but that his orders were to evacuate. He intended pulling out his corps, consisting of 1st and 50th Divisions and a brigade of the 42nd Division, within twenty-four hours, and he added that they would all be taken prisoner if they stayed for longer. Abrial's chief of staff, Captain de Frégate de Lapérouse, interjected that if Gort knew this he had lied to Fagalde. If Gort had been telling the truth, Alexander must act as ordered by Fagalde. Alexander replied that all who could be saved would be saved. 'Except honour,' replied de Lapérouse. Alexander remained silent, and Altmayer asked him to obey Abrial.

Abrial suggested that, as there appeared to be some confusion about what Gort intended, they should go and see him, as he had not yet left the bridgehead. Alexander said that Gort had already gone. The French officers made it plain that they thought he was lying. Alexander went on to say that as he was now the senior British officer in France he was the C-in-C of the BEF, and answered only to the Secretary of State for War,

35. Vice Admiral Bertram Ramsay at his headquarters in Dover Castle.

36. British troops moving along the inner pier at Dunkirk.

37. British troops of the
rearguard marching into
Dunkirk town.

38. An officer of the Royal
Ulster Rifles taking a nap in
the bottom of his trench,
outside Dunkirk.

39. 1 June 1940, soldiers of the Royal Ulster Rifles waiting to be evacuated from the beach at Dunkirk.

40. Soldiers of the BEF on the beaches near Dunkirk attempting to shoot down strafing German aircraft with their rifles.

41. British troops awaiting evacuation from the Dunkirk beaches.

42. *Opposite*. Fires at Dunkirk seen from a British destroyer during the evacuation.

43. HMS *Valorous* alongside the inner pier at Dunkirk, with a sunken trawler outboard. The destroyer *Imogen* is on the far side of the pier.

44. A destroyer arrives at Dover, her upper deck crammed with troops.

45. Bodies and wreckage at Dunkirk. Picture taken by the Germans.

46. The beach near La Panne at low tide after the evacuation.

47. A camouflaged A13 cruiser tank of the 2nd Armoured Brigade, British 1st Armoured Division at Fouacourt at the end of May 1940, during the division's operations south of the Somme.

48. Soldiers of the 7th Battalion Argyll & Sutherland Highlanders on the River Bresle, 6–8 June 1940, before the withdrawal of their division, 51st (Highland), to Saint-Valery.

Mr Anthony Eden. Fagalde said that disobeying Gort's instructions would bring shame on the British Army. Alexander agreed to consult Eden.

On his return to La Panne, Alexander telephoned Eden at 1915 hours, informing him that the French wished to hold for another three nights. He added that prolonging the evacuation would not enable more troops to get away; on the contrary the BEF would be 'wiped out'. He asked for a decision as soon as possible.

Meanwhile, Abrial had sent a signal to Weygand asking that Churchill be persuaded to order Alexander not to evacuate on the night of 1 June. Within an hour of receiving Alexander's call, Eden was back on the telephone saying: 'You should withdraw your forces as rapidly as possible on a 50–50 basis with the French Army, aiming at completion by the night of 1st/2nd June. You should inform the French of this definite instruction.'[10]

Alexander queried the '50–50 basis', which could be taken to mean that the British rate of evacuation should be slowed up until the French numbers reached parity with the British. He was told it meant equal numbers from then on. No one in the British Cabinet or War Office informed Weygand or the British liaison officer at GQG, Major General Howard-Vyse, that what Alexander had been ordered to do contradicted the arrangements agreed by the Supreme War Council in Paris.

Alexander returned to Bastion 32 at around 2300 hours and told Abrial that he would hold his sector until one minute to midnight on 1 June. By now the Supreme War Council decision had arrived at Abrial's head-quarters and was shown to Alexander. His reaction was to say that he did not serve under the Prime Minister's orders. Although this might strike one as somewhat cheeky, if not downright insubordinate, Alexander was correct. He had received instructions from Eden, who as Secretary of State for War was his political boss. The British Defence Operations Committee, acting in the absence of the Prime Minister, had approved these instructions. The decision had been taken based on considerably more up-to-date information about the true state of affairs in the Dunkirk bridgehead than was available in the fantasy world inhabited by Weygand and the French politicians. Abrial's reaction was to say that Alexander's decision dishonoured England.

The next day saw heated discussions between Paris and London. Churchill, having agreed to Abrial exercising overall command at Dunkirk, told Weygand in a telegram that

> Situation cannot be fully judged by Admiral Abrial in the fortress, nor by you, nor by us here. We have therefore ordered General Alexander, commanding British sector of bridgehead, to judge in consultation with

Admiral Abrial, whether to try to stay over tomorrow or not. Trust you will agree."

It is possible that the attitude of the British War Cabinet, and of Churchill, had been hardened by Gort's accounts of the French performance during the campaign. Gort had returned to London during the night of 31 May/1 June, and had lost no time giving ministers his opinions on, among others, Billotte, Abrial, Fagalde and the French Army's poor showing against the Germans.

The troops in the Dunkirk perimeter were unaware of the disagreements between the British and French at senior level, and it is time to return to the battle of the bridgehead.

10

THE END AT DUNKIRK

The problem facing any commander holding a bridgehead from which he wants to withdraw is maintaining a crust tough enough to resist enemy penetration, while thinning out troops to embark. From time to time he must reduce the length of the perimeter in order to release men to maintain the flow of troops back to the waiting ships and craft.

On 31 May, the day on which there was so much top-level discussion and dissension among the French and British, the Germans attacked at most points along the perimeter, but the heaviest assaults were on the eastern end. This suited the British because that sector, held by II Corps, was to be abandoned anyway that night. West of Dunkirk, the French were well protected by the maze of waterways round Mardick. The buildings of Bergues provided an easily defended anchor to the British right flank, held by I Corps.

Montgomery's plan for the evacuation of II Corps was that the Germans were to be strongly counter-attacked wherever they attempted to cross the Nieuport–Furnes Canal. After dark the 3rd and 4th Divisions were to thin out and head for the beaches of La Panne and Bray-Dunes. At 0900 hours on 31 May, Montgomery had summoned all the sappers in his corps and ordered them to construct piers at La Panne from vehicles run out into the sea. Squalls at sea brought evacuation from La Panne almost to a halt that morning, but this did not appear to worry Montgomery – he lunched with Brigadier Anderson, who had taken over the 3rd Division when Montgomery moved up to commanding the corps. At 14.30 hours, Montgomery gave his final orders for the withdrawal. He had moved corps headquarters to La Panne beach that morning where it would be in the best position to control the evacuation. He had also had reception areas set up in the dunes; soldiers were called from these down to the beach for embarkation when the beach commander summoned them. Fortunately the 3rd Division signallers had managed to bring enough telephone cable into the perimeter to link brigades with divisional headquarters and also to link reception areas with the beach commander. During the afternoon and early evening the embarkation of corps troops, administrative units and the rear-echelon elements of

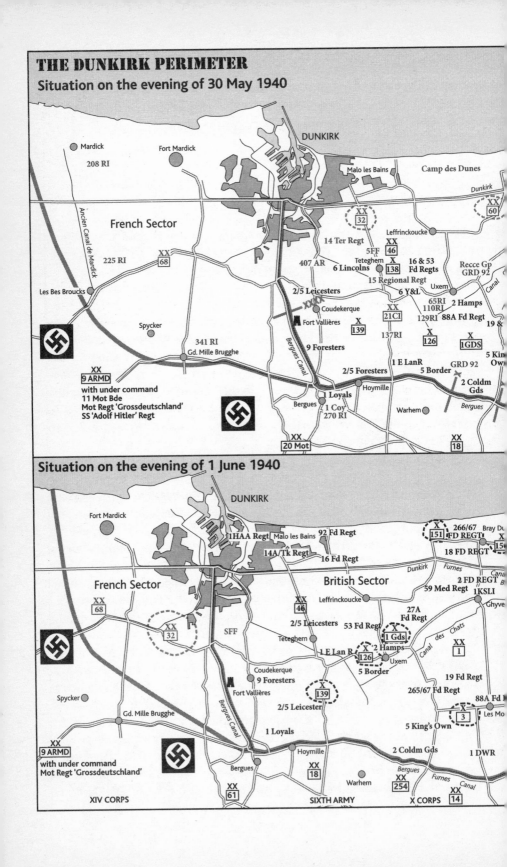

THE DUNKIRK PERIMETER
Situation on the evening of 30 May 1940

DUNKIRK

Mardick
208 RI

Fort Mardick

Malo les Bains

Camp des Dunes

Dunkirk

XX
60

French Sector

Ancien Canal de Mardick

XX
32

14 Ter Regt

Leffrinckoucke

5FF XX
46

225 RI

XX
68

Teteghem   X
6 Lincolns 138

16 & 53
Fd Regts

Recce Gp
GRD 92

407 AR

15 Regional Regt

Uxem

Canal

Les Bes Broucks

2/5 Leicesters

6 Y&L

65RI   2 Hamps
110RI

Spycker

XXXX

Coudekerque

XX
21CI

129RI 88A Fd Regt

19 &

341 RI
Gd. Mille Brugghe

Fort Vallières   X
139

137RI   X
126

X
1GDS

5 Kin
Ow

9 Foresters

1 E LanR

GRD 92

2/5 Foresters

5 Border

XX
9 ARMD

with under command
11 Mot Bde
Mot Regt 'Grossdeutschland'
SS 'Adolf Hitler' Regt

Bergues Canal

Hoymille

2 Coldm
Gds

1 Loyals

Bergues 1 Coy
270 RI

Warhem

Bergues

XX
20 Mot

XX
18

Situation on the evening of 1 June 1940

DUNKIRK

Fort Mardick

1HAA Regt Malo les Bains 92 Fd Regt

X   266/67 Bray Du
151 FD REGT   X
155

14A/Tk Regt

16 Fd Regt

18 FD REGT

French Sector

Dunkirk Furnes Cana

2 FD REGT B

British Sector

59 Med Regt 1KSLI

XX
68

XX
46

Leffrinckoucke

Ghyve

27A
Fd Regt

XX
32

SFF

2/5 Leicesters 53 Fd Regt

X
1 Gds

des Chats

XX
9 ARMD

with under command
Mot Regt 'Grossdeutschland'

Teteghem

1 E Lan R   X 2 Hamps
126 Uxem

XX
1

Coudekerque

9 Foresters

Canal

5 Border

Fort Vallières

XX
139

19 Fd Regt

Spycker

2/5 Leicester

265/67 Fd Regt

88A Fd R

Gd. Mille Brugghe

1 Loyals

X
3

Les Mo

Bergues Canal

5 King's Own

XX
9 ARMD

Hoymille

2 Coldm Gds

1 DWR

Bergues

XX
18

Warhem

Bergues Furnes Canal

XX
61

XX
254

XX
14

XIV CORPS

SIXTH ARMY

X CORPS

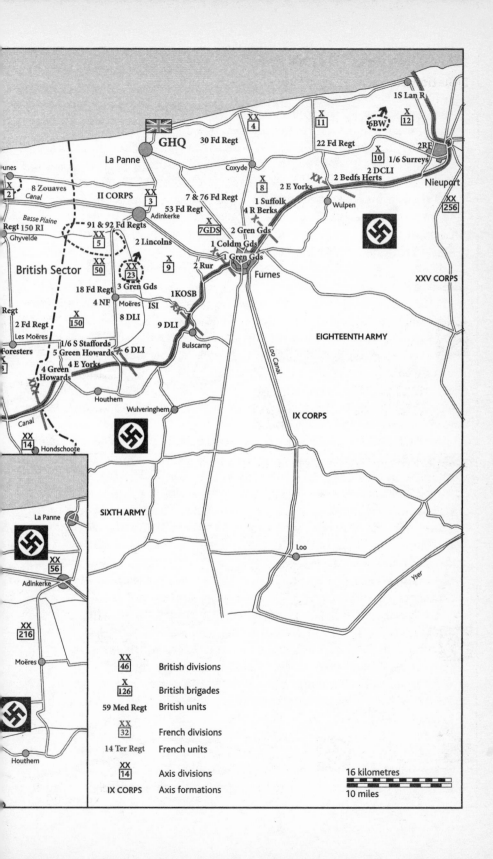

1S Lan R

XX
4

X
11

5BW

X
12

GHQ

30 Fd Regt

22 Fd Regt

2RF

La Panne

Coxyde

X
10   1/6 Surreys

2 DCLI
2 Bedfs Herts

Nieuport

unes

X
2

8 Zouaves
Canal

II CORPS

XX
3

7 & 76 Fd Regt

53 Fd Regt

X
8   2 E Yorks

1 Suffolk
4 R Berks

Wulpen

XX
256

Basse Plaine
Regt 150 RI

Ghyvelde

Adinkerke

91 & 92 Fd Regts

XX
5

2 Lincolns

X
7GDS   2 Gren Gds

1 Coldm Gds
1 Gren Gds

XXV CORPS

British Sector

XX
50

XX
23

X
9   2 Rur

Furnes

EIGHTEENTH ARMY

Regt

2 Fd Regt

Les Moëres

Foresters

18 Fd Regt   3 Gren Gds

4 NF   Moëres   ISI

X
150   8 DLI

1/6 S Staffords
5 Green Howards

1KOSB

9 DLI

6 DLI

Bulscamp

Loo Canal

IX CORPS

4 E Yorks

4 Green
Howards

Canal

XX
14   Hondschoote

Houthem

Wulveringhem

Loo

Yser

SIXTH ARMY

La Panne

XX
56

Adinkerke

XX
216

Moëres

Houthem

XX 46	British divisions
X 126	British brigades
59 Med Regt	British units
XX 32	French divisions
14 Ter Regt	French units
XX 14	Axis divisions
IX CORPS	Axis formations

16 kilometres

10 miles

II Corps went smoothly despite German shelling. At 2100 hours, as the pace of the evacuation accelerated, Montgomery and Alexander conferred and agreed that all was going to plan. Now that Gort had gone, these two had the situation well in hand. They agreed that if La Panne became unusable for any reason II Corps would use the beaches at Bray-Dunes, and if these could not be used, the port of Dunkirk would be closed to I Corps to allow II Corps to get away first – a providential decision.

The Combined Squadron of the 4th/7th Royal Dragoon Guards was sent to join the 150th Brigade in the area of Bray-Dunes. During the night German shelling blew in the windows and doors of the house where Major Frink had set up his headquarters, noting 'sixteen shells landed in field where 2 Troop and vehicles were – everyone well dug in – only one casualty, one pig – thus saving us trouble [of despatching it before eating it]'. The area in front of the squadron position was held by a French division, which Frink describes as 'excellent and efficient'.

That day on II Corps front, instead of concentrating, the Germans attacked at a number of places. German artillery observers located in Houthem brought down heavy fire on the 150th Brigade (4th East Yorks, and 4th and 5th Green Howards) holding the Furnes Canal line on II Corps' right flank. But any Germans who survived crossing the canal were eliminated or beaten back.

Within the 151st Brigade sector, the 8th DLI had been allocated a reserve location along the Ringsloot Canal about a mile north of the main perimeter line of the Bergues–Furnes Canal. The 9th DLI, the left forward battalion of the brigade, were slow getting into position up to the canal bank, and on arriving there found the Germans just on the other side. As a result the battalion suffered casualties as they were unable to dig in during the day, within full view of the enemy. If they stayed in the open they came under small-arms fire, and if they took to the houses they were mortared and shelled. With the onset of darkness, at last they could dig in.

Bulscamp provided a good covered forming-up place for German attacks, as it was close to the canal, and was also on the boundary between the 151st and 9th Brigades. From here, at first light, the enemy crossed the canal and drove a wedge between the 9th DLI of 151st Brigade and the 1st King's Own Scottish Borderers of the 9th Brigade. The two battalions counter-attacked and succeeded in regaining the home bank of the canal. In the afternoon, another attack on the left of the 9th DLI, driving back two companies, was followed by a further attack in the centre of the brigade position, and the 6th DLI on the right of the 9th had to give ground. However, the 8th DLI put in a stop position in rear, bolstered by the 3rd Grenadiers who managed to contain the enemy, while the brigade commander patched up the gaps in the left and right of his sector using the 4th Royal Northumberland Fusiliers in their scout cars and motorcycles. The movement of all this transport gave rise to scares of German tanks. As evening approached, the shelling in the 151st Brigade sector became heavier, and the machine-gunners of the 4th Gordons and 2nd Royal Northumberland Fusiliers, sent forward during the day to dig in along the Ringsloot Canal, began to lay down a stream of defensive machine-gun fire in front of the 8th DLI. Under cover of this fire, the two flank battalions, the 6th and 9th DLI, came back and reoccupied their positions. The whole 151st Brigade front was by now a jumble of platoons of several battalions intermixed.

The château which had been the headquarters of all three battalions in the 151st Brigade, in various outbuildings, now became uninhabitable thanks to shellfire, so the three COs moved out to the woods behind. All day a joint RAP had been operating in the château, where the doctors assisted by Father Duggan, the brigade Roman Catholic priest, had been doing good work keeping the wounded calm, mainly 6th and 9th DLI caught by shellfire during their temporary retirement. At this stage the brigade commander divided the brigade front into two halves in an effort to restore a modicum of control over the patchwork of sub-units holding the sector. The CO of 9th DLI took over the left half, and McLaren, still commanding the 8th, the right, irrespective of which battalion the miscellany of soldiers belonged to. In the evening, the orders were given to the 151st Brigade to retire, not for evacuation but to hold positions in the vicinity of Bray-Dunes, which would become part of the new left flank of the BEF once II Corps had pulled out that night.

The 7th Guards Brigade (1st and 2nd Grenadiers, and 1st Coldstream) had some tough fighting among the ruins of Furnes. Brigade head-quarters, dug into a dung heap in a farmyard, was treated to a heavy dose of artillery fire just as the battalion COs assembled to receive orders for the withdrawal that night. The Guards held on to enough of the town on their side of the canal to provide good observation posts for artillery and mortars, which had just sufficient ammunition for one day's shooting. The Guards had also kept some of their carriers and used these to good effect to counter-attack any attempts by the Germans to exploit their gains in the 4th Royal Berkshire sector the day before (see Chapter 9).

The main German effort along the perimeter was directed against the extreme left flank of the BEF at Nieuport. At dawn a heavy attack came in under the cover of smoke. But the brisk sea breeze dispersed the smoke and, shorn of its cover, the attackers were mown down in large numbers by Brens and Vickers machine guns. But a follow-up attack managed to penetrate south and north of Nieuport, threatening to cut off the 2nd Royal Fusiliers. A company of the 1st South Lancashires, under Captain Butler, stopped the northern penetration.

Early that morning, the 1st East Surreys had received orders to embark, and moved along the coast to Coxyde-Bains. Here to their surprise some of the seaside hotels were still open and doing business. While waiting at this seaside resort, the embarkation order was suddenly cancelled and the battalion was turned about and sent to reinforce the 10th Brigade opposite Nieuport. A dangerous situation had developed on the open flank of the 1st/6th East Surreys, whose much depleted left-hand company was holding the brickworks. The 1st East Surreys moved in their own transport, which fortunately the CO had refused to destroy despite orders to do so. The CO and intelligence officer, Lieutenant Bocquet, went ahead to meet Brigadier Barker, the commander of 10th Brigade, and carry out a reconnaissance for the counter-attack. At this juncture, Bocquet was wounded, but managed to carry on. The counter-attack was launched with B Company leading and the remainder echeloned back.

This counter-attack by 1st East Surreys stabilized the situation. At one stage, the two COs were seen firing a Bren gun together, fighting a private war of their own. In the late afternoon, the enemy could be seen forming up on the eastern side of the canal, clearly heading for another attack on the sector held by the two East Surrey battalions, when as if by a miracle eighteen Blenheim bombers and six naval Albacores flew over and bombed them. This was one of the very rare occasions when the RAF provided close air support to the BEF throughout the campaign; at this stage in the war the necessary procedures and communications did not exist, so describing this incident as a 'miracle' is not over-egging the pudding. The East Surreys certainly thought so as they stood cheering and waving in delight at seeing the Germans being treated to a dose of what they had endured at the hands of the Luftwaffe ever since 10 May. The two East Surrey battalions held the position until the 1st Battalion was ordered to withdraw at 0200 hours prior to embarkation.

This marked the fifth day of hard fighting and marching by the troops of 3rd Division, and these five days were themselves the culmination of some three weeks of marching, digging and fighting with little rest. Only when the orders for the withdrawal came through at last light did they know when their ordeal would end. As before, the task of pulling out was made easier by the German reluctance to fight at night, and the dark lines of British soldiers began to converge on the beaches. Here the evacuation was not going well, because between 2300 hours and 0300 hours the tide was too low for the makeshift piers to be used – something that the army beach staff had not foreseen, and perhaps the navy had failed to alert them to this nautical fact. From 2300 hours the troops were told to march along the beach to Bray-Dunes. Here Montgomery directed them on to Dunkirk, a march of over fifteen miles for the battalions on the left flank. He described it in his diary:

It was clearly impossible to continue embarkation at the beaches and I ordered the troops to move on to Dunkirk and embark there; this they were loath to do as they saw the ships lying off and hoped that boats would come to the shore; but no boats came.[1]

The 1st East Surreys had been told to go to La Panne, and as the coast road was under shellfire the CO ordered the companies to disperse into small parties and march clear of the road wherever possible. The CO then drove in his car with Major Bousfield and Captain Hill, OC Head-quarters Company and acting adjutant, to a bend in the road between Coxyde and La Panne, where they dismounted to see the battalion past. Unfortunately this part of the road was under intense and accurate artillery fire. The first casualty was the CO's driver, Private Dennis. The shelling continued and Major Bousfield cried that he was hit. The CO and Captain Hill hauled Bousfield into the car, and with the CO at the wheel drove into La Panne. Here Bousfield was taken into a field ambulance badly wounded. He was later killed when being taken by ambulance into Dunkirk.

At La Panne the CO assembled the 1st East Surreys in the sand dunes, disposing the battalion in defensive positions round an especially promi-nent dune, which he christened Surrey Hill. He was determined to get the battalion back to England in one body if it could be managed. Seeing an RNLI lifeboat high and dry on the beach, he decided to commandeer it as the battalion's private craft to ferry troops out to the shipping offshore. He ordered a cordon to be thrown round the vessel and the battalion fitters to get the engines going. Amid cries from the cordon of 'Anyone for the Skylark?', the two fitters descended into the engine room. They were unable to coax the diesel motors back into life, and emerged, the air blue with their opinions of marine engines and their designers. At this point, the divisional commander's ADC, or a member of his staff, appeared and said, 'The General's compliments and you are to take your battalion to Dunkirk for embarkation.'

Dunkirk was ten miles away along the sands. In the early-morning daylight, the 1st East Surreys could see the columns of black smoke rising from the town. In addition to the shelling and mortaring of the beaches, aircraft strafed the troops at low level with machine-gun fire and bombed the ships out to sea. The CO held his final O Group on Surrey Hill, stressing two points. The companies were to march well dispersed in small groups, and every man was to carry a weapon. The beaches between La Panne and Dunkirk were black with troops and long queues waded into the water chest high waiting to be picked up by boats. There was a general move towards Dunkirk, which in spite of shelling and bombing seemed to offer better chances of embarkation. The battalion set off at intervals, marching close to the water's edge where the sand was firmer. They were soon caught up in an endless procession moving slowly along towards the harbour at Dunkirk, which never seemed to get any nearer. It was a laborious march along the sand, for the day got hotter and the men were exceedingly tired. The CO insisted that the soldiers picked up every serviceable-looking Bren he spotted. One young officer, marching along behind his CO, was ordered to pick these up and pass them back down the file, where most were dumped. The soldiers were already carrying their personal weapons and there was a limit to how much extra they could lug through the sand.

When the 1st East Surreys arrived at the outskirts of Dunkirk, the CO and adjutant went forward to arrange with the embarkation staff for the battalion to be embarked in one ship. There were several ships alongside the mole, and Lieutenant Colonel Boxshall was directed to HMS *Esk*, a Hunt-class destroyer. No sooner was he aboard and trying to arrange for the whole battalion to be accommodated than the ship, which was still quite empty as far as he could see, cast off. Boxshall, horrified at the prospect of leaving his battalion behind, dashed to the bridge demanding that the ship should wait. The captain was sympathetic but replied that a transport had been bombed in mid-Channel, and he had been ordered to pick up survivors. Boxshall would willingly have swum for shore, but the destroyer was moving out fast.

Travelling at full speed, the *Esk* soon reached the stricken ship, a two-funnelled transport, carrying the French 22nd Infantry Regiment. A bomb had gone down her after funnel, exploding in the engine room, and when the *Esk* arrived she was lying on her beam ends, with French soldiers around her, holding on to anything that would float. Several small craft had begun the task of picking up the soldiers, when German aircraft appeared and bombed the rescue operations. Some of the unfortunate soldiers were swept away by the strong tide, and their cries were pitiful to hear. But the majority were rescued. The *Esk* docked in Dover later that afternoon, with Boxshall frantic with anxiety about the battalion from which he had been so abruptly snatched.

Sergeant Green with his platoon of Bedfordshire & Herefordshires, having received the order to move to the road linking Nieuport and La Panne, thought that they would all march to the vehicle jetty and embark. His platoon got cut off and they found themselves mixed up with A Company of the Duke of Cornwall's Light Infantry (DCLI). On arrival at La Panne they found the town on fire, shells dropping, vehicles and dead bodies all over the place, and men from all units trudging on towards the sea. Green led his platoon into the dunes and sat down for a rest.

By the time the 1st/6th East Surreys withdrew, there had been one case of desertion, an officer, found four miles in rear of the position. He was court-martialled on return to England, cashiered and sent to prison. No soldiers deserted. On arrival at La Panne, Captain White, the adjutant, was ordered to split up the battalion and tell them to make their way to beaches and embark where they could. White walked along the beach with Major General Johnson, the GOC of the 4th Division, who told him to take battalion headquarters towards the beach at La Panne, arriving early on 1 June. In White's opinion the embarkation was not chaotic. Although there were masses of people on the beaches and no one organized the evacuation, whenever a vessel approached, an officer or NCO would lead his group of men down to a lifeboat or small craft. There was, according to White, no panic. His party was picked up by a whaler from HMS *Speedwell*. Hanging on to the side of the boat as they could not all get in, they were rowed out to the ship. White went to a mess deck and fell asleep on the table, waking up several hours later in Dover. The remainder of his battalion embarked from the mole at Dunkirk, probably sent there by Montgomery. The problem, as White acknowledges, was the total lack of radios to companies within an infantry battalion at the time; once troops were on the move, the telephone was useless.

With the onset of darkness, McLaren had walked along the front of his half of the 151st Brigade sector. The machine-gunners of the Gordons and Northumberland Fusiliers, who had been firing almost continuously, had run out of ammunition at dusk and had pulled out. McLaren had some difficulty at first in persuading some of the DLI men not to follow, but after talking to them for a moment or two they steadied down. The German shelling of the château intensified, hitting an ammunition truck and setting it on fire, which after a huge explosion set the whole motor-transport park alight. During the night, McLaren walked up and down calming the soldiers. The Germans never came close, and the withdrawal began at 0200 hours so that all troops were clear of the position by 0230. Covered by the carriers, the 8th DLI marched north to the coast, and then along the coast to a position east of Bray-Dunes. McLaren lost his way thanks to a 'bad map' and fell into a ditch getting soaked. Eventually the battalion dug in among the dunes and had a meal.

As the last of the II Corps perimeter defences pulled out, it was vital that the complete corps should be within the sector held by I Corps by

first light. So Montgomery stayed at Bray-Dunes until 0330 hours personally directing the troops straight down the beach towards Dunkirk. While
standing on the beach, his ADC, Charles Sweeney of the Ulster Rifles,
was wounded in the head by a shell splinter. Montgomery cursed him
soundly for not wearing a steel helmet, at which Sweeney pointed out
that his general was not wearing one either. Sweeney remained with
Montgomery through much of the war, being killed, much to Montgomery's distress, right at the end in Germany in 1945. Montgomery left
Bray-Dunes and walked towards Dunkirk with Sweeney and his BGS,
Ritchie. After about an hour, they struck inland and hitched a lift in a
truck to Dunkirk. Here they embarked in the destroyer *Codrington*.

Sergeant Green became separated from his platoon among the crowds
in the dunes and managed to hitch a lift on a carrier to Dunkirk, by
which time it was daylight. Here he joined the crowd on the mole, which
included French troops, some with suitcases and even bicycles but no
weapons, in marked contrast to British troops who mostly had weapons.
Before he reached the end of the mole, an RAMC orderly came up leading
another man, about six foot six inches tall, wearing just boots, shirt and
trousers. His eyes were opaque and he moved 'like a zombie'. At the end
of the mole, Green spotted a naval party under a piece of canvas: with
'hell breaking loose all round them, they were all sound asleep'. Alongside the mole, there was a destroyer, beached and blown in half – 'you
could see straight through her'. At the end of the mole destroyers came
in with their guns pointing skywards firing at aircraft.

Green embarked on the forecastle of a destroyer by sliding down a
table-top from the mole, and the vessel slipped at about 0800 hours. He
was told to chuck his rifle down and go below. The destroyer went off at
high speed, zigzagging. Every so often there was a near miss, and the
ship lifted. After one particularly close one, Green asked a sailor if it
would take more than one bomb to sink the ship, and received the reply,
'No. One will be enough. We've only light decks over the boilers in these
ships.' One young soldier really 'went bonkers' for a minute or two,
making a dive for the ladder to get up on deck. This was a relief because
it gave the other soldiers something to do. Everyone piled on him, saying,
'Sit down, silly bugger.'

Brooke, on his arrival back at Dover the night before, had warned
Ramsay that the greatest shipping effort would be required on the night
of 31 May/1 June, and Ramsay had acted accordingly. As the exhausted II
Corps soldiers arrived at Dunkirk, they found ships waiting for them.
Some soldiers waited to join the queue at Bray-Dunes. Because there had
never been a central organization for the embarkation, with communi-

cations between embarkation points, there was no mechanism for switching the effort from beaches where embarkation was slow or completely stopped to places where it was going better.

Frink's choice of location for the night of 31 May/1 June, between an artillery battery and the main road, was not so fortunate as both were shelled continually all night, but luckily this caused no casualties to the 4th/7th squadron. 'The whole countryside was lit up by burning vehicles and villages.' The soldiers' natural inclination to appropriate any kit left lying about had not been diminished by the death and destruction all round them, and Frink's troopers found a truckload of number 9 wireless sets (the ones used in armoured vehicles), some of which they fitted to their own tanks.

With the daylight came the Luftwaffe, in larger numbers than ever before. It sank two destroyers right away, one being the *Keith*, with Admiral Wake-Walker embarked. Lieutenant Lumsden, the navigator of the *Keith*, recalled that the first three Stukas from the attacking wave missed, but the explosions from their bombs were so close that the steering gear jammed. The ship was being steered by hand from the tiller compartment when another bomb exploded and holed the starboard side between the engine boiler rooms, inflicting heavy casualties and total loss of power. The ship listed heavily and stopped. The *Keith* was anchored, and Wake-Walker and his staff boarded a launch to continue their work. Another Stuka came in and bombed the stern, starting a fire and wounding more men.

The destroyer continued to list and settle in the water, so the captain ordered abandon ship, but asked Lumsden to stay with him with a skeleton crew, in case a tow back to Dover could be arranged. A Dutch coaster took the rest of the crew to Ramsgate. As the *Keith* sank deeper, the captain summoned an Admiralty tug alongside, and she embarked the wounded and everyone else alive. As the tug pulled away, another onslaught of bombers blew the *Keith* apart, sinking her instantly; she was gone before the bomb splashes subsided.

At this point the skies seemed clear of enemy bombers, except for a lone aircraft. In case he had any bombs left, the tug skipper made a circle to starboard, and as he did so the world seemed to stand on end. The tug split in half and the forepart sank in thirty seconds, trapping all those under the forecastle. Those lucky enough to be on the bridge, including Lumsden, struck out for the beach, about three-quarters of a mile away, a laborious process in full uniform and inflated lifebelt. Lumsden, reinforcing his will to swim on by 'picturing his wife's small but beautiful backside', aimed at a redbrick fort in the dunes at Bray. About a hundred yards from the beach, he scrambled on to the deck of a wrecked yacht for a breather. Finding that he was still wearing his heavy binoculars, he hurled them into the sea.

Once he had completed the swim inshore, Lumsden was taken to the fort by some French sailors. After a rest and a fortifying cognac, he set off for Dunkirk dressed in a French sailor's uniform, complete with flat hat and pom-pom, to replace his own soaked kit. Here he found Wake-Walker in his launch alongside Dunkirk pier, who offered him a lift back to Dover.

The onset of daylight found Major Colvin, the acting CO of the 2nd Grenadiers, attempting to use the few small boats at La Panne to lift the wounded out to the destroyers offshore. After an hour spent up to his neck in water, under machine-gun and cannon attack by Messerschmitts, he abandoned the task as hopeless. He joined the crowd heading for Dunkirk, saddened by the sight of the wounded, who had to be abandoned where they had been cut down by the Messerschmitts, and who would probably drown when the tide flooded. Incoming shellfire persuaded him that a ground attack was imminent, and he decided to try another attempt at embarking from the beach as the tide was flooding strongly. With some men he had gathered he waded out to a wrecked steamer, hoping to attract the attention of a destroyer not far off. As they scrambled aboard the wreck, they saw the destroyer sunk by Stukas, and its crew being machine-gunned in the water.

Having waded back to the beach, he found an abandoned whaler, and with fourteen soldiers, none of whom could row, headed for a naval tender which was in the process of picking up sailors, many of whom were covered in oil and in some cases badly wounded. No sooner had Colvin and his party boarded the tender than three Heinkel bombers screamed in, making several runs at the tender and eventually scoring a hit with one bomb. The tender blew up, and Colvin found himself in the water with a damaged leg and surrounded by drowning soldiers. The survivors clung to pieces of wreckage and made desperate attempts to attract the attention of a passing vessel. Men were now dying from shock or drowning from cramp.

Colvin and a few others managed to swim to another wreck and drag themselves up the dangling gangway, collapsing on deck with exhaustion. The Germans bombed the wreck but missed. A passing Thames lighter spotted the survivors and coming alongside the wreck took them off. The master of the lighter insisted on heading for the beach and picking up some wounded. Fortune must have been smiling on him because the Germans were very close by now, as the beach was in Belgium. Having collected the wounded, the lighter picked up four

Belgian soldiers from a dinghy and two Grenadiers from another small boat, and returned to Dover. Colvin would almost certainly have had an easier time had he walked down the beach to Dunkirk.

There were several small parties of soldiers in the Dunkirk area who found that being separated from their unit was a disadvantage when it came to being allocated a boat or ship in which to get away. One such was Second Lieutenant McSwiney's group, which consisted of twelve gunners of his own sub-unit, 2nd Light Anti-Aircraft Battery, and about fifty 'odds and sods' added to them by a beachmaster at La Panne trying to wash his hands of them. At first McSwiney had tried marching them to Dunkirk. As they arrived there was a massive air attack, and both the town and the area near the mole were soon burning furiously. Deterred by this, he decided to return to La Panne, and on his way back tried joining several columns of troops that were embarking from small boats at the water's edge. But on each occasion that his party reached the head of the column, an officer asked what unit they were from. When he told the truth, the politest refusal he got was, 'Sorry we can't take odds and sods.' So he returned to the original beachmaster at La Panne.

After a brew of tea and a breakfast of bully beef and biscuit, they flopped down in the dunes, utterly exhausted, and slept until woken by shelling; the Germans had got the range of their section of the beach, and it created pandemonium. Men ran down to the water, tore off their clothes and started swimming to the destroyers and other craft, half a mile or more offshore; several were drowned. McSwiney managed to keep his party together with the help of a regimental sergeant major who had joined his group. When the shelling stopped, they returned to the water to try again, but the ships offshore seemed to be working with columns well to their right or nearer Dunkirk. The men were machine-gunned and bombed by aircraft at intervals. Their spirits were temporarily lifted when five of the party appeared with a quantity of tinned food, having raided a coastguard station, but the night passed slowly. It rained, and by morning they were cold and wet.

Early the next morning, McSwiney went to see the brigadier at the control centre near La Panne and told him his story. The brigadier's reply was to the effect that there were other groups like McSwiney's; he was very sorry, but they would have to fend for themselves. Either the RAF had established temporary superiority over the beaches or the Luftwaffe was busy elsewhere, for no German aircraft appeared over this section of the beach for a while. As the day wore on, McSwiney spotted what looked like three small ships' boats floating in on the tide assisted by a northerly breeze. They appeared to be empty, and he guessed that after being rowed out to one of the destroyers they had been abandoned. If his party could grab them before they reached the men on the beach, they were theirs. Three men volunteered to swim out to take possession of the boats, and managed to pull them closer in to shore. While McSwiney and two others stood up to their armpits in water to stop the boats grounding, his men piled in, cramming twenty to a boat. At this point the Luftwaffe returned to this part of the beach, bombed the nearest destroyer and missed. But one bomb fell so close that McSwiney's boat capsized. It was a case of either swimming for the destroyer, which was about 200 yards away, or clinging to the upturned boat and drifting back to the beach. Fortunately he had ordered his party to take off their boots on the beach, in case they had to swim. Three non-swimmers paddled to the destroyer on McSwiney's air bed, which he had kept in defiance of his battery commander's orders. The remainder swam. Climbing up the scrambling net was the hardest part of all. At last they flopped on the deck gasping like beached whales. The party had arrived in the late afternoon, but the destroyer, HMS *Shikari*, remained offshore until the next morning, before heading for Dover.

During the daylight hours of 1 June, Frink's Combined Squadron of the 4th/7th Royal Dragoon Guards was kept busy patrolling the area of the British perimeter. The remaining four tanks were split into two patrols of two vehicles each and sent to locate the enemy if possible, while the rest of the squadron manned OPs on roads leading into the perimeter. As the roads were cratered behind them, the patrols and OPs were withdrawn. No enemy were encountered, but their shelling and bombing was all too pervasive. All likely targets such as roads and other key points were treated to comprehensive shelling. Frink, with his usual cavalry sangfroid, had time despite the mayhem all around him to go for what he called 'a country ramble' with Major General Martell, GOC of the 50th Division.

The men of the 50th Division among the dunes around Bray-Dunes were heartened at about midday when the RAF appeared and engaged the German aircraft in a series of dogfights. Little more was seen of the Luftwaffe overhead in that sector for the rest of the day. At around 1230 hours, the commander of the 151st Brigade reorganized the brigade into a force of mobile fighting units and marching units. McLaren found himself with about a hundred Grenadiers added to his battalion. He sent men down to the beach to gather any spare weapons lying about, and they came back with a quantity of Brens. He fully expected to have to fight his way to Dunkirk

Throughout 1 June the embarkation alongside the East Mole at Dunkirk went on under heavy attacks by the Luftwaffe, mainly in the gaps between RAF fighter sweeps, which had been reduced to eight per day in order that each might be made in strength. That day the Luftwaffe sank thirty-one ships, including four destroyers. At 1800 hours, Captain Tennant decided that there would be no more daylight embarkations from Dunkirk or the remaining beaches still in Allied hands.

The 2nd Duke of Cornwall's Light Infantry arrived at Dunkirk at about midday, having walked all the way from the far end of the II Corps perimeter. While they were embarking, the DCLI were given the task of loading a hundred stretcher cases aboard the sloop HMS *Kingfisher* right at the end of the East Mole. The mole had almost been cut in half by bombing, and carrying stretchers over the narrow planking that bridged the gap was not made any easier by the attentions of the Luftwaffe. The mole was holed again while the long line of stretchers was being carried along through the debris and spray from several near misses. The ships' AA guns, as well as almost every rifle, Bren and even pistol in the battalion, added to the cacophony of noise. In a brief lull in the fire, the sloop's captain was heard shouting from the bridge, 'Get those bloody Pongos [soldiers] below, they are shooting away my aerials.' He was ignored: every man aboard was determined to do all he could to ensure that the Luftwaffe did not stop them getting away. The total number of troops evacuated during 31 May and 1 June was 132,443, of whom 40,290 were taken off the beaches and 92,153 from Dunkirk harbour. By now the accumulated total evacuated was 259,049. About 20,000 British troops remained, and a far larger number of French.

With II Corps embarked, all that remained operational of the BEF on the morning of 1 June was seven brigades under command of Alexander of I Corps. On the right were 139th Brigade (2nd/5th Leicesters, 2nd/5th and 9th Sherwood Foresters, plus 1st Loyals and C Company, 2nd Royal Warwicks), with 138th Brigade (6th Lincolns, 2nd/4th King's Own Yorkshire Light Infantry (KOYLI), and 6th York & Lancasters) in support, all under command of Major General Curtis of the 46th Division. On the left Brigadier Beckwith-Smith, the acting GOC of the 1st Division, had the 126th Brigade (1st East Lancashires, 5th King's Own and 5th Borders), 1st Guards Brigade (2nd Coldstream and 2nd Hampshires) and 3rd Brigade (1st Duke of Wellington's, 2nd Sherwood Foresters and 1st King's Shropshire Light Infantry). The 50th Division consisting of the 150th and 151st Brigades was located around Bray-Dunes behind the French 12th Infantry Division. The 5th Division had been withdrawn for evacuation. All battalions were short of men – for example, the 2nd/5th Leicesters were down to seventy all ranks. The composite regiment formed by the Combined Squadron of the 4th/7th Dragoon Guards and two squadrons of the 5th Inniskilling Dragoon Guards provided the only armoured support, having taken over all the available light tanks. The artillery consisted of elements of one medium and six field regiments. All had some ammunition, but none was plentifully supplied.

The Germans deployed four divisions against the thinly held Canal Line, and a further two on the eastern flank. Here, although the ground was seamed with ditches, there was no serious obstacle. The German 14th and 18th Divisions had fought the BEF on the Dyle, the Escaut and on each side of Ypres. Preceded by a heavy bombardment, the 18th Division thrust towards Téteghem. In some cases the Germans swam the canal and gained a foothold on the British side. Despite taking heavy losses, the Germans drove back C Company, 2nd Royal Warwicks, from the Hoymille bridge. With no reserve other than the seventy men of the 2nd/5th Leicesters, Brigadier Chichester-Constable of the 139th Brigade ordered the 1st Loyals to abandon Bergues and mount a counter-attack to clear the north bank of the canal. Under heavy shellfire which caused many casualties (one shell alone killed nine Loyals and wounded seventeen), the Loyals left Bergues to the care of a French detachment. The counter-attack through knee-deep water fizzled out. However, backed by some Inniskilling light tanks, the Loyals were eventually able to prevent the Germans from gaining any more ground. The Germans in their turn were deterred by the prospect of attacking across the same sheets of water that had hindered the Loyals, and sat back to shell the British in their exposed positions.

In the confusion, so normal in war, the medical officer of the Loyals, Captain Doll, got left behind at Bergues. Told by one of his orderlies that the battalion seemed to be leaving, he sent a runner to ask the adjutant what was happening. The reply was not very helpful: he, Doll, must take what action he thought necessary. Doll went to battalion headquarters to find that all the troops had gone. He went to see the French detachment in an effort to learn what the situation was. As he approached he was met with a blast of heat from the burning ruins of the building they had occupied. Shells were still falling as he turned back to his own RAP. Here he gathered his orderlies and wounded around him and told them they could either remain and be taken prisoner, or try to get out in a 30-hundredweight truck that had been left behind by the battalion or in his Vauxhall car. Everyone opted to go. The able-bodied and walking wounded were loaded into the truck (Doll took the casualty tags off the men who could fire their weapons, remembering, even at this tense moment, that if they were to fight they could not, under the rules of the Geneva Convention, claim to be wounded). The badly wounded were crammed into the back of Doll's car, after he had administered a large dose of morphia. He also found a motorcycle, and this was allocated to one of his orderlies, a conscientious objector, who was appointed despatch rider.

With the despatch rider leading, Doll's party set out. They soon lost their way in the ruined streets of Bergues, and then had to turn back because the bridge they had hoped to cross had been demolished. After driving uncomfortably close to the enemy, they came upon a bridge that was still intact. Shells were falling quite close and the streets were heaped with rubble. By the bridge stood two trucks that had taken direct hits from shells, and a dozen or so bodies littered the road around them. But more encouraging, and to his relief, at this point Doll encountered Captain Lascelles commanding D Company, the 1st Loyals. Doll's party was back with the battalion at last – except for the despatch rider, whom he had been unable to stop taking a wrong turning just before they saw the bridge. He turned up later, after swimming the moat surrounding the town.

Lascelles, who was about to blow the bridge, was astonished to see Doll, convinced that he had got away long before. As they were talking, another despatch rider appeared with a message for Doll from the adjutant. It was a further answer to the MO's earlier query about what he should do and ordered him to rejoin the battalion, leaving his assistant to get the wounded away as best he could. Fortunately, as Doll remarked, 'the order was now out of date'. About a mile further down the road, Doll met Major Gibson, the second-in-command, and from him learned that the battalion was involved in a counter-attack. Having found a suitable barn near the advanced battalion headquarters, he established his RAP there. He sent the lorry with all the wounded into Dunkirk. That was the last he saw of it. Apparently the driver, upon reaching the harbour, was not allowed to return. All this activity was conducted under shellfire, most of it directed randomly at the roads and key points, while the Luftwaffe seemed to be overhead for much of the time. Occasionally these aircraft were greeted by volleys of small-arms fire from the British troops in the vicinity, though it had little effect. Most of the planes were heading for, or returning from, bombing Dunkirk or the beaches and as far as Captain Doll could see did not attack troops in his vicinity. Meanwhile he busied himself using his car to ferry wounded to his RAP. From here the wounded were taken to Dunkirk by ambulances, whose drivers earned Doll's admiration for returning immediately for the next load, and not succumbing to the temptation to go straight to the beach for evacuation as soon as they had delivered the wounded to the hospital.

Further east, the German attacks threatened the 1st East Lancashires. A hefty southern Irishman, Captain Ervine-Andrews, commanded B Company, which was holding about 1,000 yards of the canal line and was cut off by enemy attacks on both its flanks. His own battalion tried but failed to gain contact with him, although Second Lieutenant Griffin got through with three carriers loaded with much-needed ammunition. Later in the day, Ervine-Andrews, learning that one of his platoons was about to be overrun, went forward and climbed on to the thatched roof of the barn which formed part of the platoon position. The Bren in this location had jammed, so he engaged the enemy with a rifle, killing at least seventeen. The Bren stoppage sorted out, it was passed up to him, and he accounted for more of the enemy, halting the attack. When the barn was set on fire, and he had run out of ammunition, he sent his wounded back in the one remaining carrier with Lieutenant Cetre to report to the CO. Cetre returned with more ammunition and orders to hold until the last round and then withdraw. With the last round fired and almost surrounded, Ervine-Andrews collected the survivors of his company and led them back. Wading through ditches, at times with water almost up to their chins, he brought them safely to another company position in rear. He was awarded the Victoria Cross. He learned about the award while dining in a restaurant in the West End of London some two months later, when the wireless was switched on for the nine o'clock news.

The German attack lapped up against the left flank of the East Lancashires and against the 5th Borders adjacent to them. Although they took their toll of the enemy, they were forced back to the Canal des Chats. This exposed the right flank of the 2nd Coldstreams, who like their sister battalion at Furnes had taken heavy losses in officers, including two company commanders. But with help from the 5th King's Own and the 2nd Hampshires they managed to cling to a foothold along the Bergues Canal, turning a cottage into a strongpoint and using the ditches to protect their flanks.

On the left flank of the Canal Line, the 1st Duke of Wellingtons had a frontage of 4,000 yards following the withdrawal of II Corps. After some bitter fighting, including a counter-attack by the 5th King's Own, the position was held. Fortunately the Dukes still had most of their carriers, and were supported by the medium machine guns of the 2nd Cheshires, as well as by some light tanks of the Inniskillings. The German attacks ground to a halt among the dykes and ditches, and their soldiers took cover on anything protruding above the flood water.

On the left flank of I Corps, the French 12th Infantry Division was able to use the existing frontier defences, dug in the previous winter. These soldiers gave such a good account of themselves that no British reserves were required to assist in the defence. Although the Germans had succeeded in penetrating the area where the BEF was making its last stand, they made no attempt to exploit their gains. With the onset of darkness came the moment for the British battalions to thin out and pull back. This was the sixth time that many of them had done this. Groggy with fatigue, their aching legs clad in sodden battledress, the BEF infantry began to pull out and head for Bray-Dunes or Dunkirk. The gunners, having fired their remaining ammunition, removed breech blocks and sights before joining the throng trudging or, in the case of the lucky ones, riding north to the sea. Eventually the German booty included 1,016 field guns and 331 mediums and heavies.

The embarkation went well that night. Inevitably there were some incidents of indiscipline. Lieutenant Nettle RNVR was sent to the beaches for the last two days of the evacuation. After watching two ships' lifeboats drifting in on the tide capsized by soldiers overloading them, he saw a third boat appear, and the troops started wading out to it. Nettle went alongside the queue shouting to them to wait until it came into shallower water. They took no notice of the young RNVR officer, so he drew his revolver and fired into the water about three yards ahead of the leading man. They all stopped, and Nettle waded across to them waving his revolver, indicating that they should all return to shore. Ingrained discipline reasserted itself, and they accepted the order, moving slowly back. Nettle detailed two men to go out and tow the boat back to shallow water so that the others could embark. He asked for two men to volunteer to row the boat back once it had delivered its load, so that it could be used for another trip. He promised that the two would go out on the next trip. But no one volunteered, and he had to rely on getting the next lift out in boats drifting on the tide.

Earlier that day, Second Lieutenant Martin with his machine-gun platoon of the 2nd Cheshires, by now exhausted and out of touch with his parent battalion, found himself without orders. So he went into Dunkirk to discover what he was to do next. He met a French soldier with one eye hanging down on his cheek, screaming for help; but could find no one in authority. So he took the platoon to the water's edge and eventually got a lift out to the destroyers, just visible offshore in the darkness, in a boat manned by some sappers, his platoon of thirty men and a padre whom he had never seen before. When the boat was about a quarter of a mile from one of the destroyers, she weighed anchor and started to steam off. The padre leaped to his feet and shouted, 'Lord, why hast thou forsaken us?' The boat was so overloaded that water was already slopping in with every stroke of the oars, so when the padre jumped up the boat rocked and water started pouring in. Everyone yelled, 'Sit down!', so loudly that the destroyer must have heard, and headed back to pick them up.

At 1430 hours, the 8th DLI were ordered to march along the dunes to the mole at Dunkirk and there lie up to await ships to take them away. All gear was destroyed, except the remaining carriers, which were used to transport wounded. The battalion set out carrying rifles, Brens and shovels to dig holes on arrival. They were machine-gunned from the air on the way, but on the whole saw little of the Luftwaffe, except for a raid on ships offshore. The beach was a scene of great confusion, a jumble of rifles, clothing, oil, bodies, all along the route. At sea the masts and funnels of sunken ships protruded above the surface, while smaller vessels and boats lay abandoned at all angles on the beach. As McLaren's battalion approached Dunkirk they were directed inland through Malo-les-Bains, which was a scene of almost total destruction at the hands of the Luftwaffe. Masses of abandoned transport cluttered the roads and spaces between the villas.

The 8th DLI arrived on the beach by the mole at about 1730 hours, and after digging holes the soldiers ate some cold food they had brought with them. There was nobody around to tell them where the battalion was to embark or when. Eventually, McLaren found the brigade major in Dunkirk and discovered what the arrangements were. On his return he found his battalion tightly packed in three ranks, heading for the mole. After dark, the battalion, in its turn, found itself on the mole edging forward with painful slowness, French on one side, British on the other, subjected to sporadic shelling. McLaren eventually boarded a minesweeper at about midnight, having felt very sick and wretched all evening. Once on board, he immediately fell asleep in an armchair, remaining there until the ship docked in Dover at around 0500 hours the next morning.

The Combined Squadron of the 4th/7th Royal Dragoon Guards was told to cover the infantry until 1900 hours, and then embark. These orders were subsequently altered because of a report of an enemy breakthrough. The squadron was sent to investigate. The 'breakthrough' turned out to be a section with a 50mm mortar, which was 'quickly disposed of'. Frink remarks dismissively in the diary, 'Reports due to a hysterical infantry subaltern who had drunk too much on an empty stomach.' By now Frink admitted to being so sleepy that he 'had to get Williams to work out the map references and orders for the withdrawal'. There were moments of humour when Lieutenant Verdin, the intelligence officer, appeared covered in black soot: he had been blown up with his carrier when a shell fell on a sapper stores dump, presumably containing much explosive.

The squadron handed over to the French on a demolished bridge and covered the last unit back at 2000 hours. By 2300 hours it had reached Dunkirk, destroyed its vehicles and guns, and joined the queue on the mole. 'Forgot to remove my gin bottle,' noted Frink. The mole was a 'seething mass of troops, mostly French'. But just before reaching the point where they hoped to embark in a ship, Frink and his squadron were told there would be no more ships that day. This 'was rather depressing' news.

Just north of Hoymille on 1 June, Captain Doll, the MO of the 1st Loyals, had finished evacuating the wounded by about 2100 hours. The counter-attack was finished and the order was given to hold their positions for one hour before withdrawing to the beaches. Doll was driving his car to battalion headquarters when the shelling intensified, seeming to keep pace with him as he drove. On his arrival, shells started falling all round him, and he jumped into a waterlogged ditch by the road, to find fifty or so other men there. Miraculously no one was scratched. When the barrage lifted, they all withdrew approximately a hundred yards from the road, and waited another half-hour until 2200 hours and the battalion's final withdrawal.

Doll kept his car as it was now the only way of evacuating wounded – he already had one wounded man with him, and picked up a further two. He also had his orderly and the battalion regimental quartermaster sergeant (RQMS) with him. As they approached Dunkirk they thought the flashes and roar of gunfire ahead must come from ships offshore, and they were considerably heartened that they were now under the protection of the Royal Navy. It transpired that what they heard were guns of the Dunkirk fort. A four-mile journey found the battalion entering Dunkirk, and the CO sent Doll ahead to locate the beach. They had been told to aim for the mole at Saint-Malo-les-Bains. Doll headed for the largest pillars of flames, which he thought would mark some part of the harbour. He wished that he had seen the place by daylight. Eventually in the glare of fires he spotted the mole some way off, and columns of French soldiers making for it. He and Pennington, the RQMS, returned to where they had left the battalion, to find that they had all gone. After driving around searching for the battalion up likely roads for about ten minutes, the two men decided to find the evacuation point for them-selves and returned to the beach, having immobilized the car as best they could. The mole, and the beach leading to it, seemed to Doll to be full of French troops, plodding slowly along in the darkness. Shells were falling at a slow but continuous rate. The French seemed to ignore them, but the only British troops he could see appeared to be separated from their units and jumped into the nearest hole in the sand at the first sound of a shell. The feeling of being cut off from their battalion made Doll and Pennington somewhat apprehensive, and soon they too made for holes, with which the sand seemed to be honeycombed. Most of them were already occupied by men who appeared to be waiting for someone to tell them what to do.

After about an hour, Doll decided that they must either push out along the mole or look for boats along the beach. He opted for the latter, and eventually he, Pennington and some soldiers who tagged along joined a queue of two or three hundred soldiers on the beach and in the water, and could see boats plying back and forth. He was delighted to see that it included two companies of Loyals and remnants of other units that had collected at Bergues, some of whom he recognized. Eventually, with water up to his chest, and up to the chins of the smaller soldiers, Doll's party reached the head of the queue and one by one were pulled over the gunwales of a boat. He was heartened to discover that in his boat was an officer from the Loyals who had been in the battalion rearguard; it was welcome proof that the battalion had got clear. Doll was rowed out to a paddle steamer and taken to the saloon, a smallish compartment containing some other officers. All seemed happy, except for an officer of the 2nd Coldstream Guards who had just seen his entire platoon killed or wounded when a shell exploded among them on one of the roads leading to the beach.

Doll soon discovered that his services were required. A sailor came to the saloon asking if there was a doctor present, and took him to a cabin where a naval medical assistant was working on some wounded soldiers on stretchers. Fortunately Doll still had plenty of morphia in his haversack, as the naval assistant had used all his. Some of the soldiers were very badly wounded, and he could not understand how they could possibly have got on board. One Coldstream guardsman, a survivor of the platoon whose officer was in the saloon, had six separate fractures in both legs; he died before the ship reached England. After seeing to the wounded in the cabin, Doll went round the ship attending to men who could not get into the cabin with the more badly wounded. He encountered one sergeant from the Loyals who at first glance seemed hardly to be hurt, until Doll cut his shirt away to reveal a shoulder almost blown off, the arm hanging by a small segment of muscle and skin.

When Doll finally came to register the time, it was 0500 hours the next day, 2 June, and the ship was well out to sea. The naval medical assistant found a bunk for him, and he fell into it, waking as the ship entered Ramsgate harbour. The other half of the 1st Loyals were not so lucky. They moved out along the mole and just missed the last ship of that night, so they had to spend another day on the beach before being taken off, but without suffering further casualties.

For at 0300 hours on 2 June, with daybreak imminent, on orders from Ramsay all the ships departed to avoid the massive losses of the previous days. The East Mole was packed with troops four abreast waiting quietly and in good order, British on the right, French on the left. The sudden departure of the ships caused some confusion. Those at the front turned about, while those at the back pressed on. It presented a juicy target for the German gunners, but only the odd shell crashed down to blast a hole in the queue. The dead were pushed over the edge of the mole or of the causeway that linked mole to beach. Eventually everyone turned and walked back into town to take cover in the dunes or cellars of Malo-les-Bains and wait for the night.

It had become clear to Alexander that, with embarkation suspended during the daylight hours, he would not be able to complete evacuation on the night of 1/2 June as originally envisaged. He thought there were about 3,000 British troops left, although according to the embarkation returns it later turned out there were more. At this stage Admiral Wake-Walker was told there were about 5,000, with an unknown number of French. Alexander formed a tight perimeter round Malo-les-Bains, with twelve 2-pounder anti-tank guns that had been manhandled through the sand dunes, sited to take on any tanks that might break through. In addition there were three 3-inch anti-aircraft guns, and four 40mm Bofors to take on the Luftwaffe.

The Combined Squadron of the 4th/7th took cover not in cellars in Malo-les-Bains but in holes in the dunes. Some enterprising soldiers found, or 'borrowed', some deserted motorcycles and 'a certain amount of relaxation was provided by motor-cycle races on the sands between bombing raids, and lively betting as to which building would be the next to go up'.[2] Frink went to see Brigadier Haydon, commanding the 150th Brigade of the 50th Division, to find out if there were any orders for the next evening evacuation, but there was no news. A number of troops, not from the 4th/7th, took to small boats, but many did not make it. Everyone was very tired, hungry and thirsty, and under almost constant bombing and shelling. 'Most of the day spent examining sea life at very close angle from the bottom of a trench so deep that the water came in,' commented Frink on this day. The 4th/7th were heartened at one stage to find A Squadron of the 5th Inniskilling Dragoon Guards under their tanks on the beach. The 4th/7th had thought up to then that they were the only squadron to miss the boat. But morale in the squadron was 'excellent', and got even better when news came in by wireless at tea time that there would be sufficient transport for all that night. The remainder of the day was spent looking anxiously at the sky wondering whether the squadron would 'get away with it till dark'.

Thanks to devoted service by the French holding the Germans at bay, no British ground units were required to engage the enemy that day. Bergues fell as late as 1700 hours after the failure of a costly counter-attack by a French training battalion. On the west side of the perimeter, the French 68th Division, firing their 75mm guns over open sights, saw off an armoured attack by the 9th Panzer Division; while the 32nd Infantry Division turfed the Germans out of Téteghem. The French 12th Infantry Division in their frontier positions repulsed all attempts to break in from the east. That the British took no part in this fighting was a breach of the promise that Churchill had made in Paris on 31 May. However, Alexander knew nothing of the pledge and was complying with the instructions given him by Eden, when he had spoken to him from La Panne on the evening of 31 May.

There were a large number of wounded in Dunkirk, and orders were that fit men would be given preference. Embarking wounded would have taken up too much time. But it was decided to try to get some wounded away in daylight in hospital ships, hoping the Germans would respect them. A hospital ship entered Dunkirk harbour in full daylight, bearing all the signs required by the Geneva Convention, and her arrival was broadcast in clear to the Germans. She was bombed and sunk. Another was so badly damaged she had to return without loading at Dunkirk. The wounded, other than those who could walk to the pier, had to be left behind. At the Casualty Clearing Station No. 12 at Château Rosendael, south of Malo-les-Bains, there were 230 stretcher cases left, with more coming in. To the surprise of the surgeons and staff, who had not expected to be evacuated, they received an order that one officer and ten orderlies would remain with the wounded and the rest would go. Three officers and thirty orderlies were chosen by ballot. Some patients made brave and sometimes poignant attempts to get to the evacuation points, knowing that only by their own exertions could they avoid capture.

At nightfall, the embarkation started, undisturbed by the Germans who had settled down for the night as was their wont. The soldiers filed quietly along the mole, by their demeanour greatly impressing Alexander. He wrote later: 'The men at no time showed fear or restlessness. They were patient, brave and obedient, and when finally ordered to embark they did so in perfectly disciplined groups, properly armed and equipped.' Throughout the day, Alexander's immaculate appearance and quiet good manners had raised the morale of all who saw him as he moved among the troops.

Frink's Combined Squadron 'formed up with the Skins [Inniskillings] Squadron and marched to the Mole at about 9 pm. Everything worked like clockwork – no shelling or bombing at what would have been a perfect target. Think largely due to the appearance of six Spitfires in the evening, about the only ones we had seen. All aboard by 1030 pm, and so to Folkestone; an unpleasant nightmare dispelled by a view of the white cliffs of Dover at dawn.'

The last of the BEF to leave were the 1st King's Shropshire Light Infantry, who had covered the withdrawal of the 1st Division the previous night. As they stood in the slowly moving queue on the mole, waiting for shells to fall on them, they were illuminated by the massive fires burning in the port and town behind them.

Just before midnight on 2/3 June, the Channel ferry *St Helier* slipped from the mole and made for England with the last of the BEF. Captain Tennant signalled Dover Command: 'BEF evacuated.' He and Alexander boarded a launch to tour the harbour and beaches in search of any remaining British troops. Alexander shouted through a megaphone, 'Is anyone there, is anyone there?' Having satisfied themselves that no one remained, they transferred to a destroyer, which was under machine-gun fire from the land.

Some 20,000 French troops were taken off in the night, and about 30,000 were left. Throughout 3 June they put up a magnificent fight. But by late afternoon the Germans were on the southern outskirts of Dunkirk, about two miles from the mole. Fagalde, however, retained a good grip on the situation, and the familiar German inertia at night allowed him to put into effect his plan for the final withdrawal. This necessitated holding an inner rearguard until 0200 hours on 4 June, and all went to plan, with no interference from the Germans other than some sporadic machine-gun fire.

It was thanks to the Royal Navy and Merchant Navy that a substantial number of French got away. It would have been unthinkable to have abandoned them, but Ramsay's sailors, both Royal and Merchant Navies, were almost at the end of their tether. There had been cases of civilian masters of merchant vessels refusing to take their ships to sea again. On 28 May, the master of the *Canterbury*, a large passenger ferry, had sailed for Dunkirk only after receiving a direct order, and with a naval officer and some ratings embarked to 'stiffen the crew'. On 29 May, after one round trip, the captain of the *St Seiriol* had refused to sail again. The ship finally sailed after the captain had been put under open arrest, and a Royal Navy party placed on board. She was hit and damaged on her way home – it was her last trip to Dunkirk. In the evening of that horrendous day, 1 June, the crew of the *Tynwald*, having completed three trips, also refused to sail. She sailed twenty-four hours later with a relief crew and a Royal Navy party, although with her chief officer as master, and five others of her ship's company. She ultimately completed five trips.[3] These were not the only examples of merchant crews refusing to sail. But those who did so were the minority.

The exhaustion of ships' companies was now the critical factor that Ramsay had to take into account when assessing how much longer

Operation Dynamo could be sustained now that most of those to be evacuated were French. He wrote in his despatch with reference to 3 June:

> No assurance could be obtained that this coming night would terminate the operation and considerable anxiety was felt regarding the effect of the gradual exhaustion of the officers and men of the ships taking part in Dynamo. This exhaustion was particularly marked in the Destroyer force the remnants of which had been executing a series of round trips without intermission for several days under navigational conditions of extreme difficulty and in the face of unparalleled air attack.
>
> The Vice-Admiral [Ramsay] accordingly represented to the Admiralty that the continuance of the demands made by the evacuation would subject a number of officers and men to a test which might be beyond the limits of human endurance, and requesting that fresh forces should be used if execution had to be continued after the coming night, with the acceptance of any consequent delay.[4]

Despite this representation, Ramsay had already issued orders for another night of operations involving all his destroyers and nine out of ten of his ferries, with the usual mixture of supporting vessels and craft. 'We arrived off Dunkirk breakwater at 11.57 pm,' recorded Captain Clarke of the passenger ferry *Princess Maud*. 'We entered the pier heads, and looked for a berth. The narrow fairway was crammed to capacity . . . Wrecks dotted the harbour here and there. The only light was that of shells bursting, and the occasional glare of fires.' She sailed loaded with French soldiers at about 0150 hours on 4 June. At 0255 hours the *Royal Sovereign* sailed, the last of the passenger ferries to leave, having completed six trips and carried a total of 6,858 soldiers in the course of the operation, one tenth of all those rescued by passenger ferries. The paddle minesweeper *Medway Queen* completed her seventh trip. The elderly destroyer *Sabre* completed her tenth sortie, having lifted a total of 5,000 men.[5]

The French Navy also played a part in the evacuation of French soldiers. Some sixty-three vessels of all kinds were involved. The Allied ships took off a further 26,175 soldiers in that final lift. The last ship to leave Dunkirk, having already completed several trips, was the *Shikari*, one of the Royal Navy's oldest destroyers dating back to 1919. At 0340 hours as the grey light of dawn began to lighten the sky through the heavy pall of smoke that hung over Dunkirk, she cast off from the East Mole with her decks crammed with French soldiers. The rattle of German machine-guns close by marked where the French rearguard still gallantly held off the Germans.

At 1423 hours on 4 June, the Admiralty made the signal ending Operation Dynamo. Originally it was thought that some 45,000 soldiers might be rescued. In the end a total of 338,226 were taken away, 308,888 in British vessels. If the troops evacuated in the week before Dynamo are included, the numbers transported to England rises to 366,162. But, as the historian Correlli Barnett has observed, the losses to the Royal and Merchant Navies were equivalent to those one might expect in a major sea battle. Of thirty-eight destroyers, six had been sunk, fourteen damaged by bombs and twelve by collision. Of forty-six personnel carriers (ferries and the like), nine had been sunk, and eleven damaged, eight so badly that they were withdrawn from service.[6]

The 1st East Surreys, whose CO had been so unceremoniously carted off to sea from the mole at Dunkirk in the destroyer *Esk*, were gathered at Axminster in Devon by 4 June. Everyone who arrived was questioned about those missing. Despite the CO's hopes, there had been no question of the battalion all embarking together, and they had been transported in a variety of ships. The medical officer stayed behind to look after the wounded, and was taken prisoner. One group of East Surreys had their ship sunk under them, but were rescued and brought safely home. One of the best athletes in the battalion, Lieutenant Hayfield, was mortally wounded in an air attack on his ship and died before reaching England.

The reception arrangements for troops returning to England were excellent. Captain White was greeted by the women of the WVS with buns and tea saying 'Well done,' which as far as he was concerned was nonsense: 'We were a defeated army.' Units were packed into trains at the port at which they disembarked and sent all over the country. The 2nd Bedfordshire & Hertfordshires whose regimental depot was in Bedford ended up at Brecon, the depot of the South Wales Borderers. It was Sunday 2 June and Sergeant Green had a big black beard. After a meal most flung themselves down on camp beds in the barracks gym, but after an hour everybody was up talking – they could not seem to relax. Second Lieutenant Martin's platoon disembarked at Margate and had their weapons removed; no reason was given. They were put on a train and found themselves in Wheaton Cavalry Barracks, between Birmingham and Stoke-on-Trent. Everybody was very ashamed of the ghastly rout, so he was surprised when everybody was assembled in the gym and told by the commandant that far from being ashamed they should all be proud of this wonderful achievement: 'We were all heroes, so we felt better.' He had broken a bone in his foot during the retreat, was sent to bed by the MO, and slept on and off for seven days. When he came to, his platoon had disappeared. Eventually he discovered that all machine-gun battalions were concentrated in Devon at Paignton, where he joined them.

Others also found their reception in England surprisingly welcoming. Lieutenant Robin Dunn with some of the 7th Field Regiment arrived in Dover on 31 May in a destroyer. After being bundled into trains, they were soon steaming through the countryside. At one station they were given hot tea, bread and marmalade, and at every stop a mass of women appeared with cigarettes, biscuits, lemonade and other food. One woman got into his carriage and insisted on feeding them and thanking them. It was astonishing to be treated thus – they had expected the population to turn their backs on them, a beaten army. Finally arriving at Shrivenham in Wiltshire, the officers were taken to a house converted into a mess and given razors, socks and underclothes. When he went into the mess for dinner, Dunn glanced at the clock – the time was 2055 hours: three weeks ago to the hour the leading gun of his troop had left the village in France in which they had been billeted, on their way to Belgium.

11

THE FINAL BATTLES

On 2 June 1940, Lieutenant General Alan Brooke just back from France, having handed command of II Corps to Montgomery, sat in the War Office in London talking to General Dill, now the CIGS. Brooke asked Dill what he wanted him to do. The CIGS replied that he wanted Brooke to return to France to form a new BEF. Brooke saw this as one of his blackest moments in the war, and there had been quite a few of those already, with many more to come. In an after-note in his diary he wrote:

> I knew only too well the state of affairs that would prevail in France from now onwards. I had seen my hope in the French army gradually shattered throughout those long winter months. I had witnessed the realization of my worst fears regarding its fighting value and morale, and now I had no false conceptions as to what its destiny must inevitably be. To be sent back into that cauldron with a new force to participate in the final stages of French disintegration was indeed a dark prospect.[1]

The force that Brooke would command consisted of the 51st (Highland) Division, the remnants of the 1st Armoured Division and an ad hoc force of lines-of-communication troops in three brigades commanded by Brigadier (later Major General) Beauman (incorrectly called Beaumont by Brooke in his diary), all of which were in France already, and corps troops consisting of artillery, engineers and machine-gun battalions in addition to those forming part of divisions. In addition he would be given the Canadian 1st Division, now based in England, and the 52nd Division (Major General Drew). Leading elements of the Canadian Division had arrived in France, and the 157th Brigade of the 52nd Division, which had already landed, had been put under command of the French Tenth Army. Under pressure, Dill agreed to give Brooke the 3rd Division, now back in England and under Montgomery's command again, when it had been refitted. On arrival in France, Brooke would take command of all British forces there, and come under the orders of General Weygand. He would take his old II Corps headquarters with him, as soon as they could be gathered together from the diverse locations they had been sent to in England after the Dunkirk evacuation.

On leaving Dill, Brooke was summoned to see Eden, the Secretary of State for War, who, after an affable greeting, asked if Brooke was satisfied with what was being done for him. Brooke astonished him by replying that he was far from satisfied, and that the mission on which he was being sent was of no value from a military point of view and would accomplish nothing. Having just escaped one disaster at Dunkirk, the British were now risking another. Brooke added that the move might have some political advantage but that was not for him to judge. It was up to Eden to decide whether the risks were justified in the hope of gaining any political advantage that might exist.

Brooke was correct in his surmise, and as the British Official History commented it was to be an unhappy story, 'relieved only by the loyalty of our intention to fight with all we had till larger forces could rejoin the battle'.[2] Demonstrating loyalty was the aim, and was to lead to more losses for no gain whatsoever.

It should be borne in mind that any action being described in this chapter that occurred before 4 June took place at the same times as, but separated geographically from, the dramatic events north of the Somme which culminated in the Dunkirk evacuation. While the BEF was fighting for its life in northern France and Belgium, there were over 140,000 British troops in France south of the Somme. As well as lines-of-communication troops in ports from Dieppe round to Saint-Nazaire, the 51st (Highland) Division, detached to the Saar front, had been cut off from the main body of the BEF by the German 'sickle-stroke' on 10 May. This division, commanded by Major General Victor Fortune, was stronger than a standard British infantry division. In addition to three full-strength brigades and the usual divisional troops (three field artillery regiments, an anti-tank regiment, three field companies and a field park company of engineers), it had been beefed up with an armoured cavalry regiment (1st Lothians and Border Yeomanry), three additional regiments of artillery, another company of sappers, two machine-gun battalions and two pioneer battalions. After 10 May the division was withdrawn, still under French command, from the Saar Line to the area of Metz.

The 1st Armoured Division, under Major General Evans, disembarked at Cherbourg between 15 and 19 May, to find the port full of troops from rear echelons saying that the war was over and trying to shove their way on board. The GSO 2 of the division, Major Charles Dunphie, a fluent French-speaker, had to push his way down the gangway to the dockside against the flow. The 1st Armoured Division was shorn of all its infantry and one of its tank battalions, diverted to Calais as described in Chapter 6. It now consisted of two armoured brigades, equipped with 143 cruisers and 114 light tanks, and a support group of anti-tank and anti-aircraft guns. After his arrival in France, Evans was given a number of missions by the French, all totally unrealistic and no longer relevant by the time he received them, reflecting the chaos caused by the rapid German advance towards the coast. These included being ordered to attack across the Somme when the Germans already held bridgeheads on that river in strength – a situation that appeared to be news to the French. In this difficult period, no fewer than three generals tried to take charge of Evans (Gort, Georges and Altmayer). Both Gort and Georges could communicate with Evans via the British Swayne Mission at Georges' headquarters. General Robert Altmayer, commanding French Group A, was merely the closest geographically, and tried to hijack the 1st Armoured Division to cover the left flank of Seventh Army in an attack on Amiens. Eventually, responding to General Gort's orders, Evans sent the 2nd Armoured Brigade to attack the German bridgeheads between Picquigny, Ailly and Dreuil on the Somme north-west of Amiens on 24 May. At the time the remainder of the division was still moving forward, with some of the administrative tail still in England. The attack failed.

That night, 24/25 May, Evans now received orders that he would be required to co-operate with the French. Meanwhile the 51st Division would be transferred from the Saar front and sent to form a group with the 1st Armoured Division, whose task would be to take up a covering position from Longpré on the Somme to the coast. In the meantime Evans, according to instructions issued by General Georges, was to hold that line until the 51st Division arrived, and establish small bridgeheads and prepare all bridges for demolition. As the Germans already held the line of the Somme in strength and had pushed their bridgeheads south by several miles, this was yet another absurd order. On 25 May, with the approval of the War Office, Evans was put under the command of the French Seventh Army (which at that stage included Altmayer's Group A).

Evans went to see Altmayer and was told that his division would be split to support a French attack on the Abbeville bridgehead on the Somme. The following day, 26 May, the orders for the attack were issued. The British 2nd Armoured Brigade, commanded by Brigadier R. L. McCreery (the Queen's Bays, 9th Queen's Royal Lancers and 10th Royal Hussars), was to come under command of the French 2nd Light Cavalry Division (DLC), commanded by Colonel Berniquet, and with this French division was to capture the high ground south of the Somme from Bray to Les Planches south of Abbeville. The French were to supply artillery and infantry.

The 3rd Armoured Brigade, commanded by Brigadier J. G. Crocker (2nd and 5th Battalions, the Royal Tank Regiment), were to come under General Chenoine, commanding the French 5th DLC, whose objective was the high ground from Rouvroy to Saint-Valery-sur-Somme. Again the infantry and artillery were to be supplied by the French. In vain, Evans tried to explain that his tanks were not heavies designed to make a breakthrough with infantry, but mainly cruisers developed to exploit a breach made by heavy armour. In short they were equivalent to a French light mechanized division, not a French armoured division. The decision by the French to break up the British armoured division in this way, and expect its brigades at little notice to co-operate successfully in its first battle with a collection of complete strangers, who did not even speak the same language, beggars belief, as do the objectives selected by the French. It illustrates the depths to which the French Army had sunk, and the unfitness for command of most, although by no means all, their senior officers. Both McCreery and Crocker were to rise to high command later in the war – unlike the French generals in the chain of command above them, who were to sink into oblivion.

The chain of command was also complicated. From division it stretched up through General Robert Altmayer's Group A (later Tenth Army) to General Frère's Seventh Army, Besson's 3rd Army Group, Georges' HQ North-East Front, finally to Weygand at the pinnacle. It was a chain of command incapable of reacting to events, and without adequate communications. It was, in a word, useless.

On 27 May the attack went in. The 2nd Armoured Brigade, told that the positions were lightly held by 'inferior troops' (how often has that phrase presaged disaster), ran into well-sited anti-tank guns covering open forward slopes. The two leading regiments, the Bays and 10th Hussars, got nowhere with heavy losses. McCreery had the good sense not to reinforce failure and did not commit his reserve, the 9th Lancers.

The 3rd Armoured Brigade made better progress, advancing about five miles and reaching the outskirts of Valery-sur-Somme and Moyenneville. The brigade lost eighteen tanks endeavouring to pin down the enemy, at which stage Crocker tried to arrange a co-ordinated attack with French infantry. But the French would not play, so Crocker pulled back.

In this battle the 1st Armoured Division lost sixty-five tanks and many crews. In addition, a further fifty-five tanks had broken down, overtaxed by the long and hasty move forward without transporters to relieve strain on tracks and drive mechanisms, and with insufficient time for maintenance – a loss of nearly 50 per cent of its armoured fighting vehicles. The 1st Armoured Division was now severely depleted after one fruitless action. The few remaining tanks of the Bays and 10th Hussars were formed into a Composite Regiment.

The French attacked on 28 May, but with markedly little success. General de Gaulle's 4th Armoured Division attacked on the next day, a much stronger formation than the partially horsed DLCs, which were used on the first day and which the British had supported. De Gaulle learned the same lessons as the British: the use of armour to attack strongly held positions without infantry and artillery support was profitless. A fourth series of attacks was mounted, but by the end of 30 May the German bridgeheads on the Somme remained untaken, and the crossings were still the enemy's for future use.

While these ineffectual efforts were being made to regain the Somme crossings, the 51st Division arrived in the area of the River Bresle from the Saar front, coming under command of the French IX Corps along with the British 1st Armoured Division. Also in the area was the improvised Beauman Division. This had been configured into three brigades, lettered A, B and C, formed from battalions on the lines of communication, from men sent out as reinforcements and from pioneer units. They had almost as many Brens or the First World War Lewis guns, and rifles, as well as anti-tank rifles, as a battalion was supposed to have at full strength. They had three improvised anti-tank gun batteries, one battery of First World War-vintage 18-pounder field guns, and some sappers, but no signallers, which made command and control difficult. Originally formed into three forces – Beauforce, Vicforce and Digforce – in some ways it was a pity that it did not continue to be called Beauforce once all three were pulled together into one formation. It would have avoided much misunderstanding on the part of the French, who thought of it in terms of a standard infantry division, which it most certainly was not. In the First World War Beauman had commanded a brigade at the age of twenty-nine.

It was decided that the British 1st Armoured, the 51st and the Beauman Divisions would operate on the extreme left of the French under their command. But British interests would be preserved by a mission with right of direct appeal to London; this task being assigned to Lieutenant General Marshall-Cornwall. He was located with Altmayer's Group A, now redesignated Tenth Army. While these moves were in train south of the Somme, the BEF was being pulled into the bridgehead of Dunkirk and evacuated to England. The conversation between Dill and Brooke with which this chapter begins took place on 2 June, by which time the BEF had been evacuated from Dunkirk.

By now Weygand had given up any ideas of attacking north of the Somme, but he still regarded the retaking of the German bridgeheads south of the river as essential to the defence against the enemy breakout and advance on Paris, which was expected any day. The British were to be involved in the last attempt to seize those vital bridgeheads.

On the morning of 4 June, the 51st Division with the Composite

Regiment of the 2nd Armoured Brigade and the remnants of the Support Group of 1st Armoured readied itself for the attempt to recapture the Abbeville–Saint-Valery bridgehead. General Fortune, GOC of the 51st, had two French divisions under command – another example of thoroughly bad French command arrangements. A divisional headquarters is not constituted to command two other divisions in addition to its own brigades, effectively three divisions in all, having neither the staff nor, more importantly, the communications. It is a job for a corps head-quarters. The British 3rd Armoured Brigade was in the midst of having its tanks repaired and therefore not available to support this scheme.

Once again a hurried attack with poor preparation ended in failure. Some units of the two French divisions moved into the area only an hour and a half before the attack began. Reconnaissance the previous after-noon had been perfunctory. There were few air photographs available. Time for briefing the troops was short, and few of the enemy positions had been identified, this despite the fact that the Germans had been holding these positions for ten days. This was very largely thanks to the loss of air superiority by the Allies resulting in a lack of air reconnais-sance. The strength of the bridgeheads had been grossly underestimated, and behind them lurked the whole of Army Group B, waiting to unleash its attack on the French.

On the right, south of Abbeville, the 152nd Brigade had 563 casualties in four hours fighting against strongly held positions. According to Captain Lang, the adjutant of the 4th Cameron Highlanders, the battalion started the attack on Caubert some 600 strong and after three hours they were down to 250 all ranks. The battalion had run into a full-strength battalion of German infantry which was itself about to attack and fully alert. A desperate struggle ensued in which the Germans had the best of it. The Camerons fell back. After dark another 130 or so men infiltrated back to the battalion; was down to two companies, with three out of the four original company commanders killed.

French heavy and light armour in support ran on to well-concealed 88mm guns, which wrought havoc. The 1st Gordon Highlanders of the 153rd Brigade had the sole success of the day, tearing into the enemy in the thick Grand Bois wood, and with excellent artillery support took the position at a cost of forty casualties. But the French 31st Infantry Division failed to take the Rouvroy ride on the Gordons' right, and since it dominated the Grand Bois the Gordons were withdrawn, considerably vexed. The British line now stretched from Caumont, four miles south of Abbeville, to Salenelle near the coast.

At 0300 hours the next day, under cover of morning mist the German attack rolled in. The Germans had made good use of the six days since the panzer divisions had been withdrawn from the battle against the BEF and French Sixth Army. They had reorganized their armour and motor infantry into five panzer corps, each made up of two panzer divisions and one motorized infantry division. Bock commanded three corps on the right of the German offensive, and Rundstedt two on the left. The two right-hand armoured formations were Rommel's 7th Panzer and Hartlieb's 5th Panzer Divisions under Hoth. From the sea to the River Meuse, the Germans deployed 104 divisions. Facing them on a front 225 miles long, the French had forty-three infantry divisions, three weakened armoured divisions and three under-strength light cavalry divisions. Twenty-five of the French divisions had been extracted from the Maginot Line, leaving another seventeen in position. The French armies in the north had either been evacuated at Dunkirk or been taken prisoner. The Germans could now concentrate their whole attention on the south.

Hitler had accurately assessed the French strength opposing his armies as sixty to sixty-five divisions. He was wrong when he declared that Weygand would 'withhold an operational assault group which is to be sought in the vicinity of Paris and eastwards. It is also to be expected that the enemy will settle down and prepare resistance further south.'[3] Weygand had actually given up all hope of defending the Somme as early as 28 May. He advised the French government that, once the defence here was breached, they should discuss the possibility of an armistice with the British government. He had mentally thrown in the towel before the final round began.

From the enemy point of view, in this chapter we are principally concerned with the actions of Bock's Army Group B, attacking across the Somme between Amiens and the sea. Kluge's German Fourth Army, consisting of two panzer divisions, six infantry divisions, one motorized division, one motorized brigade and one cavalry division, attacked from the Abbeville–Amiens area and advanced towards the lower Seine. In the sector held by the French IX Corps, which included the 51st Division, Kluge pushed four infantry divisions and a motor brigade across the lower reaches of the Somme between Abbeville and the sea, while the rest of his army, including two panzer divisions and two infantry divisions, crossed between Abbeville and Amiens. The effect was like a man smashing his opponent in the face with a shield held in his right hand, while thrusting into his side with a spear held in his left hand.

At 0400 hours on 5 June the Germans attacked along the whole of 51st Division's front. The 154th Brigade held a series of villages, too widely spaced to afford mutual support. By late afternoon the 7th Argylls had been cut off. The remnants of the battalion held out for another twenty-four hours, before being overcome. What was left of the brigade pulled back to an intermediate line between Woincourt and Eu. The 153rd Brigade on their right had a hard fight but were driven back to a line Toeufles–Zoteux–Frières. The soldiers of the 51st Division had been attacking the previous day, suffering heavy casualties. They had enjoyed very little sleep before the Germans unleashed their attack on them, accompanied by heavy artillery fire and Stukas. It was mid-summer and very hot. While they held off attackers they could see other enemy units bypassing their positions and could do little about it. Casualties were again heavy. That first day the 7th Argylls lost twenty-three officers and nearly 500 NCOs and soldiers killed, wounded or missing. They were the worst case, but the whole division had been savagely battered. With the French 31st Division they held forty miles of front, well beyond the capability of two infantry divisions. Battalions had to hold wide frontages. For instance the 1st Black Watch of the 154th Brigade defended two and a half miles of broken terrain – far too much against a powerful enemy.

During the next day the German pressure seemed to slacken, and this provided the opportunity for the 51st Division to pull back behind the River Bresle, but not before the GOC, Major General Fortune, had written a strongly worded letter to General Marshall-Cornwall demanding that part of his front be taken over. All that Marshall-Cornwall could persuade Altmayer, commanding the French Tenth Army, to agree to was that the 51st should withdraw to the Bresle, but the position was to be 'held at all costs'. The French 31st Division was to take over the sector from Senarpont to Gamaches, and the 51st was to hold from there to the sea, a sector of some twelve and a half miles.

At this stage it was apparent that the German armour had broken through on the right flank of the French IX Corps, heading in the general direction of Rouen. It was clear to the British commanders on the spot and to the War Office that unless the 51st Division and the French formations alongside them were withdrawn, they would all end up cut off in the Havre peninsula, in a replay of Dunkirk. The British informed the French, through the Swayne Mission at Weygand's headquarters, that they intended that a new BEF would form in France. As proof of that purpose, General Brooke, commanding a corps, would arrive within a week, and brigade group of the 52nd Division was to sail for France the next day, 7 June. With these plans in mind, the War Office urged that a line of withdrawal be secured for the 51st Division, not into the sack of Havre, but towards the main French forces and the British bases south of the Seine. But Weygand was in a state of paralysis and the retirement order, when it came, was too late.

By now the 51st Division was so sorely reduced in strength that

A Brigade of the Beauman Division was sent to reinforce it. This brigade, consisting of the 4th Buffs, 1st/5th Foresters and the 4th Border Regiment, was only some 900 strong, only 150 more men than one full-strength infantry battalion. The Bresle was not much of an obstacle, except where flooding had been deliberately caused along the stretches downstream from Eu. Unfortunately the Germans had managed to cross at Eu and at Ponts-et-Marais about two miles upriver from there. All day on 7 June the 4th Borders and a company of the 1st/5th Foresters tried to eliminate the crossing at these points, without success. Meanwhile the situation south of the 51st Division deteriorated rapidly as the 5th and 7th Panzer Divisions outflanked the Bresle line south of Aumale.

The British 1st Armoured Division, less the Composite Regiment with the 51st Division, was now directly under the orders of General Altmayer. Evans and Altmayer agreed that the 1st British Armoured Division should move to Gournay and, from there, strike at the flank of the German advance. Evans had forty-one cruisers and thirty-one light tanks of the 3rd Armoured Brigade plus six light tanks from the 2nd Armoured Brigade, just back from being repaired in workshops. As these moves were under way, Weygand arrived at Altmayer's Tenth Army headquarters. Here he saw Marshall-Cornwall and Evans. Weygand was emotional and clearly stressed, saying that the Tenth Army battle was the decisive engagement of the war. Major Charles Dunphie was told to ask Weygand what troops were guarding the line of the Seine. The reply was 'Deux battalions des douaniers' (two battalions of customs officials) and as, according to Weygand, there were no other French reserves available, all now depended on the 1st Armoured Division.

The division was to hold the upper reaches of the Andelle river from Nolleval to Serqueux, while French formations would counter-attack from the south. That begs the question, what French formations? Weygand had already said there was no reserve. The divisions existed solely in Weygand's imagination. Evans protested, saying that he had already had all his infantry, artillery and anti-tank guns taken from him for use elsewhere, that his cruiser tanks were totally unsuitable for static defence, and in any case were already on their way to counter-attack the enemy flank. Weygand would not alter his decision, although he conceded that if Evans was forced to withdraw from the River Andelle he should pull back across the Seine where he would still be available for counter-attacks. Evans had to issue fresh orders and pull back his units moving to attack the German flank; some were already in contact with German reconnaissance five miles north-west of Gournay.

First light on 8 June saw the panzer divisions approaching Rouen and the French IX Corps, including the 51st Division, being cut off. It was a relatively quiet day for the 51st Division, because the Germans were holding the 'shield' and not pushing too hard, while the 'spear' was hooking round the flank. It was in some ways a repeat of what had happened in northern France and Belgium in May. It would have been far better if the French Tenth Army had ordered IX Corps to fall back, using the numerous river lines as intermediate positions in order to keep contact with the French formations on their right and withdraw over the Seine. By staying put, IX Corps was in a trap.

To the south, the greatly reduced 1st Armoured Division stood on the Andelle. The division had suffered much vexation since its arrival in France. It had lost its infantry and one tank battalion to the Calais battle. It had never been allowed to fight as a division. Most of what remained of the 2nd Armoured Brigade was now reduced to a Composite Regiment which was fighting on the Bresle. All Evans had was the two tank battalions of the 3rd Armoured Brigade and some remnants of the 2nd Armoured Brigade.

The Beauman Division, less A Brigade with the 51st Division, was deployed between the River Béthune and the Andelle. On 6 June, it had been joined by more infantry. This consisted of Syme's Battalion made up of soldiers from the base reinforcement depot (commanded by Lieutenant Colonel A. G. Syme of the Royal Scots), and the 2nd/4th King's Own Yorkshire Light Infantry and 2nd/6th Duke of Wellington's, two battalions that had been involved in the fighting at Abbeville way back on 20 May. The three battalions were now deployed near Rouen: Syme's Battalion at Isneauville, the KOYLI on a bridge over the Seine, and the Dukes on the railway south of Boos. Beauman's widely scattered units hardly qualified for the name 'division'. They lacked wireless communication, artillery and other supporting arms. In some places they were intermixed with the 1st Armoured Division, and in others with French units of whose purpose and plans they had no knowledge. Beauman had no alternative but to issue orders that troops were to hold for as long as it seemed possible to do so, and commanders were given discretion to decide when to withdraw, which would be across the Seine.

The picture was further muddied by the command arrangements. The elements of Beauman's Division deployed on the Andelle Line with the 1st Armoured were under a different commander from 1st Armoured. For the three British formations were under three different commanders. The 51st Division was under the French IX Corps. The 1st Armoured Division was under Altmayer, but acting under the direct orders of Weygand. The Beauman Division was under the orders of Lieutenant General Karslake who, as commander of all British lines-of-communications troops, was under General Georges, commanding the French Armies of the North-East.

On 8 June, the German formations swinging round IX Corps on the Bresle punched through to Rouen. They were preceded by streams of French refugees, making it difficult for Beauman's soldiers to close the roadblocks they had built. The refugees were closely followed by French tanks, which were allowed to go through, but these turned out to have been captured by the Germans, and were leading the main body of enemy armoured formations. Positions held by British infantry with no means of mobility were bypassed, cut off and eventually attacked from the rear, while the main enemy force motored on. The 1st Armoured at least had some mobility, but without anti-tank guns its machine guns and some 2-pounders were outgunned and it could not hold for long. Early that morning the Composite Regiment had been ordered to rejoin the 1st Armoured Division to assist with defending the left of the Andelle Line. On arriving at L'Epinay, in the afternoon, it ran straight into German tanks followed by motorized infantry hot-foot from Serqueux, twelve miles away. A confused roughhouse followed, in which some damage was done to the enemy, but a number of British tanks were put out of action. After three hours, with the Germans almost encircling it, the Composite Regiment, or what was left of it, broke off the engagement.

The 5th Panzer Division's leading elements ran into Syme's Battalion at Isneauville at around 1600 hours. Here the battalion, which had been in existence for only a week, put up a stout fight from behind roadblocks, wire and mines, delaying the 5th Panzer Division from entering Rouen that night.

That afternoon, and during the early part of the night of 8 June, the remnants of the 1st Armoured and Beauman Divisions pulled back over the Seine. Now, too late, Weygand ordered the French IX Corps, including the 51st Division, to pull back over the Seine. General Ihler, commanding IX Corps, received these orders direct from Weygand because Ihler's immediate boss, Altmayer of Tenth Army, had precipitately withdrawn his headquarters to the vicinity of Paris and was out of communication with his subordinate formations. After the meeting between Evans, Altmayer and Weygand the previous day, Altmayer had said that he would give orders the following morning. But when Dunphie went to collect the orders Altmayer had disappeared. Such was the state of French Army command-and-control arrangements. The British Official History is scathing, but still amazingly restrained given the consequences that were to flow from the dithering by the utterly incompetent Weygand and his equally inept fellow French commanders:

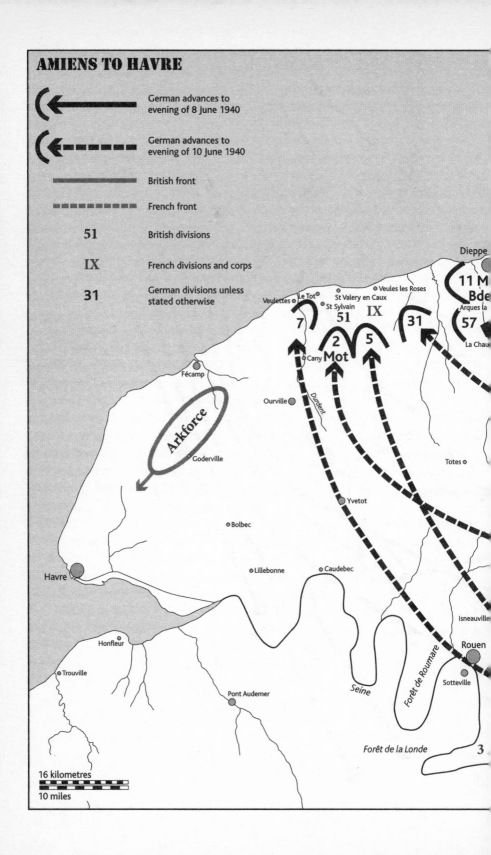

AMIENS TO HAVRE

German advances to evening of 8 June 1940

German advances to evening of 10 June 1940

British front

French front

51 British divisions

IX French divisions and corps

31 German divisions unless stated otherwise

Dieppe

11 M
Bde

Arques la

57

La Chau

Veules les Roses

St Valery en Caux

St Sylvain

Le Tot

Veulettes

7

51

IX

31

2

5

Mot

Cany

Fécamp

Durdent

Ourville

Arkforce

Goderville

Totes

Yvetot

Bolbec

Lillebonne

Caudebec

Havre

Isneauville

Honfleur

Rouen

Trouville

Forêt de Roumare

Sotteville

Pont Audemer

Seine

Forêt de la Londe

3

16 kilometres

10 miles

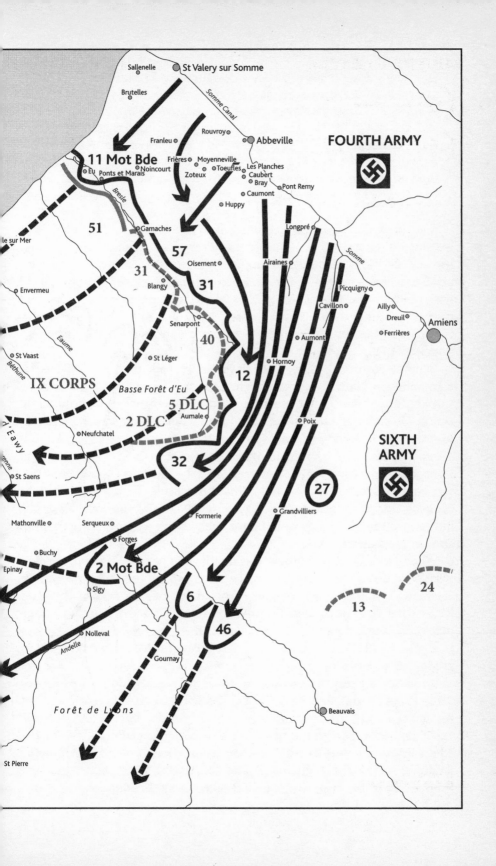

Thus there was exhibited the same initial refusal to face facts, and the same subsequent attempt to mask the consequences of delay by the issue of orders that could not be carried out, as had been displayed in connection with the Weygand Plan. The wisdom of early withdrawal from the Bresle, while it was still possible to retire behind the Seine, was not recognised: and when withdrawal could no longer be avoided the IX Corps was ordered to retire through an area which had been open to them earlier but was now occupied by the enemy.[4]

Ihler met his divisional commanders to give them his plan that evening. It envisaged a leisurely withdrawal over four days through layback positions, finally arriving at Rouen on day four. Yet another pedestrian French general had failed to grasp that enemy armour within four hours' motoring of Rouen was likely to get there first. The next morning, 9 June, the Germans entered Rouen unopposed. The French IX Corps was now cut off, as there were no bridges over the Seine below Rouen in 1940.

General Fortune had realized days before that the sluggish French command-and-control process might lead to the decision to withdraw through Rouen being left too late, but dismissed the idea of unilateral action. He addressed his brigade commanders on the afternoon of 5 June: 'Gentlemen, I know you would not wish us to desert our French comrades. We could be back in Le Havre in two bounds. But they have no transport. They have only their feet to carry them. We shall fight our way back with them step by step.' What his brigade commanders thought of this is not recorded. After their experience at the hands of the French, one conjectures that they would have been all too ready to leave them to stew in their own juice.

When the order to withdraw was finally, and belatedly, given, Fortune persuaded Ihler that the only place from which to withdraw was Le Havre, sixty miles away. He knew from naval officers who had visited him earlier that ships were waiting there, and it was the only suitable place for evacuation. He also persuaded Ihler, fresh from the Maginot Line and totally out of his depth, that a covering force would have to guard the approaches to Le Havre, between Fécamp and Bolbec. Accordingly such a force was constituted, made up of the 154th Brigade (4th Black Watch, who had switched brigades with the 1st Black Watch, and remnants of the 7th and 8th Argylls), A Brigade, the 6th Royal Scots Fusiliers, and supporting units. Commanded by Brigadier Clarke of the 154th Brigade, it was called Arkforce, having been formed at Arques-la-Bataille. During the night of 9 June the troops were pulled out and transported to Fécamp, which they reached early the following morning.

The main body of the 51st Division fell back to the Varenne during the night of 9/10 June.

Arkforce got out just in time, but not the 51st Division. At 1100 hours on 10 June, a wireless operator motoring to join Arkforce ran into the enemy at Cany on the River Durdent, and transmitted the news that he was about to be captured. In fact 7th Panzer Division, commanded by Rommel, had reached the sea at Veulettes. Fortune realized that his evacuation options had been reduced to Saint-Valery-en-Caux or Dieppe. It quickly became clear that the latter was about to fall into enemy hands, so Saint-Valery it would have to be. Saint-Valery had a tiny harbour which almost completely dried out at low water and was dominated by high cliffs on either side from which guns could fire on ships approaching the port.

The Commander-in-Chief Portsmouth, Admiral Sir William James, had arrived at Le Havre to supervise the evacuation and, realizing that the 51st Division and French IX Corps would not get there, sent a signal to the Admiralty and War Office telling them that he had made arrangements to evacuate the 51st Division from Saint-Valery, and had moved small-craft flotillas there already, adding, 'If General 51st Division will keep me informed of his intentions I will direct the evacuation forces to meet his requirements.'

The troops of the 51st Division were ordered to jettison all non-fighting equipment, such as blankets, in order to free as much transport as possible for troop-carrying so that all the men in the division could be carried on RASC trucks and in battalion transport. The move that night, 10/11 June, was a nightmare, as the allocation of roads between the 51st Division and the French units was not adhered to by the latter, and French transport, much of it horsed, kept breaking in from side roads, jamming the narrow ones. Fortunately the enemy were slow to follow up the withdrawal to begin with. This may have owed something to the efforts of D Company the 4th Border Regiment and A Company the 1st/5th Sherwood Foresters, who held two of the Bresle crossings. Orders to withdraw did not get through to them, and so, having heard nothing to the contrary, they stood fast. They denied the crossings to the enemy for six days, beating off all enemy attacks, even taking some prisoners. Only on 13 June, when the Germans brought up artillery, and when they learned that all other fighting north of the Seine had ceased, did they finally surrender.

By the morning of 11 June, Fortune had his division disposed in two parts, one facing east and the other facing west, about eleven miles apart, with a gap in the southern part which he hoped to fill with French troops, but they were in such disorder that he eventually filled it with

what he could scrape together of his own. At about 1400 hours the
German armour began to close in. The German formations surrounding
Saint-Valery consisted of two panzer divisions, 5th and 7th, 2nd Motor
Division, 11th Motor Brigade, and two infantry divisions, 31st and 57th.

Rommel's 7th Panzer Division broke through at Le Tot and seized the
cliff-tops overlooking Saint-Valery from the west. The 2nd Seaforths and
1st Gordons had valiantly fought against three German tank battalions, a
total of a hundred tanks, and had been cut off though not overwhelmed
by them, before Rommel achieved his objective. To the south of the 1st
Gordons, the 4th Camerons were positioned facing west and south. The
battalion had been reinforced by '150 Jocks and three officers, when we
paused at Dieppe on our way back from the Bresle. Within three days
they were in the bag,' remembered Captain Lang.

Meanwhile the battalions on the east side (2nd/7th Dukes, 4th Seaforths and 5th Gordons) battled on against the German 31st Infantry
Division and the 11th Motor Brigade, while the 1st Black Watch held
Saint-Pierre against the 5th Panzer Division, where they too were cut off.
Divisional headquarters, and IX Corps headquarters, had been withdrawn into the town, and from here Fortune tried to communicate with
the ships offshore. He reckoned that the best, and indeed only, night
for embarkation was that very night, 11/12 June. Shells from tanks and
artillery crashed into the town.

The rain poured down as the 4th Camerons along with other battalions
withdrew into Saint-Valery, the narrow lanes seething with disorganized
French soldiers. The fires started by shelling and bombing became an
inferno. There was no wireless communication between battalions or
from battalions to brigade headquarters. Nor was there any from brigade
headquarters to divisional headquarters. Fog crept in from the sea as
men waited to be evacuated, but the ships did not come – the fog was
too thick. The ships found the little fishing port of Veules-les-Roses, still
within the perimeter, and from here took off 1,137 British troops,
including three-quarters of the 2nd/7th Dukes, but not their CO, and
some 1,184 French troops. At 0300 hours, with no craft in sight, Fortune
gave orders for the perimeter to be manned again, in hopes of rescue the
following night. The 4th Seaforths, originally on the east side, were given
the job of driving the Germans back from the western cliff, while most
others assumed their previous locations.

The rain fell more heavily, and the fog thickened. The evacuation from
Veules-les-Roses went on, with the Germans held back by naval gunfire.
The strength of the 51st Division was considerably reduced by now, one
brigade having already been despatched to Le Havre with Arkforce. Three
battalions, 2nd Seaforths, 1st Gordons and 1st Black Watch, were cut off

in positions they were still tenaciously defending on the perimeter and could not withdraw to Saint-Valery. As the 5th Gordons approached the cliffs east of Saint-Valery to take up their positions for the forthcoming day, German tanks moved in. French troops carrying white flags chose that moment to march between the Gordons and the enemy armour, masking the Gordon Highlanders' fire. The Germans closed in and it was all over in this vicinity. Similar situations occurred in the 1st Black Watch and 4th Cameron sector. At 0815 hours a white flag was hoisted on the steeple near the headquarters of the 51st Division. Fortune ordered it cut down and whoever hoisted it arrested. The offender was a French officer acting on Ihler's orders: the flag signalled that Ihler had surrendered. This was followed by a note from Ihler to Fortune, which being translated read, 'Fire ceases at 8 o'clock'. As if to rub salt in the wounds, Ihler then asked if Fortune could transmit the surrender telegram to French headquarters, as his IX Corps had no communications.

Fortune judged that there was no possibility of holding off the enemy until nightfall, and in addition, as he was serving under French command, reluctantly came to the conclusion that he might be forced to obey Ihler's orders. But he still would not give up, signalling the War Office at 1030 hours: 'I have informed corps commander that I cannot comply with his orders until I am satisfied that there is no possibility of evacuating any of my division later.' But all French troops had ceased fire and white flags seemed to be everywhere. So, before sending the message above, he added, 'I have now ordered cease fire.' Half an hour later, he received a signal from the Commander-in-Chief at Portsmouth, 'Regret fog prevented naval forces arriving earlier off St Valery last night. SNO [Senior Naval Officer] afloat will make every endeavour to get you off and additional ships are being sent to arrive tonight.' By the time this message had been received the ceasefire had been ordered. Some troops fought on, like the 1st Black Watch who had broken out to the south. They and the 2nd Seaforths and 1st Gordons did not surrender until 1700 hours.

It is impossible to say how many of the 51st Division would have succeeded in getting away if fog had not prevented ships from going inshore that night, 11/12 June. What is certain is that German artillery and machine guns on the cliffs overlooking the narrow estuary and entrance on each side would have sunk or damaged many ships with heavy losses, and wrought similar carnage among the soldiers in these vessels or awaiting embarkation. This is borne out by Lieutenant Hawkins, of the 7th Royal Norfolks (a pioneer battalion with the 51st Division). His company was attached to Fortune's headquarters, and he was sent to meet a naval officer at Saint-Valery to arrange the evacuation.

This officer told Hawkins that it was not possible to get enough large vessels into the port to take off the number of troops that needed evacuating. In addition, from the port area Hawkins could see German tanks on the cliffs overlooking the port.

One of Hawkins's platoons managed to make its way to Veules-les-Roses while the mist was still down and eventually steal out to the ships by rowing boat. The men got home safely, but were subsequently sent to the 18th Division, which was captured in its entirety at Singapore in February 1942 – and about half of that platoon never came home. The rest of Hawkins's company, after capture by the Germans, lost only one man, to pneumonia.

Captain Lang, the adjutant of the 4th Camerons, was another of those who headed for Veules-les-Roses. With some 'Jocks', he made his way along the beach, past bodies at the foot of the cliffs. As they crept along, a German machine gun on the heights above Saint-Valery fired on them but missed. On arrival at Veules-les-Roses they found two vessels, one British, which was aground, and one French offshore. Suddenly, the French vessel was hit and blew up. This left the British vessel, packed with soldiers waiting for the tide to float her off. Germans began to close in, and tanks fired from the cliff-tops, holing the grounded vessel so that even if she had floated off she would have sunk. Lang, who had climbed on board, was firing a Lewis gun with which the vessel was armed, and was wounded just before the Germans came out on to the beach and 'rolled us up'.

The Highlanders would return to Saint-Valery in 1944 to liberate the town. The reborn 51st (Highland) Division had to complete a long journey before that great moment – all the way from Alamein in North Africa, via Sicily and Normandy. By then they were commanded by Major General Thomas Rennie, who as a major and GSO 2 to Fortune had undertaken the unpleasant task of notifying the division of the order to surrender. He subsequently escaped from the prisoner column.

Others also escaped, including Captain Lang. With two others he too broke away at night from the prisoner column in the Pas-de-Calais area. After fourteen days they reached Le Touquet, to find every boat requisitioned by the Germans. While searching for a means to get away they were recaptured. Lang made a second break, this time when being transported through Belgium. He succeeded in getting clear this time, via Paris by train to the south of France, and eventually across the Mediterranean to Syria. From here he returned to Britain and eventually commanded the 5th Cameron Highlanders with distinction when they were part of the 152nd Brigade of the resurrected 51st Highland Division in north-west Europe.

After crossing the Seine, the 1st Armoured Division withdrew to a perimeter across the Carentan Peninsula. There were no British army maps of the area, and the division was reduced to using Michelin maps when they could be found. Evans was eventually made the scapegoat for what had befallen his division.

Arkforce made it to Le Havre, and by 1530 hours on 13 June the evacuation of this port was complete. Arkforce was shipped to Cherbourg, through which port it was intended that the British should send in reinforcements and continue the fight under the command of the recently knighted Lieutenant General Sir Alan Brooke. For, although the story of the BEF's travail in the campaign of 1940 was nearly over, it had a little time to run. By now, the Italians had joined forces with Hitler, declaring war on France and Britain on 10 June 1940.

Brooke arrived at Cherbourg early in the morning of 13 June. His first order was to continue with the evacuation of lines-of-communication troops not essential for the maintenance of the 'new BEF' of four divisions. He learned that one of those divisions, the 51st (Highland), had been cut off and forced to surrender. Next he drove to the British lines-of-communication headquarters at Le Mans and met Swayne, head of the mission to General Georges (still commander of the North-East Front). After discussions with Swayne and Howard-Vyse, head of the British mission at Weygand's headquarters, who happened to be visiting the headquarters, Brooke came to the conclusion that the French could not hold out for more than another few days. This impression was reinforced when he arrived with Howard-Vyse at Weygand's headquarters at Orléans the next day after a 170-mile drive. It was clear that Weygand had given up, and he told Brooke that the French Army had ceased to be able to offer organized resistance and was disintegrating into disconnected groups. The Germans would enter Paris that day, 14 June, and their divisions were scything through France.

As far as Weygand was concerned the only military recourse was to form a redoubt in Brittany by holding forward a line just east of Rennes, with one flank on the sea at Saint-Malo and the other on the mouth of the Loire, adding that this plan had been agreed by the Supreme War Council. Subsequently Weygand was to deny that he had given Brooke such a depressing portrayal of French disarray. It is hard to believe that Brooke did not hear him aright. He was a fluent French-speaker and described the meeting in his diary that night, giving his views on the Brittany plan, which he thought 'wild' and 'quite impossible'.[5]

Brooke and Weygand then drove to Georges' headquarters, which were sited near Weygand's. During the journey, Weygand turned to Brooke and said, 'This is a terrible predicament I am in.' Brooke was about to answer that he could well understand the heavy responsibility of being entrusted with saving France in her agony when Weygand continued, 'Yes, I had finished my military career which had been a most successful one.' Brooke was astounded that all this man, on whom France had pinned her hopes, could think about was his military career. It would not have surprised General Spears, the British Liaison Officer at GQG who, as we have seen, received the same impression about Weygand when he met him on 20 May.

On arrival at Georges' headquarters, Brooke was shown a situation map, which clearly demonstrated that the French Army had lost all cohesion. He asked how Georges would find the troops to defend a front of 93 miles in Brittany, a minimum of fifteen divisions. The British were producing four. Where were the others to come from? The answer: there were none. Both Georges and Weygand considered the plan ridiculous, but as it had been agreed by the Inter-Allied Council it was an order. Brooke said he would participate in the scheme, but would report his views to the British government. Weygand did not reveal that he had already advised the French government to ask for an armistice.

Brooke sent a telegram back to London asking that the Brittany plan be reconsidered in view of Weygand's, Georges's and his opinion that it was absurd. Brooke despatched Howard-Vyse back to Britain to see General Dill, the CIGS, to tell him to stop despatching any more British troops and make preparations to evacuate those already in France. Having driven the 170 miles back to Le Mans, Brooke spoke to Dill on the telephone. He requested that the flow of British troops to France be stopped (the Canadians and corps troops). He added that there was only one course open, to re-embark the Expeditionary Force as quickly as possible. He then arranged for those troops in France not under the command of French Tenth Army, and still fighting, to be got out as quickly as possible. He sent for Marshall-Cornwall, still liaison officer with Tenth Army, and told him to discuss with the French the evacuation of British troops as soon as they could be released.

Brooke's recommendations were accepted by the War Office, as was his request that Weygand be told that the British Army would no longer remain under his command. Plans were made for the main body of the 'Second BEF' to embark at Cherbourg, while a covering force held the neck of the Cotentin Peninsula. Some lines-of-communication units would embark at the nearest convenient port, such as Saint-Malo, Brest and Saint-Nazaire.

At about 2000 hours, Brooke had another telephone conversation with Dill, who was at No. 10 Downing Street, and found himself talking to Churchill. Brooke had difficulty persuading the Prime Minister to agree to the evacuation of the two brigades of the 52nd Division that had just arrived in France. Churchill suggested that they be used to close a thirty-mile gap between the French Tenth Army and the one on its right. Brooke talked him out of it. He was forthright and firm with Churchill, whom he had never met. It was a model of how a soldier should deal with a politician at moments of great crisis. A lesser man might have lacked moral courage and resorted to telling the Prime Minister what he wanted to hear. Brooke recorded this conversation in an afternote in his diary. Having been told by Churchill that he, Brooke, had been sent to France to make the French feel that the British were supporting them, Brooke replied 'that it was impossible to make a corpse feel, and that the French army was, to all intents and purposes, dead, and certainly incapable of registering what had been done for it'.[6]

During half an hour of talking, in which Churchill implied that Brooke was suffering from 'cold feet', Brooke managed to maintain his temper by looking out of the window at the GOC of the 52nd Division sitting on a garden bench talking to one of his brigadiers, and it reminded him 'of the human element of the 52nd Div and of the unwarranted decision to sacrifice them with no attainable object in view'. At last, when Brooke was exhausted, Churchill said, 'All right, I agree with you.'[7]

The next four days were critical, and Brooke's firmness kept the British both in France and back home in Whitehall on track, a track that for the remnants of the BEF led back to Britain. He was absolutely clear that the French were about to surrender, and was determined that as few British troops as possible should be caught up in the ensuing debacle. On 16 June, with embarkation in progress, Brooke moved his headquarters to Redon, north of Saint-Nazaire. Here he learned from Dill over the telephone that Weygand was complaining about Brooke's not honouring his undertaking to hold Brittany. Weygand appeared to have forgotten that two days earlier Dill himself had told him that British troops were no longer under his command and were therefore not available to take part in the Brittany redoubt scheme – a scheme which Weygand himself had described as fantasy. Dill had referred the matter to Churchill, who said there was no such agreement between the two governments.[8]

On 17 June, Brooke heard Marshal Pétain broadcast to the French armies to cease hostilities while he negotiated with the Germans. Neither Weygand nor any other French officer had seen fit to inform the British, who still had large numbers of troops and masses of equipment in France. Instead they were still carping about Brooke's refusal to partici-pate in the impossible Brittany redoubt plan. The French excused their failure to notify their allies by claiming that they would fight on if the terms of the armistice were not honourable. But nobody, least of all

Brooke, having seen the state to which the French Army had been reduced, could possibly be persuaded that Pétain broadcasting that the fighting had to stop could mean anything other than surrender. Fighting on did not figure on the French agenda.

Brooke left France on 18 June, via Saint-Nazaire. He had arrived at the port the day before to be told that the destroyer sent to pick him up was full of survivors from the liner *Lancastria* which had just been bombed with 6,000 troops on board, sinking in fifteen minutes with the loss of 3,000 lives. He was offered an armed trawler, the *Cambridgeshire*, that could just fit in his HQ staff and was sailing at once, or the *Ulster Sovereign* sailing the next day. Conscious that Pétain's negotiations with the Germans might include the internment of British troops in France, he decided not to wait, and boarded the trawler.

The evacuations went on until 25 June, the day the armistice terms signed between France and Germany came into effect. Between 16 and 25 June, the final evacuations took place from Cherbourg, Saint-Malo, Brest, La Pallice and Saint-Nazaire. During this period a total of 144,171 British, 18,246 French, 24,352 Polish, 1,939 Czech and 163 Belgian troops were transported to Britain. Some troops were even taken from Mediterranean ports until mid-August, by which time that region of France was Vichy territory and not under German occupation.

Brooke by his appreciation of the disaster about to overtake the French and by his refusal to carry out the British government's instructions, including standing firm against Churchill himself, saved three British divisions from the fate that befell the 51st (Highland) Division. These divisions along with lines-of-communication and other Allied troops, plus nearly 300 guns were taken to England to fight again another day.

12

RECKONING

Personally, I feel happier now that we have no allies to be polite to and to pamper.

King George VI writing to his mother after Dunkirk[1]

With the fall of France, British strategy for fighting the war against Germany lay in ruins. For years the government had shied away from committing Britain to fighting alongside the French on the continent of Europe. When they finally did so in February 1939 it was on the assumption that the next war would mirror the opening years of the last one: in the event of invasion, the French would contain the Germans. This would allow the British Army to build up sufficiently in both manpower and equipment to enable it to play its full part in what would be a replay of the previous war. It took nine months to build up the BEF from its original September 1939 strength of four divisions to the ten divisions that faced the Germans on 10 May 1940, plus another three that landed in France later in May. Many of these formations were neither equipped nor trained to face a first-class enemy. During those nine months leading up to the German offensive in the west, except for patrol skirmishes in the Maginot Line sector, the BEF had not been engaged in any fighting whatsoever. Despite being granted this intermission, neither foreseen nor catered for, the time vouchsafed thereby was still insufficient to manufacture the necessary equipment, and raise and train the units required to expand the 1940 BEF into the force comparable with the BEF of fifty-six divisions that eventually fought on the Western Front between 1916 and 1918. By May 1940 much more needed to be done to bring the BEF up to full fighting efficiency, let alone expand it. But thanks to the manner in which the Germans conducted their campaign, and the swift collapse of the French Army, time was not granted.

The evacuation of the BEF at Dunkirk was spoken about as a miracle at the time, and still is depicted in those terms to this day. The only miraculous element in the operation was the weather: gales and high seas would have allowed far fewer troops to be taken off – probably none from the beaches, and drastically fewer from the seaward side of the East Mole. On the plus side, however, bad weather, especially if accompanied by bad visibility and low cloud, might have curtailed the activities of the Luftwaffe. The Dunkirk operation owed its success to the power and skill of the Royal Navy, not to any mystical intervention. The part played by the Royal Navy has been consistently underestimated; without it the considerable contribution by the RAF and the courage and skill of the BEF would have been to no avail. Ask anyone in the street what he or she knows about Dunkirk, and aside from the large number who will gaze at you blankly, most will say 'The little ships bringing the BEF home.' That the contribution of the 'little ships' to the successful evacuation from the Dunkirk beaches was significant is without doubt. But their role has become the enduring myth of the operation to the extent of obliterating the contribution of the Royal and Merchant Navies. This can be understood in the context of the time. To boost national morale and cohesion, the story of the 'little ships' was milked as hard as it could be. The facts are that more than two and a half times as many troops were taken from Dunkirk harbour as from the beaches, and of those taken off the beaches the majority were transported in destroyers or other ships, albeit in many cases ferried out to these larger vessels, either by 'little ships' or by ships' boats. The number of men taken directly from the beaches to England by the 'little ships' was small. The breakdown of figures is at Appendix C. One-third of all the troops evacuated were taken off in the fifty-six destroyers involved in the operation.

Without the Royal Navy the evacuations after Dunkirk would have been impossible too. These involved taking off some 140,000 British troops from formations and lines-of-communication units left south of the Somme after the German breakthrough. The only instance of the Royal Navy not fulfilling its obligation to the army occurred at Saint-Valery, and that was largely due to the weather and the proximity of German armour. But the Royal Navy did manage to evacuate 2,137 British and 1,184 French troops from Veules-les-Roses near Saint-Valery.

It is arguable that the defeat of the French Army in 1940, which led to the withdrawal of the British Army from the continent, was a blessing in disguise for the British – although not for the reason that King George VI gave in his letter to his mother, quoted at the head of this chapter; and it certainly would not have been seen as a godsend at the time. Indeed for reasons that will be covered later, the Fall of France was to make the British conduct of the war infinitely more difficult than envisaged by the Chiefs of Staff and politicians in 1939 and early 1940.

But there were bonuses as well. First, because there was no 1940 repeat of the events of 1914, that is an eventual halting of the German offensive in France and Flanders, there was no 1940s version of the 1914–18 Western Front, with all that would have flowed from that including massive casualties. Just over a year later, flushed with their victory in the west, the Germans invaded Russia. It was on the Eastern Front that the main body of the German Army was engaged from June 1941 until May 1945. It was here that the colossal casualties suffered by Britain and France fighting the Germans in the previous war were repeated, only on a vastly increased scale, and borne this time by the Russians. In the process the German Army was worn down, and unable to move sufficient divisions to the west to contain the British and Americans when they landed and liberated western Europe in 1944–5.

Thus Britain, because of the Fall of France, was granted some 'time out', respite from engaging the German Army. Indeed one could argue that Britain never again encountered the enemy's main effort on land for the rest of the war. There was tough fighting in several campaigns, yes, but not against the main body of the German Army; it was engaged in Russia.

The collapse of France, and the failure of the Luftwaffe to win the Battle of Britain, bought the time that Britain needed to absorb the lessons so dearly learned in France, to re-equip, and to retrain. In the process some of the dead wood among the middle-ranking and senior officers was cut out of the British Army. Generally, those who had done well were promoted, those who had failed were given administrative jobs or, if more senior, retired. On the whole, younger, fitter men commanded at all levels: most commanding officers were under thirty, some in their mid-twenties, rather than the over-forty-year-old veterans of the First World War that commanded units in 1940. Company commanders, and their equivalents, were correspondingly younger, mostly in their early twenties. These changes took time, but now there was time.

Time was also vouchsafed to get the Americans used to the idea that they might have to become involved in this war. The final catalyst was of course the Japanese bombing of Pearl Harbor in December 1941. The United States, whose army in 1939 ranked seventeenth in the world after Rumania, was, even as late as November 1942, in the words of Field Marshal Sir John Dill, 'more unready for war than it is possible to imagine'. It is therefore inconceivable that America could have played any part in stopping the expansion of the Axis had Britain given in when France fell, or made a separate peace with Hitler in 1941, as the late Alan Clark was fond of suggesting. Without Britain and her Empire and Commonwealth continuing to resist after the Fall of France, Hitler could have won the war.

Finally, still counting blessings, even the French may have benefited from their defeat in 1940 – bitter though the shame was at the time and even though the poison lingers still. But there was no equivalent to Verdun, or any of the other Western Front battles that in total cost France over six million casualties between 1914 and 1918.[2] Yes, there was the degradation of collaboration with a foul Nazi regime and all that went with it, including the labour camps and persecution of the Jews. But it is not for us to speculate on which was preferable: sparing France a second round of years of fighting on a 1940s Western Front (including the massive material damage), or the shame of defeat and all that followed. Only a Frenchman or woman can say what would have been right for France.

The debit side of the reckoning resulting from the defeat of France included a number of unpalatable realities. The French Army of ninety-four divisions was out of the equation, leaving a handful of badly equipped British, Commonwealth and Empire divisions to face some 160 German ones. Granted these would not immediately be encountered in Europe, and in Britain only if the Germans invaded. But, until Russia came into the war, as a result of German aggression (not, it must be emphasized, in order to assist the British), those German divisions were a potential threat to British interests in the Mediterranean and conceivably in the Middle East. Indeed, even when embroiled with Russia, the German Army could still spare sufficient formations to cause the British considerable grief in North Africa, Sicily, Italy, Greece and the Aegean over the ensuing years.

But more immediately menacing than the German Army were the Luftwaffe and the U-boats. With bases in France, Belgium and Holland the Luftwaffe could now reach every city in the United Kingdom and realize the nightmares with which British politicians had frightened themselves since the mid-1930s. These nightmares were to prove largely groundless until June 1940, for the simple reason that most German aircraft of that period, designed for tactical support of ground forces and not for strategic bombing, had a small radius of action, especially so in the case of their fighters.[3] To bomb London from even the nearest part of Germany would involve a 600-mile round trip. Flying from bases in Germany, the Luftwaffe simply did not have the capability to mount mass attacks on major cities and communication links in the United Kingdom. If attempted in daylight, without fighter escorts, the bombers would have been easy meat for the RAF. After the Fall of France it was very different.

From airfields in northern France to London the radius of action is 200 miles. Not only could the Luftwaffe attack the United Kingdom, it could also attack shipping in coastal waters, especially in the Channel and North Sea. The Focke-Wulf Condors could range far out into the Atlantic, not only acting as eyes for the U-boat packs, but also able to attack shipping with bombs and machine guns. Between June and November 1940, Condors operating from Bordeaux had sunk 90,000 tons of Allied shipping, and for the next three years they were, in Churchill's words, 'the scourge of the Atlantic'.

In 1917, the U-boats had nearly brought the United Kingdom to her knees. Then they had only the short stretch of Belgian coast and Germany's North Sea coast from which to operate, and access to the Atlantic trade routes involved a long trip round the north of Scotland or through the Straits of Dover. Now, from occupied France's Biscay coast, the U-boats could sortie straight out to attack shipping in both the North and South Atlantic. The occupation of Norway also gave the Germans bases from which to send out Condors to spy on and attack convoys routed as far north as southern Greenland in an attempt to keep out of the clutches of the U-boats.

The Fall of France also drastically altered the strategic balance in other ways. The Royal Navy had counted on the well-equipped French Navy to cover the Mediterranean, while it protected trade routes and fulfilled Imperial commitments elsewhere. Now the French Navy was immobilized in French ports by the terms of the Armistice Treaty with Germany. At the same time Italy had come into the war on the German side, bringing with her a powerful battle fleet and large air force. Although the latter was equipped with obsolescent types of aircraft, with numerous land bases the Italian Air Force posed a major threat to shipping transiting the Mediterranean long after the threat posed by the Italian Navy had been severely reduced by the Royal Navy. As a result of the Italian threat, the main trade route through the Mediterranean was immediately abandoned by Britain, thereby lengthening the voyage from the United Kingdom to Suez and the supply of British forces in the Western Desert and Palestine from 3,000 to 13,000 miles round the Cape of Good Hope, and similarly to Bombay and British forces in India from 6,000 to 11,000 miles.

From June 1940 to June 1941, Britain and her Empire and Commonwealth were at war without an ally against two powerful enemies, Germany and Italy, with a third lurking ever more menacingly, Japan. This was the perilous strategic state to which the United Kingdom was reduced by the Fall of France.

The losses suffered by the Royal Navy during the evacuation have already been covered. During the campaign, the Royal Air Force lost 1,526 killed in action, died of wounds or injury, lost at sea, wounded or taken prisoner. The vast majority of these were pilots and aircrew. Aircraft losses amounted to 931 failed to return, destroyed on the ground or damaged beyond repair.

British Army casualties were 68,111 killed in action, died of wounds, missing, wounded or prisoners of war. The material losses of the army were enormous, either in battle or destroyed, or left behind, as shown below.[4]

Material losses of British Army in France and Belgium, May to June 1940

	Shipped to France	Consumed and expended in action or destroyed or left behind	Brought back to England
Guns	2,794	2,472	322
Vehicles	68,618	63,879	4,739
motorcycles	21,081	20,548	533
Ammunition (tons)	109,000	76,697	32,303
Supplies and stores (tons)	449,000	415,940	33,060
Petrol (tons)	166,000	164,929	1,071

Note: Of some 170 cruiser tanks, 175 light tanks and 100 infantry tanks, only thirteen light tanks and nine cruiser tanks were brought back to England.

Until the lost equipment could be replaced by British and American industry, the British Army faced the prospect of fighting an invading German Army armed mainly with rifles and light machine guns. The 4th/7th Royal Dragoon Guards were typical. In June 1940, the regiment was equipped with a vehicle called the Beaverette, named after Lord Beaverbrooke, the Minister of Aircraft Production and member of the War Cabinet, whose 'baby' it was. The Beaverette, officially known by the grandiose title the Ironside, was an ordinary Standard 14-horsepower family car fitted with a sheet of armour plate in front and on the sides, and open at the top.[5] Each squadron was organized into five troops of four Beaverettes each, and a bus troop, which provided a dismounted party that travelled to war in a luxury coach that had once carried happy holidaymakers to the seaside. Each squadron mustered about twenty-five Brens and six anti-tank rifles. These they would take to battle in a vehicle that did not keep out even an armour-piercing rifle bullet. The regiment was not re-equipped with tanks until April 1941, and what it got was the Covenanter, already obsolete by the time it was issued.[6]

Despite these losses, the morale of the British Army was undented. The BEF came back with an unswerving belief that given equal terms it could have defeated the German Army. Let the final word on this subject be left to the enemy. In August 1940, German divisions training for the invasion of the United Kingdom were provided with a report prepared by the German IV Corps, which in Bock's Sixth Army had fought the BEF from the Dyle to the Channel coast. The report covers mainly technical detail of British fighting methods, but this is what it has to say about the British soldier (the italics are in the German original):

> *The English soldier* [sic] was in excellent physical condition.[7] He bore his own wounds with stoical calm. The losses of his own troops he discussed with complete equanimity. He did not complain of hardships. *In battle he was tough and dogged.* His conviction that England would conquer in the end was unshakeable . . .
>
> The English soldier has always shown himself to be a *fighter of high value.* Certainly the Territorial divisions are inferior to the Regular troops in training, but where morale is concerned they are their equal.
>
> In defence the Englishman *took any punishment that came his way.* During the fighting IV Corps took relatively fewer prisoners than in engagements with the French or Belgians. On the other hand casualties on both sides were high.[8]

Two other topics demand an airing in the reckoning: an assessment of Gort and an evaluation of the senior command of the French Army. Both will of necessity be short.

Gort's decision to evacuate his army at Dunkirk saved the BEF. He may not have been a brilliant army commander – his faults have been discussed already and need no repeating. But he was able to see with absolute clarity that the French high command were utterly bankrupt of realistic ideas and that consequently Allied plans would lead nowhere, and he had the moral courage and unwavering willpower to act in the face of censure and criticism, thus ensuring that the BEF was saved. There are few occasions when the actions of one man can be said to be instrumental in winning a war. This was one of those. Had the BEF been surrounded, cut off and forced to surrender, it is inconceivable that Britain could have continued to fight without an army. That is not to say that Britain would necessarily have been occupied, but a humiliating accommodation with Hitler would surely have followed. Without continuing British resistance, weak at first but daily growing stronger, Hitler would have won the war. For the reasons already given, the United States was incapable of intervening to limit Hitler's hold on Europe.

The French high command have been criticized in this book. Whatever excuses one might offer, in the end one has to ask how it was that the French Army, with better tanks and more of them than the Germans, was so utterly defeated in so short a space of time. The deficiencies of the French Army have been covered in the first chapter, and it is not intended to repeat them in detail here. The French, having been on the winning side in the First World War, were entirely content that the lessons they drew from it were the right ones. They repeated the mistake they had made after the Franco-Prussian War of 1870–1, when they applied lessons they had learned in that war to the first half of the First World War, suffering huge casualties and coming close to defeat in the process. After the First World War, believing in the power of the defence (a conclusion they had drawn from that war), they aimed to fight a static war in the next contest. Conducting operations in this way would not require good communications because the pace of events would, in their estimation, be so slow that their inadequate arrangements for radio and telephone links and rigid command-and-control organization would be able to cope. There was no point in massing their armour, they believed, because its principal role was to support the infantry in defence and in local counter-attack. Events did not go as they had foreseen, and the shock to an army whose morale was already flawed was too much. The French Army met General James Gavin's definition: 'Organisations created to fight the last war better are not going to win the next one.'

The German Army, having been defeated in the First World War, was not above analysing the lessons at the tactical and operational level, and drew the right conclusions. That their leaders, Hitler and his generals, failed to learn the strategic lessons contributed to Germany's ultimate defeat in the Second World War, as it had in the First.

Appendices

APPENDIX A

ALLIED LAND FORCE ORDER OF BATTLE AS AT 10 MAY 1940

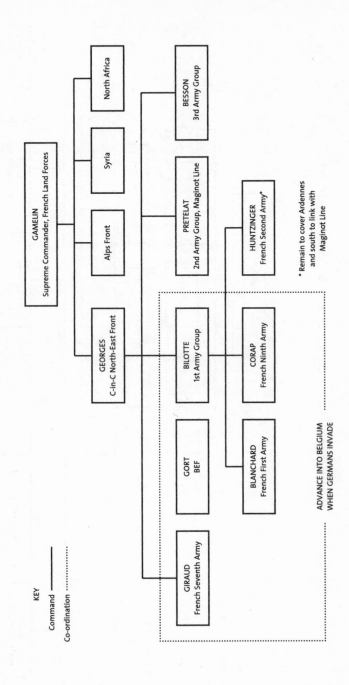

KEY

Command ———

Co-ordination ··········

GAMELIN
Supreme Commander, French Land Forces

North Africa

Syria

Alps Front

BESSON
3rd Army Group

PRETELAT
2nd Army Group, Maginot Line

HUNTZINGER
French Second Army*

GEORGES
C-in-C North-East Front

BILOTTE
1st Army Group

CORAP
French Ninth Army

GORT
BEF

BLANCHARD
French First Army

GIRAUD
French Seventh Army

ADVANCE INTO BELGIUM
WHEN GERMANS INVADE

* Remain to cover Ardennes
and south to link with
Maginot Line

APPENDIX B

ALLIED LAND FORCE ORDER OF BATTLE AS AT 12 MAY 1940

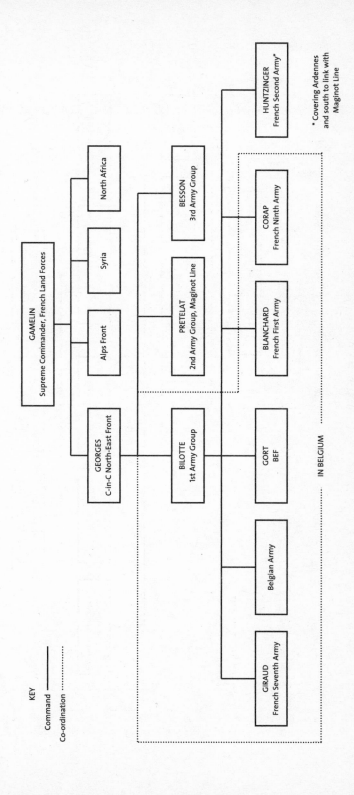

KEY

Command ———

Co-ordination ·············

GAMELIN
Supreme Commander, French Land Forces

North Africa

Syria

Alps Front

GEORGES
C-in-C North-East Front

BESSON
3rd Army Group

PRETELAT
2nd Army Group, Maginot Line

BILOTTE
1st Army Group

HUNTZINGER
French Second Army*

CORAP
French Ninth Army

BLANCHARD
French First Army

GORT
BEF

Belgian Army

GIRAUD
French Seventh Army

IN BELGIUM

* Covering Ardennes
and south to link with
Maginot Line

APPENDIX C

BRITISH AND ALLIED TROOPS LANDED IN ENGLAND FROM DUNKIRK, 27 MAY TO 4 JUNE 1940

Date	From the beaches	From Dunkirk harbour	Total	Accumulated total
May 27	Nil	7,669	7,669	7,669
28	5,390	11,874	17,804	25,473
29	13,752	33,558	47,310	72,783
30	29,512	24,311	53,823	126,606
31	22,942	45,072	68,014	194,620
June 1	17,348	47,081	64,429	259,049
2	6,695	19,561	26,256	285,305
3	1,870	24,876	26,746	312,051
4	622	25,553	26,175	338,226
Grand total	**98,671**	**239,555**	**338,226**	

Glossary

AA – anti-aircraft.

Adjutant – the CO's personal staff officer in a battalion or regiment in the British Army. In the Second World War, and for several years thereafter, there was no operations officer at this level, so the adjutant was responsible for all the operational staff work as well as discipline and all other personnel matters. Not to be confused with adjutant in the French Army who was, and is, a warrant officer.

Artillery – the BEF in 1940 had the following types of artillery:

Field Regiments – each had headquarters and two twelve-gun batteries, further sub-divided into three four-gun troops. Their armament varied. The 18-pounder gun and 4.5-inch howitzer were to be superseded by the new 25-pounder, and until this was available 18-pounders were converted into 25-pounders. Field regiments were equipped either with 18-pounders, 4.5-inch howitzers, or converted 18/25-pounders.

Medium Regiments – each had headquarters and two batteries, each of eight 6-inch howitzers or eight 60-pounders. The new 4.5-inch/60-pounders were just coming in to production.

Heavy and Super-Heavy Regiments – each had headquarters and four batteries. Each regiment had four 6-inch guns, and either twelve 8-inch or twelve 9.2-inch howitzers. Super-heavy regiments were equipped with 9.2-inch or 12-inch howitzers.

Anti-Tank Regiment – each had headquarters and four batteries each of twelve 2-pounder anti-tank guns, or some 25mm guns.

Anti-Aircraft Regiment – each had headquarters and three or four batteries of eight 3.7-inch anti-aircraft guns.

Light Anti-Aircraft Regiment – each had headquarters and three or four batteries of twelve Bofors 40mm light anti-aircraft guns.

Battalion – the organization of a 1940 British infantry battalion is shown in the chart overleaf:

The organization of a German infantry battalion varied depending on whether it was part of the rifle regiment, or motorcycle battalion of a panzer division or

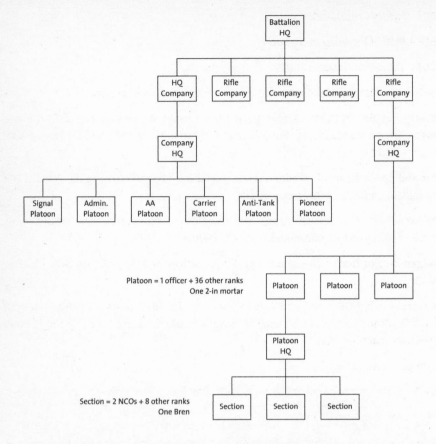

Platoon = 1 officer + 36 other ranks
One 2-in mortar

Section = 2 NCOs + 8 other ranks
One Bren

in an infantry division, but the table below shows the organization of a non-motorized German infantry battalion compared with a British infantry battalion. A German infantry battalion had three rifle companies each of three platoons of four sections, and one heavy weapons company of two platoons.

	BRITISH	GERMAN
Strength: officers andmen	21 and 752	15 and 693
CO	Lt Col	Major
Sub-machine guns	none	about 30 (scale varied)
Light machine guns	50 with rifle companies, 10 with carrier platoon 4 with AA platoon	45 (36 with rifle companies)
Heavy or medium machine guns	none organic to battalion: could be allotted from divisional machine-gun battalion	12 (2 per rifle company, 6 in heavy weapons company)
Anti-tank rifles	22 (12 with rifle companies)	9
Light mortars	12 × 2 in (used mainly for smoke)	9 × 50 mm
Medium mortars	2 × 3 mm mortars	6 × 81 mm mortars

BC – Battery Commander.

BEF – British Expeditionary Force.

BGS – Brigadier General Staff.

Bofors – a 40mm quick-firing anti-aircraft gun of Swedish design.

Bren – the British light machine gun of the Second World War and until the late 1950s. Fired a standard .303 round from a thirty-round magazine (usually loaded with twenty-eight rounds).

Brewed up – a slang expression meaning a tank on fire after being hit. An allusion to lighting a fire to brew a cup of tea.

Brigade – in the British Army, a formation of three infantry battalions or armoured regiments commanded by a brigadier.

Brigade Major (BM) – the senior operations officer of a brigade, de-facto chief of staff.

Carrier – a lightly armoured tracked vehicle, in 1940 often called a Bren-gun carrier, although it was also used in machine-gun battalions to carry the Vickers medium machine gun.

C-in-C – Commander-in-Chief.

CIGS – Chief of the Imperial General Staff, the senior soldier in the British Army.

CO – Commanding Officer.

Corps – a formation of at least two divisions commanded by a lieutenant general. Also the generic term for arms and services except armour, artillery and infantry, hence the corps of Royal Engineers, Royal Signals, Royal Army Service Corps and so on.

CRA – Commander Royal Artillery. The senior gunner in a division, and responsible for commanding and co-ordinating the artillery support of the division.

CRE – Commander Royal Engineers, the senior engineer in a division and responsible for commanding and co-ordinating the engineer support of the division.

CSM – Company Sergeant Major.

DCLI – Duke of Cornwall's Light Infantry.

DCM – Distinguished Conduct Medal. Instituted in 1854 as the equivalent of the DSO for warrant officers, NCOs and soldiers of the British Army (and Royal Marines when under Army Command). Awarded for gallantry in action, a prestigious and rare award, second only to the VC. Now discontinued.

Defensive Fire (DF) – mortar, artillery, or machine-gun fire by troops in defensive positions against attacking troops or patrols. Usually pre-registered on a number of key places, and numbered, so a particular DF can be called down quickly by reference to its number. Guns and mortars will be laid on the DF SOS when not engaged on other tasks. As its name implies the DF SOS is the target deemed to be the most dangerous to the defenders.

Dingo – small, lightly armoured, turretless, four-wheel-drive scout car.

Direct Fire – weapons aimed directly at the target as opposed to indirect-fire weapons such as artillery and mortars. Vickers machine guns can also be fired in the indirect role.

Division – formation of two or more brigades commanded by a major general.

DLC – Division Légère de Cavalerie.

DLI – Durham Light Infantry.

DLM – Division Légère Méchanique.

DSO – Distinguished Service Order. Instituted in 1886. Until the awards system was changed in 1994, it was a dual-role decoration, recognizing gallantry at a level just below that qualifying for the VC by junior officers, and exceptional leadership in battle by senior officers. Officers of all three services were and are eligible. Since 1994 it has become less prestigious by virtue of a change in the rules for its award. It is now awarded for successful leadership and command in 'operational' circumstances. What constitutes 'operations' is open to question, since DSOs appear to 'come up with the rations' after so-called operations, such as Kosovo in 1999, when hardly a shot has been fired in anger, whereas DSOs for tough fighting in Iraq (from 2003) were too sparsely awarded, and deserving cases were palmed off with lesser awards or not decorated at all.

Forward Observation Officer (FOO) – an artillery officer who directs artillery fire. Normally one with each forward rifle company and provided by artillery battery supporting the infantry battalion.

GHQ – General Headquarters. In the context of this book, Gort's headquarters.

GOC – General Officer Commanding.

GQG – Grand Quartier Général. The headquarters of the Supreme Commander French Land Forces (Gamelin followed by Weygand), in the Château de Vincennes outside Paris.

GSO – General Staff Officer, a staff officer who dealt with General (G) Staff matters (operations, intelligence, planning and staff duties), as opposed to personnel (A, short for Adjutant General's Staff), or logistic matters (Q, short for Quartermaster

General's Staff). The grades were GSO 1 (lieutenant colonel), GSO 2 (major) and GSO 3 (captain).

HE – high explosive.

HMS – His Majesty's Ship.

Jocks – slang expression for private soldiers used in Scottish regiments.

KOYLI – King's Own Yorkshire Light Infantry.

KRRC – King's Royal Rifle Corps.

Layback Position – a temporary position established in rear of a withdrawing unit or formation to ensure that enemy following up is held off while the withdrawing troops get clear. They in their turn may establish another layback position further back through which the unit or formation protecting their backs withdraws in its turn – and so on.

Limber – wheeled (usually two wheels) trailer for carrying gun ammunition, originally towed by horses, with the gun hooked on behind in the case of field artillery. In the BEF of 1940 towed by a specially designed truck in which the crew rode.

LSSAH – Leibstandarte SS Adolf Hitler.

MC – Military Cross, instituted in 1914, it was awarded to army officers of the rank of major and below, and to warrant officers, for gallantry in action. Now all ranks are eligible.

Mk – mark.

MM – Military Medal. Instituted in 1916, it was awarded to army NCOs and soldiers for gallantry in action. Now discontinued; *see* MC.

MO – Medical Officer.

MTB – motor torpedo boat.

NCO – non-commissioned officer, from lance-corporal to colour or staff sergeant. See also Warrant Officer.

OC – Officer Commanding.

O Group – short for Orders Group, the group to which orders are given at any level of command from platoon to army. For example, at platoon level the platoon commander briefing his section commanders, and at brigade level, the brigade commander briefing his battalion and supporting arms COs, and other people who need to know the plan.

OODA – Observation Orientation Decision Action.

OP – observation post.

Pioneers – the Pioneer Corps was formed at the outbreak of the Second World War to undertake unskilled labour on the lines of communication in order to relieve trained infantry or engineers of the task. In the early days of the war some TA and regular infantry were temporarily employed on these duties.

Platoon Sergeant Major – *see* Warrant Officer.

Provost – military police.

QMG – Quartermaster General. Can refer to the appointment, or to the staff branch. The Quartermaster General's branch at all staff levels dealt with what we would now call logistics.

QVR –Queen Victoria's Rifles.

RA – Royal Artillery.

Radius of Action – the distance an aircraft or ship carrying out a sortie can cover from base to a target and back without stopping to refuel. *See* Range.

RAF – Royal Air Force.

Range – the distance to a target, or the total distance an aircraft can fly or a ship steam. *See* Radius of Action.

RAP – Regimental Aid Post, the place where the Medical Officer (MO) of a battalion or equivalent-sized unit set up his aid post. Usually the requirement here was to administer 'sophisticated first aid' to stabilize the casualty sufficiently to enable him to survive the next stage of evacuation.

RE – Royal Engineers.

Regiment – originally a regiment was of horse, dragoons (mounted infantry) or foot raised by command of King, and later Parliament, and named after its colonel, usually a royal appointee. The regiment has become the basic organization of the British Army for armour, artillery, engineers and signals units equivalent to battalions in those arms in other armies. In the case of the infantry, the British Army battalion belongs to a regiment, of which in the Second World War there could be several battalions. In 1923 many British cavalry regiments were amalgamated, retaining both their old numbers, hence the 4th/7th Royal Dragoon Guards was a combination of the 4th and 7th Royal Dragoon Guards, not the 4th Battalion of the 7th Royal Dragoon Guards. In typical idiosyncratic British fashion, this rule did not apply to infantry battalions, so that the 1st/6th East Surreys was the 1st Battalion of the 6th (TA) Battalion of the East Surrey Regiment, the 6th Battalion of the East Surreys having hived off several battalions. *See* Territorial Army.

Regimental Sergeant Major – *see* Warrant Officer. It is one of the idiosyncrasies of the British Army that infantry battalions and regiments (artillery and armoured) all have a Warrant Officer Class 1 called the Regimental Sergeant Major. He is the commanding officer's right-hand man and advisor on many aspects of the battalion/regiment daily life, especially matters involving the soldiers and NCOs. The CO and the RSM have very likely known each other since the former was a second lieutenant and the latter was a young private or equivalent.

RHA – Royal Horse Artillery. In the BEF of 1940 not horsed but towed by trucks. Later in the Second World War, and thereafter, RHA regiments were often equipped with self-propelled guns to enable them to keep pace with armoured formations. The title was a hangover from horsed days. The RHA was originally formed to accompany the cavalry, and consequently consider themselves a cut above the rest of the Royal Artillery.

RM – Royal Marines.

RN – Royal Navy.

RNF – Royal Northumberland Fusiliers.

RNLI – Royal National Lifeboat Institution.

RNR – Royal Naval Reserve, usually officers of the Merchant Navy who had volunteered to serve in the Royal Navy in wartime.

RNVR – Royal Naval Volunteer Reserve, usually civilians called up for service in the Royal Navy in wartime, often with no previous maritime experience.

Royal Army Service Corps (RASC) – the administrative corps responsible for transporting supplies.

RQMS – Regimental Quartermaster Sergeant. A warrant officer class II (*see* Warrant Officer) who was the assistant to the battalion or regimental quartermaster.

RSM – Regimental Sergeant Major.

RTR – Royal Tank Regiment.

Sapper – the equivalent of private in the Royal Engineers; also a name for all engineers.

Start Line – a line in the ground, usually a natural feature, stream, bank, ridge, or fence preferably at 90 degrees to the axis of advance, which marks the start line for an attack and is crossed at H-hour in attack formation. Can be marked by tape if there is no natural feature which lends itself to being used as a start line. Now called line of departure (LOD).

Skins – 5th Royal Inniskilling Dragoon Guards.

SOS – see Defensive fire.

SS – Schutzstaffel.

SS Verfügungs – a hangover from the early days of the formation of the SS when they were known as SS-Verfügungstruppe, and eventually became the Waffen-SS or military SS. The term disappeared as the war progressed.

Territorial Army (TA) – part-time soldiers who are mobilized in war. The pre-1939 TA was a large organization consisting of regiments and battalions of all arms: armour, artillery, engineers, signals, infantry, service corps and so on.

Vickers Medium Machine Gun – a First World War-vintage belt-fed, water-cooled machine gun, rate of fire 500 rounds per minute. Maximum range with Mk VIIIZ ammunition, 4,500 yards. Last fired in action in 1962.

VC – Victoria Cross, the highest British award for bravery in the face of the enemy. To date, in the 152 years since its inception by Queen Victoria for conspicuous bravery during the Crimean War of 1854–6, only 1,358 VCs have been awarded, including a handful of double VCs, five civilians under military command, and the one presented to the American Unknown Warrior at Arlington. This figure includes the many awarded to Imperial, Commonwealth and Dominion servicemen.

VCIGS – Vice Chief of the Imperial General Staff.

Warrant Officer – since 1913 there have been two classes of Warrant Officer (WO) in the British Army: WOII, typically a company/squadron sergeant major, and WOI, usually regimental sergeant major, of which there is only one in each battalion or regiment. Just before the Second World War a WOIII, or platoon sergeant major grade was created to command platoons or troops, but it was not a success and was allowed to lapse.

A WO has a warrant signed by a government minister or representative of the Army Council, unlike a commissioned officer (of the rank of second lieutenant and above), who has a King's or Queen's commission. Those junior in rank to WOIs and WOIIs address them as sir, and Mr (Surname); those superior to them formally refer to them as Mr (Surname), but often address them and refer to them as Sergeant Major or RSM. They are not saluted by those junior to them and live in the WOs' and Sergeants' Mess.

Wehrmacht – German armed forces.

WVS – Women's Voluntary Service (later WRVS, Women's Royal Voluntary Service).

Notes

1. Twenty Wasted Years

1 Ewan Butler, *Mason-Mac: The Life of Lieutenant General Sir Noël Mason-MacFarlan* (Macmillan, 1972) p. 116.
2 Shakespeare, *Henry VI, Part 1*, Act 1, Scene 1, lines 74–7.
3 See Stephen Budiansky, *Air Power: From Kitty Hawk to Gulf War II: A History of the People, Ideas and Machines that Transformed War in the Century of Flight* (Viking, 2003), pp. 97–9. The formation of the RAF was in Budiansky's words 'a radical, indeed almost a mad step', made in a mood of panic caused by the pin-prick raids on Britain by German bombers and Zeppelins during the First World War, whose total effort *throughout the war* caused fewer casualties than one would find on a typical 'quiet day' on the Western Front. The total property damage was less than half what the First World War cost the British each day.
4 *War Diaries 1939–1945: Field Marshal Lord Alanbrooke*, ed. Alex Danchev and Daniel Todman (Weidenfeld & Nicolson, 2001), p. 18.
5 Ibid.
6 Alistair Horne, *To Lose a Battle: France 1940* (Papermac, 1990), p. 79.
7 Arthur Koestler, *Scum of the Earth* (Macmillan, 1941), quoted in *To Lose A Battle*, p. 138.
8 Winston Churchill, *The Second World War*, vol. 1: *The Gathering Storm* (Cassell, 1948) p. 442.
9 *Alanbrooke Diaries*, p. 26.
10 Ibid., p. 27.
11 Ibid., p. 4
12 David Fraser, *Alanbrooke* (Hamlyn Paperbacks, 1983), p. 137.
13 *Alanbrooke Diaries*, p. 12.
14 Ibid., p. 20.
15 Nigel Hamilton, *Monty: The Making of a General 1887–1942* (Hamlyn Paperbacks, 1982), p. 344.

2. Into Belgium: First Shocks

1 *Alanbrooke Diaries*, p. 60.
2 Ibid., p. 61.
3 L. F. Ellis, *The War in France and Flanders: 1939–1940* (HMSO, 1953), p. 42.
4 The expression 'fifth column' owes its origin to the Spanish Civil War (1936–9), when the Nationalist leader General Franco told Republicans defending Madrid that, besides having four armed columns outside the city, he had a fifth inside waiting to rise and fight for him. German propaganda used rumour to intensify fears that fifth columnists owing allegiance to them were working inside countries that they wished to conquer. This engendered panic and suspicion, even though fifth columnists were mainly a myth.
5 Ellis, *The War in France and Flanders*, p. 335. The Germans, and the French, often used the term 'England' to refer both to that country itself in a geographical sense and to the whole of the UK. They used the word 'English' in the same way regardless of whether the people to whom they were referring were English, Scots, Welsh or Irish. The French found it difficult to rid themselves of the folk memory of the English as their oldest enemy since the early Middle Ages, the alliances of the First and Second World Wars being historical aberrations. There was plenty of Anglophobia among senior French commanders, and this attribute came to the fore only too readily when things started going badly.
6 Ibid., p. 336.
7 Mungo Melvin, 'The German View', in Brian Bond and Michael Taylor (eds), *The Battle for France and Flanders: Sixty Years On* (Leo Cooper, 2001), p. 212.
8 Ellis, *The War in France and Flanders*, p. 59.
9 Winston S. Churchill, *The Second World War*, vol. II: *Their Finest Hour* (Cassell, 1949), p. 42.
10 John Terraine, *The Right of the Line: The Royal Air Force in the European War 1939–1940* (Wordsworth, 1997), p. 134.

3. Back to the Escaut and Disaster on the BEF's Southern Flank

1 *Alanbrooke Diaries*, p. 64.
2 Ellis, *The War in France and Flanders*, pp. 66–7.
3 Ibid., p. 77.
4 Now borne by their lineal descendants, the Princess of Wales's Royal Regiment.
5 Ellis, *The War in France and Flanders*, p. 81. There is no record of a XXXXI Corps

anywhere other than in Ellis. Both 6th and 8th Panzer Divisions were in Reinhardt's XLI Panzer Corps.

6 Ibid., p. 83. This is my summary of Ellis's much longer original.
7 Ibid.
8 General Robert Altmayer commanding Group A (later French Tenth Army) should not be confused with his brother General René Altmayer commanding French V Corps.
9 Ibid., p. 84.
10 Ibid., p. 85.

4. Counter-Strike at Arras

1 See Ellis, *The War in France and Flanders*, p. 87.
2 A regiment of armour in the British Army, whether tank, light mechanized cavalry or armoured car, is the equivalent of a battalion in most other armies. A regiment of artillery is the equivalent of an artillery battalion in most other armies, and is divided into gun batteries, of which in a field regiment there are three.
3 At that stage in the war, each RTR company (see note 4 below) was subdivided into five sections, each of three tanks. An RTR squadron had five troops of three tanks each. Later in the war, a squadron had four troops of four tanks each.
4 Some battalions of the RTR were divided into companies at this stage of the war, not squadrons, as the armoured cavalry were – although eventually the RTR battalions would become regiments, and their companies squadrons.
5 Horne, *To Lose a Battle*, p. 582.

5. Fighting on Two Fronts

1 The officers of the 52nd are alleged to have counted as they cleaned their teeth, 1, 2, 3 and so on to 41, 42, then *spit*, 44.
2 The expression 'ball', a hangover from the days of muskets, was still applied to the solid, pointed, metal-jacketed bullet fired by all small arms. Hence 'ball' ammunition as opposed to 'blank', or 'tracer'.
3 *Alanbrooke Diaries*, p. 67.
4 See Horne, *To Lose a Battle*, pp. 586 n. 19, and 589.
5 *Alanbrooke Diaries*, p. 68.
6 Ellis, *The War in France and Flanders*, p. 112.
7 Ibid., p. 111.
8 *Alanbrooke Diaries*, pp. 67–8.

9   Ellis, *The War in France and Flanders*, p. 142.

10   Ibid., pp. 138–9.

6. Boulogne and Calais

1   Ellis, *The War in France and Flanders*, p. 155.

2   Ibid., p. 159.

3   At this stage in the war, the RTR was in the process of reorganizing its companies into squadrons, and its battalions would shortly become regiments, bringing the RTR into line with the rest of the Armoured Corps. In May 1940, 3rd RTR, in common with the rest of the RTR, was still a battalion.

4   Ellis, *The War in France and Flanders*, pp. 159–60.

5   W. H. Close, *A View from the Turret: A History of the 3rd Royal Tank Regiment in the Second World War* (Dell & Breedon, 1998), p. 9.

6   Ibid., p. 11.

7   Airey Neave, *The Flames of Calais: A Soldier's Battle 1940* (Hodder & Stoughton, 1972), p. 53.

8   The 1st Rifle Brigade was not a brigade but the first battalion of an infantry regiment which in the idiosyncratic British fashion was called the Rifle Brigade. Both the KRRC and Rifle Brigade, having been amalgamated as the Royal Green Jackets in the 1960s, are now The Rifles.

9   Ellis, *The War in France and Flanders*, p. 163.

10   Ibid., p. 164.

11   Ibid., p. 165.

12   Ibid., pp. 165–6.

13   See Glossary for explanation of platoon sergeant major.

14   Ellis, *The War in France and Flanders*, p. 167.

15   Ibid.

16   Ibid.

17   Ibid.

18   Churchill, *Their Finest Hour*, p. 73.

19   Ibid.

7. The Withdrawal: II Corps on the Eastern Flank

1   Bernard Montgomery, *The Memoirs of Field Marshal the Viscount Montgomery of Alamein* (Collins, 1958), p. 65.

2   *Alanbrooke Diaries*, p. 71.

3   To 'refuse' a flank involves turning part of a unit or formation's front at

right angles to protect the threatened flank. In simple terms the deployment becomes like the letter L, the horizontal part of the L being the 'refused' flank.

4 *Alanbrooke Diaries*, p. 72.

5 Ibid., p. 73.

6 In the Second World War, and up to the present, a fighting unit in the British Army (infantry battalion, armoured regiment, artillery regiment, sapper squadron and so on) in war, as opposed to operations other than war (such as Iraq after the 2003 invasion) was, and is, divided into three echelons. F Echelon consists of the elements required to carry out the actual fighting, including vehicles such as carriers, tanks, armoured cars, command vehicles, gun towers and limbers, and immediate ammunition re-supply vehicles. A Echelon consists of the vehicles and men usually held in the rear of unit locations for short-notice logistic back-up, and often commanded by the unit motor transport officer. B Echelon, usually commanded by the unit quartermaster, contains the personnel (such as the armourer, vehicle mechanics and cooks) and vehicles to provide longer-term logistic support on a daily basis, for example cooking hot food (often brought up at night in special containers called hayboxes) or the repair of weapons and vehicles. Frequently all Unit B Echelons would be, and still are, centralized under brigade or divisional control, with the aim of reducing the risk of chaos caused by each unit B Echelon 'doing its own thing' at a time of its own choosing, especially on restricted lines of communication. The detailed composition of the echelons varied depending on the type of unit and the theatre of operations.

7 *Alanbrooke Diaries*, p. 72.

8 Ibid., p. 73

8. The Withdrawal: Fighting the Panzers on the Western Flank

1 A field ambulance company was capable of establishing an advanced dressing station (ADS) to which casualties were taken from unit regimental aid posts (RAPs). The field ambulance company had thirty-six stretcher bearers and eight ambulances for this purpose.

2 Originally formed as Hitler's bodyguard of about a company strong and designated Leibstandarte Adolf Hitler (LAH), it was the first of the Waffen (armed or military) branch of the SS, to distinguish it from camp guards and other SS security personnel. By 1940, with the letters SS added to their title the LSSAH was a full-sized motorized regiment. In 1941 the LSSAH became a panzer division, the 1st SS Panzer Division Leibstandarte Adolf Hitler.

3 Gregory Blaxland, *Destination Dunkirk: The Story of Gort's Army* (William Kimber, London, 1973), p. 305.

4 Ibid.
5 Ellis, *The War in France and Flanders*, p. 206, quoting German documents captured after the war.
6 Ibid., p. 208, quoting German documents captured after the war.
7 Ibid.

9. Comings and Goings at Dunkirk

1 Ellis, *The War in France and Flanders*, p. 182.
2 Ibid., p. 183.
3 J. D. P. Stirling, *The First and the Last: The Story of the 4th/7th Royal Dragoon Guards 1939–1945* (Art & Educational Publishers, 1946), pp. 25–6.
4 Ellis, *The War in France and Flanders*, p. 230.
5 Ibid., pp. 233–4.
6 Hamilton, *Monty*, p. 387.
7 Ibid.
8 Montgomery Papers, letter of 25 August 1952, Imperial War Museum.
9 Churchill, *Their Finest Hour*, p. 97.
10 Ellis, *The War in France and Flanders*, p. 240.
11 Churchill, *Their Finest Hour*, p. 101.

10. The End at Dunkirk

1 Quoted in Hamilton, *Monty*, p. 392.
2 Stirling, *The First and the Last*, p. 26.
3 Correlli Barnett, *Engage the Enemy More Closely: The Royal Navy in the Second World War* (Hodder & Stoughton, 1991), pp. 159–60.
4 Ibid., p. 160.
5 Ibid., pp. 160–1.
6 Ibid., p. 161.

11. The Final Battles

1 *Alanbrooke Diaries*, p. 74.
2 Ellis, *The War in France and Flanders*, p. 249.
3 Ibid., p. 274.
4 Ibid., p. 282.
5 *Alanbrooke Diaries*, p. 80.
6 Ibid., p. 81.

7 Ibid.
8 Ibid., p. 84.

12. Reckoning

1 Brian Bond (ed.), *The Battle of France and Flanders 1940: Sixty Years On* (Leo Cooper, 2001), p. 49.
2 The figures for French casualties in the First World War, compared with those suffered by the British Empire and Germany, are:

Country	Killed (million)	Wounded (million)	Prisoners (million)	% of forces mobilized
France	1.3	4.3	0.50	76.3
British Empire	0.9	2.0	0.19	35.8
Germany	1.8	4.2	1.20	64.9

3 Statistics for some German aircraft in service by early 1940 are shown below:

Aircraft type	Bomb load (lb)	Radius of action (miles) with full bomb load
Messerschmitt Bf 109 fighter	n/a	365–460
Messerschmitt Bf 110 fighter	n/a	528
Dornier 17 bomber	2,205	721
Junkers 87 'Stuka'	1,500	373
Heinkel He 111	1,103	745
Focke-Wulf Condor*	4,626	2,206

* Used in anti-ship attack role only.

Comparable British aircraft statistics are:

Aircraft type	Bomb load (lb)	Radius of action (miles) with full bomb load
Hawker Hurricane	n/a	460
Spitfire	n/a	395
Fairey Battle	1,000	900
Blenheim	1,000	1,950
Whitley	7,000	470*
Wellington	5,000	2,200

* 1,650 miles with bomb load of 3,000lb.

Just for comparison, the Lancaster, a true strategic bomber, which did not come into service in the RAF until 1942, could carry a 14,000lb bomb load 1,660 miles.

4 Ellis, *The War in France and Flanders*, p. 327.
5 Standard was the brand name of a range of British saloon cars in the 1940s, such as Morris and Austin.
6 Stirling, *The First and the Last*, p. 27.
7 See Chapter 2, note 5, for the German use of the terms 'English' for British and 'England' for the United Kingdom.
8 Ellis, *The War in France and Flanders*, p. 326.

Select Bibliography

Many works were consulted during research for this book, but the following were particularly valuable.

Atkin, Ronald, *Pillar of Fire: Dunkirk 1940* (Sidgwick & Jackson, 1990)

Barnett, Correlli, *Engage the Enemy More Closely: The Royal Navy in the Second World War* (Hodder & Stoughton, 1991)

Bidwell, Shelford and Graham, Dominick, *Fire-Power: The British Army Weapons and Theories of War 1904–1945* (Pen & Sword Military Classics, 2004)

Blaxland, Gregory, *Destination Dunkirk: The Story of Gort's Army* (William Kimber, 1973)

Bond, Brian and Taylor, Michael (eds), *The Battle for France and Flanders: Sixty Years On* (Leo Cooper, 2001)

Budiansky, Stephen, *Air Power: From Kitty Hawk to Gulf War II: A History of the People, Ideas and Machines that Transformed War in the Century of Flight* (Viking, 2003)

Churchill, Winston, *The Second World War*, vol. II: *Their Finest Hour* (Cassell, 1949)

Close, Bill, *A View from the Turret: A History of the 3rd Royal Tank Regiment in the Second World War* (Dell & Bredon, 1998)

Danchev, Alex and Todman, Daniel (eds), *War Diaries 1939–1945: Field Marshal Lord Alanbrooke* (Weidenfeld & Nicolson, 2001)

Ellis, L. F., *The War in France and Flanders 1939–1940* (HMSO, 1953)

Forty, George, *British Army Handbook, 1939–1940* (Sutton Publishing, 1998).

Fraser, David, *And We Shall Shock Them: The British Army in the Second World War* (Sceptre, 1988)

——, *Alanbrooke* (Hamlyn Paperbacks, 1983)

Hamilton, Nigel, *Monty: The Making of a General 1887–1942* (Hamlyn Paperbacks, 1982)

Horne, Alistair, *To Lose a Battle: France 1940* (Papermac, 1990)

Montgomery, Bernard, *The Memoirs of Field Marshal the Viscount Montgomery of Alamein* (Collins, 1958)

Moore, William, *Panzer Bait: With the Third Royal Tank Regiment 1939–1945* (Leo Cooper, 1991)

Neave, Airey, *The Flames of Calais: A Soldier's Battle 1940* (Hodder & Stoughton, 1972)

Shepperd, Alan, *France 1940: Blitzkrieg in the West* (Osprey Publishing, 1990)

Stirling, J. D. P., *The First and the Last: The Story of the 4th/7th Royal Dragoon Guards 1939–1945* (Art & Educational Publishers, 1946)

Terraine, John, *The Right of the Line: The Royal Air Force in the European War 1939–1945* (Wordsworth, 1997)

Index